T.C.J.C.-S.C.

Critical Essays on
Louisa May Alcott

Critical Essays on Louisa May Alcott

Madeleine B. Stern

G. K. Hall & Company • Boston, Massachusetts

Copyright © 1984 by Madeleine B. Stern
All Rights Reserved

Library of Congress Cataloging in Publication Data
Main entry under title:

Critical essays on Louisa May Alcott.

    (Critical essays in American literature)
    Includes index.
  1. Alcott, Louisa May, 1832-1888 — Criticism and interpretation —
Addresses, essays, lectures. I. Stern, Madeleine Bettina, 1912-   . II.
Series.
PS1018.C7 1984   813'.4   84-4499
ISBN 0-8161-8686-3 (alk. paper)

This publication is printed on permanent/durable acid-free paper
MANUFACTURED IN THE UNITED STATES OF AMERICA

CRITICAL ESSAYS ON AMERICAN LITERATURE

This series seeks to anthologize the most important criticism on a wide variety of topics and writers in American literature. Our readers will find in various volumes not only a generous selection of reprinted articles and reviews but original essays, bibliographies, manuscript sections, and other materials brought to public attention for the first time. This volume on Louisa May Alcott, edited by Madeleine B. Stern, is a welcome addition to our list. There are reprinted reviews and articles by many leading critics and writers, including Henry James, George Jean Nathan, Elizabeth Janeway, Brigid Brophy, Sean O'Faolain, Leo Lerman, G. K. Chesterton, Amy Lowell, and Ann Douglas, among others. In addition to an extensive introduction, there are original essays by Ruth K. MacDonald, Freda Baum, Martha Saxton, Joel Myerson, Adeline R. Tintner, Marie Olesen Urbanski, Mary Cadogan, and Alma J. Payne. Madeleine B. Stern is the author of numerous books about nineteenth-century America, including four concerning Alcott. We are confident that this volume will make a permanent and significant contribution to American literary study.

JAMES NAGEL, GENERAL EDITOR

Northeastern University

CONTENTS

INTRODUCTION	1
EXPERIMENTATIONS BEFORE *LITTLE WOMEN*	
Flower Fables	
Anonymous, [Review of *Flower Fables*, 1855]	23
Anonymous, [Review of *Flower Fables*, 1855]	23
Hospital Sketches and *Camp and Fireside Stories*	
Anonymous, [Advertisement for *Hospital Sketches*, 1863]	25
Anonymous, [Review of *Hospital Sketches*, 1863]	25
Anonymous, [Review of *Hospital Sketches and Camp and Fireside Stories*, 1869]	26
Bessie Z. Jones, "Introduction to *Hospital Sketches*"	27
Jan Cohn, "The Negro Character in Northern Magazine Fiction of the 1860's"	30
Abigail Ann Hamblen, "Louisa May Alcott and The Racial Question"	33
Gothics and Thrillers	
Anonymous, [Review of *Comic Tragedies Written by "Jo" and "Meg" and acted by the "Little Women,"* 1893]	41
LaSalle Corbell Pickett, [Louisa Alcott's "Natural Ambition" for the "Lurid Style" Disclosed in a Conversation]	42
Leona Rostenberg, "Some Anonymous and Pseudonymous Thrillers of Louisa M. Alcott"	43
Madeleine Stern, "Introduction [to *Behind a Mask*]"	50
Moods	
Aaron K. Loring, [A Letter to Louisa May Alcott (1864) by the Future Publisher of *Moods*]	65
Anonymous, [Review of *Moods*, 1865]	66
Anonymous, "Transcendental Fiction" [Review of *Moods*, 1865]	66
Henry James, [Review of *Moods*, 1865]	69
Anonymous, [Review of *Moods*, revised edition, 1882]	74
Ruth K. MacDonald, "*Moods*, Gothic and Domestic"	74

viii   Contents

LITTLE WOMEN

Anonymous, [Review of *Little Women*, Part I, 1868]	81
Anonymous, [Review of *Little Women*, Part I, 1868]	81
Anonymous, [Review of *Little Women*, Part II, 1869]	82
Anonymous, [Review of *Little Women*, Part II, 1869]	82
Anonymous, [Review of *Little Women*, Part II, 1869]	83
Barrett Wendell, [*Little Women* and the *Rollo* Books]	84
Anonymous, "*Little Women* Leads Poll: Novel Rated Ahead of Bible for Influence on High School Pupils"	84
Dorothea Lawrance Mann, "When the Alcott Books Were New"	85
David A. Randall and John T. Winterich, "One Hundred Good Novels"	85
George Jean Nathan, [A Dramatic Performance of *Little Women*, 12 December 1944]	88
Edward Wagenknecht, [*Little Women* and the Domestic Sentimentalists]	88
C. Waller Barrett, "Little Women Forever"	89
Brigid Brophy, "Sentimentality and Louisa M. Alcott"	93
Elizabeth Janeway, "Meg, Jo, Beth, Amy and Louisa"	97
Lavinia Russ, "Not To Be Read On Sunday"	99
Cornelia Meigs, "Introduction to Centennial Edition of *Little Women*"	103
Sean O'Faolain, "This Is Your Life . . . Louisa May Alcott"	105
Stephanie Harrington, "Does *Little Women* Belittle Women?"	110
Leo Lerman, "Little Women: Who's In Love With Miss Louisa May Alcott? I Am"	113
Patricia Meyer Spacks, [*Little Women* and the Female Imagination]	114
Thomas H. Pauly, "*Ragged Dick* and *Little Women*: Idealized Homes and Unwanted Marriages"	120
Ellen Moers, "Money, Job, Little Women: Female Realism"	126
Nina Auerbach, "*Little Women* [and *Pride and Prejudice*]"	129
Judith Fetterley, "*Little Women*: Alcott's Civil War"	140
Carolyn Heilbrun, [Jo March: Male Model—Female Person]	143
Madelon Bedell, "Beneath the Surface: Power and Passion in *Little Women*"	145

THE LITTLE WOMEN SERIES

Anonymous, [Review of *An Old-Fashioned Girl*, 1870]	153
C.L.P., [Review of *An Old-Fashioned Girl*, 1870]	155
Anonymous, [Review of *Little Men: Life at Plumfield with Jo's Boys*, 1871]	157
Anonymous, [Review of *Little Men: Life at Plumfield with Jo's Boys*, 1871]	158

Grover Smith, "The Doll-Burners: D. H. Lawrence and Louisa Alcott"	160
Henry James, [Review of *Eight Cousins; or, The Aunt-Hill*, 1875]	165
Anonymous, [Review of *Eight Cousins; or, The Aunt-Hill*, 1875]	167
Anonymous, [Review of *Eight Cousins; or, The Aunt-Hill*, 1875]	168
Anonymous, [Review of *Rose in Bloom: A Sequel to "Eight Cousins,"* 1876]	170
Anonymous, [Review of *Under the Lilacs* and *Jack and Jill*, 1905 reprints]	170
Anonymous, [Review of *Jack and Jill: A Village Story*, 1880]	171
Anonymous, [Review of *Jo's Boys and How They Turned Out: A Sequel to "Little Men,"* 1886]	171
Carolyn Forrey, "The New Woman Revisited [in *Jo's Boys*]"	172

SCRAP-BAGS AND COLLECTIONS

Anonymous, [Review of *Aunt Jo's Scrap-Bag*, I, 1872]	177
Anonymous, [Review of *Aunt Jo's Scrap-Bag*, II, 1872]	177
Anonymous, [Review of *Aunt Jo's Scrap-Bag*, III, 1874]	178
William Henry Harrison, ["Transcendental Wild Oats," 1873]	178
Anonymous, [Review of *Silver Pitchers: And Independence, A Centennial Love Story*, 1876]	179
Anonymous, [Review of *Proverb Stories*, 1882]	180
Anonymous, [Review of *Lulu's Library*, I, 1886]	180
Joy A. Marsella, "The Promise of Destiny [in *Aunt Jo's Scrap-Bags*]"	181

DEVIATIONS FROM THE PATTERN

Work

Anonymous, [Review of *Work: A Story of Experience*, 1873]	185
Anonymous, [Review of *Work: A Story of Experience*, 1873]	186
Anonymous, [Review of *Work: A Story of Experience*, 1873]	187
Sarah Elbert, "Introduction to *Work: A Story of Experience*"	191

A Modern Mephistopheles

Anonymous, [Review of *A Modern Mephistopheles*, 1877]	203
Anonymous, [Review of *A Modern Mephistopheles*, 1877]	204
Edward R. Burlingame, [Review of *A Modern Mephistopheles*, 1877]	204
Anonymous, [Review of *A Modern Mephistopheles*, 1877]	206

APPRAISALS AND REAPPRAISALS

Ednah D. Cheney, ["Her Works Are a Revelation of Herself"]	211
Anonymous, "Books That Separate Parents from Their Children"	212
G. K. Chesterton, "Louisa Alcott"	212
F. B. Sanborn, "Reminiscences of Louisa M. Alcott"	215
Amy Lowell, "Books for Children"	216
Katharine Fullerton Gerould, "Miss Alcott's New England"	217
Elizabeth Vincent, "Subversive Miss Alcott"	222
Thomas Beer, [The Influence of Louisa Alcott]	225
Eleanor Perényi, "Dear Louisa"	227
Ann Douglas, "Mysteries of Louisa May Alcott"	231
Madeleine B. Stern, "A Writer's Progress: Louisa May Alcott at 150"	240
Freda Baum, "The Scarlet Strand: Reform Motifs in the Writings of Louisa May Alcott"	250
Martha Saxton, "The Secret Imaginings of Louisa Alcott"	256
Joel Myerson, " 'Our Children Are Our Best Works': Bronson and Louisa May Alcott"	261
Adeline R. Tintner, "A Literary Youth and a Little Woman: Henry James Reviews Louisa Alcott"	265
Marie Olesen Urbanski, "Thoreau in the Writing of Louisa May Alcott"	269
Mary Cadogan, " 'Sweet, If Somewhat Tomboyish': The British Response to Louisa May Alcott"	275
Alma J. Payne, "Louisa May Alcott: A Bibliographical Essay on Secondary Sources"	279
INDEX	287

INTRODUCTION

The cloud that often obscures the reputation of an author from the eyes of his contemporaries is, it has been said, "finally scattered by the patient work of critics and scholars, but even then, the figure that reappears is never that which his contemporaries saw."[1] For much of her life Louisa May Alcott was regarded as "The Children's Friend" and such stature as she attained was that of America's best-loved author of juveniles. Today, thanks to "the patient work of critics and scholars," she is viewed as an experimenting, complex writer, and her work has become fertile ground for the exploration both of literary historians and of psychohistorians. Indeed, it might be said that America's best-loved author of juveniles may today have lost some of her childhood readership but has gained a substantial critical readership. Both her stature and her audience have undergone a metamorphosis, and for this certainly "the patient work of critics and scholars" is responsible. Their work has had interesting side effects also, for it has unfolded, in the course of reappraisal of a career, Alcott's experiences with publishers, the complexities of her character, and, to some extent, the development of her literary techniques as a professional writer. All these aspects of Alcott's life and work emerge in varying degree from this volume of *Critical Essays* which reflects her expanding reputation, her increased stature, and finally her secure place in American literary history.

The first review of an Alcott book appeared in December 1854 and concerned a volume of fairy tales entitled *Flower Fables* which the twenty-two-year-old author had imagined for Emerson's daughter Ellen. The *Boston Evening Transcript* found her work "agreeable" and "adapted to the capacity of intelligent young persons,"[2] an innocuous enough dismissal that gave no hint of the zealous investigation to which the Alcott oeuvre would one day be subjected.

That oeuvre began with a germinal period of experimentation which produced not only the "agreeable" *Flower Fables*, but the more realistic *Hospital Sketches* of 1863, the flamboyant Gothic thrillers of the 1860s, and the author's first novel, *Moods*. Those works preceded, and to some extent laid the ground for, the creation of *Little Women*, the Alcott masterpiece. The critical comments those early writings evoked from contemporary and later reviewers clearly indicate the initial stages in the shaping of a literary reputation.

The decade of the 1860s was especially productive for an author essaying a variety of genres. Her *Hospital Sketches* (1863), a quasi-humorous, quasi-realistic record of her experience as a nurse in the Union Hotel Hospital, Georgetown, D.C., aroused enthusiastic immediate response, contemporary reviews finding its "graphic" description and "quiet . . . humor" meritorious. "The reader," according to the *Waterbury American*, "is alternately moved to laughter and tears" — early indication of a skill that would become characteristic. By the time a century had passed, critics began to find in *Hospital Sketches* something more than mere Civil War memorabilia. Besides classifying it as "one of the earliest first-hand reports of personal experience with the wounded," Bessie Z. Jones noted that the work spares us the "false pieties" of other Civil War reminiscences and "merits a permanent place in the literature of military medicine and the impact of women on the practices related to it."

Both *Hospital Sketches* and the related *Camp and Fireside Stories* became by the 1970s sources of considerable cogitation regarding Alcott's attitudes toward the blacks. Jan Cohn in 1970 analyzed Alcott's "confusion in the face of the black man, who was . . . neither a respectable adjunct to Boston's abolitionist societies nor a realization of Mrs. Stowe's Uncle Tom." Discussing her "tentative probings into the problem of miscegenation" in her story of a slave rebellion, "An Hour," and in "My Contraband," he concluded that, despite the noble abolitionist attitudes of the North in general and of Alcott in particular, "the North remained complacently racist . . . throughout its decade of independent examination of the black character in fiction." Abigail Ann Hamblen is kinder to Alcott and her views of race relations. Conceding that she "passes over any theory that might oppose hers," that there is condescension in her attitudes, and that there are "facets of the Negro-slavery question" that she ignores, Hamblen finds that she bent "a great talent . . . to the ends of propaganda" in her "violently partisan" war stories, and, comparing her work with that of James Gould Cozzens and Hamilton Basso, concludes that Alcott "has undeniable relevance for her own troubled period."

The year of publication of *Hospital Sketches* (1863) also saw publication of the first of the so-called Alcott thrillers. Turning her hand not only to realistic war stories but to Gothic romances dominated by manipulating heroines whose feminist fury triggers a course of violence and revenge, Alcott continued her literary experimentations during the 1860s. Those sensational stories appeared for the most part anonymously or pseudonymously in popular journals and called forth no traceable contemporary reviews. Indeed, their very existence was generally unknown, though suspected, during the author's lifetime. Even after her death, when the *Comic Tragedies* of her salad days was published, it was regarded merely as "a curiosity," although a canny reader might surely have detected in those early melodramas of deceit and vengeance many an ingredient that would be stirred in the cauldron of Alcott's later sensational stories. In the course of an interview with LaSalle Corbell Pickett—not published until 1916—Alcott revealed her fascination with sensational themes, declaring, "I think my natural ambition is for the lurid style. I indulge in gorgeous fancies and wish that I dared inscribe them upon my pages and set them before the public." The fact that she had indeed dared to inscribe them upon her pages and set them—albeit clandestinely—before her public, was not substantiated until Leona Rostenberg discovered the Alcott pseudonym of A. M. Barnard, the titles of the thrillers, and the periodical in which they had appeared. Her discovery was announced in 1943 in the *Papers of the Bibliographical Society of America*, where the letters of publisher James R. Elliott of Boston to Miss Alcott—the letters that disclosed the secrets—were also printed for the first time.

Not until 1975–76 did Madeleine Stern actually gather the Alcott thrillers together and make them public. Their titles alone suggested the violence of themes that ranged from mind control to madness, from the machinations of manipulating heroines to hashish experimentation and opium addiction: "Pauline's Passion and Punishment," "A Whisper in the Dark," "V.V.: or, Plots and Counterplots," "A Marble Woman: or, The Mysterious Model," and "Behind a Mask: or, A Woman's Power." Stern's introductory analysis of the collection considered "not only the nature of the creation but the nature of the creator," pointing out the personal humiliations and tribulations that were transmuted into the motivations of fictional *femmes fatales*, and tracing the development of Alcott's skill in dialogue, plotting, and characterization. According to Stern, "her gallery of *femmes fatales* forms a suite of flesh-and-blood portraits. Her own anger at an unjust world she transformed into the anger of her heroines. . . . The psychological insights of A. M. Barnard disclose the darker side of the character of Louisa May Alcott." Thus the corpus of Alcott thrillers is "rich with interest for those in search of current themes and preoccupations as well as for those in search of Louisa May Alcott." Indeed, the publication of Alcott's sensational narratives in 1975 and 1976 was to prove pivotal to much of the Alcott reevaluation that followed.

Meanwhile, also in the 1860s, Alcott produced her first novel, *Moods*. The experimenting author was to some extent guided by the suggestions of her publisher, A. K. Loring of Boston, who demanded "Stories of the *heart*," stories of "constant action," and stories that "teach some lesson of life." If her novel of marital relations that ends in the death of the heroine bears traces of her melodramatic tales of passion and punishment, it also looks forward to those "stories of the heart" that "teach some lesson of life" which would punctuate her career in maturity. Contemporary reviewers of *Moods* stressed the author's delicate rendering of the "conflict of passion" and expressed the belief that "greater experience and resolute study" would "correct the imperfect literary art." Classifying the novel as "Transcendental Fiction," an English periodical, the *Reader*, commented that, despite its originality, it invested marriage with sanctity and so left "society with its old frontiers." In the *Nation*, the twenty-two-year-old Henry James expressed more ambivalence regarding the worth of the book than regarding the worth of the writer. The novel he found "innocent of any doctrine whatever," and its hero, Adam Warwick, merely "the inevitable *cavaliere servente* of the precocious little girl." Although the author was ignorant of human nature and self-confident "in spite of this ignorance," James still felt there was "no reason why Miss Alcott should not write a very good novel, provided she will be satisfied to describe only that which she has seen. . . . With the exception of two or three celebrated names, we know not, indeed, to whom, in this country, unless to Miss Alcott, we are to look for a novel above the average."

It was certainly in an effort to make *Moods* more natural, more descriptive of "that which she had seen," that in 1881 Louisa Alcott revised her first novel for an edition published the following year by Roberts Brothers. In the revision much of the metaphysical and much of the morbid were eliminated; her heroine, motivated more by principle than by impulse, met with a less extravagant fate, and *Moods* was reshaped into a more wholesome fiction. The revision of *Moods* gave to the critic of Alcott's first novel an opportunity to examine the author's maturing techniques and attitudes. As Ruth K. MacDonald notes, the two editions "do much to explain Alcott's developing literary style and changing perceptions of romantic love." Despite the more realistic and conventional touches in the revised edition of this novel on "the relationships between the sexes," MacDonald finds that the author does not abandon the radicalism of her earlier views on marriage and divorce. In brief, the modern critic sees in the revision of *Moods* an abandonment of the Gothic in favor of the realistic.

With this corpus of experimental publications behind her—the "agreeable" *Flower Fables*, the more realistic *Hospital Sketches*, the gaudy and gruesome thrillers, the first edition of the novel *Moods*—Louisa Alcott in 1868 sat down to write the girls' story that was to mark the climax of her professional life. In *Little Women*, as in the later revision of *Moods*, she abandoned the Gothic in favor of the realistic, and produced a domestic novel for the young that was also a portrait and a nostalgic re-creation of nineteenth-century New England family life.

At first she had been reluctant to write the story for girls suggested by Thomas Niles of the Boston publishing house Roberts Brothers. And once having written it, basing its characters—the four March girls—upon the four Alcott sisters, and their lives upon the lives the sisters had led, she was ambivalent about its worth. Her journal entries have become part of the history of the book:

> *May*, 1868. — . . . Mr. N[iles]. wants a *girls' story*, and I begin "Little Women." . . . I plod away, though I don't enjoy this sort of thing. Never

liked girls or knew many, except my sisters; but our queer plays and experiences may prove interesting, though I doubt it.

June. — Sent twelve chapters of "L.W." to Mr. N. He thought it *dull*; so do I. But work away and mean to try the experiment; for lively, simple books are very much needed for girls, and perhaps I can supply the need. . . .

August 26th. — Proof of whole book came. It reads better than I expected. Not a bit sensational, but simple and true, for we really lived most of it; and if it succeeds that will be the reason of it.[3]

The public agreed with the author's August rather than her June judgment. After publication of Part I in October 1868, Part II was demanded for spring, and on 1 November the author recorded in her journal: "Began the second part of 'Little Women.' I can do a chapter a day, and in a month I mean to be done."[4] In April 1869, Part II, carrying the March sisters to young adulthood, was published, and a book that had begun as an unwelcome assignment on the part of an author who had tried her ink-stained fingers on many genres as she struggled to find her style, was on its way to becoming history.

The phenomenal sales of *Little Women* have engaged the attention of critics almost since the time of publication. Its worldwide reputation too has puzzled reviewers who have addressed themselves to the question why a sentimental domestic novel for girls should have been exalted into a "perennial classic." Nineteenth-century and early twentieth-century critics have been, by and large, content to base the book's enormous popularity as well as its worth upon its verisimilitude in reanimating New England family life of the 1860s. Later critics, detecting subtler merits in *Little Women*, have fixed upon its feminist themes and have almost succeeded in converting Louisa Alcott's classic story for girls into a feminist tract for her times.

Contemporary reviewers found *Little Women* "an agreeable little story" or "the best Christmas story which we have seen for a long time." However, they were astute enough also to perceive that, although it was "well adapted to the readers for whom it is especially intended," it "may also be read with pleasure by older people," and that, although "it deals with the most ordinary every-day life," "it never gets commonplace." Publication of Part II stirred up more enthusiasm: "The varied emotions of the young heart are here caught and transfixed"; the Alcott genius was evinced in the ability not only to entertain children but to portray them. And so contemporary reviews laid the groundwork for the criticism that would follow after the author's death: the view of *Little Women* as the pleasing record of a New England family. Barrett Wendell, for example, writing in 1900, compared Jacob Abbott's pictures of Yankee life in the *Rollo* books of the 1840s with Alcott's portrait of a generation later, a portrait more assertive but "just as sweet and clean."

The phenomenal continuing circulation of *Little Women* seemed to substantiate this opinion. By 1927 it was rated ahead of the Bible for its influence upon high school pupils, and two years later its sales were announced as legendary while its translations gave it a worldwide readership. Its bibliographical points were enumerated by the bookseller-scholar David A. Randall in 1939, and the history of its generation and publication was traced by the collector John T. Winterich, who pronounced Alcott's own comment—"It reads better than I expected. . . . we really lived most of it; and if it succeeds that will be the reason of it"—"the most accurate tabloid review and prognosis of a book ever written."

By the 1940s criticism of *Little Women* consisted almost entirely of hymns of praise. A dramatization of the novel called forth George Jean Nathan's comment that it was "still serviceable theatre, and a felicitous journey out of the hard-boiled present into the lace-valentine yesterday." By the following decade Edward Wagenknecht saw *Little Women* itself as a "hymn in praise of family life," an American *David Copperfield* and hence perhaps a "sign of the 'feminization' of life and letters"—the first inkling that *Little Women* would one day provide the basis for a corpus of feminist criticism. Meanwhile, the collector C. Waller Barrett sang his own hymn in praise of *Little Women* in "Little Women Forever," where he recapitulated its genesis, its public appeal, and its position in "the front rank of best-sellers of all time."

It was not until the early 1960s that *Little Women* was subjected to the keen analysis of Brigid Brophy who, in the first serious modern criticism of the book, dissected the characters of the four March sisters and the Alcott sentimentality in which Brophy found an "absence of intellectual content" but a "craftsmanship . . . to be . . . legitimately enjoyed."

The year 1968, marking *Little Women*'s centennial, opened the floodgates of Alcott criticism much of which apotheosized Alcott's alter ego, Jo March. With Elizabeth Janeway's "Meg, Jo, Beth, Amy and Louisa," the feminist shock of recognition in *Little Women* may be said to have begun. According to Janeway, it was the character of heroine Jo alone that converted the novel into a "perennial classic." Jo was "a unique creation: the one young woman in 19th-century fiction who maintains her individual independence, who gives up no part of her autonomy as payment for being born a woman—and who gets away with it." This view of Jo March as "the tomboy dream come true," "an idealized 'New Woman,' capable of male virtues but not . . . 'unsexed,' " would be questioned by feminist critics, but it laid the ground for feminist criticism of *Little Women*.

Lavinia Russ pursued a somewhat similar vein of thought in "Not To Be Read On Sunday," emphasizing Jo as the rebel, "with rebels for parents. . . . rebels who looked at the world as it was, saw the poverty, the inequality, the ignorance, the fear, and said, 'It isn't good enough' and went to work to change it."

Two other articles have been rescued from the critical flood of 1968 because of the variety of their viewpoints. In her introduction to the Centennial Edition of *Little Women*, Cornelia Meigs harked back to Alcott's lack of pretense and the influence of Bunyan's *Pilgrim's Progress* upon an author whose "counterpart was Mr. Valiant-for-truth." Sean O'Faolain, on the other hand, found the clue to the popularity of *Little Women* in its honorable escapism. The author, he concluded, had glossed over the hardships of her life, watered down the "bitter wine of . . . poverty and . . . misery," made a mere shadow of the atypical paterfamilias, and had lifted "those genteel muslin curtains of Boston just enough . . . to let us guess the whole truth about her period." She had also created "a new kind of heroine, who . . . grins across the ages at many an American girl of today."

By the 1970s it was that "new kind of heroine" who commanded the attention of Alcott critics. Dramatizations of *Little Women*, the acceleration of the feminist movement, and the subsequent publication of the unknown Alcott thrillers—all helped to trigger the critical reaction to *Little Women* in which feminist insights were pivotal. In 1973 Stephanie Harrington touched off that feminist theme with her "Does 'Little Women' Belittle Women?" deciding that, despite the sentimentality and domestic homilies rejected by today's feminists, the March sisters do think, grow, and "stand as moral actors in the context of their world." To "Jo March–Louisa May Alcott" Leo Lerman, who rereads *Little Women* annually, wrote a "love letter" singing of his enchantment, as "a first generation American," with the Americanism, the optimism, the "life" that "pulsates in these long-lived pages." By 1975 *Little Women* became a feminist tract for and against the times. Patricia Meyer Spacks claimed that "Louisa May Alcott's ideas about what women should and can be, and what men naturally are, shape the . . . narrative structure" of her fiction. *Little Women*, according to Spacks, teaches repression of female emotions, passivity in male relations, service and self-subordination—all of which conflict with Jo's rebellion. As a result, Jo's "yearning for a man's freedom" ends in a "punitive marriage" to the authoritarian Professor Bhaer. As the author sums up, "Jo is a dangerous figure. She reveals her creator's awareness that women have needs deeper than Mrs. March allows herself to know."

A similar attitude is conveyed by Thomas H. Pauly in his comparison of Alger's *Ragged Dick* with Alcott's *Little Women*. Both books, he finds, "mirror a society firmly committed to a sharp differentiation of the sexes," and Alcott, like Alger, "resisted the marital responsibilities essential to the familial happiness her book strives to project." In other words, nonconformist Jo, who refused to marry Laurie but did marry the professor, advocates a Victorian home but rejects the role it imposed upon its women.

The concept of *Little Women* as a salute to women's solidarity appears in the criticism of Ellen Moers who finds in Alcott's fiction a "curious modernity." She also compares Alcott's exaltation of "work as an act of faith" with that of Simone Weil, "the modern philosopher of work," and reminds us that "the importance of work in America's favorite girl-child's classic [as contrasted with the importance of play in the boy's *Tom Sawyer*] is worth pondering." Nina Auerbach, too, in her comparison of *Little Women* with

Pride and Prejudice, finds in the former "a community of new women," a "militant vision of permanent sisterhood" as "a felt dream." Indeed, Auerbach attributes the continued popularity of *Little Women* to the fact that "Mrs. March allows her girls a great freedom . . . the freedom to remain children and, for a woman, the more precious freedom *not* to fall in love" — a reference to Jo March's attitude toward marriage.

By 1979, Judith Fetterley examined the feminism of *Little Women* in the light of Alcott's thrillers. "Alcott's sensation fiction," she wrote, "provides an important gloss on the sexual politics . . . of Jo's relation with Professor Bhaer." Indeed, she finds the continued interest in and influence of *Little Women* "the result of . . . internal conflict" between the overt and the covert, a conflict that ended in compromise. Alcott's "true style," Fetterley concludes, "is rather less than true." Carolyn Heilbrun is more affirmative, claiming that Jo March's was "one of the most revolutionary voices in American fiction about family roles and the expectations of girls in confronting them." Although Jo March could not reinvent womanhood, she did reinvent girlhood, appropriating "the male model without giving up the female person." As Madelon Bedell puts it in the final selection concerned with *Little Women*, the book "has survived the successive waves of both American feminism and antifeminism, . . . emerging fresh, whole — and different — for the next generation of women." Thus, Jo March is Alcott's persona, and *Little Women* "may be *the* American female myth." The feminists, whether for or against that persona and that myth, have proven their fascination with both.

Bedell questions the inner contentment of the Jo March who is converted into the Mrs. Jo Bhaer of the sequels, *Little Men* and *Jo's Boys*. After the success of *Little Women*, Louisa Alcott felt compelled to continue in the vein in which she had triumphed, and though she too occasionally rebelled against writing what she once called "moral pap for the young,"[5] she supplied her publishers and her public with the so-called Little Women Series — seven additional novels in the genre of *Little Women*. *An Old-Fashioned Girl*, *Little Men*, *Eight Cousins*, *Rose in Bloom*, *Under the Lilacs*, *Jack and Jill*, and *Jo's Boys*, published between 1870 and 1886, were stories "about Young America, for Young America."[6] Although none of them ever attained the stature of *Little Women*, they all helped maintain the author's popularity and in time yielded their own harvest of critical comment.

An Old-Fashioned Girl which in 1870 followed close upon the heels of *Little Women* crusaded against the fashionable absurdities of the day, and in the character of Polly, the "old-fashioned girl," shaped a new but still womanly woman. As an anonymous reviewer observed in the *Nation*, while Alcott assisted her reader "to reproduce his youth," writing "not so much for children as about them," her characters "exist for their creator's purposes, not their own; they all are made that they may point a moral." The moral — that frivolous materialism and the caprices of fashion were to be abjured — was, according to *Lippincott's Magazine*, a vital one for the author's "fellow-women of America." "Miss Alcott," the critic decided, "writes like an honest and fearless woman."

Indeed, her fearlessness led to raised eyebrows on the part of the *Harper's* reviewer who in 1871 challenged some of the liberties allowed the pupils in *Little Men*. That pedagogical novel was based in part upon Bronson Alcott's educational methods, and at Plumfield self-knowledge, self-help, and self-control were deemed more important than Latin and Greek. One incident in *Little Men* has given rise to considerable critical probing, the incident of the ritual sacrifice of "the things we like best" to placate the imaginary "Naughty Kitty-Mouse." The sacrifice is proposed to his twin sister Daisy by Demi (perhaps influenced by his "grandfather" — Bronson Alcott's — discipline in denial), and the immolation of toys that follows terminates with the burning of Daisy's favorite doll. Contemporary reaction to that incident, represented by the *Overland Monthly*'s review, was simply that the sacrifice was "a capital bit of fun, and a truthful illustration of the wonderful power of imagination in children." By 1958, when Grover Smith addressed himself to the episode of "The Doll-Burners," he found a parallel between it and a passage in D. H. Lawrence's *Sons and Lovers*, where the victim is a doll owned by Paul Morel's sister. Smith hazards the guess that "Lawrence saw in the doll-burning a symbol of male retaliation against female domestic ascendancy." Moreover, he judges the narration "less horrible" in Lawrence than in Louisa Alcott, who fanned "the balefire of her jolly moral tale."

In its way *Eight Cousins* (1875) is also a pedagogical novel in which the heroine Rose is taught by her Uncle Alec, a crusader against convention, to shed life's shams. Championing the new enlightenment in schooling, food, and clothing, Alcott establishes herself as an advocate of children whom, according to the *London Athenaeum*, she considered "generally in the right." The thirty-two-year-old Henry James, however, reviewing *Eight Cousins* for the *Nation*, regarded it as "a very ill-chosen sort of entertainment to set before children." "What," he pined, "have become of the 'Rollo' books," which, unlike Barrett Wendell, James regarded as "an antidote to this unhappy amalgam of the novel and the story-book."

Among the objections to later books in the Little Women Series — *Rose in Bloom* (sequel to *Eight Cousins*), *Under the Lilacs*, and *Jack and Jill* — were the author's use of slang and "untidy English," as well as the introduction of "amateur lovemaking" into her narratives. The former violation of contemporary taste was forgiven as time went on, but the latter was not. According to the 1876 *Nation*, in *Rose in Bloom*, "Mac's declaration and subsequent courtship take us to the utmost verge of fiction for minors." Five years later, the *Atlantic Monthly* condemned the "suppressed love-making" of the "young people" in *Jack and Jill*, and as late as 1905, when reprint editions of *Under the Lilacs* and *Jack and Jill* were reviewed anonymously in the *Nation*, it was considered that "the lovemaking" in the Alcott books "remains a distinct blot on girl and boy literature."

The final novel in the Little Women Series was *Jo's Boys* (1886), upon which the author labored on and off for several years. The sequel to *Little Men*, the story also marks the fall of the curtain on the March family saga. Although Alcott repeats herself in *Jo's Boys* and stereotypes her incidents, she reweaves in the fabric of her novel the thread of her memories and the thread of her crusades, feminist and otherwise. In 1974, Carolyn Forrey, writing on "The New Woman Revisited," remarked that "A reader who knows Louisa May Alcott only as the author of *Little Women* might do well to look at *Jo's Boys* . . . in which her sympathies for the New Woman are quite evident." It is in the character of Nan, the once untamed tomboy who becomes a doctor, that Forrey finds the "strongest New Woman figure in the novel." In the character of the once wild boy Dan who dies defending the Indians, Madelon Bedell discovered Jo March's alter ego, and, in the "symbol-laden conclusion to Dan's story . . . the hidden end of the *Little Women* legend."

The reworking of the *Little Women* legend between 1868 and 1886 had resulted in eight narratives that became a fertile field for critical comment. During their creation the prolific tale-spinner also produced a succession of short stories that appeared in contemporary periodicals and were subsequently reintroduced to her avid public as collections. These too evoked assessment.

The six volumes of *Aunt Jo's Scrap-Bag*, appearing over the Roberts Brothers imprint between 1872 and 1882, formed a repository for Alcott reprints from periodicals and new tales. The *Scrap-Bag* in her hands became a dispensary for sugar-coated pills that encased many of the reforms of the day, from temperance to women's rights. The criticism the series evoked upon publication was generally approving. "For the little ones," according to *Godey's Lady's Book*, "there is plenty of incident and adventure, for the elders, a thoughtful portraiture of character; and a verisimilitude that appeals to both." On the other hand, *Harper's New Monthly Magazine* regarded the Alcott style as "always vivacious, but not always natural and simple." A century after their publication, Joy A. Marsella, in *The Promise of Destiny: Children and Women in the Stories of Louisa May Alcott*, provides a keenly analytical study of the moral code and the roles of women and children as reflected in the Scrap-Bag Series.

Many of the Alcott short stories, like her novels, are imbedded in her autobiography. One of them has commanded special attention, "Transcendental Wild Oats." First published in the *Independent* in 1873, this bowdlerized account of her father's utopian experiment in Harvard, Massachusetts, in the early 1840s has been reprinted six times. One of the recent reprints, by the Harvard Common Press, includes a critical preface by William Henry Harrison who indicated that, while the author Louisa Alcott emphasized the absurdities and freakish aspects of Bronson Alcott's community of Fruitlands, she de-emphasized the ideology behind his new Eden. "The transition from 'Fruitlands' to 'Apple Slump' was not as dramatic an event as Louisa describes it." She was, by her own confession, no biographer, but as a professional writer she had her hand on the public pulse.

"Transcendental Wild Oats" had been reprinted earlier, in 1876, in another Alcott story collection, *Silver Pitchers*, whose title narrative was concerned with temperance — a simpler, more objective reform than utopian society for Alcott to handle. *Silver Pitchers*, and other collections that followed — *Proverb Stories* in 1882, *Spinning-Wheel Stories* in 1884, and the three-volume series of *Lulu's Library* between 1886 and 1889 (told and named for her niece, May's daughter, after May's death) — interwove the thread of autobiography with the thread of reform and helped sustain the author's now exalted reputation. Some critics, here represented by an 1882 reviewer in the British *Saturday Review of Politics, Literature, Science, And Art*, still found an excess of "love-making" in stories intended for children. Four years later, however, another anonymous reviewer in the same journal astutely observed that "Miss Louisa Alcott has made her specialty of those years in a girl's life that come between the time of the doll and the time of the lover."

That specialty, as it turned out, had not prevented the author from attempting other specialties as well. Although, as she had stated, "biography is not in my line," autobiography certainly was. All the *Little Women* novels are in some sense autobiographical, but it was in her novel *Work: A Story of Experience* (1873) that Alcott created a largely autobiographical fiction geared to feminist ends. Another novel that she produced in the 1870s represented for her, in part at least, a return to her experimentations of the past. In *A Modern Mephistopheles*, published anonymously in 1877, Alcott reverted to the sensational techniques of A. M. Barnard to narrate the conflict of good and evil, crime and punishment. Both those novels, directed to adult readerships, mark deviations from the pattern established by America's best-loved author of juveniles. They — and the criticism they gave rise to — disclose interesting aspects of a complex professional writer.

Work: A Story of Experience, published in 1873, had been begun in 1861 as *Success* — a transformation in title that was itself a commentary upon the author's changing attitudes. The experience upon which it was based was, for the most part, Louisa Alcott's, and her labors as domestic servant, actress, companion, seamstress, and military nurse all became episodes in the progress of her heroine Christie Devon. In the same way, the author's feminist inclinations were imparted to Christie, who takes charge of her dead husband's greenhouse business and joins an association of working women. The earnest life of Christie Devon failed to rouse enthusiasm on the part of reviewers accustomed to *Little Women, An Old-Fashioned Girl* and *Aunt Jo's Scrap-Bag*. Indeed, the *London Athenaeum* found the succession of hardships endured by the heroine almost unnatural. "The story of 'Work' is too restless; and the result is so fatiguing, that we should not be surprised if the reader, after finishing it, gives up, and refuses to do anything whatever for the rest of the day." *Harper's Magazine* classified this episodic fiction as a didactic essay on the subject of woman's work and pontificated, "The book would not have made her reputation, but her reputation will make the book." With some astuteness the reviewer objected to the lack of cohesion in *Work*. "Miss Alcott appears to have sat down to write the first chapter without knowing what the next chapter would be, and to have drifted along in the current of her own thoughts till she found a novel growing under her hands." The *Lakeside Monthly* was even more vehemently condemnatory, objecting to the apotheosis of "Madam Work," a gospel overpreached in New England during the last half-century, castigating the novel's events as incredible and absurd improbabilities, and concluding that *Work* was "the story of a female who was not a woman, married to her choice who was not a man, . . . this book has not a heart. We trust the author has."

Not until 1977, when Sarah Elbert wrote the introduction to a new edition of *Work*, did that fiction receive the modern reading it deserves. Elbert views *Work* as "an expression of Alcott's feminist principles" in which "she broadened the scope of her fiction from the domestic relations she excelled in portraying, to an urgent, passionate portrait of the female life cycle in all its complexity." This is a large claim, but Elbert proceeds to substantiate it. She perceives in the nineteenth-century background of *Work* "the injustices of developing industrialism," the patriarchal system that precluded woman's independence, and the sisterhood of women workers that eventually emerged. Christie's awareness of all this is part of the process that expanded "individual salvation" into "social reform." There is much else to engage the attention of the careful critic of *Work*—the question of racial integration in Christie's friendship with the black cook Hepsey Johnson and the portraits of David Sterling based upon Thoreau and of Mr. Power based upon Theodore Parker. Basically, however, *Work* describes, as Elbert puts it, "Alcott's sense of the formation of women's consciousness in the nineteenth century." As a result, it "deserves a modern audience, not only as an historical document and a minor literary achievement, but . . . as a key to understanding. . . ."

Work: A Story of Experience has had the modern readings it merits. Alcott's other major deviation from her established pattern—*A Modern Mephistopheles*—has not yet been subjected to the modern criticism it deserves. This novel that seeks to penetrate "the mysterious mechanism of human nature"[7] depicts the Mephistophelian sybarite Jasper Helwyze in the role of manipulator of his victim Felix Canaris. *A Modern Mephistopheles* stirs in its crucible borrowings from the thrillers of the author's salad days, including an experiment with hashish, along with more metaphysical borrowings from Goethe and Hawthorne. It was published anonymously as a volume in the "No Name Series" sponsored by Roberts Brothers, and upon its appearance in 1877 Alcott wrote in her journal: " 'M.M.' appears and causes much guessing. It is praised and criticised, and I enjoy the fun, especially when friends say, 'I know *you* didn't write it, for you can't hide your peculiar style.' "[8]

She had apparently hidden it well, for contemporary reviewers failed to penetrate not only the secrets of its text but the secret of its authorship. It was to the latter that they gave much of their attention. The *Atlantic Monthly* credited Julian Hawthorne with authorship of "this peculiar production" of "signal force." *Godey's Lady's Book* deduced it had been written "by a young person, probably a girl, with much literary facility and fluency, and an excellent grasp of plot, but with little experience of life," adding that, "With advancing years and a larger experience the author may make her mark." Edward R. Burlingame, writing for the *North American Review*, cogitated upon the "psychological experiment" portrayed in *A Modern Mephistopheles* but dismissed the result as "a fresh and dainty fantasy" that bore "both the defects and merits of a woman's pen."

As a feminist document, *Work* has captured the thoughtful attention of modern critics. Although it lacks the feminist theme, *A Modern Mephistopheles* is no less deserving of attention. Alcott's first major deviation from her pattern—*Work*—helped raise woman's consciousness. Her second—*A Modern Mephistopheles*—explored "the mysterious mechanism of human nature" and in so doing revealed much of her own. It should be reexamined.

Unlike the absence of modern treatment accorded *A Modern Mephistopheles*, general appraisals and reappraisals of the Alcott canon have not been wanting. Indeed, they have punctuated the years since her death, increasing qualitatively and quantitatively with the passage of time. Practically every decade has yielded up its quota of pros and cons as critics have tried to explain the continuing popularity of Louisa May Alcott and to penetrate the moral influence of one who was less artist than professional writer.

Alcott's first biographer, Ednah D. Cheney, pointed out shortly after her subject's death that the Alcott writings were a recapitulation of the Alcott autobiography. "Her works," she asserted, "are a revelation of herself." Cheney's eulogy of those works was offset by the iconoclastic remarks quoted in the *New York Times Saturday Review* in 1898: " 'I am sorry to be obliged to be sorry that Miss Alcott ever wrote.' " The following decade saw publication of G. K. Chesterton's playful essay on "the famous books of Miss Alcott" in the course of which he announced his discovery that, to his "immeasurable astonishment, . . . they were extremely good." Comparing the Alcott talent with that of Jane Austen, Chesterton found its vitality in a lack of pretense, in a re-creation of life "even where it is not literature." Franklin B. Sanborn, the family friend who became Bronson Alcott's biographer, went further in 1912 when he recalled Louisa's addiction to the theatre and saw "the laurel . . . prophetic" on her head. Seven years later, the laurel was removed by the poet Amy Lowell who condemned the "very bad English" and untruth to life in the Alcott books which she did "not at all recommend."

By 1920, critics began to address themselves seriously to Alcott's continuing fascination. Their explanations for that phenomenon were based upon the positive and the negative aspects of her work. Katharine Fullerton Gerould, for example, concluded that the very paradoxes in the Alcott oeuvre contributed to its successful re-creation of "mid-century New England." The bad grammar coupled with the literary background; the social *laissez-aller* coupled with the moral purity; the plain living coupled with the high thinking; the omnipresent morality coupled with the absence of religion; the abundance of sentiment coupled with the lack of passion; the breath of reform hot upon the pages — all helped make of the Alcott legacy a "genuine document," an accurate reconstruction of the "quintessential New England village."

In her clever article for the *New Republic* in 1924, "Subversive Miss Alcott," Elizabeth Vincent fashioned a different answer to the same question: Alcott was still read because she was bad for her readers. The persistent moralizing was irresistible. "Could any but pernicious influence hold such a fascination for so long?" As for Thomas Beer, author of *The Mauve Decade*, he perceived Alcott's books as conveying a matriarchal, not a patriarchal, message — "God's ministrant is always female" — and found her influence "familiar as a corset." In 1955, Eleanor Perényi formulated for *Harper's Magazine* her answer to the intriguing puzzle, suggesting that it was Alcott's regional interest and liberalism, her "capitalistic conscience," her "anti-classical" pragmatic pedagogy — in short, her modernity — that contributed to the durability of her influence. "It has been her lasting legacy to mirror for young Americans certain more or less permanent attitudes inherent everywhere in American culture, but most particularly in New England culture."

Whatever the reasons for Alcott's continuing influence — and they certainly embraced all those proffered by perplexed critics — that influence has persisted. More recent commentators have accepted the fact without concerning themselves with attempted explanations, and have gone on to examine other aspects of the Alcott canon. In 1978, Ann Douglas, reviewing the Martha Saxton biography *Louisa May* which followed "logically upon Madeleine Stern's critical . . . republication of Alcott's lost 'thrillers,' " addressed the paradoxes in Alcott's career, the disparity between "the different influences of her parents," the sensational and the domestic threads in the fabric of her writing, and the "discrepancy between the literary persona and the reality of Louisa May Alcott."

Departing from an attempt to analyze the persona of Louisa Alcott, Madeleine Stern, on the occasion of the author's 150th birthday in 1982, summed up the Alcott oeuvre, tracing the development of her craftsmanship by tracing "the stages in her writer's progress," from her output as "Flora Fairfield" to her output as "Nurse Tribulation Periwinkle," from the Walpurgis Night of "A. M. Barnard" to the creations of "The Children's Friend."

Essays written expressly for this volume include Freda Baum's "The Scarlet Strand," a study of the reform motifs that punctuate Alcott's writings and make of them "important cultural artifacts"; Martha Saxton's investigation of the dark undercurrents in Alcott's work; penetrating analyses of the influence of and the interrelations between three great contemporaries and Alcott: Joel Myerson on Bronson Alcott and his daughter; Adeline Tintner on Henry James and Louisa Alcott; and Marie Olesen Urbanski on Henry David Thoreau and Alcott. In each case the critic has brought his/her particular expertise to bear upon a previously unexamined or insufficiently examined subject. Mary Cadogan's " 'Sweet, If Somewhat Tomboyish' " encapsulates British response to "The Children's Friend"; finally, Alma J. Payne's bibliographical essay on secondary sources traces the assessment and reassessment of Alcott as revealed in successive biographies and critical analyses during the century since the writer's death.

In Payne's bibliographical essay the major Alcott biographies are briefly described: the earliest by Ednah D. Cheney, the tribute entitled *Louisa May Alcott: The Children's Friend* (1888) as well as her still indispensable edition of *Louisa May Alcott: Her Life, Letters, and Journals* (1889); the reminiscences of Annie M. L. Clark in *The Alcotts in Harvard* (1902) and of Clara Gowing in *The Alcotts as I Knew Them* (1909); "the first noteworthy attempt at a biography," Belle Moses' *Louisa May Alcott, Dreamer and Worker* (1909); Cornelia Meigs' *The Story of the Author of Little Women: Invincible Louisa* (1933) which "provided background valuable for an in-depth understanding of Alcott's works"; Katharine S. Anthony's psychological study *Louisa May Alcott* (1938); Madeleine B. Stern's *Louisa May Alcott* (1950, reprinted 1971), "a sound critical biography, readable but important for its bibliography and notes on sources"; Marjorie Worthington's *Miss Alcott of Concord* (1958) which "reworked material from Cheney's edition, with the addition of some personal experience"; Helen Waite Papashvily's *Louisa May Alcott* (1965) which "expanded the earlier material [from Papashvily's *All the Happy Endings* (1956)] into a biography by making use of . . . primary materials"; Martha Saxton's *Louisa May: A Modern Biography of Louisa May Alcott* (1977) which followed Stern's publication of the unknown Alcott thrillers and used them as a basis for reinterpretation of the Alcott life; and finally Madelon Bedell's *The Alcotts, Biography of a Family* (1980) which traced Alcott family development to the mid-century.

Payne also cites the major Alcott bibliographies including Lucile Gulliver's *Louisa May Alcott: A Bibliography* (1932); Judith C. Ullom's *Louisa May Alcott: A Centennial for "Little Women"* (1969); the bibliographies in

Stern's *Louisa May Alcott* (1950 and 1971) and in Madeleine B. Stern's *Louisa's Wonder Book — An Unknown Alcott Juvenile* (1975); and Alma J. Payne's *Louisa May Alcott: A Reference Guide* (1980).

Some of the critical items cited by Payne have been reprinted in these pages, and a few others — also cited by Payne — would have been included had not the exigencies of space prevented. A word or two might be added about the Alcott criticism not included either in Payne's bibliographical essay or in *Critical Essays on Louisa May Alcott* — omissions for which, once again, the limitations of space are responsible. Jeanne F. Bedell's "A Necessary Mask: The Sensation Fiction of Louisa May Alcott"[9] dilated upon the image of the author during her early period of experimentation. The already large corpus of articles on *Little Women* in this volume might have been expanded by inclusion of the following: John T. Winterich's chapter on that masterpiece in his *Twenty-Three Books and the Stories Behind Them*[10] which stresses its desirability as a collectible; Margery Fisher's comments on the book's continuing popularity in *Intent upon Reading;*[11] Margaret Crompton's "Little Women: The Making of a Classic";[12] Sara Innis Fenwick's "American Children's Classics: Which Will Fade, Which Endure?"[13] There Fenwick considers both *Little Women* and *Little Men*. In 1978, Ann Boaden viewed freedom for woman's development as the major theme in *Little Women*, where it is communicated by the use of "certain patterns and techniques of comedy."[14] Anne Hollander's thoughtful reflections on Alcott's masterpiece concern the attitude of the Marches toward marriage and money, consider Jo's retreat from sex, and conclude that "Jo can write as a true artist only later, when she finally comes to terms with her own sexual self."[15]

Sarah Elbert's examination of *Work* would have been richly complemented by Jean Fagan Yellin's analysis of that autobiographical novel in the *Massachusetts Review* of 1980.[16] With Elbert, Yellin found in *Work* reflections of the varied aspects of ninteenth-century radicalism, from abolition to utopian collectivism, from economic feminism and woman's rights to a struggle against the double sexual standard. But Yellin, who addresses herself to the novel as a literary achievement — albeit a flawed one — probes more deeply into matters of literary structure, tracing the shift and breaking of text in part to the interrupted history of its creation, in part to the attempted use of the sentimental novel as a vehicle for social criticism. "*Work,*" she muses, "is most interesting where most flawed," and this novel of a woman who struggled to lead an autonomous life in nineteenth-century America she finds a durable achievement.

Writing for the *New York Times Magazine* in 1938, Mildred Adams posed an interesting answer to the question that still perplexed the critics: "how it is that the simple annals of the March family have continued to charm generations of children from the end of the Civil War to the second decade after the World War" despite the differences between the America for which Alcott wrote and the America of 1938.[17] Either, she pondered, "there must have been the stuff of greatness in her books . . . or else the difference in surfaces is less important than it looks." Adams attributed the phenomenon to the fact that Alcott wrote "when the tide was turning toward . . . newer virtues" and she managed to combine the old and the new, the "homely humanity" and the "new naturalism." In so doing she "opened all the windows . . . and let the cold outside air rush into stuffy parlors and stuffier heads."

The diversities of the Alcott canon are surveyed by Iola Haverstick in her *Saturday Review* article, "To See Louisa Plain,"[18] while Martha Shull's dissertation, "The Novels of Louisa May Alcott as Commentary on the American Family,"[19] studies the influence exerted upon family life by succeeding generations of Alcott readers. Eugenia Kaledin examined for *Women's Studies* the Alcott achievement as well as Alcott's literary concessions in her "Louisa May Alcott: Success and the Sorrow of Self-denial."[20] In 1977, Suzy Goldman considered Alcott's attitude toward the arts in her study of Alcott's treatment of a career in the arts combined with marriage, or, indeed, with femininity,[21] and more recently Janice M. Alberghene discussed Alcott's approach to the artist's life in a paper delivered before the Children's Literature Association.[22]

A charming reminiscent essay recalling a meeting with Alcott was presented as a fortnightly theme by student Florence Phillips to her instructor William Vaughn Moody. Not until 1980 did Professor George Arms publish both theme and corrections in an article entitled "The Poet As Theme Reader: William Vaughn Moody, A Student, and Louisa May Alcott."[23]

Feminist investigation of Alcott's work might have been extended with the remarks of Sharon O'Brien in her "Tomboyism and Adolescent Conflict: Three Nineteenth-Century Case Studies,"[24] and with Jane Van Buren's almost clinical analysis, "Louisa May Alcott: A Study in Persona and Idealization," a study that perceived Alcott as suffering "an existential crisis of non-being" that imposed upon her the "total separation of the sentimental and the Gothic genres."[25] Finally, *Critical Essays on Louisa May Alcott* would have been enriched by inclusion of several of Elizabeth Keyser's fine yet unpublished writings on individual Alcott stories: "Little Women in Louisa May Alcott's *Little Men*" and " 'Nothing But Love': Louisa May Alcott's 'Cupid and Chow-chow.' "[26]

For more than a century Alcott has survived, until today she engages the attention not only of the youthful reader to whom much of her work was directed but also of the mature scholar. The variety of her oeuvre has disclosed the complexities of her nature, and considerable attention has been paid to reconstructing the life from the fiction. As a result, Alcott's own feminist fury—or lack of it—has been analyzed and even psychoanalyzed, the conflicts between the sentimental and the Gothic, between domesticity and crusading reform have all been subjected to critical study by reviewers who judge the autobiography from the literary production. All this is, of course, a tribute not only to Alcott's interest as a persona but to the stature of her output. There is opportunity still for future critics to work more closely from the life to the fiction, to seek more understanding of the work from the facts of the autobiography. Specifically there is need for critical new editions of *Moods* and of *A Modern Mephistopheles*. Studies of the fatherless home and the independent spinster in Alcott fiction would be welcome. Finally, although Louisa Alcott was herself many things — sentimentalist and reformer, exalter of family sweetness and explorer of individual darkness — she was basically a professional writer whose works have endured. What is due to all such professional writers is also due to her: more keen critical analysis of her narrative technique, her methods of characterization, and her craftsmanship. Her themes have been explored. Her techniques still demand further perceptive investigation. Their study will clarify the ways and means by which she who reached a mass audience in the nineteenth century still challenges the literary critic of the twentieth.

Madeleine B. Stern

Notes

1. Frank O'Connor, "A Writer Who Refused to Pretend," *New York Times Book Review*, 17 January 1960, quoted in James Matthews, *Voices: A Life of Frank O'Connor* (New York: Atheneum, 1983), p. 376.

2. Unless otherwise indicated, all quotations are from reviews and essays reprinted in the present volume.

3. Ednah D. Cheney, ed., *Louisa May Alcott: Her Life, Letters, and Journals* (Boston: Roberts Brothers, 1889), pp. 198-99.

4. Cheney, p. 201.

5. Cheney, p. 296.

6. Louisa May Alcott, *An Old-Fashioned Girl* (Boston: Little, Brown & Co., 1920), p. 231.

7. Louisa May Alcott, *A Modern Mephistopheles and A Whisper in the Dark* (Boston: Roberts Brothers, 1889), p. 46.

8. Cheney, p. 297.

9. Jeanne F. Bedell, "A Necessary Mask: The Sensation Fiction of Louisa May Alcott," *Publications of the Missouri Philological Association*, 5 (1980), 8–14.

10. John T. Winterich, *Twenty-Three Books and the Stories Behind Them* (Philadelphia: J. B. Lippincott Co., 1939), pp. 195–204.

11. Margery Fisher, *Intent upon Reading: A Critical Appraisal of Modern Fiction for Children* (Leicester: Brockhampton Press, 1961), pp. 297–98.

12. Margaret Crompton, "Little Women: The Making of a Classic," *Contemporary Review*, 218 (February 1971), 99–104.

13. Sara Innis Fenwick, "American Children's Classics: Which Will Fade, Which Endure?" *Wilson Library Bulletin*, 47 (October 1972), 179–81.

14. Ann Boaden, "The Joyful Woman: Comedy as a Mode of Liberation in *Little Women*," in *The Masks of Comedy: Papers Delivered at the Humanities Festival, 1978, Augustana College* (Rock Island, Ill.: Augustana College Library, 1980), pp. 47–52; 56–57.

15. Anne Hollander, "Reflections on *Little Women*," *Children's Literature*, 9 (1981), 28–39.

16. Jean Fagan Yellin, "From *Success* to *Experience*: Louisa May Alcott's *Work*," *Massachusetts Review*, 21 (1980), 527–39.

17. Mildred Adams, "When the Little Angels Revolted," *New York Times Magazine*, 6 March 1938, pp. 10–11, 24.

18. Iola Haverstick, "To See Louisa Plain," *Saturday Review of Literature*, 51 (19 October 1968), 35, 52.

19. Martha Irene Shull, "The Novels of Louisa May Alcott as Commentary on the American Family," Diss. Bowling Green State University 1975.

20. Eugenia Kaledin, "Louisa May Alcott: Success and the Sorrow of Self-denial," *Women's Studies*, 5 (1978), 251–63.

21. Suzy Goldman, "Louisa May Alcott: The Separation between Art and Family," *Lion and the Unicorn: A Critical Journal of Children's Literature*, 1 (1977), 91–97.

22. Janice M. Alberghene, "Alcott's Psyche and Kate: Self-Portraits, Sunny-side Up," *Proceedings of the Eighth Annual Conference of the Children's Literature Association, March 1981* (1982), 37–43.

23. *Toward a New American Literary History: Essays in Honor of Arlin Turner*, ed. Louis J. Budd, Edwin H. Cady, and Carl L. Anderson (Durham: Duke Univ. Press, 1980) pp. 140–53.

24. Sharon O'Brien, "Tomboyism and Adolescent Conflict: Three Nineteenth-Century Case Studies," in *Woman's Being, Woman's Place: Female Identity and Vocation in American History*, ed. Mary Kelley (Boston: G. K. Hall & Co., 1979), pp. 362–72.

25. Jane Van Buren, "Louisa May Alcott: A Study in Persona and Idealization," *Psychohistory Review*, 9 (Summer 1981), 282–99.

26. To these might be added Elizabeth Keyser, "Alcott's Portraits of the Artist as Little Woman," *International Journal of Women's Studies*, 5 (November–December 1982), 445–59, and "Women and Girls in Louisa May Alcott's *Jo's Boys*", ibid., 6 (November–December 1983). I should like to thank Mr. Greg Anderson, reference librarian, the Library of Congress; Dr. Robert Burkholder, Pennsylvania State University; Professor Joel Myerson, University of South Carolina; and Ms. Betty-Carol Sellen, acting chief librarian, Brooklyn College Library for their help in supplying photocopies of materials reprinted in this volume.

EXPERIMENTATIONS BEFORE *LITTLE WOMEN*

Flower Fables

[Review of *Flower Fables*, 1855] Anonymous*

Messrs. George W. Briggs & Co. have published an illustrated work entitled *Flower Fables*, by Louisa May Alcott. It contains several agreeable sketches, in prose and verse, adapted to the capacity of intelligent young persons.

[Review of *Flower Fables*, 1855] Anonymous*

Very sweet are these little legends of faery land, which those of our young friends, who are so fond of tales of enchantment, will, we are sure, peruse with avidity. The interest which children take in fairy tales is well known, and the infant mind is more susceptible to truths under such a guise, than in the more direct tales of a moral character.

---

*Reprinted from the *Boston Evening Transcript*, 20 December 1854, p. 1.

*Reprinted from the *Saturday Evening Gazette* (Boston), 23 December 1854, p.[2].

Hospital Sketches and *Camp and Fireside Stories*

[Advertisement for *Hospital Sketches*, 1863]

Anonymous*

THE BOSTON TRANSCRIPT

Productions of uncommon merit . . . Fluent and sparkling in style, with touches of quiet humor and lively wit, relieving what would otherwise be a topic too sombre and sad, they are graphic in description and exhibit the healthful sentiments and sympathies of the cheerful heroism that would minister to the sick and suffering. The contrast between the comic incidents and the tragic experience of a single night, given in No. 2 of the series, is portrayed with singular power and effectiveness. 'The death of John' is a noble and touching feature.

— — —

THE WATERBURY AMERICAN

Graphically drawn . . . Exceedingly well written—and the graver portions of thrilling interest. There is a quiet vein of humor, too, running all through them, so that the reader is alternately moved to laughter and tears.

[Review of *Hospital Sketches*, 1863]

Anonymous*

Hospital Sketches, by Louisa Alcott (Roberts Bros.), is the first and best of Miss Alcott's books. Written in and of the war, full of pathos, wit, and fire, it has now, and will retain the first place among the memorabilia of these times.

*Reprinted from an undated (1863) clipping in Louisa May Alcott Papers (bMS Am 800.23), Houghton Library, Harvard University.
*Reprinted from an undated (1863) clipping from *Zion's Herald* in Louisa May Alcott Papers (bMS Am 800.23), Houghton Library, Harvard University.

[Review of *Hospital Sketches and Camp and Fireside Stories*, 1869]

Anonymous*

These "Hospital Sketches" were originally written as letters from Washington when Miss Alcott was engaged as nurse in one of the army hospitals there in the winter of 1862–3. They were printed at that time in the *Boston Commonwealth*, and were received with warm commendation by the public. Miss Alcott possesses the rare gift of presenting a cheerful view to even the saddest of scenes, and so these "Sketches" excite smiles as well as tears. Some have objected to these descriptions of hospital life as having a "tone of levity." To such she says in her preface "that the wish to make the best of everything and send home cheerful reports even from that saddest of scenes, an army hospital, probably produced the impression of levity upon those who have never known the sharp contrasts of the tragic and comic in such a life.

"That Nurse Periwinkle gave no account of her religious services, thereby showing a 'sad want of Christian experience,' can only be explained by the fact, that it would have as soon occurred to her to print the letters written for the men, their penitent confidences, or their dying messages, as to mention the prayers she prayed, the hymns she sung, [sic] the sacred words she read; while the '*Christian experience*' she was receiving then and there was far too deep and earnest to be recorded in a newspaper."

The touching story of the brave John's struggle and triumph cannot soon be forgotten by those who read it. The lesson, too, which Miss Alcott teaches of our Christian duties to the colored people is most timely and valuable.

[Lengthy quotation deleted]

The "Camp and Fireside Stories," eight in number, make up the rest of the volume. They were originally published as magazine contributions and were received with much favor. Their collection in one volume, with the "Sketches," will afford much additional pleasure to the numerous readers of *Little Women*, into whose hands the book will be sure to go.

*Reprinted from the *National Anti-Slavery Standard*, 30 (18 September 1869), [3].

Introduction to *Hospital Sketches*   Bessie Z. Jones*

Since 1868 Louisa May Alcott has been virtually identified with Jo March, topsy-turvy sister of Meg, Beth, and Amy, beloved of Laurie, wife of the unromantic Professor Bhaer, mother of little men, and foster-mother of an assortment of Jo's boys at Plumfield. Yet her bibliography runs to more than 250 items, including, besides well-known stories short and long, various nonfictional pieces, poems, plays, and three serious novels for adults.[1] *Hospital Sketches* (1863), the result of her brief tour of duty as a volunteer nurse in the Civil War, is of all her books perhaps the least familiar. As one of the earliest first-hand reports of personal experience with the wounded, it won a wider audience than her few tales had then attracted, it brought her to the attention of the publisher chiefly responsible for her success, and it is one of the most illuminating accounts we have of hospital practices in the Civil War and of the unprecedented work of women in it.

[Sections deleted concerning Alcott's early writings, biographical details, and especially Civil War background.]

She fell ill of typhoid fever a month after her arrival — hardly a surprise to her father, who, on January 8, 1863, had entered in his journal: "Letters come from Louisa, giving lively descriptions of hospital scenes. She seems active, interested, and, if her strength is adequate to the task, could not better serve herself or the country. But I fear this will end in her breaking down presently."

When she recovered, she set about arranging for publication in the *Commonwealth* the letters she had sent home, the original suggestion coming from Moncure Conway and repeated by F. B. Sanborn, the new editor. She did not agree that her letters were either witty or pathetic, but she wanted money. Much to her surprise, they made a hit, and "people bought the papers faster than they could be supplied." She forgot in her modesty the intense interest such lively, straight-from-the-front reports would arouse in families hungry for every scrap of information about the fate of their boys.

The *Commonwealth*, an anti-slavery paper, was a natural medium. Its contributors had familiar names — Julia Ward Howe, Elizabeth Peabody, Moncure D. Conway, Lydia Maria Child, Channing, Redpath, and the Alcotts. The first sketch appeared on May 22, 1863, followed by others on the 29th, and on June 12 and 26. The "Postscript," she thought, ended the subject. Luckily, she proved a bad prophet. The sketches met with instant suc-

---

*Reprinted from Louisa May Alcott, *Hospital Sketches* (Cambridge: Belknap Press of Harvard Univ. Press, 1960), pp. [vii], xl–xliv. The numbering of the notes has been changed to take into account those deleted. Reprinted by permission of the publishers from *Hospital Sketches*, by Louisa May Alcott, ed. Bessie Z. Jones (Cambridge: Belknap Press of Harvard Univ. Press); © 1960 by the President and Fellows of Harvard College.

cess and were copied in papers all over the North. Praise she cherished came to her from Henry James, Senior:

> It would be tedious to you to hear how much pleasure an old man like me has taken in your charming pictures of hospital service, . . . and how refreshing he found the personal revelation there incidentally made of so much that is dearest & most worshipful in woman; so I will not dwell on those particulars, but say all I have to say in this summary form, to wit: that I am so delighted with your beautiful papers, & the evidence they afford of your exquisite humanity, that I have the greatest desire to enroll myself among your friends.[2]

Even more rewarding was a confession from one of the Union Hotel Hospital surgeons:

> To say that I thank you for writing them from the bottom of my heart, would but poorly express the sentiment which dictates to me this minute, & to say that I feel humbled by the lesson which they teach me, is to pay a tribute to them which I fancy will be rather unexpected. . . . These papers have revealed to me much that is elevated, and pure, and refined in the soldiers' character which I never before suspected. It is humiliating to me to think that I have been so long among them with such mental or moral obtuseness that I never discovered it for myself, and I thank you for showing me with how different eyes and ears you have striven among "the men" from the organs which I used on the very same cases and at the same time.

Others spoke of the graphic descriptions, the moving blend of comic and tragic, and the touching features of particular episodes, particularly "A Night."

When both James Redpath and Thomas Niles of Roberts Brothers asked permission to issue the sketches in book form, Louisa chose her old abolitionist associate, not realizing how shortsighted she was: "Little did you dream [she commented in her journal] that this same Roberts Bros. were to help you make your fortune a few years later. The 'Sketches' never made much money, but showed me 'my style,' and taking the hint, I went where glory awaited me." The glory was of course the publication of *Little Women* by Roberts Brothers in 1868.

First copies of *Hospital Sketches* reached her late in August 1863, "a neat green-covered 18mo of 100 pages," her father noted, "likely to be popular, the subject and style of treatment alike commending it to the reader." She wrote Redpath to say how much they all liked the book and what satisfaction they had in seeing townsfolk "buying, reading, laughing & crying over it wherever we go."

The library of Civil War experience contains longer, fuller accounts by and about women and their work, some uncritical or sentimental, others of great historical import.[3] Miss Alcott's *Hospital Sketches*, however brief, impress us by their unpremeditated art — the deft, rapidly paced prose, the beautiful balance of pathos and humor, the variety of impressions packed into so small a container: conditions of travel, Dickensian notes on her fellow-passengers, glimpses of the countryside and of cities passed through; the shabby, unfinished grandeur of Washington; the crowded comings and goings outside the hospital, of ambulances, doctors, amputees, carriages, overdressed fancy ladies in three-tiered bonnets who walked like ducks; the carnival air of the gold-braided officers; the mud, the animals; above all, the Negroes, so different from those she had known in the North. Her preface to the 1870 edition comments on but does not apologize for alleged levity of tone. Happily her gift for the light touch and her decent reticence about the last moments of her men have spared us the false pieties that mar many other Civil War reminiscences. "For God's sake, give me air," her blacksmith cries. Contrast this with: " 'Tis a privilege even thus to die for one's country"; "Tell my mother I love Jesus and hope to meet her in Heaven"; "I had a praying mother. O that I might meet her!"; "I am trying to think of my Saviour"; "It is growing dark. Can it be death?" She could never have written of a sister nurse: "The frail tenement of her soaring spirit was tottering," or of another who "when the spirit seemed almost gone, earth receding, and heaven opening . . . bent over him and imprinted one last kiss on the marble brow. The thin fingers that she held quivered, the eyes faintly opened, and the shadow of a smile flitted over the pale face." Yet these are actual quotations from other accounts.

For its truth, its charm, and its picture of a side of the war largely overshadowed by the military and political emphases historians have given the conflict, Miss Alcott's book merits a permanent place in the literature of military medicine and the impact of women on the practices related to it.

Notes

1. *Louisa May Alcott: Her Life, Letters, and Journals*, ed. Ednah D. Cheney (Boston, 1916), *passim*. The most recent and best documented biography is Madeleine B. Stern, *Louisa May Alcott* (Norman, Oklahoma, 1950), which includes an excellent description of sources and a detailed list of Miss Alcott's works.

2. This and the following letter appear in a clipping in the Alcott collection, Houghton Library.

3. See George Barton, *Angels of the Battlefield: A History of the Labors of the Catholic Sisterhoods in the Late Civil War* (Philadelphia, 1897); Emma S. Edmonds, *Nurse and Spy in the Union Army* (Hartford, 1865); Mrs. A. H. Hoge, *The Boys in Blue* (New York, 1867); Mrs. H[olstein], *Three Years in Field Hospitals of the Army of the Potomac* (Philadelphia, 1867); Frank Moore, *Women of the War* (Hartford, 1866); Mgr. Frank O'Brien, *Forgotten Heroines* (Lansing, Michigan, 1916), on Catholic Sisters; Theophilus Parsons, *Memoir of Emily Elizabeth Parsons* (Boston, 1880); William H. Reed, *Hospital Life in the Army of the Potomac* (Boston, 1866); Adelaide W. Smith, *Independent Volunteer: Reminiscences of an Army Nurse During the Civil War* (New York, 1911); *South after Gettysburg: Letters of Cornelia Hancock from the Army of the Potomac*, ed. Henrietta Stratton Jaquette (Philadelphia, 1937); Annie Wittenmyer, *Under the Guns* (Boston, 1895); Katharine Prescott Wormley, *The United States Sanitary Commission* (Boston, 1863) and *The Other Side of the War* (Boston, 1889); and Anon., *Notes on Hospital Life* (Philadelphia, 1864).

The Negro Character in Northern
Magazine Fiction of the 1860's
Jan Cohn*

> But more interesting than officers, ladies, mules, or pigs, were my colored brothers and sisters, because so unlike the respectable members of society I'd known in moral Boston.
>
> — Louisa May Alcott

In 1862 Louisa May Alcott enlisted for a short tour of duty as an Army nurse in Washington; her experiences are recounted in *Hospital Sketches* (1863) and used as the basis for *Camp and Fireside Stories* (1869). As a self-declared "red-hot abolitionist," she felt the appropriate antipathy for the rebel, the requisite sentimental admiration for the Northern soldier, but a frank confusion in the face of the black man, who was, after all, neither a respectable adjunct to Boston's abolitionist societies nor a realization of Mrs. Stowe's Uncle Tom. Miss Alcott, though confused by "the genuine article," the Southern Negro, did, like many of her fellow writers from the North, find him "interesting."

[Deleted passages concern the Negro as a fictional type in the 1860s and 1870s.]

There are . . . two stories by Louisa May Alcott which make tentative probings into the problem of miscegenation. These stories suggest an attraction between black and white characters, an attraction with subtle, perhaps unconscious, sexual overtones altogether alien to the portrayal of any love relationships in magazine fiction. Furthermore, Miss Alcott's black characters have some black characteristics, both physical and psychological; while they are far from being realistic Southern Negroes, they are strikingly different from the fair octoroon of the period.

"An Hour" (*Camp and Fireside Stories*) is a melodrama of slave rebellion. The white hero is named, symbolically, Gabriel; he is "the child of a Northern mother, bred at the North by her dying desire, summoned home to take the old man's place and receive a slave-cursed inheritance into his keeping." As his father lies dying, the rebellion begins at their island home. Suddenly Gabriel must protect the white population from the black; he becomes responsible for his stepmother and her two daughters, three shrill and querulous females reminiscent of Cinderella's steprelations. Cinderella herself is suggested by the beautiful slave, Milly:

> She was only a servant, with the blood of a despised race in her veins. More beautiful than either of her young mistresses, she looked like some brilliant flower of the tropics beside two pale exotics, and the unavoidable consciousness of this showed itself in the skill with which she made her simple

*Reprinted from the *New England Quarterly*, 43 (December 1970), 572, 588–92.

dress a foil to her beauty, in the carriage of her graceful head and the sad pride of her eyes, as if, being denied all the other rights of womanhood, the slave clung to and cherished the one possession which those happier women lacked.

Having discovered the rebellion, Gabriel can save the women only with Milly's help. He tries to mitigate the arrogance of his stepmother and promises freedom for all the slaves, but Milly's acquiescence at last depends on her secret love for Gabriel: she ". . . knew that the few black drops in her veins parted herself and Gabriel more hopelessly than the widest seas. . . ." Gabriel could love Milly as well; his father had bought her, "that his son, seeing slavery in such a lovely form, might learn to love it." During his visits, however, Gabriel "soon convinced his father that no temptation could undermine his sturdy Northern sense of right and justice, and though he might learn to love the beautiful woman, he could not learn to oppress the slave. . . ." Love, established as a motivating principle, is almost immediately distorted. When Milly agrees to go to the mainland for help (thereby conveniently leaving the story), Miss Alcott describes her parting gesture in a tableau that underplays the romance while insisting on the mutual devotion of master and slave:

> He silently held out his hand, as if pledging his word to obey and trust. With the warmth and grace of her impulsive temperament, Milly bent her head, laid her cheek against that friendly hand, wet it with her grateful tears, kissed it with loving lips, and went her way, feeling as if all things were possible to her for Gabriel's sake.

Such loving submission is accorded Gabriel by the other slaves as well. The rebellion has been instigated by Prince, a man with "the limbs of an ebony Hercules." Reminiscent of the chained giant Atufal in "Benito Cereno," Prince wears an iron collar riveted about his neck, "a shameful badge of serfdom," and comes "from one of those tribes whose wills are never broken — who can be subdued by kindness, but who often kill themselves rather than suffer the degradation of the lash." His influence is counteracted by that of Blind Cassandra, the pious old slave whose loyalty is unshaken by the cruelties meted out to her. "Old Massa" has worked her hard for thirty years, sold all of her ten children — the girls to New Orleans, shot her husband for refusing to whip her himself, and finally caused her blindness; yet she nursed him when he had fever and has forgiven him now: " 'fergived him . . . right hearty, fer though dey took my eyes away dey couldn't bline my soul, and in de darkness I hab seen de Lord.' "

As the story moves away from the dangerous mutual attraction of Gabriel and Milly, it details the stereotypes of black revolutionary and counter-revolutionary only to end in an orgy of white self-congratulation. At the climax, Gabriel enters the slave meeting — Prince Charming as the Archangel:

> Out from the darkness Gabriel came among them. To their startled and superstitious eyes he seemed no mortal man, but a beautiful, benignant angel, bringing tidings of great joy, as he stood there, armed with no weapon but a righteous purpose, gifted with no eloquence but the truth. . . .

When he aids Cassandra in stilling the rebellion, when he promises the slaves their freedom, they respond with "wild abandonment," and a "wave of gratitude and love rolled up and broke at Gabriel's feet," while fifty slaves were "clinging to his garments, kissing his feet and pouring blessings on his head. . . ."

The miscegenation motif may be noted again in "My Contraband." Nurse Dane, one of Miss Alcott's several portraits of the artist as cheerful, spinster nurse, is asked to attend a Rebel typhoid victim. Bob, a contraband, assists her. The melodramatic plot reveals that Bob and the Rebel are half brothers and that the Rebel has stolen Bob's wife from him. In revenge, Bob seizes this opportunity to attempt murder. Nurse Dane, waking from a nap, finds that her morose and sullen contraband has locked them all in together, has disposed of the Rebel's medicine and water, and now waits to watch the painful death. Her initial terror fades as she develops sympathy for Bob's story; nevertheless, she knows that she must prevent this murder and she finally persuades Bob to the noble course, arranging to send him off to "good old Massachusetts."

From the early part of the story, Bob both attracts and frightens Nurse Dane. She cannot lose her awareness of his huge, brooding presence. There are sexual overtones from the beginning, implicit, for example, in Miss Alcott's description of Bob:

> . . . the profile which I saw possessed all the attributes of comeliness belonging to his mixed race. He was more quadroon than mulatto, with Saxon features, Spanish complexion darkened by exposure, color in lips and cheek, waving hair, and an eye full of passionate melancholy. . . .

In the critical scene, there is emphasis on physical contact; Nurse Dane and Bob try to persuade one another by touching, by gripping one another's arms. Finally, Bob intensifies the passion of his recital by revealing the wounds from his beatings: "With a sudden wrench he tore the shirt from neck to waist, and on his strong, brown shoulders showed me furrows deeply ploughed, wounds which, though healed, were ghastlier to me than any in the house." The sexual aspect of this scene is enforced by the unusual violence of the language: wrench, tore, furrows, ploughed. This unconscious sexuality is resolved in the final scene. Months later, Bob, now a Union soldier, is brought to another hospital, mortally wounded by his half brother whom he has killed in battle. Nurse Dane, in the tradition of the sentimental love story, is with him when he dies; for she has found him in a hospital bed under his new name: Dane. As in "An Hour," the expression of black gratitude carries sexual ambiguity.

Louisa May Alcott points out that Bob is no Uncle Tom; yet she converts him to a comfortable Christianity that forswears revenge until the battlefield sanctifies it. The reformed black man may be no great deviation from the sentimental stereotype of the noble slave, but the mixture of a Christian potential for renunciation with the brooding, even savage, sensuality of Bob, and of Milly, suggests the possibility of a new type of black character in the Northern imagination. Even with this suggested new direction and in the most theoretically radical of the fiction writers, racism remains unshamefacedly apparent; the white hero or heroine descends from a moral heaven to aid, to uplift, even in the religious sense to save. If, as one supposes, popular literature reflects the attitudes of the popular audience, then the North remained complacently racist, if nobly abolitionist, throughout its decade of independent examination of the black character in fiction.

Louisa May Alcott and The Racial Question   Abigail Ann Hamblen[*]

In *Hospital Sketches* Louisa Alcott remarks fiercely that she is a child of "two generations" of Abolitionists — and reports that she once picked up and kissed a black baby under the horrified eyes of a contemptuous Virginia woman. Always honest and at the same time mindful of the dramatic, she is completely in character here. For birth and nurture had conditioned her to abolition. She could no more have been unaware of the movement, and unaffected by it, than she could have controlled the color of her eyes, or the shape of her determined mouth.

The very year she was born — 1832 — saw the establishment in Boston of an Anti-Slavery Institution. (Garrison had begun publication of *The Liberator* the year before.) Her family's closest associates during her childhood and adolescence were the Concord group whose most impassioned words were concerned with slavery. Everyone about her was tacitly in agreement with Emerson when he said in 1844, "It is a doctrine alike of the oldest and the newest philosophy, that man is one, and that you cannot injure any member, without a sympathetic injury to all the members. America is not civil, whilst Africa is barbarous."[1]

In 1862, when she goes to Washington to help nurse the wounded soldiers, she has her first real exposure to Negroes and to slavery itself. She is surprised, for the blacks she sees look "as if they had come out of a picture book, or off the stage, but not at all the sort of people I'd been accustomed to see at the North."[2] But, though the colored help at the hospital frequently

[*]Reprinted from the *University Review — Kansas City*, 37 (1971), 307–13.

annoy her with their slothfulness and sauciness, she insists that she really "likes" them. All that is needed to bring out their "better traits" is a "show of interest or friendliness."

At midnight, January 1, 1863, she is seriously ill, yet when she hears the bells ring, and knows that the Emancipation Proclamation has gone into effect, she "electrifies" her roommate "by dancing out of bed, throwing up the window, and flapping my handkerchief, with a feeble cheer, in answer to the shout of a group of colored men below."[3]

Her interest in John Brown and his fate had been intense; the whole affair was closely followed by everyone in Concord. In October, 1859, Brown, a dedicated Abolitionist, with a few followers, for a short while controlled the small town of Harper's Ferry, Virginia (later West Virginia), where a government arsenal held a large number of rifles. Finally overpowered by federal troops, Brown was wounded and captured, then tried, and sentenced to death. (Two of his sons were killed).

Horace Greeley, who wrote of the matter (calling it "beyond dispute") said, "Virginia had but this alternative—to hang John Brown, or to abolish slavery. She did not choose to abolish slavery. . . ."[4] He also quotes Brown's statement in court: "I feel no consciousness of guilt. I have stated from the first what was my intention and what was not. I never had any design against the life of any person, nor any disposition to commit treason, or excite slaves to rebel, or make any general insurrection. I never encouraged any man to do so, but always discouraged any idea of that kind."[5]

These words are surprisingly mild and unwarlike in view of John Brown's previous career, and those of his followers. Absolutely committed to the cause of abolition, this man had helped countless slaves escape to freedom; he had—if not urged on, at least condoned and taken part in a great deal of the guerrilla fighting that had taken place on the Kansas-Missouri border in the years preceding Harper's Ferry. Certainly the raid of the latter place was to provide him and those of his persuasion with arms for further fighting. And one wonders if he did not have hopes that his bold move would not inspirit colored men in the vicinity?

Be that as it may, not even his enemies can deny that he was a completely brave man, entirely under the influence of one consuming ambition, to end slavery in the United States. Louisa Alcott, reared with that goal constantly before her, and herself an ardent admirer of courage, would naturally be passionate in her approbation of him.

Her Journal (November, 1859) says, "The Harper's Ferry tragedy makes this a memorable month. Glad I have lived to see the Antislavery movement and this last heroic act in it. Wish I could do my part in it."

The next month, December, she writes, "The execution of St. John the Just took place on the second. A meeting at the hall, and all Concord was there. Emerson, Thoreau, Father and Sanborn spoke, and all were full of reverence and admiration for the martyr.

"I made some verses on it, and sent them to the 'Liberator.' "[6]

Hospital Sketches is a lively account of her experiences nursing the wounded, experiences cut short by a bad case of typhoid pneumonia. Weakened by the strenuous work and emotional stress, she was forced to return home, there to battle for her life. She lived — but her health was never again as vigorous as it had been.

Her zeal in the cause of Abolition — and in the interests of the colored race — was undiminished, however. And her gift for narration, developed by practice and spurred on by her passion, resulted in some very colorful short stories. These stories, quite as heated as anything Harriet Beecher Stowe produced, deserve a brief examination. For they show a great talent bent to the ends of propaganda, and they tell us a good deal about Louisa Alcott, herself.

An especially good example is "M.L.," which ran in the *Boston Commonwealth* from January 24 to February 21, 1863. The story was written before the war, and in her Journal an entry dated February, 1860, says, "Mr. — — — won't have 'M.L.', as it is anti-slavery, and the dear South must not be offended." Copies of the *Commonwealth* in which it finally appeared are now rare, but the tale has been reprinted in L. D. Turner, *Anti-Slavery Sentiment in American Literature Prior to 1865*, pp. 126–152, and in *The Journal of Negro History*, Vol. XIV, No. 4, (October, 1929).

As in most stories written to promote the cause of Abolition, "M.L." is concerned with both white and colored people who suffer because of slavery, and the theme is race prejudice. Paul, a gifted young octoroon, loves and is loved by Claudia, a wealthy young woman, who is at first ignorant of his race. When she discovers the secret of his blood, and learns of his horrible sufferings prior to his gaining his freedom, she refuses to break their engagement. As he has foretold, most of her friends drop away after the marriage.

But, as the years go on, the two find themselves welcomed into a world far different from that of wealth and fashion. Here Claudia finds "a finer rank than any she had left, for men whose righteous lives were their renown, whose virtues their estate, were peers in this realm, whose sovereign was Truth, whose ministers were Justice and Humanity, whose subjects all 'who loved their neighbors better than themselves.' "[7]

When Paul achieves fame in his profession (music) "false friends" urge them back into society, but Claudia, whose values have been purified, "only touched the little heads, looked up into her husband's face, and answered with a smile of beautiful content, 'I cannot give the substance for the shadow — cannot leave my world for yours. Put off the old delusions that blind you to the light, and come up here to me.' "[8]

One sees that Claudia and Paul make an unusual couple, possessing, each of them, all the great virtues, including courage and the instinct for self-sacrifice; and they are further distinguished by perfect physical beauty, and compelling personalities.

When Claudia first hears Paul sing, his voice's "subtle softness wrapped her senses in a blissful calm, its passion thrilled along her nerves like south winds, full of an aroma fiery and sweet."[9] And when she speaks, it is in the approved heroine-accents: " 'Yes, I like that face, less for its beauty than its strength, I like that austere simplicity of dress, that fine unconsciousness of self. . . .' "[10]

"M.L." differs from other stories of its kind in one interesting way. Much anti-slavery fiction of the time deals with liaisons between white masters and Negro slave girls. Very rarely is there a combination of white woman and black man, as in Paul's and Claudia's case, and almost nowhere do we find a plot developing toward a legal, church-sanctioned *marriage* between the races, as in "M.L."

Here Louisa Alcott rises neatly above all the problems usually considered attendant on miscegenation. She mentions the falling away of Claudia's "false friends," but she makes the point very definite that because of this marriage Claudia finds a new "world," infinitely superior to her former fashionable circle with its narrow views on race. Furthermore, she is mentally and spiritually enriched: "This was the lesson she needed, it taught her the value of true friendship, showed her the poverty of old beliefs, the bitterness of old desires, and strengthened her proud nature by the sharp discipline of pain."[11]

The phrase, "touched the little heads," tells the reader clearly that Claudia and Paul are parents. The future of the children is not mentioned, the possibilities of their knowing the heart-breaking impact of prejudice. Apparently they are never to step out of their mother's and father's "world."

"My Contraband," published first in the *Atlantic Monthly* for November 1863, under the title, "The Brothers," is another good example of Alcott propaganda fiction. The tale concerns two patients in the hospital: one is a seriously ill Confederate officer of twenty, who in his fevered ravings betrays the dissoluteness and worthlessness of his past life, and one is a fine, handsome octoroon, badly, but not fatally, wounded.

The latter is assigned as an attendant to Miss Dane, the nurse who is caring for the white man, and she is impressed with the character and dignity of this former slave. The climax of the story comes when the contraband, Bob, tell her that the young captain is his half brother, son of his dead master, who was his, Bob's, father also. The captain had taken away Bob's lovely young slave wife, who had thereupon killed herself rather than live with her shame. Now Bob is going to murder "Marse Ned" in his bed.

Miss Dane has to talk fast to keep him from his purpose, and she is hard put to it to find arguments that will convince him. "Should I have urged the beauty of forgiveness, the duty of devout submission? He had no religion, for he was no saintly 'Uncle Tom,' and Slavery's black shadow seemed to darken all the world to him and shut out God."[12]

However, she does succeed in dissuading him. With the help of friends, she sends him off to Massachusetts, where he promptly enlists in the famous

54th Regiment under young Col. Robert Shaw. Some time later the Confederate prisoner is discharged and exchanged.

Time passes, and then she learns the fate of the two ill-assorted brothers. With dramatic nicety, they meet in hand to hand conflict during the terrible storming of Fort Wagner. The white man is killed by the octoroon, who is himself mortally wounded. Vengeance has been done at last.

As we might expect, all of Miss Alcott's war tales are violently partisan in every sense of the word. For instance, she shows a strong tendency to portray Southerners all evil and Northerners all good. In "An Hour," for one, the young slave-owner who wishes to free his slaves is the son of a Northern mother and has been reared in the North. In "The Blue and the Gray," a Rebel, lying beside a Yankee in a hospital ward, is vindictive enough to try to poison the latter's mug of water, though the Yankee is a model of patience, friendliness, and good temper, and is dying anyway. In the long and extremely romantic "Love and Loyalty," much is made of the bad treatment Northerns are accorded in Southern hospitals as contrasted to the kindliness shown the Southern wounded in the North.

"My Contraband" is perhaps the most marked example of her passionate adherence to one side of the conflict. Here she is explicit in pointing out the faults of both brothers: Marse Ned is selfish, authoritarian, dissolute; Bob is bitter, vengeful, murderous. The former she dismisses simply as a being of unmitigated evil; the latter, however, shows what nobility he might have been capable of had he not been blighted by slavery, crushed by the iron hand of his owner. In other words, this octoroon is the product of the "peculiar institution."

The reflective reader is willing to admit the truth of her assertion. But he might wonder about Marse Ned, and *his* character. If Bob is the result of slavery, is not his young master equally the result? If his formative years had made Bob what he is, have not Ned's done the same for him?

But Miss Alcott gives him no quarter. She is not interested in excusing the misdeeds of white men—only in applauding the good deeds of blacks. For her, Fort Wagner marks an important epoch: "The future must show how well that fight was fought; for though Fort Wagner still defies us, public prejudice is down; and through the cannonsmoke of that black night the manhood of the colored race shines before many eyes that would not see, rings in many ears that would not hear, wins many hearts that would not hitherto believe."[13]

Her first glimpse of Bob shows her that he has "an eye full of passionate melancholy which in such men always seems to utter a mute protest against the broken law that doomed them at their birth." At first reading, one imagines that she is referring to miscegenation—"the broken law." But recalling "M.L." with its picture of black man and white woman happily made parents, we realize that the "broken law" must mean slavery. Such a name for it shows the Northern attitude only; if in Northern eyes the South broke some "law" in upholding slavery, it must be recalled that many an honest Southerner felt that divine approval hallowed the institution. Again, in the true spirit of the dedicated propagandist, Miss Alcott passes over any theory that might oppose hers.

For all Louisa Alcott's burning sincerity in the struggle for Abolition of slavery, just what was her position when it came to the barriers of class? As we have noted, all Negroes are to her wronged noblemen, either pitifully crushed by generations of slavery, or strongly, proudly rising above their fate. Reared in the tradition of the anti-slavery movement, as we have shown, she could hardly have felt otherwise.

At our distance, however, we see an almost amusing paradox in her character: despite her fierce defense of the inherent nobility of the blacks, she remained what she was born to be—an aristocrat. Her feeling for "family" is one of the most pronounced traits in her strong personality. Louisa Alcott never forgot that through her mother she was a descendant of the Mays, the blue-blooded Mays, whose name had been part of Boston history for many generations.[14] In *An Old Fashioned Girl* the grandmother tells an old anecdote that mentions Col. May by name, along with the Quincys, the Hancocks, and the Marquis de Lafayette.

Mrs. Bhaer of *Jo's Boys* explains to Nat why her sister is not altogether pleased with the idea of his marrying her daughter: " 'She does not despise your poverty or your past; but mothers are very tender over their daughters, and we Marches, though we have been poor, *are*, I confess, a little proud of our good family. We don't care for money; but a long line of virtuous ancestors *is* something to desire and to be proud of.' "

Nat replies that he has "looked up" his own family, and found they "were a good lot. . . . Not one was ever in prison, hanged, or disgraced in any way. We used to be rich and honored years ago, but we've died out and got poor. . . ."

Miss Alcott's feeling of class consciousness perhaps accounts for the condescension shown toward minority groups other than Negroes. For, though in *Work* the black cook is portrayed as a courageous, aspiring member of a down-trodden race, the heroine will not consider working in the company of an Irish servant girl, an acknowledged inferior.[15] When the Irish are not deprecated in Alcott fiction, they play comedy parts, invariably speaking in a thick brogue. In *Hospital Sketches* the Irish soldiers are described in vivid terms: during the painful wound-dressing several of them "anathematized the doctors with the frankness of their nation, and ordered the Virgin to stand by them, as if she had been the wedded Biddy to whom they could administer the poker, if she didn't. . . ."

Writers today have often showed the Southern viewpoint sympathetically. A random example may be found in James Gould Cozzens' *Guard of Honor*, where a conversation occurs between Captain Wiley, from the

South and the young liberal, Lieutenant Edsell. The latter says, " 'I can see the captain is from the South; so I'll only point out to him that, like too many Southerners, he is under a grave misapprehension. The dangerous idea is his. It is very dangerous to deny people their rights. It means that, in the long run, you drive them to take their rights by force. Is that what the captain wants?' "

Captain Wiley is ready: " 'That, friend, they never will do, because they can't,' he said. 'What you're trying to say is that a Negro is equal to a white man. Don't you see that if he was equal, you wouldn't have to be demanding "rights" for him? Like you say, he'd have them by force, if no other way. He hasn't got them, though they gave them to him, and more, after the War Between the States. But he couldn't keep them; he wasn't up to it. That's where the North was wrong then, and where you're wrong now. The two races just aren't equal. Anyone who says they are, either doesn't have good sense, or doesn't know Negroes.' "[16]

Hamilton Basso, in his Civil War novel, *The Light Infantry Ball*, lifts the curtain for a moment on the stark horror that so often haunted the white man living with slavery. Eighteen-year-old Missy suddenly bursts out to her brother: " 'I hate it, Johnny, I hate it! I hate what it did to Mama all her life, ever since she was a little girl and that bad thing happened right before her eyes, and I hate how Papa sold four of our Rosebank people all the way to Mississippi that time just to *oblige* somebody, and I hate wondering where all the mulatto children come from and having to pretend sometimes that I don't *know*, just because I'm not supposed to know anything about things like that, least of all that we live surrounded by prostitutes and concubines like poor Mama once said, because she *did* say it in just those words, though I wasn't suppose to hear — oh, I hate it, I hate it, I hate it! It's a curse, that what it is, a curse!' "[17]

The above quotations illustrate facets of the Negro-slavery question that Louisa Alcott ignored. In all probability, they were unknown to her; if they had been brought to her attention, she would have been unable to give them credence. After all she, too, we must reiterate, was a product of her time and place.

Even so, she has undeniable relevance for her own troubled period. The young militants shouting "Freedom Now!" and "Reparations!," the demanding demonstrators with their occasional violence, are part of the legacy she and her associates have bequeathed us. Much of that legacy is good; much is evil. How good, and how evil, depends, of course, on where one takes his stand.

No matter where this is, one cannot ignore the problem of race relations. And so, no matter what one's persuasion, one cannot help respecting a writer who both sincerely and relentlessly took up the cudgels in a battle which she confidently expected to end in victory for the "right." She could not foresee that a hundred years later it would still be raging.

Notes

1. Quoted in Turner, Lorenzo Dow, *Anti-Slavery Sentiment in American Literature Prior to 1865*, Washington, D. C., The Association for the Study of Negro Life and History, Inc., 1929, p. 49. A century later, Ernest Hemingway was to popularize John Donne's similar statement, "No man is an island. . . ."

2. *Hospital Sketches*, N.Y., Sagamore Press Inc., 1957, pp. 50–51.

3. *Ibid.*, p. 130.

4. "John Brown: Kansas and Harper's Ferry," in *The Tragic Conflict*, Ed., by William B. Hesseltine, N. Y., George Braziller, 1962, pp. 94–95.

5. *Ibid.*, p. 96.

6. Cheney, Ednah D., *Louisa Alcott, Her Life, Letters and Journals*, Boston, Little, Brown and Co., 1925, p. 105.

7. Turner, p. 152.

8. *Ibid.*, p. 152.

9. *Ibid.*, p. 126.

10. *Ibid.*, p. 129. The sexual overtones which we find here would surprise us if we were not sure that Louisa Alcott was quite unaware of them herself. All the passion of this writer's strong nature was at the service of the anti-slavery cause. (Later, there would be others). And she was to remain a spinster all her life.

11. *Ibid.*, p. 151.

12. P. 591. This may very well be the first time that a submissive, religious black man is called an "Uncle Tom."

13. "My Contraband" p. 593.

14. Mrs. Alcott was born Abigail May. Her grandfather was "Squire" Samuel May (1723–1794) with a mansion on Washington Street when it was still called Orange Street. This was on Boston Neck, and his land went to the water's edge where he had a dock of his own to which his ships came. Her father was his son, Col. Joseph May (1760–1847); her mother was Dorothy Sewall (1758–1825).

15. This seems to have been the usual attitude of the "yankee" toward the immigrant laboring class which began coming to America in great numbers after 1846, driven from home by the terrible Irish famine.

16. N. Y., Harcourt, Brace and Co., 1948, pp. 337–338.

17. N. Y., Doubleday, 1959, pp. 299–300.

Gothics and Thrillers

[Review of *Comic Tragedies Written by "Jo" and "Meg" and acted by the "Little Women,"* 1893] Anonymous*

When the Alcott girls were young and dwelt in Concord, and were living through those events that afterward were narrated in *Little Women*, they were all stagestruck in a sort of rural, harmless way, and, either in the garret or the barn, they had frequent dramatic performances. Like those of the ancient Greeks, their plays were written for two actors only, who performed all the characters with frequent changes of costume, it being necessary, of course, to have an audience, and the younger girls cheerfully accepting that task and leaving the fun of acting to their older sisters, known in the books as "Jo" and "Meg." Where these children got their crude knowledge of the theatrical stage and their dramatic instincts it is hard to say. The "Foreword," by Meg in this volume, to which one naturally turns for some light on this interesting point, takes no note of it at all. The second sister of Miss Alcott seems to think it was perfectly natural for children living in a Massachusetts hamlet in the first half of this century to write plays in fun that have all the bloodthirsty spirit and romantic symbolism of the old school of melodrama, and to act the parts in them in those leisure hours when children might be better employed playing games of romp in the open air.

As a sort of companion to the late Miss Alcott's works, these seven amateur plays are now published. Most of them were written by Louisa Alcott herself, and they are all alike and all like the plays of Mr. Fitzball and Mr. Moncrieffe in little. Blood is shed in almost every scene, the course of true love never does run smooth, and the language is appropriately stilted and bombastic. The subjects of the plays and some of their theatrical devices suggest that the girls must have had access to some bound volumes of real plays, quite apart from Shakespeare, for there is nothing at all Shakespearean in these infantile works.

The most amusing piece is an operatic tragedy called "Bianca," in which the words were committed to memory while the music was com-

*Reprinted from the *New York Times*, 5 November 1893, p. 19.

posed and sung as the performance proceeded. This volume, at its best, is a curiosity which may attract the notice of people whose childhood was made brighter by the "Little Women" books.

[Louisa Alcott's "Natural Ambition" for the "Lurid Style" Disclosed in a Conversation] LaSalle Corbell Pickett*

Speaking of *Little Women* I said:

"The story is so natural and lifelike that it shows your true style of writing, — the pure and gentle type, with innocent young lives and the events that would inevitably befall bright girls and boys with the thoughts and feelings befitting a quiet loving home circle."

"Not exactly that," she replied. "I think my natural ambition is for the lurid style. I indulge in gorgeous fancies and wish that I dared inscribe them upon my pages and set them before the public."

"Why not?" I asked. "There seems to be no reason why you should not be gorgeous if you like."

"How should I dare to interfere with the proper grayness of old Concord? The dear old town has never known a startling hue since the redcoats were there. Far be it from me to inject an inharmonious color into the neutral tint. And my favorite characters! Suppose they went to cavorting at their own sweet will, to the infinite horror of dear Mr. Emerson, who never imagined a Concord person as walking off a plumb line stretched between two pearly clouds in the empyrean. To have had Mr. Emerson for an intellectual god all one's life is to be invested with a chain armor of propriety."

"The privilege of having such a Titan of intellect to worship is worth being subjected to some trammels of propriety."

"And what would my own good father think of me," she asked, "if I set folks to doing the things that I have a longing to see my people do? No, my dear, I shall always be a wretched victim to the respectable traditions of Concord."

*Reprinted from *Across My Path: Memories of People I have Known* (New York: Brentano's, 1916), pp. 107–08.

Some Anonymous and Pseudonymous Thrillers of Louisa M. Alcott

Leona Rostenberg[*]

When Jo March, dressed in her best, entered the office of the "Weekly Volcano" she found herself confronted by three men "sitting with their heels rather higher than their hats" and smoking long black cigars. Jo had come to offer her latest thriller to the condescending Mr. Dashwood and his partners, the editors of the "Weekly Volcano."

How exactly Louisa M. Alcott has revealed her experiences and tribulations as a writer of sensational fiction in *Little Women* cannot be determined. Nevertheless there is sufficient indication that in reality she had aspired as Jo, had known the counterpart of the critical Mr. Dashwood and his associates and had seen the pages of an authentic "Weekly Volcano" emblazoned with her thrillers.

Although Miss Alcott during the early years of her literary career contributed to the popular *Boston Saturday Evening Gazette* and the proud young *Atlantic Monthly*, she did not disdain publications of lesser repute. By 1862 she wrote regularly for *Frank Leslie's Illustrated Newspaper*, a small folio journal selling at ten cents a copy, replete with alluring pictures, New York gossip, murder trials and ringside bouts. Leslie considered her tales "so dramatic, vivid and full of plot"[1] that he announced her anonymous story, *Pauline's Passion and Punishment*, appearing in January, 1863, as a prize winner.[2] Her tale, *Enigmas*, was published in the May issues of 1864.[3] In Miss Alcott's opinion this thriller was much liked by readers of "sensation rubbish, but having gotten my fifty dollars I was resigned."[4] By her own admission, however, Louisa Alcott enjoyed writing tales injected with the "lurid" not only because of the lucrative rewards, which she sorely needed, but because of "her passion for wild adventurous life and even melodramatic action."[5] The realization that the publication of her stories in Leslie's paper and others of such character would not enhance her reputation may have induced her "resignation." Despite this attitude *Enigmas* was not to be her last tale of blood and thunder.

Shrouded in pseudonymity, Louisa Alcott's stories appeared during the 'sixties in the Boston penny dreadful, *The Flag of Our Union*. Founded by Fred Gleason in 1842 and later sold to the enterprising Maturin Murray Ballou, this weekly in 1863 passed into the hands of James R. Elliott, William H. Thomes and Newton Talbot, the first two of whom had worked with Frank Leslie for Gleason's publications.[6] Of the three partners the best known is William H. Thomes, author of several successful adventure stories. Originally from Portland, he drifted to Boston and took to sea during the early 'forties. Back in Boston and ready for new adventure, he formed

[*]Reprinted from *Papers of the Bibliographical Society of America*, 37 (2nd Quarter 1943), 131–40.

the Boston and California Joint Stock Mining Company whose members were "to take their Bibles in one hand and their great New England civilization in the other and conquer all wickedness that stood in their path."[7] Thomes appears to have conquered neither wickedness nor the West, for he was back in Boston in 1857 to become a reporter for the *Herald* until 1860.[8] The following year he associated himself with James R. Elliott as co-publisher of *The American Union* with offices at 100 Washington Street.[9] Prior to his partnership with Thomes, Elliott had published *The True Flag* with W. U. Moulton and M. V. Lincoln.[10] It appears that with the transfer of *The Flag of Our Union* to Elliott and Thomes, Talbot, who had worked as cashier for the Ballou publications, decided to continue his connections and hence became the third partner in 1863.[11]

The firm, located first at 118 Washington Street and later at 63 Congress Street, issued not only *The Flag of Our Union* but other former cheap Ballou periodicals, *The Dollar Monthly, The Monthly Novelette* and *The American Union.* Among their contributors were the popular Sylvanus Cobb, Junior, Francis Durivage, Rochester and Amanda Hale whose stories bristled with the tales of the South Seas, mulattos, banishment, love and crime. *The Flag of Our Union*, which Gleason claimed had enjoyed a circulation of 100,000 and brought its owner a yearly income of $25,000, had increased from four to sixteen pages under Elliott's management.[12] Although it originally prided itself on containing no advertisements it now brought to the public's attention the soothing properties of "Redding's Russia Salve" and "Wistar's Balsam." Under the direction of Elliott, Thomes and Talbot the annual subscription rate had risen from two to four dollars annually. It was described by the editors as the "Best Literary Journal" with a corps of contributors embracing "The Best Writers in the Country."

Miss Alcott's contributions to *The Flag*, tales of violence and revenge peopled with convicts and opium addicts, appeared anonymously, and pseudonymously as the products of A. M. Barnard. This name may have been suggested either by fancy or a chain of associations. The A may have been derived from any one of the family names, Amos, Abba or Anna. The M more than likely represented her mother's maiden name, May, likewise Miss Alcott's middle name. Her father claimed Henry Barnard, the Connecticut schoolmaster, as a close friend and the suitability of this surname may have attracted his inspired daughter. Miss Alcott's choice of a pseudonym for her stories to *The Flag* again betrays her own attitude toward the penny dreadfuls and her own thrillers. Although Elliott had written to her that *The Flag* was "a literary paper that none need to blush for, and a credit to contribute to its columns rather than otherwise," Miss Alcott was unwilling to risk a reputation already founded upon *Flower Fables* and *Hospital Sketches.*[13] Since she permitted poems to appear under her own name, it would seem that she did not altogether condemn the periodical but was loath to link her name with the sensational stories she had contributed. Elliott, however, did not fully share her attitude. He was eager for her stories to appear under her own name but consented to her pseudonym "A. M. Barnard or 'any other man' " with which she wished "to father" her tales as long as she would contribute to his publications.[14]

The exact number of stories written by Louisa Alcott for *The Flag of Our Union* and their dates of appearance cannot be accurately determined at the present time. The most complete run of this periodical owned by the Library of Congress has now been stored away for safe-keeping with the result that a thorough investigation of the stories by A. M. Barnard is now impossible. The issues of 1865 owned by the Boston Public Library and the few odd numbers at the Widener Library have contributed to the identification of three works and have corroborated Miss Alcott's choice of the pseudonym, A. M. Barnard.

In a letter of January 5, 1865, Elliott referred to the coming publication of Miss Alcott's story, *V. V. or Plots and Counterplots*, which was to appear in *The Flag* "By a Well Known Author" in four installments during February, 1865.[15] Elliott remarked that he intended to print it in *The Flag* "in place of publishing it as a novelette in cheap style." Had Miss Alcott consented to the use of her own name the story would have brought her an additional twenty-five dollars.[16] It appears either that Elliott decided to return to his original plan of issuing *V. V.* in novelette form or that the tale enjoyed considerable popularity for the firm published it at a future time as a ten-cent novelette in their series of "Standard American Authors." Hence it appeared in octavo size, 100 pages in length and bound in blue wrappers bearing the caption "V. V. By A. M. Barnard complete" centered within a medallion on the front cover. According to the Union Catalogue there is only one copy of this publication in an American library, which is catalogued in The New York Public Library under the name of A. M. Barnard.[17]

That Elliott was satisfied with the suitability of *V. V.* for *The Flag* is indicated in a letter of January 7, 1865, in which he begged for additional material. "I should be pleased to have you write me some stories for the 'Flag' of about 25 to 40 pages of such MSS. as 'V. V.' " Again he entreated her to have the story appear under her own name. According to Elliott, the offer of sixteen dollars would equal the price paid for a first page story by *The American Union* to which he believed Miss Alcott had formerly contributed.[18] In the same letter he requested a poem or two for *The Flag*. A postscript adds, "I will purchase another novelette of you at any time you may wish to dispose of one."[19] A letter addressed to Miss Alcott two weeks later reiterates the same request. "You may send me anything in either the sketch or novelette line that you do not wish to 'father' or that you wish A.M. Barnard or 'any other man' to be responsible for and if they suit me I will purchase them." He now promised three dollars a column run inside length for sketches written under her own name.[20] Although Miss Alcott's published journal makes no reference to Elliott's repeated demands, she accepted his offer since her story, *A Marble Woman Or The Mysterious Model, A Novel of Absorbing Interest by A. M. Barnard, Author of "V. V. or Plots and Counterplots"* appeared in *The Flag* in four installments from May 20 to June 10, 1865.[21] Elliott's proposal of "a poem or two . . . under your own name" was also met since her poems, *In The Garret* and *The Sanitary Fair*, appeared in March and April, 1865.[22]

Miss Alcott's facility in dashing off these saleable thrillers stimulated Elliott's desire for additional material. In a letter of June, 1865, he asked for another sensation story of about 145 to 150 pages, "such MSS. as your last 'The Marble Woman' so that I can have it by the middle of July."[23] Intensely eager now for her stories, he had become less insistent about her identity and did not care about the use of "any particular name, if you prefer any other nom de plume . . . use it, as it is for one of my cheap novelettes."[24] Although he appeared to be indifferent to her choice of a pseudonym there is some indication that he had boasted the author of *A Marble Woman* and Miss Louisa M. Alcott to be one. In a somewhat apologetic tone to the irate authoress he regretted that she should have any feeling in regard to her nom de plume. "I am sure that I have not given currency to the idea that 'A. M. Barnard' and yourself are identical."[25]

There is no proof whether Elliott had turned a journalistic Judas, but there is indication that his enthusiasm for Miss Alcott's thrillers had not waned during her year's absence abroad. From July, 1865, to August, 1866, she vacationed in Europe, strolling along the shores of Lake Leman, sailing at Vevey, where she met her golden-haired Laurie, quite unmindful of the weekly issues of *The Flag of Our Union*.

A diary entry written shortly after her return at the beginning of August, 1866, refers for the first time to Elliott as "E."; "Found plenty to do as orders from E[lliott] and L[eslie] . . . waited for me."[26] She apparently set to work immediately and completed within a short time *Behind a Mask* which appeared in *The Flag* after August 11, 1866.[27] In Elliott's opinion this was a story of peculiar power. "[I] have no doubt that my readers will be quite as much fascinated with it as I was myself while reading the manuscript."[28] He now offered the fairly popular authoress sixty-five dollars for this story and five dollars for each poem signed "by Miss Alcott," asking for another thriller to be ready by the twentieth of September.[29] His offer of sixty-five dollars was apparently rejected since Miss Alcott's journal for the period states that she received seventy-five dollars from E. for a story as well as five dollars for a poem.[30]

Elliott's demand for another story for September twentieth was also met. Miss Alcott writes, "E. . . . wanted a long story in 24 chapters and I wrote it in a fortnight 125 pages."[31] Apparently in her fervor she had not realized that even *The Flag of Our Union* had set certain limits to the sensational character of its contributions, for much to her own surprise she records in September, 1866, "E. would not have it saying it was too long and sensational."[32] But A. M. Barnard was not to be balked. She curbed her passion somewhat for the too bloody and the too thunderous and submitted another tale, *The Abbot's Ghost or Maurice Treherne's Temptation*, the last issue of which is to be found in *The Flag of Our Union* of January 26, 1867.[33]

It cannot be determined at the present whether other of Miss Alcott's stories appeared in later issues of *The Flag of Our Union*. With the publication of *Little Women* in October, 1868, Miss Alcott could have easily afforded to sever all association with A. M. Barnard. To Jo now was relegated the task of submitting her thrillers to the firm of Dashwood and Company. It was her progenitor who could now smile with some sympathy at her heroine's sallies into the domain of blood and thunder and who could recall, perhaps with some reluctance, the career of A. M. Barnard, successful contributor to penny dreadfuls.

FIVE LETTERS FROM JAMES R. ELLIOTT TO LOUISA M. ALCOTT[34]

I

Journal Building,
118 Washington Street, Boston
Jan. 5. 1865.

Louisa M. Alcott
Dear Madam,

I forward you this evening the 3 first copies of the "Flag" in its new form.

I think it is now a literary paper that none need to blush for, and a credit to contribute to its columns, rather than otherwise. Now I have a proposition to make you. I want to publish your story "V. V." in it, in place of publishing it as a Novelette in cheap style, as I had intended, and will give you $25. more for the story provided I can publish it under your own name.

Please look the "Flag" over & let me know as early as Saturday, & oblige.

Very Truly Yours
J.R. Elliott
Editor

II

118 Washington Street,
Jan. 7. 1865.

Dear Miss Alcott,

I should be pleased to have you write me some stories for the Flag, of about 25 to 40 pages of such Ms. as "V. V." I want them over your own name of course, & will give you $2.00 a column (short columns you will notice) for them. That rate will be fully equal to $16.00 for a first page story in the "American Union" which paper I think you contributed to while it was under the management of Messres. Graves & Weston. Will you not contribute a poem or two for the "Flag" also? I do not know as that is in your line, if it is I shall be glad to recieve [sic] poems from your pen. I have entered your name on our *gratis* list, & you will receive the "Flag" regularly.

Very Truly Yours
J. R. Elliott.

P.S. I will purchase another Novelette of you at any time you may wish to dispose of one. "V. V." will be commenced in No. 5 about two weeks. What title would you suggest in place of "V. V.?" Or what for a second title? Please answer at your earliest convenience

J. R. E.

III

Boston Jan. 21, 1865

Dear Miss Alcott

You may send me anything in either the sketch or Novelette line that you do not wish to "father", or that you wish A. M. Barnard, or "any other man" to be responsible for, & if they suit me I will purchase them.

I will pay for poems under your own name. Also I will give you $3.00 per column (run in inside length) for sketches under your own name.

Let me hear from you.

Very Truly Yours
J. R. Elliott

IV

63 Congress Street,
June 15, 1865

Dear Miss Alcott,

Have you written anything in the novel line you would like to have me publish "by A M. Barnard, author of "V. V." "The Marble Woman" &c. &c.? If not can you furnish me with a sensation story of about 145 to 150 pages such Mss. as your last "The Marble Woman" so that I can have it by the middle of July? I don't care about even *any* particular name, if you prefer any other nome [sic] de plume for this one story, use it, as it is for one of my cheap Novelettes.

I will give you $50. for such a story, & don't want it to exceed 150 pages of Mss. the size of "The Marble Woman," 140 pages will answer, or 145 will be better.

By the way my friends think the "Marble Woman" is just splendid; & *I* think no author of novels need be ashamed to own it for a bantling. I am sorry you should have had any feeling in regard to the nome de plume. I am sure that I have not given currency to the idea that "A. M. Barnard" & yourself were identical.

Please let me hear from you by return mail, if possible, in regard to the short novel.

Very Truly Yours
J. R. Elliott

V

63 Congress Street,
Aug. 11 1866

Dear Miss Alcott

The story entitled "Behind A Mask" is accepted. I think it a story of peculiar power, and have no doubt but my readers will be quite as much fascinated with it as I was myself while reading the Ms. I will give you $65. for it. That am't awaits your order.

I should like another by the 20th of September.

Can I have one? I sh'd be happy to pay you $5. each for two or three poems by *Miss Alcott*.

Very Truly Yours
J. R. Elliott

Notes

1. Ednah D. Cheney, editor. *Louisa May Alcott Her Life, Letters and Journals*. Boston, 1920, p. 131.

2. A letter written by Leslie's editor, E. George Squier, is dated December 18, 1862: "My Dear Madame, Your tale 'Pauline' this morning was awarded the $100 prize for the best short tale for Mr. Leslie's newspaper, and you will hear from him in due course in reference to what you may regard as an essential part of the matter. I presume that it will be on hand for those little Christmas purchases. Allow me to congratulate you on your success and to recommend you to submit whatever you may hereafter have of the same sort for Mr. Leslie's acceptance. Truly yr. obdt. servant. E. G. Squier." *Manuscript in Orchard House, Concord, Mass.* Miss Alcott writes in April, 1863: "Received $100 from F. L. for a tale which won the prize last January." Cheney, op. cit., p. 151. *Pauline's Passion and Punishment* appeared in *Leslie's Illustrated Newspaper*, Vol. XV, nos. 379 & 380, January 3 and 10, 1863.

3. *Enigmas* by Miss L. M. Alcott in *Frank Leslie's Illustrated Newspaper*, Vol. XVIII, nos. 450 & 451, May 14 & 21, 1864.

4. Cheney, op. cit., p. 158.

5. Ibid., pp. 63 and 105.

6. Frank Luther Mott. *A History of American Magazines from 1741 to 1885*. New York, 1930-1938, Vol. II, pp. 31, 35, 36, 64, 411.

7. For an account of Thomes's Western adventures and literary activity, see George R. Stewart, *Take your Bible in One Hand, The Life of William Henry Thomes*. San Francisco, 1939.

8. *The Boston Directory*, 1858-1860.

9. Ibid., 1861.

10. Ibid., 1858-1860.

11. Ibid., 1858-1862.

12. George W. Browne. *Pioneers of "Popular Literature."* In: *Granite State Magazine*, February, 1907, III, no. 2.

13. Letter I, January 5, 1865.

14. Letter III, January 21, 1865.

15. *The Flag of Our Union*. Vol. XX, no. 5, February 4, 1865, pp. 73-75; no. 6, February 11, 1865, pp. 88-91; no. 7, February 18, 1865, pp. 105-107; no. 8, February 25, 1865, pp. 121-123.

16. Letter I, January 5, 1865.

17. *V. V.* was copyrighted by Thomes & Talbot in 1865. *The Flag* had a special column under the heading of "Ten Cent Novelettes" advertising these cheap thrillers. To date the announcement of *V. V.* has not been traced. It is listed, however, as number 80 on the novelette cover. Two later thrillers by Miss Alcott, appearing under her own name, were published in this series. *The Skeleton in the Closet*, included in Perley Parker's *The Foundling*, pp. 77-99, was issued in November, 1867, as no. 49 and *The Mysterious Key* followed as no. 50 in December, 1867. There is one copy of the former work in a private collection; of the latter there are three known copies, the deposit copy in the Library of Congress and two in private collections.

18. Letter II. *The American Union*, a four-page periodical, had been purchased from Graves and Weston by Ballou from whom Elliott and Thomes bought it in 1861.

19. Letter II.

20. Letter III, January 21, 1865.

21. *The Flag of Our Union.* Vol. XX, no. 20, May 20, 1865, pp. 313-315; no. 21, May 27, 1865, pp. 329-330; no. 22, June 3, 1865, pp. 345-347; no. 23, June 10, 1865, pp. 361-364.

22. Both poems appeared under Miss Alcott's own name in *The Flag of Our Union*, Vol. XX, no. 11, March 18, 1865, p. 166, and no. 16, April 22, 1865, p. 254.

23. Letter IV, June 15, 1865.

24. Ibid.

25. Ibid.

26. August, 1866, Cheney, op. cit., p. 184.

27. Letter V, August 11, 1866.

28. Ibid.

29. Ibid.

30. August, 1866: "One [tale] for E. for which he paid $75, also a bit of poetry for $5." Cheney, op. cit., p. 184.

31. Ibid.

32. Cheney, op. cit, p. 185.

33. *The Abbot's Ghost, or Maurice Treherne's Temptation. A Christmas Story by A. M. Barnard, Author of "V. V.," "A Marble Woman," "Behind A Mask," etc. etc.* Vol. XXVII, no. 4, January 26, 1867.

34. Louisa M. Alcott Manuscripts, Box II. Houghton Library, Harvard College, Cambridge.

Introduction
[to *Behind a Mask*]   Madeleine Stern*

> I intend to illuminate the Ledger with a blood & thunder tale as they are easy to "compoze" & are better paid than moral & elaborate works of Shakespeare so dont be shocked if I send you a paper containing a picture of Indians, pirates, wolves, bears & distressed damsels in a grand tableau

*Reprinted from *Behind a Mask: The Unknown Thrillers of Louisa May Alcott*, ed. Madeleine B. Stern (New York: William Morrow & Co., 1975), pp. vii-xxii, xxvii-xxxiii. Deletions necessitated the renumbering of some notes.

over a title like this "The Maniac Bride" or The Bath of Blood A Thrilling Tale of Passion.

The quotation is not by a writer associated with the gore of Gothic romance but by the future author of a domestic novel known to all the world as *Little Women*. On June 22, 1862, Louisa May Alcott wrote those lines to a young man named Alf Whitman, whose charms she would one day incorporate into the fictional character of Laurie.[1]

The statement itself evinces her powers, for within the briefest compass it touches upon her facility in composition, her ostensible motive, and the type of periodical or audience at which she aimed. The fact that Louisa May Alcott—"The Children's Friend"—let down her literary hair and wrote blood-and-thunder thrillers in secret is in itself a disconcerting if titillating shock to readers in search of consistency. Like Dr. Johnson's dog that stood upon its hind legs, it is *per se* remarkable. Equally remarkable is the story of their discovery, an intriguing byway in literary detection. Most remarkable of all perhaps is the fact that those gory, gruesome novelettes—written anonymously or pseudonymously, for the most part—were and still are extremely good: well paced, suspenseful, skillfully executed, and peopled with characters of flesh and blood.

Now, for the first time, after more than a century, they are reprinted—a belated though well-deserved tribute to a multifaceted genius who hailed from Concord, Massachusetts. They merit not only the avid attention of the general reader, whose appetite will grow with what it feeds on, but closer study by the astonished yet delighted critic, who may wonder precisely why and when, how and for whom these colorful forays into an exotic world were written. The analysis will disclose not only the nature of the creation but the nature of the creator, for Louisa May Alcott brought to this genre of escapist literature both an economic and a psychological need.

There is no doubt the economic need was there. The four "little women" whose name was not March but Alcott—Anna, Louisa, Abby, and Elizabeth—grew up not only in the climate of love but in the colder climate of poverty. Their father, Amos Bronson Alcott, the Concord seer, who was sometimes regarded as a seer-sucker, had many gifts but none for making money. As Louisa put it in a letter to a publisher: "I too am sure that 'he who giveth to the poor lendeth to the Lord' & on that principle devote time & earnings to the care of my father & mother, for one possesses no gift for money making & the other is now too old to work any longer for those who are happy & able to work for her."[2]

[Passage deleted regarding Alcott poverty.]

To solve the mundane question of ways and means, to pay the family debts and end the necessity for a charitable Alcott Sinking Fund, Louisa May Alcott was prepared to do any kind of work that offered, menial or mental. "Though an *Alcott*"—and Louisa underlined not the condition but the name — she would prove she could support herself. "I will make a battering-ram of my head," she wrote in her journal, "and make a way through this rough-and-tumble world."[3]

She tried what was available, and what was not she tried to make available: teaching, working as a seamstress or as second girl, doing the wash at two dollars a week. At midcentury the family poverty had never been more extreme. At this juncture Louisa went out to service and garnered from her experience no money but a villain for her tales and a consuming inner fury to explode.

The full story of what might be entitled "The Humiliation at Dedham" has never been told, although Louisa herself years later wrote a bowdlerized account of it in "How I Went Out to Service." Since it was grist for the mill of a writer of thrillers, it merits recounting.[4] At the difficult midcentury the Alcotts lived for a time in Boston, for it was better to be earning a living in a city than to be starving in a country paradise. Mrs. Alcott, the Marmee of the as yet unwritten *Little Women*, worked as a city missionary and opened an intelligence office. When an ancient gentleman from Dedham applied for a companion for his sister, Louisa decided to take the position herself. The gentleman — now for the first time identified as the Honorable James Richardson, Dedham lawyer, president of a local fire-insurance company, author of several orations, and devotee of the Muses — seemed to her tall, ministerial, refined. Waving black-gloved hands about, he assured her that his home was graced by books and pictures, flowers, a piano, the best of society. She would be one of the family, required to help only in the lighter work.

Fortified by those assurances, Louisa in 1851, age nineteen, went out to service. The Richardson home was not precisely as it had been represented. The light housework included not only bed making but the kindling of fires and the destruction of cobwebs. What was more, Louisa was expected to play audience to Hon. James Richardson, who invited her into his study for oral readings or metaphysical discussions. The aged Richardson's attentions soon became maudlin. He plied her with poems while she washed the dishes and he left reproachful little notes under her door. Stranded on an island of water in a sea of soapsuds, Louisa finally delivered an ultimatum: she had come to serve as companion to Hon. James Richardson's sister, not to him. As a result of her display of independence, all the household work was assigned to her: digging paths through the snow, fetching water from the well, splitting the kindling, and sifting the ashes. The final degradation was the command to polish the master's muddy boots with the blacking hose, at which the young domestic balked. After seven weeks of drudgery she announced her intention of leaving. Richardson shut himself up in sulky retirement while his sister tucked a sixpenny pocketbook into Louisa's chilblained hands. The pocketbook contained four dollars, which the outraged Alcotts returned to Dedham. Although Louisa subsequently made light of this experience in "How I Went Out to Service," there can be no doubt that from her humiliation an anger was born that would express itself both obliquely and directly when she sat down to write her blood-and-thunder tales.

Another devastating experience a few years later could also be caught in a net of words, provided the author remained anonymous. Frustrated in her attempts to find work — teaching Alice Lovering, sewing for Mrs. Reed or Mrs. Sargent — Louisa found that her courage had all but failed. As she looked at the waters of the Mill Dam she was tempted to find the solution of her problems in their oblivion. Though her immediate problem was resolved, surely that "Temptation at the Mill Dam," however fleeting, became, along with the "Humiliation at Dedham," part of the psychological equipment of a young woman who would shortly take her pen as her bridegroom.[5]

[Passages deleted concerning other influences at work on Alcott.]

Bronson Alcott called his scribbling daughter "an arsenal of powers."[6] In that arsenal was stored still another personal source for stories. All her life the redoubtable Louisa May Alcott had gone barnstorming and all her life she had dreamed of the ten dramatic passions.[7] The "Louy Alcott troupe," of which Louisa May, age ten, was author-director, gave way to family tableaux and dramatic performances in the Hillside barn. At fifteen Louisa dipped her pen into gaudy ink as, with her sister Anna, she wrote the scripts of a succession of melodramas whose titles and subtitles foreshadow those of the thrillers that were to come: "Norna; or, The Witch's Curse"; "The Captive of Castile; or, The Moorish Maiden's Vow." The props and appurtenances, the backgrounds and characters of these early plays staged for the Concord neighbors are familiar to readers of blood-and-thunder tales: ghosts and stolen scrolls, duels and magic potions, dungeon cells and gloomy woods, murder and suicide.

Throughout her life Louisa carried the theater with her wherever she went. She took the roles of director, author, and actress in drawing-room charades or plays in the Boston kitchen. With lightning changes of costume she ranged from a prince in silver armor to a murderer in chains, until she confided to her journal that she would be a Siddons if she could. From her later work in the Amateur Dramatic Company of Walpole and the Concord Dramatic Union, Louisa gained a certain professionalism in her attitude toward the theater. In 1860 her farce, *Nat Bachelor's Pleasure Trip*, was actually staged at the Howard Athenaeum, Boston, and the playwright received a bouquet as she viewed the performance from a private parlor box. Louisa received more than a bouquet from her experience in theatricals and her romance with greasepaint. She developed a skill in lively dialogue, in suspenseful plotting, and in broad-stroke character delineation, skills she would one day apply to her blood-and-thunder tales. "I fancy 'lurid' things," she wrote in her 1850 journal, "if true and strong also"[8] — a fancy she would gratify a decade later. Like many of the episodes of her life, Louisa's addiction to the theater provided both a source and a training ground for what would follow.

So too did her reading. Dickens she devoured, reading aloud with her sister Anna the dialogue of Sairey Gamp and Betsey Prig, thrilling to the tale of Reuben Haredale's murder, reinaugurating the Pickwick Club in Concord. Books from Emerson's study could be borrowed: Dante and Shakespeare, Carlyle and Goethe. "R.W.E. gave me 'Wilhelm Meister,' " she noted, "and from that day Goethe has been my chief idol."[9] (Her chief idol, it needs no reminding, had delved into matters alchemical and antiquarian, and his Faust had made a world-famous pact with the devil.) *The Heir of Redclyffe* was a favorite of Louisa's and so too was Hawthorne's *Scarlet Letter*. Indeed, she was so enthralled by novels that in one lofty moment she "made a resolution to read fewer novels, and those only of the best."[10]

There can be no doubt at all that the fiction addict Louisa Alcott dipped from time to time into the gore of the Gothic novel. In America that type of romance was so enthusiastically received that as early as 1797 both "dairymaid and hired hand" amused themselves "into an agreeable terror with the haunted houses and hobgoblins of Mrs. Radcliffe."[11] By the time she had become an omnivorous reader a host of Gothic novels was available to her in English or in English translation. In their pages Louisa could envision settings, mouth language, and cogitate themes. She could wander from ruined abbey to frowning castle, from haunted gallery and feudal hall to pathless forest and chilly catacomb. She could savor romantic words—*repasts, casements, chambers*. She could revel in unholy themes—deals with the devil and the raising of the dead, secret sects and supernatural agencies. Horace Walpole's marvelous machinery, Mrs. Ann Radcliffe's ghosts, Monk Lewis's horrors, William Beckford's Oriental terror, Ludwig Tieck's vampires were all available to her. So too, of course, were the strange stories of Washington Irving, the haunting stories of Nathaniel Hawthorne, the subtle tales of Poe the master, whose horrors were the unknown horrors of the mind.[12]

Probably Louisa Alcott had been moved to write as soon as she had learned to read. The compulsion was hers early to combine threads of her own experience with the threads of the books she had read and interweave them into a fabric of her own creating.[13]

[Passages deleted concerning early Alcott writings.]

Seated at her desk, an old green-and-red party wrap draped around her as a "glory cloak," Louisa pondered in groves of manuscripts. In 1855 her earnings included fifty dollars from teaching, fifty dollars from sewing, and twenty dollars from stories.[14] Yet she not only preferred pen and ink to birch and book—or needle—she was committed. Her pen was never and would never be idle. She lived in her inkstand. Some years later, when she supplied *The New York Ledger* with an article on "Happy Women,"[15] she would include a sketch of herself as the scribbling spinster.

The scribbling spinster had already had a variety of writing experience. From flower fables to realistic hospital sketches, from tales of virtue rewarded to tales of violence, she had tried her ink-stained hand. Now, in her early thirties, she would attempt still another experiment. The letter to Alf Whitman revealed the plan: "I intend to illuminate the Ledger with a blood & thunder tale as they are easy to 'compoze' & are better paid than moral . . .works." For Louisa May Alcott they were indeed easy to compose. She could stir in her witch's caldron a brew concocted from her own experience, her observations and needs, as well as from the books she had read, for, like Washington Irving, she had "read somewhat, heard and seen more, and dreamt more than all." Louisa's blood-and-thunder tales would be not only "necessity stories" produced for money — from fifty to seventy-five dollars each — but a psychological catharsis. What is more, although their author never publicly acknowledged them, these experiments would stand the test of time. The future author of *Little Women* added much of her own to the genre. Indeed, had she persisted in the writing of thrillers, the name of Louisa May Alcott may well have conjured up the rites of a Walpurgis Night instead of the wholesome domesticities of a loving family.

In 1862, in the midst of the Civil War, *Frank Leslie's Illustrated Newspaper*, a popular New York weekly devoted to alluring pictures, gossip, and murder trials, offered a one-hundred-dollar prize for a story. To pay the family debts and at the same time to give vent to the pent-up emotions of her thirty years, Louisa Alcott wrote the first of her blood-and-thunder tales. Though it would be published anonymously, "Pauline's Passion and Punishment"[16] bore the stamp of its author, who immediately developed her own technique and outlined a theme to which she would often return. While her plots were violent enough and her backdrops remote enough to merit classification in the Gothic genre, Louisa was principally concerned with character. Of all the characters she adumbrated in these narratives the one who came most completely to life and who obviously was as intriguing to her author as to readers was the passionate, richly sexual *femme fatale* who had a mysterious past, an electrifying present, and a revengeful future. In such a heroine — so different from the submissive heroine of the Gothic formula — Louisa May Alcott could distill her passion for dramatics and her feminist anger at a world of James Richardsons. At the same time she could win a sorely needed hundred dollars.

In "Pauline's Passion and Punishment," as in all the Alcott thrillers, the reader is immediately introduced to problems of character rather than of plot. The suspense lies less in what the heroine will *do* than in what the heroine *is*, although both considerations become entwined as the character develops and the plot advances. In a fascinating opening, the anonymous author places onstage her Pauline, a proud and passionate woman who has lost all—fortune and, as a result of one man's perfidy, love. She is left with her fury and her desire for revenge, emotions which become the motivating forces in an ironic plot.

Against the background of an exotic paradise, a green wilderness where the tamarind vies with the almond tree, the spotlight falls upon Pauline Valary, pacing "to and fro, like a wild creature in its cage," a "handsome woman, with bent head, locked hands, and restless steps." She is a woman scorned by her lover, Gilbert Redmond, who has abandoned her for a moneyed bride. In swift course she arouses the devotion of the sensitive, young, southern romantic Manuel, who, attracted by her implicit sexuality, becomes not only her husband but her accomplice in the intended destruction of Gilbert Redmond. She does not plan Gilbert's murder but some more subtle revenge. "There are fates more terrible than death, weapons more keen than poniards, more noiseless than pistols. . . . Leave Gilbert to remorse—and me." And so, on page 1 of her thriller, the already skillful author has sketched in her characters, spotlighted her heroine, set her scene, and suggested a suspenseful plot.

The suspense mounts in the search for Gilbert and the dramatic encounter with him and his bride. The character is embroidered as Pauline's "woman's tongue" avenges her and "with feminine skill" she "mutely conveys the rebuke she would not trust herself to utter, by stripping the glove from the hand he had touched, and dropping it disdainfully." The meeting of Gilbert and Pauline is the meeting of man and woman, a meeting in which Pauline silently accepts Gilbert's challenge to the "tournament so often held between man and woman—a tournament where the keen tongue is the lance, pride the shield, passion the fiery steed, and the hardest heart the winner of the prize, which seldom fails to prove a barren honor, ending in remorse." And so faint alarms and excursions subtly suggest without overtly revealing the denouement.

Pauline's inexorable anger intensifies until she is possessed by a devil—not one with a cloven hoof but a subtle psychological force for evil. Her little stage performance and "drama of deceit"—all Louisa's heroines are actresses on the stage or off—her machinations to bankrupt Gilbert "in love, honor, liberty, and hope" fail utterly in the end.

The winner of Frank Leslie's one-hundred-dollar prize adopted the pseudonym of A. M. Barnard for a tale she submitted to another flamboyant weekly, *The Flag of Our Union*. Despite her preoccupation with passionate and angry heroines, Louisa was already too skillful a writer to repeat herself without variation. "The Abbot's Ghost: or, Maurice Treherne's Temptation"[17] is set in no exotic Cuban paradise but a haunted English abbey replete with screaming peacocks, thick-walled gallery and arched stone roof, armored figures and an abbot's ghost. A Dickensian flavor attaches to these Gothic appurtenances as, sitting round the hall fire, the dramatis personae tell tales of ghosts and coffins, skeletons and haunted houses. The star of that dramatis personae is less the hero of the title than the magnificent Edith Snowden, a strong-willed woman burdened by a heavy cross, a mysterious past, and jealousies that conflict with "contending emotions of . . . remorse and despair." "The Abbot's Ghost" is filled with psychological insights that illuminate the subtle relationships of the characters. The plot, revolving principally about the sudden cure of the crippled Maurice Treherne and ending with a triple wedding in the abbey, is basically a love story narrated against a strongly Gothic background. It comes to life through the brilliant depiction of a woman of passion and power whose furies are banked by her innate nobility.

Unlike the anonymous "Pauline's Passion" and the pseudonymous "Abbot's Ghost," *The Mysterious Key*[18] has a male hero, a charming young Italianate Englishman, and unlike either of those narratives, *The Mysterious Key* was published over the name of Louisa May Alcott. The possibility suggests itself that Louisa insisted upon secrecy less for her blood-and-thunder stories in general than for her passionate and angry heroines in particular.

The hero of *The Mysterious Key* combines a touch of that Polish boy who, with Alf Whitman, was to become the Laurie of *Little Women*, and a strong hint of the pale and ardent Italian patriot Mazzini. Paul's appearance at the Trevlyn home in Warwickshire—an estate adequately equipped with haunted room and state chamber—touches off an elaborate plot. Well paced, it depends for its unfoldment upon a prophetic rhyme and a mysterious black-bearded visitor, a sealed letter and an ancient family volume, pretended sleepwalking, a touch of bigamy and a blind ward, Helen. The silver key that opens the Trevlyn tomb and discloses a mildewed paper proving Helen's identity is less mysterious and less intriguing than the hero Paul who, as Paolo, had been—like Mazzini—a hero in the Italian Revolution. All loose ends—and there are many—are neatly tied as the silver key slips into the door of a grisly tomb unlocking "a tragedy of life and death."

Between "Pauline's Passion," written in 1862, and *The Mysterious Key*, which appeared in 1867, Louisa wrote other gaudy, gruesome, and psychologically perceptive thrillers. Sitting incognito behind her pen, she produced "V. V.: or, Plots and Counterplots," an involved tale about a danseuse, Virginie Varens, whose flesh bore the tattooed letters *V. V.* above a lover's knot. A mysterious iron ring, drugged coffee, four violent deaths, and a viscount parading as a deaf-and-dumb Indian servant were the ingredients of this heady witch's broth. Poison vied with pistols or daggers for "the short road to . . . revenge," garments were dyed with blood, the heroine concluded her dark bargain, and the author doubtless recalled with nostalgia the comic tragedies of her childhood. This flight into the all-but-impossible not only emblazoned the pages of a sensational newspaper but was reprinted as a ten-cent novelette.[19]

Like "V. V.," "A Marble Woman: or, The Mysterious Model"[20] was filled with a variety of plots and counterplots as well as a colorful cast of characters that included a sculptor, Bazil Yorke, and an opium-eating heroine. The plight of Mme. Mathilde Arnheim was pursued by the indefatigable writer in *The Skeleton in the Closet*,[21] the narrative of a woman married to an idiot husband and bound to him by a tie which death alone could sever.

Of all the blood-and-thunder tales conceived by Louisa May Alcott when her hair was down and her dander up, the most extraordinary — in this critic's opinion at least — is the one that gives this book its title. "Behind a Mask: or, A Woman's Power"[22] is not only *per se* a suspenseful story recounted in a masterly manner; it fuses in its crucible many of the elements that had gone into the life of its author. It engrosses the reader while it makes use of and reflects the experiences and emotions of its creator. "Behind a Mask" is therefore a Gothic *roman à clef*, a fast-moving narrative whose episodes unlock the past not only of the heroine Jean Muir but of the writer Louisa Alcott. Behind this mask, perhaps, the future author of *Little Women* sits for a dark but revealing portrait.

Jean Muir is many things: a woman bent, like Pauline Valary, upon revenge; a woman who, to achieve her ends, resorts to all sorts of coquetries and subterfuges including the feigning of an attempted suicide; a woman filled with anger directed principally against the male lords of creation. But she is primarily an actress.

The arrival of a new governess at the ancestral Coventry estate in England — a role played by Jean Muir — sets the plot in motion. She appears, pale-faced, small, and thin, not more than nineteen years old, and the first scene she enacts is an effective, sympathy-arousing faint. "Scene first, very well done," murmurs the astute Gerald, to which she replies, "The last scene shall be still better."

The mystery is suggested, the suspense begun, the plot laid down when, in the privacy of her room, Miss Muir proceeds to open a flask and drink "some ardent cordial," remove the braids from her head, wipe the pink from her face, take out "several pearly teeth" and emerge "a haggard, worn, and moody woman of thirty. . . . The metamorphosis was wonderful. . . . her mobile features settled into their natural expression, weary, hard, bitter. . . . brooding over some wrong, or loss, or disappointment which had darkened all her life."

Very gradually Miss Muir's transformation is made intelligible until she develops into one of Miss Alcott's most fascinating heroines. Like Pauline Valary she is, of course, a *femme fatale* with whom every male member of the Coventry household, including the fifty-five-year-old Sir John Coventry, falls madly in love. Her background is mysterious. She has lived in Paris, traveled in Russia, can sing brilliant Italian airs and read character. Her powers are fatal. She confesses to one of her lovers, "I *am* a witch, and one day my disguise will drop away and you will see me as I am, old, ugly, bad and lost."

Jean Muir is indeed a psychological if not a Gothic witch. Proud and passionate, mysterious and mocking, she wields a subtle spell. Motivated like Pauline by thwarted love, she carries out her intention of ruining the

Coventry family with deliberation, using all the dramatic skills known to the theater. She lies or cries at will, feigns timidity or imperiousness to suit her needs. In a remarkable episode, when impromptu tableaux are performed in the great saloon of Coventry Hall, Miss Muir darkens her skin, paints her brows, and writes hatred on her face. Success crowns all her efforts for she captures her prize—the middle-aged head of the House of Coventry and with him a title and an estate. Meanwhile her secret is out. And what a feminist secret it is!

The temptation at the Mill Dam, the humiliation of Dedham, the theatrical barnstorming, the readings in Gothic romances were all stirred in the caldron of "Behind a Mask." So too were Louisa's conflicting emotions, her hates and her loves, her challenge to fortune. Weaving from these varied threads a tale of evil and passion, of fury and revenge, A. M. Barnard had used her sources well.

Just why Louisa May Alcott selected that pseudonym remains conjectural. "A.M." were her mother's initials—Abigail May; "Barnard" might have been suggested by the distinguished Connecticut educator Henry Barnard, who was a family friend. For the most part, the thrillers, whether pseudonymous, anonymous, or upon one or two occasions in her own name, were issued by two publishing firms. One of them boasted an editor who was as much of a *femme fatale* as L. M. Alcott could conjure up. The other included a partner whose life strongly suggested the episodes of a sensational novel. In her editorial and publishing negotiations therefore, A. M. Barnard—whether she was aware of it or not—was among kindred spirits.

"Wrote two tales for L.," Louisa noted in her 1862 journal. "I enjoy romancing to suit myself; and though my tales are silly, they are not bad; and my sinners always have a good spot somewhere. I hope it is good drill for fancy and language, for I can do it fast; and Mr. L. says my tales are so 'dramatic, vivid, and full of plot,' they are just what he wants." And a few months later: "Rewrote the last story, and sent it to L., who wants more than I can send him."[23] . . .

The "L." of Louisa's journal, to whom she offered "Pauline's Passion" in competition for the announced hundred-dollar prize, was well aware of this need. Frank Leslie,[24] publisher of *Frank Leslie's Illustrated Newspaper*, had his hand on the public pulse. He had begun life as Henry Carter, wood engraver in England, adopted the pseudonym of Frank Leslie, and migrated to America. Ruddy, black-bearded, aggressive, dynamic, he had in 1855 launched his *Illustrated Newspaper*, a project that was to make him a power on New York's Publishers' Row. With its graphic cuts of murders and assassinations, prizefights and fires, the weekly was to dominate the field of illustrated journalism for nearly three-quarters of a century. It sported just enough text to float the pictures instead of just enough pictures to float the text. Thanks to a clever and ingenious device, Leslie was able to produce his pictures—sometimes mammoth double-page engravings—with unprecedented speed. Thanks to his editorial staff, he was able to select text that titillated an ever-expanding readership whether it gathered at hearth or campfire.

It was E. G. Squier who wrote to Louisa May Alcott in December, 1862, when she herself was nursing at the Union Hotel Hospital: "Your tale 'Pauline' this morning was awarded the $100 prize for the best short tale for Mr. Leslie's newspaper, and you will hear from him in due course in reference to what you may regard as an essential part of the matter. I presume that it will be on hand for those little Christmas purchases. Allow me to congratulate you on your success and to recommend you to submit whatever you may hereafter have of the same sort for Mr. Leslie's acceptance."[25] . . .

[Deleted passage concerns Miriam Follin Squier of the Leslie firm.]

With the new year of 1863 *Frank Leslie's Illustrated Newspaper* announced that, after deliberating over the moral tendency and artistic merit of over two hundred manuscripts, the editor had decided to award the first prize to "a lady of Massachusetts" for "Pauline's Passion and Punishment."[26] In the next number, the first half of a story of "exceeding power, brilliant description, thrilling incident and unexceptionable moral" was anonymously published, with appropriate illustrations of "Manuel reading Gilbert's Letter" and "Gilbert's Despair at Pauline's Final Rejection." "Received $100 from F.L.," Louisa commented in her journal, "for a tale which won the prize last January; paid debts, and was glad that my winter bore visible fruit."[27]

Other seasons also bore visible fruit that ripened in the Leslie periodicals. "A Whisper in the Dark,"[28] a tale too mild for A. M. Barnard but too lurid for L. M. Alcott, and "Enigmas,"[29] a mystery about Italian refugees, a spy and a woman disguised as a man, made their bows in the *Illustrated Newspaper*. In 1866 Miriam Squier reminded Louisa May Alcott that Frank Leslie would be glad to receive a sensational story from her every month at fifty dollars each.[30]

By that time the tireless author was receiving between two and three dollars a column for thrillers produced for a Boston publishing firm headed by yet another remarkable trio. In the ears of those three gentlemen the call of the wild still echoed, for one had edited tales that embodied it, a second had yielded to it by sailing to New Granada aboard the *Crescent City*, and a third had been the hero of a sensational novel, which, if written, would have included chapters on the conquest of California, gold digging, a jaunt to the Sandwich and Fiji islands, China, and Australia. If A. M. Barnard was ever at a loss for a plot she needed merely to hearken to the lives of Messrs. Elliott, Thomes, and Talbot of Boston.[31] William Henry Thomes, who had succumbed to gold fever, had also encountered Indians, coyotes, and grizzlies, had sailed aboard an opium smuggler that plied between

China and California, and was himself a mine of suggestions for authors whose thrilling romances he would publish. As publisher of the *True Flag*, James R. Elliott had edited the type of story William Thomes had lived. The two formed a publishing partnership in 1861, a year after the New York firm of Beadle had introduced their dime-novel series to an avid American reading public. Joined by Newton Talbot, who had listened to the call of the wild by sailing to New Granada, the trio set out their shingle on Boston's Washington Street and, like the House of Leslie in New York, proceeded to issue a chain of periodicals and novelettes that would bring adventure and romance to a nation at war.

The mainstay of their business was *The Flag of Our Union*,[32] a miscellaneous weekly designed for the home circle. Though, according to its publishers, it contained "not one vulgar word or line," it did seem to specialize in violent narratives peopled with convicts and opium addicts. It was for that periodical that Louisa May Alcott under the pseudonym of A. M. Barnard produced her bloodiest and most thunderous thrillers.

[Deleted passages quote the correspondence between Alcott and her publishers, discuss the discovery of those letters and of the Alcott thrillers by Leona Rostenberg, and consider Alcott's avowed addiction to the "lurid style."]

Like all the authors of sensational literature, Louisa Alcott was equipped with a riotous imagination, a dramatic instinct, and an indefatigable right hand. If she borrowed from other Gothic romancers the trappings of a rich aristocracy in which she could forget her own penury, if her language upon occasion was high-style pompous and her themes ghostly-gruesome, she nonetheless added much of her own to the genre she had adopted. Her plotting was tight and well paced and she used the serial form to heighten the mounting suspense of her narratives. Her characterizations were natural and subtle and her gallery of *femmes fatales* forms a suite of flesh-and-blood portraits. Her own anger at an unjust world she transformed into the anger of her heroines, who made of it a powerful weapon with which to challenge fate. The psychological insights of A. M. Barnard disclose the darker side of the character of Louisa May Alcott, and so her stories must appeal enormously to all who have been enthralled by the life and work of the author of *Little Women*. Since those same psychological insights reveal her as intensely modern, intensely if obliquely feminist, her stories must command an immediate response today. They are rich with interest for those in search of current themes and preoccupations as well as for those in search of Louisa May Alcott. And for those who seek merely the thrills of the cliff-hanger, they bring the delights of the suspenseful tale well told.

[Deletion.]

Here her "gorgeous fancies" and her flamboyant characters do "cavort at their own sweet will." And here, in an extraordinary union, the excitements of escape are coupled with the excitements of self-discovery. She writes in a vortex behind her mask and she proves, if proof is needed, that "the writers of sensation novels are wiser in their generation than the children of sweetness and light."[33]

Notes

1. Louisa May Alcott to Alf Whitman, Concord, 22 June [1862] (Houghton Library, Harvard University).

2. Louisa May Alcott to James Redpath, n.p., n.d. (New York Historical Society).

3. Ednah D. Cheney, ed., *Louisa May Alcott: Her Life, Letters, and Journals* (Boston: Roberts Brothers, 1889) p. 89 (hereinafter Cheney). For biographical details about Alcott see also Madeleine B. Stern, *Louisa May Alcott* (Norman: University of Oklahoma Press, 1971).

4. Louisa May Alcott, "How I Went Out to Service," *The Independent*, XXVI: 1331 (June 4, 1874); Stern, *Louisa May Alcott*, pp. 64–66. The Dedham family was identified with the help of the late Mr. Frank W. Kimball and Dr. Arthur M. Worthington, both of Dedham, Mass. In *An Address . . . before . . . the Massachusetts Charitable Fire Society* (Boston, 1810), James Richardson announced, "Benevolence is both a sentiment and a duty." See also Alvan Lamson, *A Discourse on The Life and Character of Hon. James Richardson* (Boston, 1858).

According to "Gossip," *Frank Leslie's Lady's Journal*, XIX: 476 (December 25, 1880), p. 115, Louisa May Alcott had worked as a servant in a former Senator's household. A young theological student who boarded with the family asked her to black his boots shortly after her term as a servant had expired. Her reply was that while studying divinity he should have learned humanity. Despite inaccuracies, this is an interesting record, especially since it appeared in a Leslie periodical.

5. Stern, *Louisa May Alcott*, pp. 89–91.

6. A. Bronson Alcott to Mrs. A. Bronson Alcott, St. Louis, November 30, 1866, in Richard L. Herrnstadt, ed., *The Letters of A. Bronson Alcott* (Ames, Iowa [1969]), p. 397.

7. *Comic Tragedies Written by "Jo" and "Meg" and Acted by the "Little Women"* (Boston, 1893); Stern, *Louisa May Alcott, passim*; Madeleine B. Stern, "Louisa Alcott, Trouper," *The New England Quarterly*, XVI:2 (June, 1943); Madeleine B. Stern, "The Witch's Cauldron to the Family Hearth: Louisa M. Alcott's Literary Development, 1848–1868," *More Books, The Bulletin of the Boston Public Library* (October, 1943), p. 363.

8. Cheney, p. 63.

9. *Ibid.*, p. 45.

10. *Ibid.*, p. 68.

11. Edith Birkhead, *The Tale of Terror: A Study of the Gothic Romance* (New York [1920]), p. 197.

12. For a fine anthology of Gothic novels with extremely informative introductions, see Peter Haining, ed., *Gothic Tales of Terror*, I and II (Baltimore, 1973).

13. For Louisa May Alcott's writings, see the Bibliography appended to Stern, *Louisa May Alcott*, pp. 342–360; Madeleine B. Stern, *Louisa's Wonder Book: A Newly Discovered Alcott Juvenile* (Mount Pleasant, Mich., 1975); Jacob Blanck, *Bibliography of American Literature* (New Haven, 1955), I, 27–45.

14. Cheney, p. 80.

15. Louisa May Alcott, "Happy Women," *The New York Ledger*, XXIV: 7 (April 11, 1868).

16. "Pauline's Passion and Punishment," *Frank Leslie's Illustrated Newspaper*, XV:379 and 380 (January 3 and 10, 1863). Published anonymously. Now reprinted from issues at the New York Public Library and the New York Historical Society Library.

17. "The Abbot's Ghost: or, Maurice Treherne's Temptation," *The Flag of Our Union*, XXII: 1, 2, 3, and 4 (January 5, 12, 19, 26, 1867). Published under the pseudonym of A. M. Barnard. Now reprinted through the courtesy of Mr. William Matheson, Chief, Rare Book Division, Library of Congress.

18. L. M. Alcott, *The Mysterious Key, and What It Opened* (Boston: Elliott, Thomes & Talbot, [1867]). Issued as No. 50 in the *Ten Cent Novelettes* of *Standard American Authors* series. Reprinted as No. 382 in *The Leisure Hour Library* by F. M. Lupton of New York, ca. 1900. For bibliographical details, see Blanck, *op. cit.*, No. 152 and No. 231. Now reprinted through the courtesy of Dr. Julius P. Barclay, Curator of Rare Books, and Miss Joan Crane, Alderman Library, University of Virginia. The copy at the University of Virginia had belonged to Carroll Atwood Wilson.

19. "V. V.: or, Plots and Counterplots," *The Flag of Our Union*, XX:5, 6, 7, 8 (February 4, 11, 18, 25, 1865). Reprinted as No. 80 in the *Ten Cent Novelettes* of *Standard American Authors* series under the pseudonym of A. M. Barnard. For bibliographical details, see Blanck, *op. cit.*, No. 165.

20. "A Marble Woman: or, The Mysterious Model," *The Flag of Our Union*, XX: 20, 21, 22, 23 (May 20, 27, June 3, 10, 1865). Published under the pseudonym of A. M. Barnard.

21. L. M. Alcott, *The Skeleton in the Closet*. Published with Perley Parker, *The Foundling* (Boston: Elliott, Thomes & Talbot [1867]), as No. 49 in the *Ten Cent Novelettes* of *Standard American Authors* series. For bibliographical details, see Blanck, *op. cit.*, No. 151.

22. "Behind a Mask: or, A Woman's Power," *The Flag of Our Union*, XXI: 41, 42, 43, 44 (October 13, 20, 27, November 3, 1866). Published under the pseudonym of A. M. Barnard. Now reprinted through the courtesy of Dr. Marc A. McCorison, American Antiquarian Society, Worcester, Mass.

23. Cheney, p. 131.

24. For details of Frank Leslie and his *Illustrated Newspaper*, see Frank Luther Mott, *A History of American Magazines 1850–1865* (Cambridge, Mass., 1957) II, 452–465; Madeleine B. Stern, *Imprints on History: Book Publishers and American Frontiers* (Bloomington, Ind., 1956), pp. 221–232; Madeleine B. Stern, *Purple Passage: The Life of Mrs. Frank Leslie* (Norman, Okla., 1970), *passim*; John Tebbel, *A History of Book Publishing in the United States* (New York and London, 1972) I, 357–358.

25. E. G. Squier to Louisa May Alcott, ca. December 18, 1862 (Orchard House, Concord, Mass.). Quoted in Leona Rostenberg, "Some Anonymous and Pseudonymous Thrillers of Louisa May Alcott," *Papers* of the Bibliographical Society of America, XXXVII: 2 (1943). See also Stern, *Louisa May Alcott*, p. 123.

26. Stern, *Louisa May Alcott*, p. 128.

27. Cheney, p. 151.

28. "A Whisper in the Dark," *Frank Leslie's Illustrated Newspaper*, XVI:401 and 402 (June 6 and 13, 1863). Reprinted in *A Modern Mephistopheles and A Whisper in the Dark* (Boston, 1889).

29. "Enigmas," *Frank Leslie's Illustrated Newspaper*, XVIII:450 and 451 (May 14 and 21, 1864).

30. Miriam F. Squier to Louisa May Alcott, New Rochelle, September 17, 1866 (Houghton Library, Harvard University). See also Stern, *Purple Passage*, p. 220.

31. For Elliott, Thomes & Talbot, see Rostenberg, "Some Anonymous and Pseudony-

mous Thrillers of Louisa M. Alcott," *passim;* Stern, *Imprints on History,* pp. 206–220; Tebbel, *A History of Book Publishing in the United States* I, 438–440.

    32. The periodical ran from 1846 to 1870. See Mott, *A History of American Magazines* II, 35.

    33. Dorothy L. Sayers and Robert Eustace, *The Documents in the Case* (New York, [1972]), p. 81.

Moods

[A Letter to Louisa May Alcott (1864) by the Future Publisher of *Moods*]   Aaron K. Loring*

A. K. Loring entered the publishing field in 1863 with *Faith Gartney's Girlhood* by Mrs. A. D. T. Whitney. Sometime during the following year, in an undated letter to another of his authors, Louisa May Alcott (now at the Alderman Library, University of Virginia), Loring formulated his publishing demands and credo: "I judge a book by the impression it makes and leaves in my mind, by the *feelings* solely as I am no scholar. — A story that touches and moves me, I can make others read and believe in. — What I like is conciseness in introducing the characters, getting them upon the stage and into action as quickly as possible. — Then I like a story of constant action, bustle and motion. — Conversations and descriptive scenes are delightful reading when well drawn but are too often skipped by the reader who is anxious to see what they do next, and its [sic] folly to write what will be skipped in reading. The books you have read and admired, the poetry you love, the music that has enchanted, Paintings and Sculpture admired, the heroic words uttered by earnest thinkers who sway the world rightly introduced add greatly to the enjoyment of the story as they revive and refresh the memory of every reader. . . . I like a story that starts to teach some lesson of life [and] goes steadily on increasing in interest till it culminates with the closing chapter leaving you spell bound, enchanted and exhausted with the intensity with which it is written, the lesson forcibly told, and a yearning desire to turn right back to the beginning and enjoy it over again. . . . Stories of the *heart* are what live in the memory and when you move the reader to tears you have won them [sic] to you forever."

*Reprinted from *Publishers for Mass Entertainment in Nineteenth Century America*, ed. Madeleine B. Stern (Boston: G. K. Hall & Co., 1980), p. 192.

[Review of *Moods*, 1865]

Anonymous*

 Moods, by Louisa M. Alcott (Loring, Boston). This is a short story of great power and absorbing interest by a new writer, whose *Hospital Sketches* were remarkable for a humor and insight which ought to have made them much more widely known. In the present tale the conflict of passion in noble characters is drawn with great delicacy and skill, and with a freedom and firmness which promise remarkable works hereafter. *Moods* is neither sentimental nor morbid nor extravagant. It has freshness and self-reliance. Greater experience and resolute study will correct the imperfect literary art; nor is it a disheartening failure not to have succeeded in a satisfactory discrimination between the two heroes of the tale. Such likeness in unlikeness demands a Shakespearian subtlety of skill fully to delineate. It is something to have suggested it. After Hawthorne we recall no American love-story of equal power.

Transcendental Fiction [Review of *Moods*, 1865]

Anonymous*

 Miss Alcott, hitherto known to the readers of American books as the writer of a series of spirited sketches drawn from her own experiences in a military hospital at Washington, has in this volume made her first appearance as a writer of fiction. The work has attracted considerable attention in her own country, and passed through several editions. It may be classified as belonging to the transcendental school of novels, and bears upon its title-page the following sentence from Emerson: 'Life is a train of moods like a string of beads; and as we pass through them they prove to be many-coloured lenses, which paint the world with their own hue, and each shows us only what lies in its own focus.' It is, however, the work of an original and somewhat daring mind. Of speculations which find their type in Goethe's 'Elective Affinities' there are few representatives in English fiction. Our writers, being reluctant to enter upon paths which lead over stone walls and through swamps to doubtful lands, have contented themselves with portraying and analysing the characters formed amid the trials and passions generated by the imperfect but disciplinary conditions of society and its institutions. Miss Alcott boldly grapples with the institutions themselves; and though she cannot be denied a partial success, it must be confessed that she faints at last, and leaves society with its old frontiers.

---

*Reprinted from *Harper's Weekly*, 9 (21 January 1865), 35.
*Reprinted from the *Reader*, 5 (15 April 1865), 422–23.

It is an old battlefield on which the encounter occurs—a false marriage. In Sylvia Yule, the youngest child of a loveless marriage, are

> Mysteriously blended the two natures that had given her life, although she was born when the gulf between regretful husband and sad wife was widest.

[Quotation and comments on Sylvia's character deleted.]

She is eccentric, even to the extent of running about her flower-garden dressed in a suit of boy's clothing, and choosing as her pets the more desolate and ugly creatures, as a caterpillar or fieldmouse. Sylvia is little more than a child when she meets the two young men with whom her destiny is bound up, Geoffrey Moor and Adam Warwick. They have been friends at college; since then Moor has passed his time in Europe, and Warwick in Cuba. In Cuba, Warwick has formed a hasty engagement of marriage with a fascinating woman, of which he deeply repents, but can only obtain her consent to the test which a year's absence may give to her feelings towards him, and, with a vow to return at the end of the year, leaves Cuba to become the guest of his old friend Moor, who lives upon his inherited estate, close to Mr. Yule's residence. The young men are also the friends of Sylvia's brother Mark. . . .

[Quotation deleted.]

It is not wonderful that these personages should be wafted into the region of tender emotions. Moor and Warwick cannot resist the charms of their fair companion. Warwick knows that if he shall remain near Sylvia, Moor's hope will be ruined; and, believing that Sylvia does not yet consciously love him, resolves to sacrifice his own love to that of his friend. He then goes off to fulfil his vow of meeting again the Cuban beauty, whom, however, he has resolved never to marry; at length, however, she is kind enough to marry another.

Warwick subsequently learns that Sylvia has declined an offer from Moor, and resolves to return and make his love known. But, meanwhile, Sylvia has learned of Warwick's engagement with the Cuban lady, and hearing that the latter is married, supposes that it is to Warwick. The love that Warwick supposed unaroused has long been awake, and she has been expecting his return; but now, when she believes he is married, she becomes weak and weary, and is easily persuaded to marry Moor, who is entirely unaware of any attachment between her and Warwick. The wedding of Moor with Sylvia is followed by an excursion among the mountains. On one occasion, when Sylvia has separated from the rest of the party, Warwick meets her. He has not heard of her marriage, and pours forth his protestations of love. Sylvia, overwhelmed with grief, finds that her love for Warwick is unconquerable. There is a tragical parting. But when the wedding party has returned home, Warwick, with a judicious friend—Faith

Dane by name—visits the Moors, and they accept an invitation to remain some days. It is evident to him that Sylvia's marriage is a loveless one, and that, despite Geoffrey Moor's devotion to her, she is unhappy. On a certain evening at Moor's house the company fall to discussing the best method of retrieving a false marriage, *apropos* of the recent occurrence of the elopement of a wife in the neighbourhood. Sylvia has ventured some ejaculation of pity for the woman, which has much shocked her sister Prue, who appeals to Warwick on the general subject.

[Deleted passages contain lengthy quotations from the book.]

The author is, however, not prepared to have her characters put into practice these theories, which really constitute the moral aim of the book. Sylvia confesses her love for Warwick, but when she has separated from her husband, agrees with her lover upon a renunciation. This renunciation, however, rests not at all upon the fact of the previous marriage, but upon some formidable transcendental ideas urged by Miss Dane, concerning a natural incongruity of both Sylvia and Warwick for marriage. We think we recognize in this Miss Dane, beneath all her philosophy, a New-World edition of our very potent friend, Mrs. Grundy. Moor starts for Europe, and Warwick joins him. They remain devoted friends to the last. Warwick fights well in a battle, and receives the praise of Garibaldi. Moor receives a call to come home from his wife, and, believing that she has learned to love him, starts with Warwick for America. When in sight of the shore, Warwick, in saving his friend's life, after the ship has sunk, loses his own. Moor returns home only to be the friend of his wife in her father's house for the few months of life left to her.

Whilst we cannot discover from this volume that the New World has anything to add in the way of solving the sad problems with which it deals, we acknowledge the benefit of having our problems themselves stated so bravely and chastely. The right putting of a question is the most important step towards obtaining the right answering of it. "The world's great bridals," of which Tennyson sings, and the nobler race to spring from them, are not yet so near that we can fail to heed any earnest voice that would prepare their way; for we know that great ultimate steps cannot be taken except as the summing up of many intervening ones. As Browning has said—

> God has conceded two sights to a man—
> One, of men's whole work, time's completed plan;
> The other, of the minute's work, man's first
> Step to the plan's completeness.

With reference to the question of divorce, in itself, nothing is intimated in the volume which would help us on the positive side. No one can think that there is any gain to virtue or to society in having two persons remain in the closest relation who have no real attraction but the iron rivets of law. But the hostility of society to divorce is a part of that general economy of nature which insists that the paramount care shall go for the protection and development of the fruit. Severe divorce laws are the thorny burrs that are meant to protect the child, and preserve a home and training for it. If it were not for children, divorce laws and social customs would be sufficiently facile for all cases. But no philosopher has yet presented a new marriage theory that included a sufficient protection to the child. Until this is done marriage will remain, as it is now, the most fortified of human institutions. Marriage, so far from being assailed in the volume before us, is invested with the utmost sanctity.

A rich vein of humour pervades this book. There is a description of a Golden Wedding in a farm-house of New England that has a subtlety of humour and wit not unworthy of Charles Lamb, alternating with passages of pathos and true feeling which warrant the largest hope from the author. The work as a whole lacks the completeness of its separate scenes. Probability — as in a certain somnambulistic adventure of Sylvia's — is sometimes strained; and there are a few other things which may be attributable to the first effort at a sustained work of fiction, and require rather to be pointed out than to be severely criticised. These defects are, however, very slight in the presence of a story of such thrilling and varied interest, written in a style so graphic and simple.

[Review of *Moods*, 1865] Henry James[*]

Under the above title, Miss Alcott has given us her version of the old story of the husband, the wife, and the lover. This story has been told so often that an author's only pretext for telling it again is his consciousness of an ability to make it either more entertaining or more instructive; to invest it with incidents more dramatic, or with a more pointed moral. Its interest has already been carried to the furthest limits, both of tragedy and comedy, by a number of practised French writers: under this head, therefore, competition would be superfluous. Has Miss Alcott proposed to herself to give her story a philosophical bearing? We can hardly suppose it.

We have seen it asserted that her book claims to deal with the "doctrine of affinities." What the doctrine of affinities is, we do not exactly know; but we are inclined to think that our author has been somewhat maligned. Her book is, to our perception, innocent of any doctrine whatever.

The heroine of *Moods* is a fitful, wayward, and withal most amiable young person, named Sylvia. We regret to say that Miss Alcott takes her up in her childhood. We are utterly weary of stories about precocious little

[*]Reprinted from the *North American Review*, 101 (July 1865), 276–81.

girls. In the first place, they are in themselves disagreeable and unprofitable objects of study; and in the second, they are always the precursors of a not less unprofitable middle-aged lover. We admit that, even to the middle-aged, Sylvia must have been a most engaging little person. One of her means of fascination is to disguise herself as a boy and work in the garden with a hoe and wheelbarrow; under which circumstances she is clandestinely watched by one of the heroes, who then and there falls in love with her. Then she goes off on a camping-out expedition of a week's duration, in company with three gentlemen, with no superfluous luggage, as far as we can ascertain, but a cockle-shell stuck "pilgrim-wise" in her hat. It is hard to say whether the impropriety of this proceeding is the greater or the less from the fact of her extreme youth. This fact is at any rate kindly overlooked by two of her companions, who become desperately enamored of her before the week is out. These two gentlemen are Miss Alcott's heroes. One of them, Mr. Geoffrey Moor, is unobjectionable enough; we shall have something to say of him hereafter; but the other, Mr. Adam Warwick, is one of our oldest and most inveterate foes. He is the inevitable *cavaliere servente* of the precocious little girl; the laconical, satirical, dogmatical lover, of about thirty-five, with the "brown mane," the quiet smile, the "masterful soul," and the "commanding eye." Do not all novel-readers remember a figure, a hundred figures, analogous to this? Can they not, one of his properties being given, — the "quiet smile" for instance, — reconstruct the whole monstrous shape? When the "quiet smile" is suggested, we know what is coming: we foresee the cynical bachelor or widower, the amateur of human nature, "Full of strange oaths, and bearded like the pard," who has travelled all over the world, lives on a mysterious patrimony, and spends his time in breaking the hearts and the wills of demure little school-girls, who answer him with "Yes, sir," and "No, sir."

Mr. Warwick is plainly a great favorite with the author. She has for him that affection which writers entertain, not for those figures whom they have well known, but for such as they have much pondered. Miss Alcott has probably mused upon Warwick so long and so lovingly that she has lost all sense of his proportions. There is a most discouraging good-will in the manner in which lady novelists elaborate their impossible heroes. There are, thank Heaven, no such men at large in society. We speak thus devoutly, not because Warwick is a vicious person, — on the contrary, he exhibits the sternest integrity; but because, apparently as a natural result of being thoroughly conscientious, he is essentially disagreeable. Women appear to delight in the conception of men who shall be insupportable to men. Warwick is intended to be a profoundly serious person. A species of prologue is prefixed to the tale, in which we are initiated into his passion for one Ottila, a beautiful Cuban lady. This chapter is a literary curiosity. The relations of the two lovers are illustrated by means of a dialogue between them. Considering how bad this dialogue is, it is really very good. We mean that, considering what nonsense the lovers are made to talk, their conversation is quite dramatic. We are not certain of the extent to which the author sympathizes with her hero; but we are pretty sure that she has a secret "Bravo" in store for him upon his exit. He talks to his mistress as no sane man ever talked to a woman. It is not too much to say that he talks like a brute. Ottila's great crime has been, that, after three months' wooing, he has not found her so excellent a person as he at first supposed her to be. This is a specimen of his language. "You allured my eye with loveliness, my ear with music; piqued curiosity, pampered pride, and subdued will by flatteries subtly administered. Beginning afar off, you let all influences do their work, till the moment came for the effective stroke. Then you made a crowning sacrifice of maiden modesty, and owned you loved me." What return does she get for the sacrifice, if sacrifice it was? To have her favors thrown back in her teeth on the day that her lover determines to jilt her. To jilt a woman in an underhand fashion is bad enough; but to break your word to her and at the same time load her with outrage, to call her evil names because she is so provokingly in the right, to add the foulest insult to the bitterest injury, — these things may be worthy of a dissolute adventurer, but they are certainly not worthy of a model hero. Warwick tells Otila that he is "a man untamed by any law but that of [his] own will." He is further described as "violently virtuous, a masterful soul, bent on living out his aspirations at any cost"; and as possessed of "great nobility of character, great audacity of mind"; as being "too fierce an iconoclast to suit the old party, too individual a reformer to join the new," and "a grand man in the rough, an excellent tonic for those who have courage to try him." Truly, for her courage in trying him, poor Ottila is generously rewarded. His attitude towards her may be reduced to this: — Three months ago, I fell in love with your beauty, your grace, your wit. I took them as a promise of a moral elevation which I now find you do not possess. And yet, the deuse take it, I am engaged to you. *Ergo*, you are false, immodest, and lacking in the "moral sentiment," and I will have nothing to do with you. I may be a sneak, a coward, a brute; but at all events, I am untamed by any law, etc.

Before the picnic above mentioned is over, Warwick and Moor have, unknown to each other, both lost their hearts to Sylvia. Warwick may not declare himself, inasmuch as, to do him justice, he considers himself bound by word to the unfortunate beauty of the Havana. But Moor, who is free to do as he pleases, forthwith offers himself. He is refused, the young girl having a preference for Warwick. But while she is waiting for Warwick's declaration, his flirtation with Ottila comes to her knowledge. She recalls Moor, marries him, and goes to spend her honeymoon among the White Mountains. Here Warwick turns up. He has been absent in Cuba, whether taking back his rude speeches to Ottila, or following them up with more of the same sort, we are not informed. He is accordingly ignorant of the change in his mistress's circumstances. He finds her alone on the mountain-side, and straightway unburdens his heart. Here ensues a very pretty scene, prettily told. On learning the sad truth, Warwick takes himself off, over the crest of the hill, looking very tall and grand against the sun, and leaving his mistress alone in the shadow. In the shadow she passes the rest of her brief existence. She might have lived along happily enough, we conceive, masquerading with her gentle husband in the fashion of old days, if Warwick had not come back, and proffered a visit, — his one natural and his one naughty act. Of course it is all up with Sylvia. An honest man in Warwick's position would immediately have withdrawn, on seeing that his presence only served seriously to alienate his mistress from her husband. A dishonest man would have remained and made love to his friend's wife.

Miss Alcott tries to persuade us that her hero does neither; but we maintain that he adopts the latter course, and, what is worse, does it like an arrant hypocrite. He proceeds to lay down the law of matrimonial duty to Sylvia in a manner which, in our opinion, would warrant her in calling in her husband to turn him out of the house. He declares, indeed, that he designs no "French sentiment nor sin," whatever these may be; but he exerts the utmost power of his "masterful soul" to bully her into a protest against her unnatural union. No man with any sense of decency, no man of the slightest common-sense, would presume to dogmatize in this conceited fashion upon a matter with which he has not the least concern. Miss Alcott would tell us, we presume, that it is not as a lover, but as a friend, that Warwick offers the advice here put into his mouth. Family friends, when they know what they are about, are only too glad to shirk the responsibility of an opinion in matrimonial differences. When a man beats, starves, or otherwise misuses his wife, any judicious acquaintance will take the responsibility of advising the poor woman to seek legal redress; and he need not, to use Miss Alcott's own preposition, have an affinity "for" her, to do so. But it is inconceivable that a wise and virtuous gentleman should deliberately persuade two dear friends — dear equally to himself and to each other — to pick imperceptible flaws in a relation whose inviolability is the great interest of their lives, and which, from the picture presented to us, is certainly one of exceptional comfort and harmony.

In all this matter it strikes us that Sylvia's husband is the only one to be pitied. His wife, while in a somnambulistic state, confesses the secret of her illicit affection. Moor is, of course, bitterly outraged, and his anger is well described. Sylvia pities him intensely, but insists with sweet inflexibility that she cannot continue to be his wife, and dismisses him to Europe, with a most audacious speech about the beautiful eternity and the immortality of love. Moor, who for a moment has evinced a gleam of natural passion, which does something towards redeeming from ludicrous unreality the united efforts of the trio before us, soon recovers himself, and submits to his fate precisely like a morbidly conscientious young girl who is engaged in the formation of her character under the direction of her clergyman. From this point accordingly the story becomes more and more unnatural, although, we cheerfully add, it becomes considerably more dramatic, and is much better told. All this portion is, in fact, very pretty; indeed, if it were not so essentially false, we should call it very fine. As it is, we can only use the expression in its ironical sense. Moor consents to sacrifice himself to the beautiful ethical abstraction which his wife and her lover have concocted between them. He will go to Europe and await the dawning of some new abstraction, under whose starry influence he may return. When he does return, it will not be, we may be sure, to give his wife the thorough rating she deserves.

At the eleventh hour, when the vessel is about to start, Warwick turns up, and thrusts himself, as a travelling companion, upon the man he has outraged. As Warwick was destined to die a violent death, we think Miss Alcott might have here appropriately closed her book by making Moor pitch Adam into the water for his impertinence. But as usual, Warwick has his own way.

During their absence, Sylvia sinks into a rapid decline. After a certain interval they start homeward. But their ship is wrecked; Warwick is lost in trying to save Moor's life; and Moor reaches home alone. Sylvia then proceeds to put him and every one else in the wrong by dying the death of the righteous.

The two most striking facts with regard to *Moods* are the author's ignorance of human nature, and her self-confidence in spite of this ignorance. Miss Alcott doubtless knows men and women well enough to deal successfully with their every-day virtues and temptations, but not well enough to handle great dramatic passions. The consequence is, that her play is not a real play, nor her actors real actors.

But beside these facts are others, less salient perhaps, upon which it is pleasanter to touch. Chief among these is the author's decided cleverness; that quality to which we owe it that, in spite of the absurdities of the action, the last half of her book is replete with beauty and vigor. What shall we call this quality? Imagination does not seem to us too grand a word. For, in the absence of knowledge, our authoress has derived her figures, as the German derived his camel, from the depths of her moral consciousness. If they are on this account the less real, they are also on this account the more unmistakably instinct with a certain beauty and grace. If Miss Alcott's experience of human nature has been small, as we should suppose, her admiration for it is nevertheless great. Putting aside Adam's treatment of Ottila, she sympathizes throughout her book with none but great things. She has the rare merit, accordingly, of being very seldom puerile. For inanimate nature, too, she has a genuine love, together with a very pretty way of describing it. With these qualities there is no reason why Miss Alcott should not write a very good novel, provided she will be satisfied to describe only that which she has seen. When such a novel comes, as we doubt not it eventually will, we shall be among the first to welcome it. With the exception of two or three celebrated names, we know not, indeed, to whom, in this country, unless to Miss Alcott, we are to look for a novel above the average.

[Review of *Moods*, revised edition, 1882]

Anonymous*

The differences in the two editions of Miss Alcott's *Moods* are slight, but interesting, as showing how little essential to the novelist's art are the conditions on which the novelist is apt to rely. The entire omission of the most dramatic episode in the earlier book — probably the episode on which Miss Alcott most prided herself at the time — is found to leave the little story just as interesting and much more dignified; while the cheerful solution of Sylvia's difficulties at the close of the present edition is far more acceptable to readers who could not hope for consolation or help in their own troubles from the dramatic ending of the first edition. We cannot all die when death would be the easiest relief from our tragedies; but we may live and make them considerably less tragic if we will. Miss Alcott does well to enforce this change of moral, and we commend the confession and correction of a literary and moral mistake.

Moods, Gothic and Domestic

Ruth K. MacDonald*

When Louisa May Alcott first started work on *Moods*, the only public appearance of her work was a volume of fairy tales and some sentimental short stories. Between 1860, when she began it, and 1865, when it was first published,[1] the novel underwent several revisions. The most dramatic of these was dictated by the publisher, A. K. Loring, who advised Alcott to cut the description and dialogue in favor of emphasizing action. But Alcott's own writing had been tending in that direction anyway. *Hospital Sketches* (1863) is a lively narrative series about her experiences as a Civil War nurse. It had little in common with the transcendental metaphysics of *Moods*. The warm critical reception of *Hospital Sketches* and the praise it garnered for its lively, realistic portrayal of the war perhaps prepared Alcott for the sacrifice of her first born to the editor's unmerciful cuts.

By 1881, when the novel was completely revised and reissued, Alcott had already gained fame and fortune as a writer of realistic novels for children. Loring's return of the copyright to her occasioned the revision and the explanatory preface that indicated the author's mode of working during the revision:

> Several chapters have been omitted, several of the original ones restored; and those that remain have been pruned of as much fine writing as

*Reprinted from the *Critic*, 2 (20 May 1882), 139.

*This essay was written for this volume and appears here for the first time by permission of the author.

could be done without destroying the youthful spirit of the little romance. At eighteen death seemed the only solution for Sylvia's perplexities; but thirty years later, having learned the possibility of finding happiness after disappointment, and making love and duty go hand in hand, my heroine meets a wiser if less romantic fate than in the former edition.[2]

The gothic "potboilers" of her early career were well on their way to literary obscurity, and Alcott had abandoned the gothic mode in favor of the realistic and domestic. Alcott's other adult novel, *Work* (1873), had permitted her opportunity to experiment more realistically with the relations between grown men and women. Framing as they do Alcott's literary career and rising reputation, the two editions of *Moods* do much to explain Alcott's developing literary style and changing perceptions of romantic love.

Certainly the most shocking revision Alcott made was in the ending. At the end of a stormy life whose tempest culminates in a triangular love affair, Sylvia Yule, the heroine, rejects both husband and lover and chooses to devote herself to her father. She contracts an unnamed, fatal, but morally improving disease, and dies as her husband returns to her, sentimentalized but compensating for the harm she has done both husband and family by showing them her example of selfless living in her last months. Martha Saxton posits that the idea for concluding the novel with Sylvia's death came from Alcott's gothic thriller, "V. V., or Plots and Counterplots."[3] In that story, the heroine chooses suicide instead of sacrificing herself to the law for her misdeeds. Since Alcott went immediately to the end of *Moods* after finishing the short story, the speculation is an interesting one. But both novel and short story end somewhat ambiguously: is there no way that a life begun with one misstep can be redeemed?

Perhaps it was simply age and experience. Perhaps it was her writing about such faulty couples as Meg and John Brooke in *Little Women*, Christie and David Sterling in *Work*, and Jo and Friedrich Bhaer in the three March family novels. In any case by the time that Alcott returned to *Moods* for the revision, she had managed to imagine for Sylvia Yule a future of domestic happiness with a husband who was not, perhaps, the dominating passion of her life, but whose caring, thoughtful attitude and true love for her will make him a reliable, supportive partner for many years to come.

Even Sylvia's lover, Adam Warwick, becomes much more realistic in the revision. The opening chapter of the first edition shows Warwick breaking an engagement with a passionate, immoral Cuban beauty. The marriage proposal was elicited from him in a moment of weakness, when the lady misrepresented her moral self to an unsuspecting celibate. Warwick's manner of rectifying the situation is brutal if truthful. By opening the novel with this scene, Alcott shows clearly the parallel between *Moods* and her gothic short stories, which are often set in foreign climes. The high-flown diction—"Only a month betrothed, and yet so cold and gloomy, Adam!" (1865 edition, p. 8)—indicates that the mode of writing is not realistic, and that the emotions and characters are as overwrought as the rhetoric. Opening the novel with Warwick as the focus also misleads the reader, for the real protagonist is Sylvia Yule, not her lover. Exposition about her character, the personality dominated by the moods of the title, is therefore delayed until the second chapter.

In the second, revised edition, Alcott wisely places the former second chapter at the beginning of the novel. With equal wisdom, she eliminates the entire Cuban entanglement from Adam's situation. In its place are several scenes in which Sylvia and Adam are given a chance to talk, to get to know each other, to fall in love with some reasonable predication for doing so. It is impossible to know whether these scenes were in the original novel and were cut at the editor's direction. The original manuscript is no longer available. But since these scenes are so focal to the entire triangle, it seems unlikely for Loring to have made such a suggestion. Without the courtship situations, Adam seems to fall in love with Syliva, and she with him, on the barest of acquaintances. Such an attachment seems an improbable basis for the persistent, destructive passion which develops between them. Rather, it appears in the first novel as an inexplicable, unrealistic obsession that bears little relationship to reality or real love.

The revision gives Sylvia and Adam a chance to know each other enough that a realistic affection can develop between them. Adam has a chance to show the reader his growing interest in Sylvia, and his largeness of spirit in absenting himself from Sylvia so that his friend and rival for Sylvia's affection can press his own suit for her affections and eventually marry her. Adam is also shown laughing and crying from recognizable human feelings. Without this kind of background information, his feelings for Sylvia resemble demonic possession. The only revelation of his character comes from indirect reports, rather than from action observed by the reader. Perhaps the revision of Adam's character was influenced by Alcott's imaginative conception of David Sterling, the hero of *Work*. Like Adam, David is modeled after Thoreau, with his sympathy and understanding for nature and brooding personality. But Christie, the heroine of *Work*, cannot get David to be a hero, to aspire to greatness. Instead, he remains a home-body, a man with a problem. But the problem is not so all-consuming that he becomes obsessed by it, as the first version of Adam Warwick is in his desire for truth and self-respect. The new Adam is not only manly and heroic. He is also fun to be with, available enough to others so that they, as well as the reader, can get to know him as a man worthy of Sylvia's love.

The one change that Alcott does not make in the revision is in a rather remarkable exchange of views in the novel about divorce and remarriage. Warwick advocates breaking up ill-conceived marriages of poorly matched partners with little concern for the wronged partner or the regard of the world. Whereas this course might be appealing for both him and Sylvia, Sylvia is persuaded by her husband's arguments and those of a friend that the straying partner should do all in his or her power to try to love the chosen mate, and to leave the marriage only if this is impossible. But the friend, a wise spinster who hints later that she too has been disappointed in affairs of the heart, pushes her point even further, saying that there are those who should never marry, like herself and Sylvia, because they are unsuited for the institution. To start a new marriage then is not the solution to Sylvia's dilemma. Perhaps celibacy, or learning to be a better partner, are better ways.

Public acceptance of the subject of divorce was probably greater in the 1880s than it was in the 1860s. But even though Alcott invents a more realistic, even if somewhat conventional ending for her heroine in the revision, she does not abandon her radical stance about divorce and woman's vocation outside of marriage. Sylvia may return to her marriage, but at least she is not forced to do so, nor is she denied the privilege of considering other alternatives, including divorce. Though Alcott's revised ending, with Sylvia returning to her husband, chastened, improved, and compromised in her vision of love, may be stereotypic to some extent, Alcott does not back down from the radical views she expressed about marriage earlier in her life. She does not give in to her public, but rather submits to her own common sense. There are certainly examples of Alcott giving in to public expectations about her characters' marriages. *Good Wives* and the second half of *An Old-Fashioned Girl* were both composed to satisfy her public rather than the demands of her narrative. Alcott understood how to pander to her public in order to keep sales up. But this is one instance where she did not refrain from stating her point of view at the risk of offending.

For all of Alcott's disavowals, the theme of the novel, both before and after the revision, is really marriage, or more broadly, the relationships between the sexes. There are a number of marriages, both happy and otherwise, held up for inspection during the novel. The revision eliminates none of them. And for all of Sylvia's moodiness in both versions, the fact that in the first case she dies from inability to cope with marriage, and lives in the second case so that she can continue her marriage, says as much about her mature consideration and satisfaction from the institution as it does about her growing stability. For all that characters like Warwick are given to disclaimers about the importance of marriage, for all that Sylvia and her spinster friend may consider themselves inappropriate for married life, there are many satisfactions to be found in marriage. Though Sylvia is not allowed to pursue Warwick, the grand passion of her life, she is allowed to find happiness in what might otherwise be seen as a compromise in her life's goals. Perhaps this is the mature Alcott's consideration of what she missed in her life — a happy, steady homelife with a man to support and encourage her in her middle age.

Notes

1. Louisa May Alcott, *Moods* (Boston: A. K. Loring, 1865).
2. Louisa May Alcott, *Moods* (Boston: Roberts Brothers, 1882), p. vi.

3. Martha Saxton, *Louisa May: A Modern Biography of Louisa May Alcott* (Boston: Houghton Mifflin, 1977), p. 274.

LITTLE WOMEN

[Review of *Little Women*, Part I, 1868]

Anonymous*

Miss Alcott's new juvenile is an agreeable little story, which is not only very well adapted to the readers for whom it is especially intended, but may also be read with pleasure by older people. The girls depicted all belong to healthy types, and are drawn with a certain cleverness, although there is in the book a lack of what painters call atmosphere — things and people being painted too much in "local colors," and remaining, under all circumstances, somewhat too persistently themselves. The letterpress is accompanied by four or five indifferently executed illustrations, in which Miss May Alcott betrays not only a want of anatomical knowledge, and that indifference to or non-recognition of the subtle beauty of the lines of the female figure which so generally marks women artists, but also the fact that she has not closely studied the text which she illustrates.

[Review of *Little Women*, Part I, 1868]

Anonymous*

This is decidedly the best Christmas story which we have seen for a long time. The heroines (there are four of them) are the "little women" of the title, ranging from twelve to sixteen years of age, each interesting in her way, and together enacting the most comical scenes and achieving most gratifying results. The father is in the army, and it is to please him that his daughters make an effort of a year to correct certain faults in their dispositions. In this they are quite successful, and the father comes home, after many sad war scenes, to find his little ones greatly improved in many respects, a comfort and joy to both their parents. The book is most originally written. It never gets commonplace or wearisome, though it deals with the

*Reprinted from the *Nation*, 7 (22 October 1868), 335.
*Reprinted from *Arthur's Home Magazine*, 32 (December 1868), 375.

most ordinary every-day life. Parents desiring a Christmas book for a girl from ten to sixteen years, cannot do better than to purchase this.

The writer almost promises, as the story is concluded, to follow this volume with others of similar character. We sincerely hope she will.

[Review of *Little Women*, Part II, 1869]

Anonymous*

No reader of Miss Alcott's *Little Women*, published some months since by Roberts Brothers, but will desire to possess the "second part" of the charming sketches which she has just given to the public through the same publishers. The first series was one of the most successful ventures to delineate juvenile womanhood ever attempted; there was a charm and attractiveness, a naturalness and grace, about both characters and narrative, that caused the volume to become a prime favorite with everybody. This issue continues the delight — it is the same fascinating tale, extended without weakening, loading the palate without sickishness. The varied emotions of the young heart are here caught and transfixed so that we almost note the expression of the face upon the printed page. Surely Miss Alcott has wonderful genius for the portraiture, as, years ago, we knew she had for the entertainment, of children. Lee & Shepard have the volume.

[Review of *Little Women*, Part II, 1869]

Anonymous*

The second part of this charming story is out, and all who followed the four sisters and their brother-friend through their childish years, will be eager to follow their various experiences through maidenhood, in college, abroad, and later, in the new home centres they all, save one, helped to make. It would not be fair to those who will read the book, and whose eyes may fall upon this notice to tell any of the story. It is enough to say that the second part perfectly fulfills the promise of the first, and one leaves it with the sincere wish that there were to be a third and a fourth part; indeed he wishes he need never part company, with these earnest, delightful people.

One thought ought to be sown broadcast, till it supplants the heresy that "boys *must* have wild oats to sow," with the truth that purity and virtue are not less the birthright of the brother than of the sister. Of Laurie she says

*Reprinted from the *Commonwealth*, 7 (24 April 1869), 1.
*Reprinted from *National Anti-Slavery Standard*, 29 (1 May 1869), [3].

The poor fellow had temptations enough from without and from within, but he withstood them pretty well, — for much as he valued liberty he valued good faith and confidence more, — so his promise to his grandfather, and his desire to be able to look honestly into the eyes of the women who loved him, and say 'All's well,' kept him safe and steady.

Very likely some Mrs. Grundy will observe, "I don't believe it; boys will be boys, young men must sow their wild oats, and women must not expect miracles." I dare say *you* don't, Mrs. Grundy, but its [sic] true, nevertheless. Women work a good many miracles, and I have a persuasion that they may perform even that of raising the standard of manhood by refusing to echo such sayings. Let the boys be boys, — the longer the better — and let the young men sow their wild oats if they must, — but mothers, sisters, and friends may help to make the crop a small one, and keep many tares from spoiling the harvest, by believing, — and showing that they believe, — in the possibility of loyalty to the virtues which make men manliest in good women's eyes. If it *is* a feminine delusion, leave us to enjoy it while we may — for without it half the beauty and the romance of life is lost, and sorrowful forebodings would embitter all our hopes of the brave, tender-hearted little lads, who still love their mothers better than themselves, and are not ashamed to own it.

Miss Alcott could crave no richer harvest than that which is sure to come from her sowing. Thousands of young people will read her story of these healthy, happy homes, and their standard of home and happiness must in many cases be raised. This is a blessed thing to accomplish in these days of extravagance, when the highest ideal of home is more and more seldom realized.

[Review of *Little Women*, Part II, 1869]

Anonymous*

Little Women, Part II, by Louise M. Alcott, is a rather mature book for the little women, but a capital one for their elders. It is natural, and free from that false sentiment which pervades too much of juvenile literature. Autobiographies, if genuine, are generally interesting, and it is shrewdly suspected that Joe's experience as an author photographs some of Miss Alcott's own literary mistakes and misadventures. But do not her children grow rather rapidly? They are little children in Part First, at the breaking out of the civil war. They are married, settled, and with two or three children of their own before they get through Part Second.

---

*Reprinted from *Harper's New Monthly Magazine*, 39 (August 1869), 455–56.

[*Little Women* and the *Rollo* Books] Barrett Wendell*

Miss Alcott's *Little Women* does for the '60's what *Rollo* does for the '40's.

Mr. Jacob Abbott's "Rollo Books," . . . remain, with their unconscious humour and art, such admirable pictures of Yankee life about 1840. Twenty-eight years later, Louisa Alcott, the admirably devoted daughter of that minor prophet of Transcendentalism, published a book for girls, called *Little Women*, which gives almost as artless a picture of Yankee life in the generation which followed Rollo's. A comparison between these two works is interesting. Comically limited and consciously self-content as the world of Rollo is, it has a refinement which amounts almost to distinction. Whatever you think of the Holiday family and their friends, who may be taken as types of the Yankee middle class just after Gilbert Stuart painted the prosperous gentlemen of Boston, they are not vulgar. The world of *Little Women* is a far more sophisticated world than that of Rollo, a bigger one, a rather braver one, and just as sweet and clean. But instead of unquestioning self-respect, its personages display that rude self-assertion which has generally tainted the lower middle class of English-speaking countries.

Little Women Leads Poll:
Novel Rated Ahead of Bible for
Influence on High School Pupils Anonymous*

Louisa May Alcott's *Little Women* is still one of the favorite books of American childhood, according to a poll just completed by Current Literature among high school classes. The pupils were asked "What book has interested you most?" The Alcott novel was the first choice.

Next in order came the Bible, *Pilgrim's Progress*, Helen Keller's *Story of My Life*, *Polyanna*, E. J. Copus's *As Gold in the Furnace*, *Romona* [sic] *Ben-Hur*, Bruce Barton's *The Man Nobody Knows*, *The Bent Twig*, *So Big*, and *Trail Makers of the Middle Border*.

An essay contest was conducted at the same time, with fifteen prizes for the best written essays on the subject of the book selections. The first prize went to Mildred Childs of Gray, Ga., who chose *Little Women*.

---

*Reprinted from *A Literary History of America* (New York: Charles Scribner's Sons, 1900), pp. 237, 337.

*Reprinted from the *New York Times*, 22 March 1927, p. 7. Copyright 1927 by the New York Times Company. Reprinted by permission.

When the Alcott Books Were New

Dorothea Lawrance Mann*

There are best sellers and best sellers, but the sales of *Little Women* are now mounting up toward the three million mark.

[Passage on biographical background deleted.]

Little Women was translated into French, German and Dutch, and was well known in England and on the continent. In Holland the first book was published under the title, *Under the Mother's Wings*, while the second part was known as *On Their Own Wings*. In 1890, when he was in Athens, Frank Sanborn found a copy of it in modern Greek. Just a few years ago *Little Women* was translated into Chinese by the Misses Sung Tsing-yung and Martha E. Pyle, and appeared in red-linen covers with golden Chinese characters and a fanciful colored-picture in time to be a gift for the Chinese New Year. The fame of the book is world-wide. In the Royal Free Hospital of London not so long ago there was established a *Little Women* bed.

One of the remarkable things about *Little Women* has been the way in which its sales have gone on increasing. Great as was its success during its author's lifetime, it did not touch its fame or its sales in the succeeding years. In 1921 it was selling better than it did in 1896, twenty-five years earlier. The delegates to the American Library Convention held in Detroit in June, 1922, and the delegates to the National Educational Association in Boston the same year were given a ballot bearing the names of one hundred books considered to be the children's favorites. They were asked to indicate twenty-five books which they would consider the best for a one-room country school. When the vote was tabulated the result showed that *Little Women* headed the list, with Lewis Carroll's volume containing the two stories, *Alice's Adventures in Wonderland* and *Through the Looking Glass* second.

One Hundred Good Novels

David A. Randall and John T. Winterich*

Little Women

Little Women / Or, / Meg, Jo, Beth And Amy / By Louisa M. Alcott / Illustrated By May Alcott / Boston / Roberts Brothers / 1868.

*Reprinted from *Publishers' Weekly*, 116 (28 September 1929), 1619, 1623, 1624. Excerpted from the *Publishers' Weekly* of September 28, 1929, published by R. R. Bowker Company. Copyright 1929. Used by permission.

*Reprinted from *Publishers' Weekly*, 135 (17 June 1939), 2183–84. Collations by Randall; notes by Winterich.

Collation: [I]–21⁸, 22⁶. Size: 6½ x 4⅜ inches.

Contents: Brown coated on white endpaper; fly-leaf; frontispiece, inserted; [i], title-page, as above; [ii], Entered according to Act of Congress, in the year 1868, by / Louisa M. Alcott, / In the Clerks office of the District Court of the District of Massachusetts. / Stereotyped By Innes & Regan, / 55 Water Street, Boston. / (Rule) / Presswork by John Wilson and Son. [iii]–iv, Contents; [v], Preface (12 lines) Adapted From John Bunyan; [vi], blank; 7–341, text; [342], blank; [343–348], Advertisements of Roberts Brothers Publications, numbered 3, 2, 11, 12, 8, 11; fly-leaf; endpaper, as above.

Illustrations: Frontispiece, and facing pages 116, 135, and 320 all inserted.

Binding: Noted in several colors of cloth, no priority. Front cover: Blind rectangular border rule with a gilt oval in the center and lettered in gilt within the oval: Little / Women / (Rule) / L. M. Alcott. Back cover with a blind rectangular border rule, otherwise blank. Spine ruled and lettered in gilt: (Rule) / (Wave design) / (Double rule) / (Oval design enclosing lettering as on front cover) / Boston / Roberts Bros. / (Double rule) / (Wave design) / (Rule).

Note: The first issue of the first edition does not have an announcement of *Little Women, Part Two*, at the foot of the last page of text, and *Part One* does not appear on the spine.

Louisa May Alcott was of that glorious company of authors who are not satisfied with the mere production of material designed for publication, but who observe a perpetual busman's holiday by writing letters and keeping a diary. Sometimes such collateral productivity is not of much help to anybody except perhaps a roving psychoanalyst. Miss Alcott, however, competently self-critical and always thoroughly honest, fairly exploded source material in her communings with her relatives and with herself.

We know, therefore, that it was in May, 1868, that she began to write "Little Women"; that in June she sent twelve chapters to Mr. Niles of Roberts Brothers of Boston, who "thought it *dull*" (Miss Alcott's italics); that by July 15th she had finished the task and sent off the 402 pages of manuscript; that on August 28th the proofs arrived. By this time Miss Alcott, who had at first agreed with Mr. Niles, had revised her opinion, as had Mr. Niles. "It reads better than I expected," she confided to her diary. "Not a bit sensational, but simple and true, for we really lived most of it; and if it succeeds that will be the reason of it." And there is the most accurate tabloid review and prognosis of a book ever written.

On October 30th the energetic Mr. Niles was able to report "good news of the book. An order from London for an edition came in. First edition gone and more called for. Expects to sell three or four thousand before the

New Year. Mr. N. wants a second volume for spring." Two days later she began Part Two, planning to write a chapter a day, "and in a month I mean to be done." Actually she took two months, for the manuscript was not sent to Mr. Niles until New Year's Day of 1869. On January 22nd she wrote her Uncle [sic] John Pratt that Roberts Brothers had paid her three hundred dollars for the first three thousand copies — they had made her an outright offer for the story but had advised her to keep the copyright, and fifteen years later she footnoted in her diary: "An honest publisher and a lucky author, for the copyright made her fortune."

"The fifth thousand is now under way," she told Uncle John. "He (Mr. Niles) says as it goes so well there is no reason why it should not run to ten thousand. It is selling in England, and though I get no copyright it helps to make 'my works' known. The sequel is in press. . . . I don't like sequels, and don't think No. 2 will be as popular as No. 1, but publishers are very *perverse* and won't let authors have thier (*sic*) way, so my little women must grow up and be married off in a very stupid fashion."

It will be noted that Miss Alcott took the large view of overseas piracy, just as Mr. Dickens had taken the small view, and Miss Alcott never went to England to lecture.

The first edition of "Little Women" contains four illustrations by Louisa's sister, May Alcott, which are pretty awful. They were quickly replaced (there is evidence that May Alcott was fully alive to her artistic shortcomings) by a set of drawings by an unidentified hand which were better only in that they were obviously the work of a professional if uninspired hand. The 1880 quarto edition (Parts One and Two) with more than 200 illustrations by Frank T. Merrill was the first to be competently illustrated.

"Little Women" has been translated into French, German, Czech, Hungarian, Italian, Finnish, Dutch, Swedish, Norwegian, Spanish, Polish, and Japanese. Alexander Woollcott has recorded: "When I made a speech one day at a girls' school in Tokyo they understood all my little jokes, and when, in comparing their school to the one which Jo March launched in 'Little Women,' I groped through my memory for the name of it, my rescuing prompter was a round, dusky little Japanese girl who helped me out by supplying 'Plumfield' in a stage whisper."

[A Dramatic Performance of *Little Women*, 12 December 1944]

George Jean Nathan*

[Discussion of the performance deleted.]

Little Women, believe it or not, is, in short, still serviceable theatre, and a felicitous journey out of the hard-boiled present into the lace-valentine yesterday. The argument that it is overly sentimental is true. But it could not well be otherwise, since it happens to deal with overly sentimental people. As soundly argue that *The Lower Depths* is overly cynical.

There are some people, critics among them, who insist upon a villain in even something like *Ode To A Nightingale*.

[*Little Women* and the Domestic Sentimentalists]

Edward Wagenknecht*

Little Women is about as close as we have come to creating an American *David Copperfield*; is this fact a sign of the "feminization" of life and letters which some persons are sure has taken place in America? Except for *Tom Sawyer*, it may well be the most beloved American book. It needs— and is susceptible of—little analysis; critics have, therefore, generally neglected it. Collectors, like readers, have been wiser. One night in 1929, Carolyn Wells got A. Edward Newton out of bed in the middle of the night with a telegram in which she asked him whether she should pay the $1,600 she was being asked for a first edition. "Yes," he replied, "and be quick about it."

[Biographical background deleted.]

Little Women itself accepts the limitations of the domestic sentimentalists and imposes charm and common sense upon them. It is, as has been said, an idyll, a hymn in praise of family life, not a literal transcription of domestic experiences: "I do think that families are the most beautiful things in all the world!" Nevertheless, it is honest. "Amy teased Jo, and Jo irritated Amy, and semi-occasional explosions occurred, of which both were much ashamed afterwards." Again we are told that "Every one seemed rather out

*Reprinted from *Theatre Book of the Year: 1944-45* (New York: Knopf, 1945), p. 197. Reprinted by permission of Associated University Presses, on behalf of Fairleigh Dickinson University Press.

*Reprinted from *Cavalcade of the American Novel From the Birth of the Nation to the Middle of the Twentieth Century* (New York: Henry Holt & Co., 1952), pp. 88, 89. Copyright 1952 by Henry Holt and Company, 1952; renewed, 1980, by Edward Wagenknecht.

of sorts, and inclined to croak." The Marches are a religious family, but the daughter of a Transcendentalist philosopher could have no truck with bigotry. Tears are shed, but there is no masochistic desire to "kiss the rod"; Mrs. March craves happy, useful lives for her daughters "with as little care and sorrow to try them as God sees fit to send." Beth even dies realistically. "Seldom, except in books, do the dying utter memorable words, see visions, or depart with beatified countenances. . . ."

Little Women Forever

C. Waller Barrett[*]

Early in October of 1868 an unpretentious volume in a variety of cloth bindings—green, terra cotta, and purple—began to appear on the book counters of Boston. The publishers, the well-known firm of Roberts Bros., had been in no special rush to deliver this work into the hands of the booksellers. The manuscript had been in their offices since the middle of July and the firm did not entertain the slightest suspicion that they were to produce what was to become the most popular and most beloved book for girls ever written. A first printing of 2,000 copies is evidence of the caution that tempered their modest hopes. The volume was priced at $1.25 and the distinguishing feature of the first printing is the notice in the advertisements at the back showing this price. The book naturally did not show the words Part One on the backstrip, since the publishers had no glimmering of the fact that Part Two was to be written and published within a few months, in response to an insistent demand.

The consistently favorable reception accorded the work caused the publishers to raise the price promptly to $1.50, and later printings show this price increase in the advertisements. At the time this rather modest markup was determined, they would have been astonished had they been able to foresee that seventy-seven years later a rather ordinary copy would be sold at auction in New York for $750.

The genesis of *Little Women*, or *Meg, Jo, Beth and Amy*, has often been described as occurring in 1868, the year of publication. Actually, however, the book went through a gestation period of at least ten years in the mind of Louisa Alcott in the form of a vague plan to write the story of *"The Pathetic Family,"* i.e. the Alcotts. Whether or not this plan would have ever been carried out without some outside stimulus is a moot point, but happily the impetus was supplied by Thomas Niles, the literary partner of Roberts Bros., who twice in 1867 suggested to Louisa that she write a book for girls. Another circumstance which moves back the chronological record of the

---

[*]Reprinted from William Targ, *Bibliophile in the Nursery: A Bookman's Treasury of Collectors' Lore on Old and Rare Children's Books* (Cleveland: World Publishing Co., 1957), pp. 378–86.

book's creation is the discovery of a letter, here published for the first time, from Louisa's father, Bronson Alcott, to Louisa, dated February 19, 1868, which reads in part:

> After leaving you yesterday I called at "Roberts Brothers" . . . I spoke of "The Story for the Girls" which R. Bs. asked you to write and find that they expect it and would like to have it ready by September at longest. They want a book of 200 pages or more just as you choose. Mr. Niles, the literary partner spoke in terms of admiration of your literary ability, thinking most highly of your rising fame and prospects. He obviously wishes to become *your* publishers and *mine*. Now I suppose you will come home from ( ) and write your story. My last visit to Boston apparently opens a brighter world for us personally and pecuniarily.   Your Father.

This letter interestingly bears an asterisk in the hand of Louisa changing the title from "The Story for the Girls" to "Little Women."

It was not until May of that year, however, that Louisa was galvanized into what she described as "one of those work-deliriums" and within six weeks had completed and delivered the manuscript. Her journal records that in June she "sent twelve chapters of L.W. to Mr. N. He thought it dull; so do I. But work away and mean to try the experiment; for lively, simple books are very much needed for girls, and perhaps I can supply the need."

Mr. Niles, one of fifteen children and "a confirmed bachelor," read these chapters and wrote frankly to Louisa expressing his doubts about the success of the book but asked to see the remainder. On July 15th Louisa's journal records: "Have finished Little Women and sent it off, — 402 pages. May is designing some pictures for it. Hope it will go, for I shall probably get nothing for "Morning Glories." Very tired, head full of pain from overwork, and heart heavy about Marmee, who is growing feeble." In 1876 Louisa made the following notation: "Too much work for one young woman. No wonder she broke down."

Once again Mr. Niles expressed disappointment and perhaps even considered abandoning publication. Before doing so he wisely determined to seek the opinion of the kind of girl at whom the story was aimed. He gave the manuscript to his young niece Lily Almy, who thereupon achieved the distinction of being the first girl to read *Little Women*. A charming description of this incident has been left by a friend of the family, Miss Lurabel Harlow:

> The little girl in a very short time was wholly absorbed in the story. She heard nothing and saw nothing but the pages where the delightful story was progressing. Now she laughed gaily, or again her eyes were filled with tears. Intent and engrossed, she read on till the tale was done, and then laid down the last sheet with the utmost praise for the story, and the deepest regret that it was finished.

His niece's overwhelming approval overcame all of Mr. Niles's misgivings and in August Louisa's journal records that: "Roberts Bros. made an offer for the story, but at the same time advised me to keep the copyright; so I shall." In 1885 Louisa made the following notation: "An honest publisher and a lucky author, for the copyright made her fortune, and the 'dull book' was the first golden egg of the ugly duckling." On August 26th, Louisa noted in her Journal:

> Proof of whole book came. It reads better than I expected. Not a bit sensational, but simple and true, for we really lived most of it; and if it succeeds that will be the reason of it. Mr. N. likes it better now, and says some girls who have read the manuscripts say it is "splendid." As it is for them, they are the best critics, so I should be satisfied.

The success of the book was almost instantaneous and the demand was not confined to young girls. Staid bankers and merchants would greet each other on the street with the query: "Have you read *Little Women?*" The publication of a sequel or second part became a foregone conclusion; people simply had to know what had happened to the March girls, and on November 1st Louisa's Journal contains this notation:

> Began the second part of *Little Women*. I can do a chapter a day, and in a month I mean to be done. A little success is so inspiring that I now find my "Marches" sober, nice people, and as I can launch into the future, my fancy has more play. Girls write to ask who the little women marry, as if that was the only end and aim of a woman's life. I *won't* marry Jo to Laurie to please any one.

An account in a local newspaper is typical of the overwhelming demand for the second part, accompanied by a consuming curiosity to learn the future of the March girls:

> *Little Women*. The publication of the second part of Miss Alcott's popular story is postponed to April 15th, as it has been found impossible to get ready the large edition needed by the first of that month. In the meantime the publishers hope to hear from the old lady in the country who is "a reading of it" (the first part) and means to send her opinion "soon's ever she can stop laughing and crying over it." The curiosity to learn the denouement of *Little Women* amounts to an epidemic, and one tender-hearted little damsel goes quite beyond the book and wishes to know "where she can find a Laurie, for he just suits her, and she is dying to find just such a delightful boy." This lad may do as much mischief out of the book as he did in it; a result not contemplated by the author when she drew the character.

Naturally a work which attracted so much notice received attention from the critics and reviewers in periodicals all over the country. The reports were almost uniformly favorable but there was an occasional sour note such as the one that appeared in *Zion's Herald* which today cannot be read without a smile:

> *Little Women*, by Miss Alcott, (Roberts Bros.,) is a vivacious story of four girls and their hardly older mother, judging from the picture. What she

should know of poverty is hard to conceive. We dislike the disspiritualizing in it of Bunyan's great Allegory. No child should be taught any less evangelism than that. The fight with Apollyon is reduced to a conflict with an evil temper, and the Palace Beautiful and Vanity Fair are made to be only ordinary virtues or temptations. We cannot commend the book as its quality merits. It is without Christ, and hence perilous in proportion to its assimilation to Christian forms. Don't put in the Sunday School library.

However, regardless of reviews favorable or unfavorable the book steadily made its way into the hearts of the people. It was purchased and read by people who never glanced at the literary notes in newspapers and other periodicals. A Boston correspondent of the *New York Evening Mail* wrote:

A lady was reading it when a great gale came and was so absorbed that she paid no heed to the rain or wind, which was snapping trees like pipestems, until she came to a wedding or the end of a chapter, when the spell was temporarily broken and she flew upstairs to shut the windows. Question for a debating society — ought Miss Alcott repay for the damage done to the carpets?

As the sales mounted steadily toward fifty thousand, the financial tribulations of the "pathetic family" were at an end and Louisa was able to do those things for her father and mother and sisters that she had so longed for. One dearest wish came to a prompt realization. She was able to send the youngest sister, May, who had considerable artistic talent, to Europe to continue her studies, and May was later to achieve the success of having a picture accepted and hung in the Paris Salon. As noted in Louisa's Journal, May did the illustrations for the first part of *Little Women* but unhappily they were among her inferior sketches. May was aware of her deficiencies as is shown by a letter to Mr. Niles dated July 26, 1868, which reads in part:

As my sister decidedly prefers the accompanying sketch to the orchard scene I have ventured putting it on block though the other would have been by far the most effective if I could have done it justice. *This one certainly surpasses the former ones for utter flatness* and my only hope is to do better on a fairy book, that kind of fanciful drawing being much more to my taste.

A tactful change was made for Part Two by securing the services of Billings, the well-known illustrator. A letter from Louisa dated April 1st, 1869, shows that she was not completely enraptured with his efforts:

Oh Betsey! such trials as I have had with that Billings no mortal creter knows! He went & drew Amy a fat girl with a pug of hair, sitting among weedy shrubbery with a lighthouse under her nose, & a mile or two off a scrubby little boy on his stomach in the grass looking cross, towzly, & about 14 years old! It was a blow, for that picture was to be the gem of the lot. I bundled it right back & blew Niles up to such an extent that I thought he'd never come down again. But he did, oh bless you, yes, as brisk &

bland as ever, & set Billings to work again. You will shout when you see the new one for the man followed my directions & made (or tried to) Laurie "a mixture of Apollo, Byron, Tito & Will Greene." Such a baa lamb! hair parted in the middle, big eyes, sweet nose, lovely moustache & cunning hands; straight out of a bandbox & no more like the real Teddy than Ben Franklin. I wailed but let go for the girls are clamoring & the book can't be delayed. Amy is pretty & the scenery good but — my Teddy, oh my Teddy!

As the years went on, this astonishing book not only maintained but increased its hold on the affections of the reading public, particularly girls. Publication in London had speedily followed the issuance in Boston and it evoked the same enthusiastic response. Translations were made into many foreign languages. Since the fifty-six years of copyright protection expired some time ago, it is difficult to estimate the total number which have been sold, as many editions at various prices have been available. Little Brown & Co., the authorized publishers, reported in 1932 the sale of over 1,500,000 copies in the United States alone. It seems safe to say that the total sales of the book (including translations) have been more than 3,000,000 copies, which puts it into the front rank of best-sellers of all time. (The veteran publisher of *Publishers' Weekly*, Mr. Frederic G. Melcher, estimates that the figure is nearer 5,000,000.)

Sentimentality and Louisa M. Alcott

Brigid Brophy[*]

Who's afraid of Louisa M. Alcott? Well, Louisa M. Alcott, for one; and, for another, me.

I'm afraid of her in a quite straightforward way — because she makes me cry. Being myself an almost wholly unsentimental writer, I'm not a bit afraid of her example, which doesn't tempt me. It's not as a writer but as a reader that I fear her.

Her own fear of herself was, however, more ambiguous. She is, I suppose, of all writers the one whose name *means* sentimentality: and yet sentimentality is what she and her characters most dread. Indeed, the very reason why Josephine March preferred to be known as Jo (and I would guess the nickname was the final simple stroke which turned her into one of the classic characters of popular-cum-nursery culture, up there with Sherlock Holmes and Little Miss Muffet) is that she found the name Josephine 'so sentimental'.

I was driven back to Louisa M. Alcott, whom I hadn't read since I was fourteen, by the recent revival on television of the old film of *Little Women*.

[*]Reprinted from *Don't Never Forget: Collected Views and Reviews* (London: Jonathan Cape, 1966), pp. 113–14, 117–20.

By the old film I mean the one with the young Katharine Hepburn—and there I instantly caution myself not to render unto Alcott credit which belongs to Hepburn. The cinematic personality of Katharine Hepburn (for which I imagine the credit belongs to the real-life personality of Katharine Hepburn) is one of those purely poetic literary inventions like Rosalind or the very idea of a seraph. Tears shed over Hepburn are diamonds, cutting clean and deep lacerations into the cheeks they course down. They have no connexion at all with the synthetically pearled snail-track left by the tears of sentimentality. It was just Louisa M. Alcott's good posthumous luck that Hepburn played Jo and that the high ruffled necks of 'period' clothes (to use the word in its purely evocative or estate agent's sense) set off to perfection the essentially tragic sinewiness of the Hepburn throat.

And yet: one can't say Alcott did *nothing* to deserve her luck. Hepburn was never so ideally cast again. It's already something that Alcott created the character which most perfectly became her. And then—the clinching point—the film provoked tears even when Hepburn was not on the screen.

It also brought back enough memory of the text for me to think that it was sticking fairly reverently to Alcott situations and dialogue—which I soon afterwards confirmed by getting hold of the book or, rather, books; the film is in fact taken from both *Little Women* and *Good Wives*. Buying them turned out to be an exercise in itself in nostalgia for a pre-war childhood. They are pretty well the last genuine *books*, with binding and dust wrapper, to be had for a paperback price. Presumably, therefore, they still sell in commercially worthwhile quantities (though as they are out of copyright there is no author's royalty to add its mite to the selling price). Indeed, perhaps they still sell as a going contemporary concern: for though the publishers admit, by the clothes on the pictorial wrappers, that the stories themselves are 'period', there is nothing to make it unequivocally clear that they weren't written yesterday. You have to consult a reference book to discover that *Little Women* was first published in 1868. The blurb of one edition still speaks of 'Miss Alcott'—which seems to surrender the advantages of suggesting she's immortal in favour of those of suggesting she's still alive.

Having re-read them, dried my eyes and blown my nose (it is itself a sentimentality that this less dignified aspect of weeping is so seldom mentioned: one day I shall go through the fiction in the public library and to every 'His eyes filled' add 'so did his nose'), I resolved that the only honourable course was to come out into the open and admit that the dreadful books are masterpieces. I do it, however, with some bad temper and hundreds of reservations.

[Comments on sentimentality deleted.]

You can measure Alcott's technical skill by asking any professional novelist how he would care to have to differentiate the characters of four adolescent girls—particularly if he were confined to a domestic setting, more-or-less naturalism and the things which were mentionable when Alcott wrote. Greater scope in at least the first and last of those departments has not prevented more than one recent novel from making a hash of almost the identical technical problem. Alcott, of course, triumphed at it (that is why we have heard of her), incidentally turning out for one of her four, Meg, a brilliant portrait of the sort of girl whose character consists of having no character. Girls of this sort are the commonest to meet in life and the rarest in literature, because they are so hard to depict (the problem is a variant of the old one about depicting a bore without being boring): usually it takes the genius of a Tolstoy (who specialised in them) to bring them off.

Whereas Meg was a commonplace of Alcott's own—or any—time, in Amy Alcott actually shewed sociological prescience. Or, rather, I think, it shewed despite her. Try as she will to prettify and moralise, she cannot help making Amy the prototype of a model which did not become numerous in the United States until the twentieth century—the peroxided, girl-doll gold-digger. *Of course* it's Amy who gets Laurie in the end (he's rich, isn't he?): she's had 'Good pull-in for Laurie' emblazoned on her chest from the moment her chest began to bud.

With Beth, I admit, Alcott went altogether too far. Beth's patience, humility and gentle sunniness are a quite monstrous imposition on the rest of the family—especially when you consider at what close, even cramped, quarters they live (two bedrooms to four girls): no one in the household could escape the blight of feeling unworthy which was imposed by Beth. I concur in the judgment of the person with whom I watched the film (and who wept even more than I did) in naming her the Black Beth. (I also concur in his naming Marmee Smarmee.) I think Louisa Alcott may herself have had an inkling that in designing a fate for Beth she was inspired by revenge. She seems, perhaps through suspicion of her own motives, to have faltered, with the result that she committed the sort of blunder only a very naïve technician would fall into and only a very self-assured one could, as she does, step out of in her stride. She brings Beth to the point of dying in *Little Women*, and then lets her recover; whereupon, instead of washing her hands—as not ruthless enough to do it—of the whole enterprise, she whips the situation up again in *Good Wives* and this time does ('As Beth had hoped, "the tide went out easily" ') kill her off.

As for Laurie: well, of course, Laurie is awful, tossing those awful curls (though in *Good Wives* he has them cropped and is told off for it): yet though I will go to my death (may the tide go out easily) denying that Laurie has a millionth part of the attractions he thinks he has and the girls think he has, I cannot deny that he is lifelike. If you want to see the romanticised implausibility which even an intelligent woman of the world (and great novelist into the bargain) could make of a curly-haired young man, look at George Eliot's Will Ladislaw. Laurie by contrast is—if awfully—probable.

In the most important event affecting Laurie, the fact that Jo refuses him, Alcott goes beyond verisimilitude and almost into artistic honesty. No doubt she found the courage for this, which meant cutting across the cliché-lines of the popular novel and defying her readers' matchmaking hopes, in the personality of Jo. Jo is one of the most blatantly autobiographical yet most fairly treated heroines in print. All that stands between her and Emma Woodhouse is her creator's lack of intellect. Alcott is not up to devising situations which analyse and develop, as distinct from merely illustrating, her characters.

And in fact absence of intellectual content is the mark of the sentimental genre; conversely it is because of her intellect that Jane Austen is never sentimental. I think, incidentally, that the word 'sentimental' may have been in bad repute with Louisa Alcott because in 1868 it still wore eighteenth-century dress. And the reason, of course, why the eighteenth-century sentimental mode, unlike the nineteenth-century one, no longer works on us (the death of Virginie in *Paul et Virginie* really can't be read without laughing) is that the eighteenth century was so double-dyed intellectual that it *couldn't* put aside intellect when it took out its handkerchief: its many attempts to be affectingly simple were made self-conscious and absurd by its (perfectly correct) suspicion that it was being a simpleton.

As sentimentalists go, Louisa M. Alcott is of the gentler and less immoral sort. Beth's is the only really lushed-over death (the canary who dies in Chapter Eleven of *Little Women* is virtually a throw-away): on the whole, Alcott prefers to wreak her revenges on her characters by making them unhappy in their moments of happiness. (They make it easy for her to do so, through their own proneness to sentimentality.) Even here, one can morally if not aesthetically justify her. It's all, so to speak, between consenting adolescents. All four girls are quite masochists enough to enjoy what she does to them.

I rest on Louisa M. Alcott my plea—hedged about with provisos, reduced, indeed, to a mere strangled sob—that we should recognise that, though sentimentality mars art, craftsmanship in sentimentality is to be as legitimately enjoyed as in any of those genres (thrillers, pornography, ghost stories, yarns, science fiction—whichever way your taste lies) which, because they suppress some relevant strand in artistic logic, are a little less than literature. The spasm across the eyelids is not inherently more despicable than the frisson of the supernatural or the muted erotic thrill imparted by a brilliant sado-erotic literary craftsman like Raymond Chandler. It is, however, more dangerous. One should take to heart this stray little fable by Kierkegaard (whose personality is, indeed, to be taken to heart in all contexts): 'In itself, salmon is a great delicacy; but too much of it is harmful, since it taxes the digestion. At one time when a very large catch of salmon had been brought to Hamburg, the police ordered that a householder should give his servants only one meal a week of salmon. One could wish for a similar police order against sentimentality.'

Meg, Jo, Beth, Amy and Louisa

Elizabeth Janeway[*]

Meg, Jo, Beth and Amy are 100 years old on Oct. 3, and except for Natasha Rostova, who is almost exactly their contemporary (*War and Peace* appeared over the years 1865 to 1869), the Marches must be the most read about and cried over young women of their years. In my time we read *Little Women* of course, but we liked to think it was because our sentimental mothers had loved the book so and urged it on us. For all I know, this is still the cover story today, but just the same, the answer to "Have you read *Little Women*?" is still "Of course." In the last week I've heard it from three Americans, an Italian and an English girl, all in their twenties—the English girl quoted the whole opening: "Christmas won't be Christmas without any presents," it begins, in case you've forgotten—and a mother of teen-agers assured me that her daughters were even now devouring the works of Miss Alcott. Read *Little Women*? Of course.

Why? It is dated and sentimental and full of preaching and moralizing, and some snobbery about the lower classes that is positively breathtaking in its horror: that moment, for instance, when old Mr. Laurence is improbably discovered in a fishmarket, and bestows his charity on a starving Irish woman by hooking a large fish on the end of his cane, and depositing it, to her gasping gratitude, in her arms. It is as often smug as it is snug, and its high-mindedness tends to be that peculiar sort that pays. Brigid Brophy, writing in *The New York Times Book Review* a few years ago, called it a dreadful masterpiece, and the judgment stands (though not, I think, quite on Miss Brophy's grounds). And yet, here it is in a new and handsome centennial edition (Little, Brown, $5.95), as compulsively readable as it was a century ago when publisher Thomas Niles's nieces overrode their uncle's doubts and urged him to bring it out.

Its faults we can see in a moment. They cry to heaven, and when Miss Brophy dwelt at length on the literary sin of sentimentality which falsifies emotion and manipulates the process of life, she hardly had to cite evidence. *Little Women* does harp on our nerves, does play on our feelings, does stack the cards to bring about undeserved happy outcomes here and undeserved comeuppance there. But that is not the whole story, and couldn't be, or there wouldn't be all those girls with their noses in the book right now, and all those women who remember the supreme shock of the moment when Jo sold her hair; when Beth was discovered on the medicine chest in the closet with scarlet fever coming on; when Meg let the Moffats dress her up; when Amy was packed off, protesting and bargaining, to Aunt March's stiff house.

No, *Little Women* does manipulate life, but it is *about* life, and life that is recognizable in human terms today. Miss Alcott preached, and the

---

[*]Reprinted from the *New York Times Book Review*, 7 (29 September 1968), 42, 44, 46. © 1968 by the New York Times Company. Reprinted by permission.

conclusions she came to are frequently too good to be true; but the facts of emotion that she started with were real. She might end by softening the ways to deal with them, but she began by looking them in the eye. Her girls were jealous, mean, silly and lazy; and for 100 years jealous, mean, silly and lazy girls have been ardently grateful for the chance to read about themselves. If Miss Alcott's prescriptions for curing their sins are too simple, it doesn't alter the fact that her diagnoses are clear, unequivocal and humanly right. When her girls are good, they are apt to be painful; but when they are bad, they are bad just the way we all are, and over the same things. It must have been a heavenly relief 100 years ago to learn that one's faults were not unique. Today I suspect that it is a relief to be told to take them seriously and struggle with them; that it is important to be good.

This general background of human interest makes *Little Women* still plausible, but it is hardly enough to keep it a perennial classic. The real attraction is not the book as a whole, but its heroine, Jo, and Jo is a unique creation: the one young woman in 19th-century fiction who maintains her individual independence, who gives up no part of her autonomy as payment for being born a woman — and who gets away with it. Jo is the tomboy dream come true, the dream of growing up into full humanity with all its potentialities instead of into limited femininity: of looking after oneself and paying one's way and doing effective work in the real world instead of learning how to please a man who will look after you, as Meg and Amy both do with pious pleasure. (So, by the way, does Natasha). It's no secret that Jo's story is the heart of *Little Women*, but just what that story represents has not, to my knowledge, been explored, and I think it is worth looking at.

[Details of biographical background deleted.]

The subtlety of Miss Alcott's character drawing (or self-knowledge, if you will) comes through here, for Jo is a tomboy, but never a masculinized or Lesbian figure. She is, somehow, an idealized "New Woman," capable of male virtues but not, as the Victorians would have said, "unsexed." Or perhaps she is really archaic woman, re-created out of some New-World-frontier necessity when patriarchy breaks down. For Jo marries (as we all know! Who can forget that last great self-indulgent burst of tears when Professor Bhaer stops, under the umbrella, and asks "Heart's dearest, why do you cry?"). Yes, Jo marries and becomes, please note, not a sweet little wife but a matriarch: mistress of the professor's school, mother of healthy sons (while Amy and Laurie have only one sickly daughter), and cheerful active manager of events and people. For this Victorian moral tract, sentimental and preachy, was written by a secret rebel against the order of the world and woman's place in it, and all the girls who ever read it know it.

Not To Be Read On Sunday
                                            Lavinia Russ[*]

Nineteen sixty-eight seems a strange time to talk about *Little Women*, and I seem a strange choice to do the talking. Of course there is an obvious reason for the date: October 3, 1968, will make it a neat one hundred years since *Little Women* was first published—published because an editor, Thomas Niles, nagged, in a Boston gentleman's kind of way, at Louisa M. Alcott to write the book. "I think, Miss Alcott," he told her, "you could write a book for girls. I should like to see you try it." He had to ask her twice. Her swift reaction the first time was that she knew nothing about girls, that she understood boys better. Circumstances—her family's—were on Mr. Niles's side when he asked her the second time. Her family, who always lived on the edge of economic disaster, was teetering perilously then, and she agreed to try. So Louisa M. Alcott, who before that had saved the family she loved by writing wild tales of blood and thunder, rescued them this time by writing about them—rescued them and created immortality for them. And for herself.

But 1968 seems a strange year to talk about the books she sent Mr. Niles at Roberts Brothers (*Little Women* was originally two books), strange to talk about these books in this year of violence that has already seen the most terrifying of all the faces of violence—assassination—not once, but two times. To think, let alone to write, about a book remembered as a story of a loving New England family in the nineteenth century seems about as timely as a history of antimacassars.

And I seem a strange choice to be writing about it. Though I write some reviews of children's books, I am no authority on children's literature, am not equipped by degrees to evaluate *Little Women* academically, nor by temperament—I loved it too much when I was young to evaluate it dispassionately, loved it so much when I was a girl that Jo was the second most important person in my life.

She must have been loved by other girls, millions of other girls, for Jo's book—and *Little Women is* Jo's book—has survived one hundred years. Survived! It has flourished like a New England oak! There are no exact figures available. Publishers did not keep sales figures back in the nineteenth century; and Little, Brown and Company did not take it over from Roberts Brothers until 1898. And nowadays with the countless editions of *Little Women* around, both in hardback and paperback, a search for the sales figures for one year would be a five-year project.

But Augusta Baker, Coordinator of Children's Services of the New York Public Library, who *is* an authority, told me that the two most circulated titles on the New York City Public Library's shelves are *The Diary of Anne Frank* and *Little Women*.

And Virginia Haviland, head of the Children's Book Section of the Li-

---

[*]Reprinted from the *Horn Book Magazine*, 44 (October 1968), 521–26.

brary of Congress, who is *also* an authority, sent me a list of the countries, and in some instances the languages, in which *Little Women* has been published. Listen to their names. Together they form a musical wreath around the world—Argentina, Belgium (Flemish), Brazil, Czechoslovakia, Denmark, Egypt (Arabic), Eire, England, Finland, France, Germany, Greece, Hungary, Iceland, India (Urdu), Indonesia, Israel, Italy, Japan, Korea, Netherlands, Norway, Persia, Poland, Portugal, Russia, Spain, Sweden, Taiwan, and Turkey.

Not everybody loves *Little Women*. Brigid Brophy didn't love it—she took six full columns in the *New York Times Book Review* to say why, ending her blast against sentimentality by calling it "a masterpiece, and dreadful," a blast which shot her readers straight to their bookshelves to reread their copies of *Little Women*.

Ernest Hemingway did not love the idea of it—in Paris, when he and this century were young, Hadley and he once asked me up to their flat. When I walked in with a copy of Ibsen's plays under my arm, Ernest put me down with "You're so full of young sweetness and light you ought to be carrying *Little Women*." (He had never read it.)

The unknown critic who wrote one of its first reviews didn't dislike *Little Women*, but did not announce the birth of a masterpiece with any ruffle of drums. "Louisa Alcott is a very spritely and fascinating writer, and her sister, May Alcott, always makes beautiful pictures to illustrate the books. Their books and stories are always interesting and instructive about everyday life. They are not religious books, should not be read on Sunday, and are not appropriate for the Sunday School. This is the character of the book before us. It is lively, entertaining, and not harmful."

Why did *I* love it? Why did all the millions of girls who have read it in the last hundred years love it? Why do all the girls who are reading it all around the world today love it? To find out, I reached for my copy of *Little Women* with its title page "Little Women or Meg, Jo, Beth and Amy, by Louisa M. Alcott, with illustrations in color by Jessie Wilcox Smith, Boston, Little Brown and Company, 1915," with its inscription on the fly leaf from the most important person in my life—"Lavinia Faxon—To a Little Woman—Father." And for the first time in fifty years, I read it straight through, from the very beginning—" 'Christmas won't be Christmas without any presents,' grumbled Jo, lying on the rug"—to the very end, to the sunny afternoon at Plumfield, where all the Marches had gathered to celebrate Marmee's sixtieth birthday with presents and songs—"Touched to the heart, Mrs. March could only stretch out her arms as if to gather children and grandchildren to herself, and say, with face and voice full of motherly love, gratitude, and humility, 'Oh my girls, however long you may live, I never can wish you a greater happiness than this!' "

I read it all, and I found out, I found out why I loved it. I had a strong hunch I had found out why when I read earlier Cornelia Meigs's splendid biography of Miss Alcott, *Invincible Louisa*, and when I read *Louisa M.*

Alcott: Her Life, Letters and Journals, edited by Ednah D. Cheney. I found out later for sure when I reread *Little Women*. I loved it because Louisa M. Alcott was a rebel, with rebels for parents. I found out why other girls loved it — because Jo was a rebel, with rebels for parents. Not the rebels of destruction — they never threw a brick — but rebels who looked at the world as it was, saw the poverty, the inequality, the ignorance, the fear, and said, "It isn't good enough" and went to work to change it.

They did not attack poverty by buying a ticket to a charity ball at the Waldorf. Poverty was their neighbor, often their star boarder. Charity was no Lady Bountiful; charity was another name for compassion.

Mrs. Alcott ran an informal employment service, "a shelter," Louisa Alcott describes in her journal, "for lost girls, abused wives, friendless children, and weak or wicked men." In her journal Louisa tells how "One snowy Saturday night, when our wood was very low, a poor child came to beg a little, as the baby was sick and the father on a spree with all his wages. My mother hesitated at first, as we also had a baby. Very cold weather was upon us, and a Sunday to be got through before more wood could be had. My father said, 'Give half our stock, and trust in Providence; the weather will moderate, or wood will come.' Mother laughed, and answered in her cheery way, 'Well, their need is greater than ours, and if our half gives out we can go to bed and tell stories.' "

The Alcotts attacked inequality by working for Abolition. Louisa, who had a memory, so far back in her childhood that she couldn't remember where or when, of finding a slave hidden in the vast oven of one of the houses they lived in, wrote of a meeting to protest the return of a runaway slave, which she went to when she was nineteen — "I should be horribly ashamed of my country if this slave is taken back."

Louisa M. Alcott was among the first to work for suffrage for women. In an 1881 letter to Mr. Niles — "I can remember when Antislavery was in just the same state that Suffrage is now, and take more pride in the very small help we Alcotts could give than in all the books I ever wrote or ever shall write." Then in characteristic salty fashion she adds, "I, for one, don't want to be ranked among idiots, felons, and minors any longer, for I am none of the three, but very gratefully yours, L. M. A."

The Alcotts attacked ignorance with truth — truth they looked for constantly and found in the inward life, not in the established manners and mores of their time. Always with Ralph Waldo Emerson nearby to offer advice, encouragement, and practical help, they sought for truth. Louisa's father, Bronson Alcott, taught truth as he found it. He was one of the first teachers to respect his pupils and to trust their instincts as he respected and trusted the instincts of his own children. He found such joy in learning that to teach was a joyful experience, and he taught children that to learn was a joyful experience.

They attacked fear with faith. And laughter. When poverty threatened to change from a familiar who was a constant annoyance to have around, to an enemy who could destroy them, they routed him with faith. When Bronson Alcott came back from what we would now call a lecture tour, Louisa recorded in her journal, "In February Father came home. Paid his way but no more. A dramatic scene when he arrived in the night. We were waked by hearing the bell. Mother flew down crying 'My husband.' We rushed after her, and five white figures embraced the half frozen wanderer, who came in hungry, tired, cold and disappointed, but smiling bravely and as serene as ever. We fed and warmed and brooded over him, longing to ask if he had made any money, but no one did till little May said after he told all the pleasant things, 'Well, did people pay you?' Then with a queer look he opened his pocketbook and showed one dollar, saying with a smile that made our eyes fill, 'Only that. My overcoat was stolen and I had to buy a shawl. Many promises were not kept, and traveling is costly. But I've opened the way and in another year shall do better.' I shall never forget how beautifully Mother answered him, though the dear hopeful soul had built much on his success. With a beaming face she kissed him, saying, 'I'd call that doing *very well*. Since you are safely home, dear, we don't ask anything more.' Anna and I choked down our tears and took a little lesson in real love which we never forgot. Nor the look that the tired man and the tender woman gave one another. It was half tragic and half comic, for Father was very dirty and sleepy, and Mother in a big nightcap and funny old jacket."

And when death knocked uninvited at their door, they welcomed him, serene in their faith that death was not an enemy, but the darker brother of life.

Brigid Brophy was wrong about *Little Women*. A girl in Russia cries over Beth's death, not because it is sentimental, but because it is brave. And a girl in India cries when Jo refuses Laurie, because she realizes suddenly that life is not going to hold a neat, happy ending for her.

Ernest Hemingway was wrong about *Little Women*. If he had read *Little Women*, he would have realized that it is not "sweetness and light," it is stalwart proof of his definition of courage: grace under pressure.

Its early reviewer was wrong about *Little Women*, because if religion is living Faith, Hope and Charity every minute of your life, the Alcott-Marches were a truly religious family.

Above all, girls are right to love *Little Women*, every word of it, because it is a story about *good* people. And if there is one generality that is true (and it is the only generality I will ever make about them), it is that young people love goodness. And if there is one hope for us in 1968, the only one, it is that the young recognize the power of goodness, and the responsibility that goodness demands of men and women of good will — the responsibility to their brothers, the responsibility to look at the world as it is — at the poverty, the inequality, the ignorance, the fear — and to say "It isn't good enough" and go to work to change it.

Introduction to Centennial Edition of *Little Women*

Cornelia Meigs[*]

With what qualities was that story of *Little Women* endowed, begun as it was with little confidence, finished in three months and brought out with doubts on the part of both the author and the publisher, to be met with an instant success which was to last for a hundred years? Louisa Alcott could never explain the reasons nor did she ever attempt to do so. Can we, looking back upon her with interested affection, examine what she was doing and thinking and writing in just those crucial years and come to any conclusion as to what brought about these remarkable and happy results? There can be satisfaction at least in trying.

[Discussion of earlier literary experiences deleted.]

She contributed not only sympathy and understanding to her characters but also a complete and generous honesty which gave the book its strong sense of reality. She pretended nothing and concealed nothing; all of her persons were fully and frankly themselves. People who read the book could see reflected their own failings, their own small and secret temptations, and be reassured by the account of other people trying to get the better of their shortcomings. Particularly in relation to herself, Miss Alcott showed Jo in all her hasty-tempered errors, all her doubts and hesitations and her many failures in trying to avoid them. With her instinctive keenness of observation she was able to describe how people could and did change, could develop and make the most of themselves as they went forward. Louisa, whose father was a philosopher, whose intimate family friend was Ralph Waldo Emerson, one of the greatest thinkers of his time, had unconsciously learned the full importance and meaning in the progress of daily life.

In certain ways the book inevitably shows that it was written in another age, one in which people felt free to express their feelings and their spiritual and inner thoughts more fully than they would today. In spite of that, the book showed a long step forward for its time. In books for young people it was then the custom to weigh down the narrative with moral platitudes, strewn with an all too heavy hand. Louisa was fully aware of the dangers of too much preaching. She says of Jo at one point when things were not going happily for her: "Now if she had been the heroine of a moral storybook, she ought at this period of her life to have become quite saintly, renounced the world and gone about doing good in a mortified bonnet with

---

[*]Reprinted from Louisa May Alcott, *Little Women or Meg, Jo, Beth and Amy* (Boston: Little, Brown & Co., 1968), vii, x–xiv. From *Little Women*, by Louisa May Alcott, Introduction by Cornelia Meigs, Centennial Edition. © 1968 by Little, Brown and Company (Inc.). Reprinted by permission of Little, Brown and Company.

tracts in her pocket." Miss Alcott makes it plain that such was not the case and that Jo was "sad, cross, listless or energetic, as the mood suggested."

Mrs. March's occasional little lectures have their own solid worth; they are, actually, only made up of matters that all parents would like to put before their children. Jo's mother, when the two consult together over Jo's impulsive difficulties in the conduct of her life, does not hesitate to meet her troubled daughter on her own ground and exposes all of her own failures in learning to control a hot and explosive temper.

The natural progress of events which is involved in the growing up of four lively girls and the boy who lives next door would make plot enough, but the course of the story follows a more distinctive pattern which should not be overlooked. There is an illuminating scene in the earlier part of the book which ought not to be too hastily passed over. On a certain summer afternoon Laurie sees the girls going up the hill behind the house, wearing big hats, with bags hanging on their shoulders and with staffs in their hands. When he joins them he finds that they are playing a game which they have been fond of since they were small children, that of being people in *Pilgrim's Progress*, the book to which every one of the Alcotts was so devoted. Sitting on the grass the girls and Laurie fall to talking of the future and each one voices his or her ambition, telling of the thing that is at the back of every growing young person's mind, "What would I like to be?"

Meg has arrived somewhere near the fulfillment of her wish, although she only speaks of it cautiously as "To have a lovely house, full of luxurious things" and containing "pleasant people." Jo is also somewhat indefinite. "I want to do something splendid . . . something heroic and wonderful that won't be forgotten after I'm dead. I don't know what, but I'm on the watch for it and mean to astonish you all some day. I think I shall write books and get rich and famous: that would suit me, so that is *my* favorite dream." Beth is too shy to tell what is her real desire, although we learn of it later. All that she will own to now is the wish "that we may all keep well and be together; nothing else."

Amy has "ever so many wishes; but the pet one is . . . to go to Rome and do fine pictures and be the best artist in the whole world." Laurie is not far behind her. "I'm to be a famous musician myself and all creation is to rush to hear me; and I'm never to be bothered about money or business, but just enjoy myself and live for what I like." He adds reflectively, "We're an ambitious set, aren't we? Every one of us but Beth wants to be rich and famous, and gorgeous in every respect. I do wonder if any of us will ever get our wishes."

While the reader is not aware of it, one of the things that holds the story together is the fact that all these cherished schemes do, in actual fact, come to their desired ends but only after each person has accepted the modification and compromise that circumstances and his or her own character have made inevitable. The happy and irresponsible materialism and youthful vanity that clothe these ambitious plans are shed away and replaced by something far more valuable. It is the highest proof of Louisa Alcott's mastery of storytelling that none of us realize this until we look back long after we have read the book.

[Biographical details deleted.]

There also is an element in the very atmosphere of *Little Women* which, it would seem, makes it stand somewhat apart from Louisa Alcott's other books. When good Mr. John Bunyan sat in his dark prison at Bedford and wrote down the matchless tale of *Pilgrim's Progress* he had very little idea of how directly he was laying the foundation for this very different story that was to come so long after him and was to travel almost as widely. The reading of Bunyan's book was interwoven with the whole course of the Alcott girls' growing up as it had been with their father's. Its whole substance was a household word with them. With every year that they grew older they came to understand it more and feel its deeper meaning coloring their own thinking. There is splendor in the unfolding story of every person's life, its joy or pain or despair, if the whole of it can be told truly. That is what John Bunyan taught Louisa.

Young readers of our own time may occasionally be puzzled by the chapter heads, which had direct reference to Bunyan's book: "Amy's Valley of Humiliation," "Jo Meets Apollyon," "Meg Goes to Vanity Fair." There is no more terrible battle described in English literature than that when Christian is attacked by Apollyon with his darts of temptation. Young readers will go on, however, and look back at the end to see how a stout will and firm belief in the good can get the better of adversity. There are a multitude of figures in *Pilgrim's Progress*, so many that we can usually find the likenesses of ourselves and our friends in it. One need not look far to see that Louisa's counterpart was Mr. Valiant-for-truth.

This Is Your Life . . . Louisa May Alcott
Sean O'Faolain*

A lot of novels besides *Little Women* are still read a hundred years after they were written. I doubt that any is read as widely, remembered as fondly and preserved as loyally, often in a much-thumbed copy that has been around the house since long before one was born. The centennial of its appearance this year will see a special edition in celebration of its long life, and doubtless many essays. Though not as good, by a long chalk, as *Treasure Island* or *Robinson Crusoe* or *The Three Musketeers*, it must rank beside them in popularity. And I think the reason for the popularity of those

*Reprinted from *Holiday*, 44 (November 1968), 18, 22, 25–26.

four books, and of a few others of the same order, is that we escape with them honorably. I would not much like to be caught in my study deep in *Beau Geste* or *The Beloved Vagabond* or Vicki Baum's *Grand Hotel;* if I were surprised with *Little Women*, I could hold it up with, at most, a self-deprecating smile or an At-My-Age shrug and go on escaping, unabashed.

Miss Alcott's formula for escape was, however, a little more complicated than most. The formula of most escapist novels is anything from five to twenty-five grains of truth, and the rest plain water. No sugar required. Omission is, of its nature, saccharine. But the reader knows or can guess what has been left out of such novels. In fact, he has to, because it is what is left out that validates what is left in. I am, say, reading a novel about Hong Kong's spies, pirates, sampans, Oriental junks, drugs, brave men, kind whores, true lovers, graft, filth and magnificent sunsets. I can believe every word of it simply by saying to myself, "Well, yes, *all* this—and all the rest that he has left out and that I don't want to consider for the time being." The essential that is left out, however, is not more facts—it is the personality of the writer. This has to be left out, because if the author put it in, his nonsense would become real, his book would no longer be escapist; it would, in fact, if the fellow could write at all, become a good book. In the personality of a writer lies the sole reality of his life and the quality of his work.

Miss Alcott's technique of escape was quite different. Her personality is all over *Little Women*. She fibbed about almost all the facts. She had lived for years the life of a galley slave, toiled in the utmost poverty, humiliation and hardship, looked on hopelessly while her impractical father brought his family to the ground, wept over the misery of her mother and sisters. Being as honest a woman as was ever shaped by the best Puritan traditions of New England, she did not want to obliterate that sadder side of her life or of life at large. At the same time, being also a very gallant young woman, without an iota of self-pity in her composition, she wanted to present life in a heroic glow. She solved her problem by sheer force of character. She exorcised her miserable past by recording it with more gaiety and gusto than she can possibly have felt while living it.

To have done this was, it must be agreed, in the nature of, bordering on or actually a fib; but whichever it was—and her degree of fibbery varies enormously throughout her book—no modern, hard-boiled novelist has the right to take a lofty attitude about it. Gusto and disgust come from the same root. If any reader feels that he should lay aside *Little Women* because there is too much happiness in it, he should also think how little happiness there is in *Ulysses, The Sound and the Fury* or *The Group*. I will not quarrel with any reader's right to lay her book aside because there is too much sweetness and light in it, but I do feel that the balance she strikes between the dark and bright sides of life is more true to common experience than the opposite imbalance of our so-called realists. And she did, despite all her regrettable factual reticences, lift those genteel muslin curtains of Boston just enough, in hints and clues scattered through every chapter, to let us guess the whole truth about her period—one of the least attractive in the history of America.

[Lengthy discussion of biographical background deleted.]

Very quickly the dominant theme of the novel is struck: the conflict in these four young souls between self-love and self-sacrifice, between the poverty of the body and the riches of the heart, between courage and the challenges of life. So, having gloated over the presents they mean to buy themselves, the four suddenly think of mamma, who is out in the cold at that very moment packing boxes of quilts to be sent to the army in the South, and they at once agree to sacrifice their few coins to buy presents for her.

On Christmas morning they will go even farther. They will sacrifice their entire breakfast of buckwheat cakes, hot muffins and cream, gruel and tea to feed a starving German family in a nearby slum—six children in one bed, no fire, and a newborn baby crying with the cold. And as the five return home that cold morning through the dark back streets, there will not be "in all the city four merrier people than the hungry little girls who gave away their breakfasts and contented themselves with bread and milk on Christmas morning."

As we read on, we realize that all this is based on idealized recollections of that one happy if hard year in Concord before their unfortunate father. . . .

But here we stop. What has she done with papa? He is, apparently, the one character she could not deal with. She has packed Bronson off the scene to the war—as a chaplain; nor does she permit him to appear until the very end of the book, a mere shadow of reality.

Once we observe this obliteration—and we do so on page one—we realize that *Little Women* presents us with two considerations that help us measure its quality, both by the pleasure it gives us and the pain it denies us. The novel is patently and undeniably true to life insofar as we are delighted to accept, from the first page, that there really was such a family, at that time, in that place, close-knit, hard-pressed, loving and loyal. Having acknowledged this, in admiration and gratitude, we come up against the second consideration, possibly put into our heads by that passing glance at the starving German immigrants. It is that the background picture is regrettably incomplete in almost all the more interesting social aspects of the life of New England in her time.

I imagine that my experience of reading *Little Women* must be similar to that of most others. When I first read it, many years ago now, it made me feel an enormous increase of affection for the city in which it is placed. It was many more years before I delved into the memoirs and biographies of those scholars who, like Leona Rostenberg and Madeleine Stern, have uncovered the cold facts about that happy family. Thereafter whenever I have reread or remembered the novel, that appealing urban facade of ruby houses lining the green Common, and the society it symbolized for so many generations, have come back to me in a slightly darker, if not sinister, light. I think how effectively Boston imposed its own polite reticences and devious evasions on a novelist who, in her private life, hardly knew what those words meant.

The key to these reticences is, surely, that primal omission of the father. It was his hopeless, gallant struggle with Boston's (and, by inference, America's) philistinism and provincialism that started her whole life story. In leaving him out, she deflected the loyalty of the family from him to their mother. She simply had to leave him out, not so much — though that, no doubt, too — because the memory of his follies and his apparent indifference or blindness to the unhappiness of his wife had hurt her cruelly, but because if she had left him in, his accusing finger would have offended her readers on every page. (She could, of course, have put him in and softened all the oddity and humanity out of him, and where he does fleetingly come in at the end of the first part of the novel — and as fleetingly again in its sequel — that is precisely what she did.)

Unfortunately, by so idealizing the kindness of the mother she had to slide over the loyalty of the wife — a theme any serious writer would have wanted to depict in full. From this deflection we also get the watering down of the bitter wine of the actual poverty and dire misery the entire family suffered over many years. But what I, for one, regret most of all is that we only barely guess what we now know — the magnitude of Louisa Alcott's heroism in her chosen role as the spinster breadwinner and ultimate savior of what she once called The Pathetic Family.

She was wise to throw the book a little backward in time. It enabled her to invoke an older, sterner, simpler morality than that of the full-blast steam age, even if we must observe that it was a morality or theory of life with as many holes in its gleaming surface as melting ice. She constructed her novel on the principle that good girls always get on. So after these good girls give up their breakfast on Christmas morning to the raggedness of the unhappy German immigrants, what happens? Great rewarding dishes of ice cream, the daintiest French bonbons and four large bouquets of hothouse flowers appear that very Christmas night — the gift of a God-the-Father figure, old Mr. Lawrence in the big house next door. In the same way, when two of the girls bravely attend a big New Year's dance in their slightly tarnished dresses, with odd gloves and borrowed shoes, they pick up one of the nicest boys at the party and come home in a carriage attended by their "maid." Because Beth makes slippers for God-the-Father, she gets a present of a new piano. Because Amy is so sweet and generous at Mrs. Chester's fair, and Jo is haughty and rude, Aunt Carrol decides to take Amy abroad with her and leaves Jo behind. So far as I can recall, only one large incident in the novel occurs outside this convenient theory of Happy Causation: it occurs, that is, inexplicably or, in the real sense of the word, tragically: the death of

Beth. We cannot, however, be too rigid about Louisa's (Boston's) morality. There are also many times when the prize to goodness is not material reward but inner happiness.

If I were asked what her gravest fib was, after her denial of her papa, I think it was her overworking of a theme that must have enchanted her publisher and given much pleasure to upper, lower and middle Boston—the theme of hardworking Respectability. It is not the hard work one dislikes; it is rather her attitude to Respectability, that universal obsession of the middle classes the world over. She has no reservations about it. Indeed, she again fibs about papa to advance its worthiness, explaining that the reason why "the two eldest girls *begged* to be *allowed* to do *something* for their own support *at least*" was that their father (in real life a society-scorning, rebellious, penniless, Owenite socialist) had once been rich, but had lost all his property in trying to help a friend. Not that Bronson might not have done such a thing, but that he did not—he had no property at all.

There were, however, some things that Louisa would not surrender, even to please the Boston Beast growling at her door. One of these self-assertions must have greatly worried Mr. Niles and given much satisfaction to her father. It is that all the "correct" things are done during the Christmas season except one—no member of the family goes to church. As one might expect of any of Bronson Alcott's children, Louisa did not believe in any form of organized religion whatever.

But the most fascinating of all her stubborn self-assertions was her firm refusal to marry her heroine, Jo March, to Laurie Lawrence, a decision which may well be one of the main reasons why the book has always appealed so much to young girls. Throughout most of *Little Women* Jo is at that familiar girlish stage that rejects girlishness. She several times wishes she were a boy. In my country, girls at this age frequently become what we call horsey: they long to possess a horse, wear jodhpurs, let their hair grow tangled and slosh around in stables. It is a form of sex-rejection. At one time, with a charming pre-Freudian innocence of what she is doing, Jo actually wanted to be a horse, and pranced and neighed like a horse as she ran. For Jo to marry like any other girl would have been the sort of fib Louisa simply could not tell. We remember how she hated it when Meg was found courting; and we remember (another unconscious Freudian symbol?) how offended she was when Mr. Brooke was found to have secreted Meg's glove in his pocket, and how much she hated all that soppy courting stuff, and how unromantically her own engagement to old (old to her), bearded, Jovelike Professor Bhaer is managed in that tender little scene under the umbrella in the rain. "Heart's dearest, why do you cry?" he asked, and Jo, too frank to dissemble, said weepingly, "Because you are going away," thus opening the way for his final declaration of his love.

Without Jo March *Little Women* would really be nothing at all. Countless young people, male as well as female, must have taken her to their hearts because she was so "unsoppy," so full of high boyish spirits, so hot-tempered, independent, unconventional, with plenty of grit and lots of go, her loose-limbed body always in movement, her lovely long hair either tumbling down or flowing in the wind. She gives us the impression of being boxed up in that house, of belonging more to the river and the fields. In a Boston suburb—though a Boston much smaller than ours, much nearer to the wild, open country—she gives us the impression of being at heart an open-air girl, matching the open-air men of the era before hers, whom Matthew Brady or Southward and Hawes photographed and Eakins and Mount painted as farmers, soldiers, fishermen, lumbermen, under the vast, cold, cloudless skies of a wider America. In her is centered the nostalgic appeal of an age passing away even while she lived, and today, ironically, as hard to find as a steam engine. Before *Little Women* there had been boys like Jo March; in her we meet for the first time a new kind of heroine, who, allowing for the changes of fashion and of morals since then, grins across the ages at many an American girl of today.

So it may not be entirely through folly or sentimentality or advancing senility that I sometimes see, through the masks of so many girls I meet in your streets, campuses and subways, at least the potential of another Jo March. An admirable, if idealized, Miss America?

Does *Little Women* Belittle Women?
Stephanie Harrington[*]

The women's movement is several television seasons old now and each season more and more column inches are written protesting the medium's caricature of women as a gaggle of witless wonders endowed with the intelligence, independence and emotional maturity of retarded guppies. But, as Judy Klemesrud pointed out on this page a few weeks ago ("TV's Women Are Dingbats"), relief is not even in sight—unless, in the shadow of the television stereotype, we look in unlikely places and revise a few prejudices. For, in contrast to the weekly humiliation of Edith Bunker, whose victimization is a matter for therapy not comedy, *Little Women* (the BBC production of which is currently being serialized in nine installments on WCBS, Sundays at 5 P.M.) takes on the force of a feminist tract.

And that is really saying something about the way television writers, producers and directors treat women in the standard fare they serve up because, taken on its own and not compared with currently prevailing caricatures, Louisa May Alcott's story of the four March sisters of Concord, Mass., and how they grew, might understandably strike a contemporary woman

[*]Reprinted from the *New York Times*, 10 June 1973, Sec. 2, pp. 19, 37. © 1973 by the New York Times Company. Reprinted by permission.

with only fellow-traveling ties to the movement as a perfectly disgusting, banal, and craven service to male supremacy. For Alcott is at all times careful to keep the development of her characters safely hemmed in by comfortable moralisms that make it perfectly clear that even Jo, the most "unfeminine" and independent of the March sisters, will come eventually to rest in the snug harbour of "Kirche, Küche und Kinder."

Marriage is anointed as "the sweetest chapter in the romance of womanhood," motherhood as "the deepest and tenderest [experience] of a woman's life," and the combination of these two circumstances as "the sort of shelf on which young wives and mothers may consent to be laid, safe from the restless fret and fever of the world, finding loyal lovers in the little sons and daughters who cling to them, undaunted by sorrow, poverty, or age; walking side by side, through fair and stormy weather, with a faithful friend, who is, in the true sense of the good old Saxon word, the 'houseband'...." Yuchhh! But as if that is not enough, Meg, the oldest March sister and the first to marry, having weathered the initiation to her role, also learns "that a woman's happiest kingdom is home, her highest honor the art of ruling it, not as a queen, but as a wise wife and mother."

Jo, the second oldest and most stoutly independent of the March sisters, who works hard at being a writer, insists she will never marry and speaks her mind no matter what the social cost, eventually comes to value the traditionally feminine determination of Amy to be agreeable, to please people. For Amy, the youngest, who wants to marry well (and she does) and move in elegant circles, agreeableness is at first a socially expedient tool, but as the young woman matures she develops her desire to please into what, in Louisa May Alcott's moral universe, is considered admirable selflessness.

Though Jo never attains Amy's state of grace, with slow, painful effort she does temper her willfulness with increasing patience and understanding. Eventually she even finds fulfillment as a wife and mother and proclaims her old dream of a solitary writer's life as "selfish, lonely and cold." She is helped to this conclusion by the death of her younger sister Beth, a saintly creature who seemed too fragile for this life and who devoted her existence to the loving care of others. On her deathbed Beth implored Jo to take her place as companion and comfort to their parents, assuring her older sister that she would be "happier in doing that, than writing splendid books or seeing all the world; for love is the only thing that we can carry with us where we go...."

These are, of course, precisely the kinds of sentiments (or sentimentality) and conclusions that today's feminists reject, illusions that have served the feminine mystique and kept women in their place. As early as page three of *Little Women* Jo's independence and ambition are passed off as unnatural for a girl: "I can't," says Jo, "get over my disappointment in not being a boy." But she does, and, we are told, she is much the happier for it.

But, although the March sisters wage their inner struggles and work out their designs for living within a moral framework that renders their conclusions foregone, though the questions of individual character that absorb them may seem banal diversions from the weighty matters reserved for men, and their acceptance of their "given" roles a disappointing capitulation, they are at least presented as representatives, and not caricatures, of the women of their time and place. They at least think. They at least, in their own terms, grow. By comparison to the heroines of TV Land, who are bounced back and forth between "situations" like Ping-Pong balls, rarely even capable of reflexes, let alone intelligent volition, the March sisters stand as moral actors in the context of their world.

And the BBC-TV version now being shown on Channel 2 is, from a feminist point of view, more palatable than the novel. It is necessarily pared down, and in adapting the novel for television, writers Denis Constanduros and Alistair Bell stripped it of the author's moral kibitzing, sparing us the homilies with which she rationalizes the eventual domestication of all, including the strong-minded Jo.

Thus edited, *Little Women* can be viewed as a toney and not terribly offensive little soap opera, competently acted and directed. The British cast speaks "American" so well that what traces of accent there are seem more a matter of breeding than nationality. At times, though, the performances are so studied that there is no question that a proscenium arch separates the actors from your living room.

And the typecasting is almost too perfect, the actors fitting Alcott's descriptions of her characters down to the last blush and curl. Stephen Turner, for instance, looks exactly as Theodore Laurence (Laurie) should, but his performance is too stiff and tentative to convey the mischief in Laurie's soul. And while Janina Fay, as Amy, is perfectly pretty and spoiled, she is so perfect in that single dimension that Amy's efforts to vanquish her own selfishness with generosity seem more of a public relations gesture than an inner struggle. But Angela Down's Jo is, in looks and performance, Alcott's word-picture come to life—shattering forever my childhood conviction, held firmly since the children's matinee of *Little Women* at the Parkway movie theater in Mount Vernon, that June Allyson was Jo March.

The BBC production was filmed in England in 1970, and though the social consciousness of the novel is attuned to the 1860's, this version does include lines in which the March sisters object to being considered men's playthings and insist that they will go on with their work, Jo with her writing and Amy with her painting, even if they do marry.

Hardly militant sentiments for our time. But *Little Women* was first published in 1869, and Jo March is a far more liberated woman for those days than Edith Bunker is for these. And if Marlo Thomas, who played a cuddly little eyelash-batting kewpie doll of a woman on "That Girl," can emerge in 1973 as a militant feminist, why not Louisa May Alcott, who at least refers to her characters as women? No, we have not come a long way, baby. Nobody ever called Jo March baby.

Little Women: Who's In Love With Miss Louisa May Alcott? I Am

Leo Lerman*

When Miss Louisa May Alcott was late in years, world famous she was, The Concord Scheherazade, she told a female journalist, "I have often thought that I may have been a horse before I was Louisa Alcott. . . . Now, I am more than half-persuaded I am a man's soul put by some freak of nature into a woman's body." It is not pertinent, in this love letter to Miss Alcott and her *Little Women*, to pursue her along the highways and byways of Freudian understanding (she was, thank the Lord, pre all that, anyway), but both her equine and male sensibilities are very Jo — Jo, as in the tomboy, harumscarum heroine of that unique book, Miss Alcott's masterpiece, *Little Women*, Parts I and II. I fell in love, at a very early age, with Jo, Meg, Beth, Amy, Laurie, Marmee, Hannah, Prof. Bhaer—all of the Marches, their friends, relatives, their Civil War and post Civil War lives in transcendental Concord. Jo did go off to be a governess in New York City, Amy went abroad as a companion to Aunt March . . . I fell irrevocably in love with all of them whether they remained in their very New England nest or fared abroad, for to me, a first generation American, raised in an Orthodox Jewish household where more Yiddish was spoken than English, everything about *Little Women* was exotic. It was all so American, so full of a life I did not know but desperately hoped to be part of, an America full of promises, hopes, optimisms, an America where everyone had a chance to become somebody wonderful like Jo March-Louisa May Alcott who (I had discovered that the Marches and the Alcotts were almost identical) did become, with this story book that I adored, world famous.

The optimism continues to enchant me. No matter what happens in the passing American scene, I continue to believe deeply in the promises, the optimisms which brought us to these American shores. Indeed, I am the result of those promises and optimisms. But what really makes me reread *Little Women* annually, so that it is not so much a rereading but revisiting a house I know intimately, filled with friends whose being is part of my being, is still the life Miss Alcott recreated, the happy, sad, unceasing flow. . . . Jo sits in her attic hideyhole, munching apples, writing her melodramas; Amy sucks limes and is punished; Meg sighs for beautiful clothes; Beth tends her raggle-taggle doll family; Marmee puts all to rights with ever-loving sagacity and thought for moral improvement; Laurie, that rich, handsome boy next door, enraptures all hearts, breaks a few; Jo sells her hair. But these are little things . . . daily junketings, to-and-froings. Death takes over. Deep love. Compassion. We find, and this is unusual in fictions written for young people during the nineteenth century, that goodness, purity, diligence is not always rewarded in just measure. Beth does not get Laurie: Beth dies, her death caused, albeit remotely, by an act of goodness in which her sisters

*Reprinted from *Mademoiselle*, 78 (December 1973), 40. © 1973 Leo Lerman.

refused to partake. So life pulsates in these long-lived pages: kisses, unladylike slaps, a riot of Christmases with glorious unexpected treats to eat and jokes galore and sometimes such presents! The dark side, the bright side, but always the loving heart beating hopefully through the laughter and the tears. You see, Miss Alcott knew life, she lived it, loved it realistically: she could, and did, prick the bubble of conceit, flatten the foible of affectation — she saw these clearly but she also cherished people for themselves, for what they were. There is such understanding in this book . . . such goodness, such a humor of being. Here is a scrap, pulled out at random: " 'Jo! Jo! where are you?' cried Meg, at the foot of the garret stairs. 'Here!' answered a husky voice from above; and running up, Meg found her sister eating apples and crying over the 'Heir of Redcliffe', wrapped up in a comforter on an old three-legged sofa by the sunny window." It isn't much, just set down out of context, but it is immediate, as immediate as a snapshot or even a moving picture. It is living by people over one hundred years ago and, miracle of miracles, clear for us to see, to feel, to smell and to taste because a New England spinster lady had the genius and the wit and the ambition and the need to write it all down. So, whether Miss Louisa May Alcott thought she'd been a horse or that she was inhabited by the soul of a man, I love her, and to her, wherever she is, from this now ample-sized, gray-bearded Jewish boy who has become part of her enormous American — no — global family, the loveliest of Christmases, the brightest of New Years, dear Jo March, dear, very dear Miss Louisa May Alcott.

[*Little Women* and the Female Imagination]   Patricia Meyer Spacks*

"When I was in fourth grade I was a horse. I was a stallion, I was the one that led the herd and everything. The thing was, I always thought of myself in the masculine position. A year or so later I started to write a book about being an Indian, and I was the boy. I just thought I could get more accomplished that way."

That was a characteristic response to reading *Little Women*, which about half my students had first encountered as children. Some confessed to weeping again over the death of Beth, some professed to be cynical. Some thought it was "a really good book," at least for children, some thought it sentimental, or too moralistic. But all agreed that they had identified with Jo. Not with noble Beth, or domestic Meg, or artistic Amy on her jaunt to Europe, but with boyish Jo, striving for masculine achievement, yearning

*Reprinted from *The Female Imagination* (New York: Alfred A. Knopf, 1975), pp. 95–101. From *The Female Imagination*, by Patricia Meyer Spacks. © 1972, 1975 by Patricia Meyer Spacks. Reprinted by permission of Alfred A. Knopf, Inc.

for masculine freedom. I never asked my students how many of them wished they were men, or had wished it, but their reaction to *Little Women* suggested that all of them yearned somehow to be boy and girl simultaneously. Who can blame them?

The difference between boy and girl is strongly marked in *Little Women*. It is spelled out in an account of Meg's twins, a boy and a girl, who from infancy define themselves according to sex:

> At three, Daisy demanded a "needler," and actually made a bag with four stitches in it; she likewise set up housekeeping in the sideboard, and managed a microscopic cooking stove with a skill that brought tears of pride to Hannah's eyes, while Demi learned his letters with his grandfather. . . .
> The boy early developed a mechanical genius which delighted his father and distracted his mother, for he tried to imitate every machine he saw, and kept the nursery in a chaotic condition, with his "sewin-sheen" . . . ; also a basket hung over the back of a big chair, in which he vainly tried to hoist his too confiding sister, who, with feminine devotion, allowed her little head to be bumped till rescued. . . . Of course, Demi tyrannized over Daisy, and gallantly defended her from every other aggressor; while Daisy made a galley slave of herself. . . . A rosy, chubby, sunshiny little soul was Daisy, who found her way to everybody's heart, and nestled there.

This distribution of virtues seems invented for the purpose of being attacked by feminists: a textbook example of damaging assumptions about the nature of the female, and of the way a girl learns to be charming because she's not allowed to be intelligent or inventive. The patterns of life for bigger girls and boys in the book are what one might predict from this version of babyhood.

Little Women is usually remembered, sometimes even referred to in print, as a study of four girls with an absent father. In fact, the father is on hand for half the narrative. He provides spiritual advice to his daughters (his tone and language eerily identical with his wife's), confiscates the wine at Meg's wedding, teaches his grandson the alphabet: guide, rebuker, pedagogue — man. Yet he seems invisible: in a deep sense this is a women's world. On the other hand, there is no doubt about which sex really *does things*. The novel — one hesitates to call it that, since the narrative complexity is on the level of a child's story: all, of course, it purports to be — exhaustively examines the feminine role of "taking care," yet makes clear from the outset that the masculine kind of taking care — providing financial and serious moral support — is the kind that counts. The girls dispute about who is to have the privilege of buying their mother some new slippers. Jo wins, saying, "I'm the man of the family now papa is away, and I shall provide the slippers, for he told me to take special care of mother while he was gone." Unfortunately for her psychic well-being, she can only temporarily occupy the comforting role of "man of the family"; her father returns to supplant her.

The book is not one an adult is likely to reread with pleasure, yet children — even college students — still respond strongly to Jo as a fictional character. And the pure didacticism that governs the narrative gives it special clarity as a revelation of nineteenth-century feminine assumptions about feminine nature and possibility. Louisa May Alcott's ideas about what women should and can be, and what men naturally are, shape the simple narrative structure, which moves from one "lesson" to another. These pieces of didacticism reveal how completely women can incorporate unflattering assumptions about their own nature, using such assumptions as moral goads. The assumptions, and the lessons drawn from them, are only cruder in presentation than Mrs. Gaskell's: at core they are virtually identical.

The nature of women, this book suggests, is to be frivolous, foolish, vain, and lazy. They must be laboriously taught to be otherwise. Only in relative isolation can they learn to be good, since female society is thoroughly corrupt. Confining themselves within the family, learning at the knee of a virtuous mother, controlled from afar by a vague but stern father, they may hope to acquire goodness, which will be rewarded, at best, by marriage or at least by the opportunity to exercise positive influence on a man. Boys, on the other hand, are naturally enterprising, gay, and bold. Masculine society may lead a young man to play pranks; such boyish high spirits will be admired and envied by young women, who beg to be told of them. At worst, such society leads the man to drinking — but a word from a good woman will make him swear off. A man may fall into depression; a woman can bring him out of it. Such power is her highest achievement. In most cases her other nondomestic accomplishments represent only ways of passing time until she is married. It is true that Jo writes successfully — but Jo is a special, and complicated, case.

Given such unpromising raw material as four daughters, the virtuous mother (who has presumably received rigid early training from *her* mother, and who at one point explains how her husband has helped to train her) must struggle to inculcate the proper values. Beth is a saint, rewarded by dying young. The other three, left to their own devices, will glory in laziness, valuing a vacation week of no responsibilities. They are of course wrong: Beth's canary dies as a result (even she succumbs to inertia and neglects her bird) and everyone agrees at the week's end that it's really more fun to have little tasks to do. Meg shows a reprehensible interest in finery, regretting the poverty that deprives her of clothes as attractive as her peers': but she learns that there are more important things in life. Amy, at a school where all the other girls trade pickled limes, wants to have contraband pickled limes too. She is discovered and punished, thus learning that one is not to value pickled limes. Jo's special lessons are more interesting — all lessons in self-control, a virtue highly valued for everyone. Because she says what she thinks, tactlessly, she is deprived of a trip to Europe. She learns that one should be careful about saying what she thinks.

"To be loved and chosen by a good man is the best and sweetest thing which can happen to a woman; and I sincerely hope my girls may know this beautiful experience. . . . I'd rather see you poor men's wives, if you were happy, beloved, contented, than queens on thrones, without self-respect and peace." So speaks the mother: the first and great commandment for girls is to value the love of a good man. The problem is, how to win it. Ignorance is the first article of virtue. No matter that Meg is ill equipped, as a result, to deal with the malice of acquaintances who accuse her and her mother of plotting to ensnare a rich husband—her total ignorance, which her mother would call innocence, makes her automatically the moral superior of those who accuse her. Such superiority demands no effort on the part of its possessor, and this is part of its attraction. Passivity in sexual matters is highly valued. "Better be happy old maids than unhappy wives, or unmaidenly girls, running about to find husbands." Like Molly in *Wives and Daughters*, Miss Alcott's heroines learn that they must sit at home and wait.

And they too must learn to repress emotion, specifically anger. The expression of anger, it seems, is always unforgivable. When Meg's husband brings home an unseasonable guest, she reveals her anger and frustration in an explosion. He conceals his, so he wins: she apologizes. When Meg is extravagant with her husband's money, he says almost nothing, but quietly sacrifices his winter overcoat. He wins. Mrs. March has learned almost total repression of hostile emotions: this is a source of her power. She urges the lesson on Jo particularly, whose curse is a temper. Girls are not expected, not *allowed*, to have tempers. When a boy, their neighbor Laurie, has a fit of temper, Jo goes over to soothe him and his grandfather and bring them together by feminine wiles. No one objects to the boy's directly expressed resentment and hostility. When Jo has a fit of temper, her sister almost dies as a result. Her mother reveals that she has once had the same fault, but "I've learned to check the hasty words that rise to my lips and when I feel that they mean to break out against my will, I just go away a minute, and give myself a little shake, for being so weak and wicked." It is "weak and wicked" for a woman ever to express hostility . . . ever to express even vitality, except in limited prescribed forms. Jo's mother has learned from her husband to be good. "He never loses patience—never doubts or complains—but always hopes, and works, and waits so cheerfully that one is ashamed to do otherwise before him." For men virtue seems natural; for women, in most cases, it must be bitterly acquired.

If girls are to be passive in their relations with men, repressed in their emotional lives, they yet are allowed that familiar sphere of service to others. The glorification of altruism as feminine activity in *Little Women* reaches extraordinary heights. The good woman *serves*, she subordinates herself always to the will of others—to husband, to employer, but also to the poor family down the street—she demonstrates her worthiness by sacrificing her self, in the most literal sense: one comes to feel that no *self* remains for the book's ideal woman. Beth, exemplifying the ideal, quietly fades away. As she points out soon before her death, she has never had plans for the future, as the other girls have: she is a model of selflessness. What can she do but die? True, the most powerful explicit argument for altruism is that it generates a sense of self: "Work is wholesome, and there is plenty for everyone; it keeps us from ennui and mischief, is good for health and spirits, and gives us a sense of power and independence better than money or fashion." But such language does not correspond to actuality. Although service to others may make the server smug, it seems ill-adapted to generating real power and independence—or even a convincing illusion of their presence.

In the context of these precepts and assumptions, Jo is remarkable. She is of course a version of the author herself: if we didn't know that, we'd be forced to surmise it. Her fictional vitality comes from the fact that she alone is in essential conflict with herself. The other girls, with superficial conflicts, deeply accept the values inculcated by their mother. Jo, more ardent than the rest in her resolutions to do good, her professions of virtue, her efforts to control her temper, cook dinners, be agreeable to her disagreeable aunt, fails no more often than anyone else. Still, she is different. The difference is exemplified by her reservations about being a girl. At the very beginning, she observes, "It's bad enough to be a girl, anyway, when I like boys' games and work and manners! I can't get over my disappointment at not being a boy; and it's worse than ever now, for I'm dying to go and fight with papa, and I can only stay at home and knit, like a poky old woman!" Her rebellion, childish and ill-considered in articulation, is yet profound. She learns to behave more like a girl; her father congratulates her at length, when he returns, on having become more womanly. But her preference for boys' work and manners stems from a deep awareness of how the limitations on feminine possibility make it difficult for her to express what's in her. Indeed, she is, as a girl, constantly being told that she is not supposed to express what's in her—yet her vocation is to be a writer.

Next-door Laurie, in a bad temper, tempts Jo to run away with him. She wants to do so, longing—as well she might—for "liberty and fun"; but she observes, "If I was a boy, we'd run away together, and have a capital time; but as I'm a miserable girl, I must be proper, and stop at home." *Miserable* is precisely the right adjective. She means by it something like "worthless," a valuation that she applies by implication to her sex in its entirety—girls are generically worthless by comparison with boys. But she also conveys the dull suffering, the consciousness of always being in the wrong, that seems the very foundation of the girl's lot in life. Boys are allowed to "have a capital time": girls are not. Seeing the division of roles in this way, Jo is necessarily doomed to suffering.

Writing provides the promise of escape. She justifies the activity on altruistic grounds—if she earns money by her writing, she can help her parents and the other girls—but the need for it is far deeper than the need to earn money. It appears to be a quite genuine vocation, although Jo has no guidance about how to develop it and promptly falls into the corruption of writing sensational stories, a trap from which she is rescued, of course, by a wiser man. The writing of trash appeals to her because she is paid for it — and to be paid is to be valued. She is interested in the occupation in itself, unlike Amy, for example, whose narcissistic desire to paint disappears promptly when she is married. But she is also interested in being valued. To be valued for expressivity contradicts what she has been taught at home: the conflict becomes ever more intense.

My students resented the way Jo is finally disposed of. Meg marries the tutor next door, and bears the charming twins, acquiring a new and attractive identity in marriage and motherhood. Amy marries the wealthy, handsome neighbor who has previously proposed to Jo and been rejected. Her mother provides the rationale for the rejection, explaining that both Laurie and Jo have strong tempers and will therefore constantly clash — an impossible basis for marriage. In other words, Jo's failure at self-repression makes a glamorous marriage out of the question for her. Instead, Miss Alcott assigns her to a poor German professor more than twice her age and allows her to open with him a school (for boys!) and to be very happy. But my students felt — rightly, I think — that this was something of a sell. Why, after all, shouldn't Jo have charming, rich Laurie? Why should she be subjected to a father figure? Would she really be as happy as the author claims?

It seems, in an odd way, despite all the professions of happiness, a punitive marriage. Jo's "problem" is self-control . . . repression. If she is so bold as to continue yearning for a man's freedom, a man's happiness, a man's possibilities, if she insists on expressing herself, will not settle down in a predictable role — if she is like this, she must be given a man who can control her. She "proves" her womanliness by nursing Beth tenderly until her death, then remaining at home to comfort her parents. Then Professor Bhaer shows up once more, and marries her, providing from without the authority she needs to keep her in check.

Louisa May Alcott does not enter deeply into the problems of marriage, although she examines Meg's match on a ladies' magazine level (what do you do when your currant jelly refuses to jell? what do you do when your husband starts spending the evening elsewhere?). She . . . sees marriage as reward for virtue and as enlarged sphere for feminine activity; but she also sees it as discipline. Mrs. March's husband helps her control her temper; Meg's husband by example teaches her the beauties of self-sacrifice and self-control; Amy's husband insists that she help him spend his money doing good; Jo's husband, after all, is a middle-aged professor who has begun his relationship with the girl by showing her that she is wrong to write newspaper fiction. Discipline, *Little Women* suggests, is what women little and big require. They must be controlled or their passion for pickled limes and finery and freedom will precipitate chaos. Jo is a dangerous figure. She reveals her creator's awareness that women have needs deeper than Mrs. March allows herself to know.

Ragged Dick and *Little Women*: Idealized Homes and Unwanted Marriages

Thomas H. Pauly*

Published within a year of each other, Horatio Alger's *Ragged Dick* (1867) and Louisa May Alcott's *Little Women* (1868) both became runaway best-sellers overnight[1] and went on to establish themselves as landmarks in the history of children's literature. While the success of these books has been traditionally explained by the captivating appeal they held for adolescent readers from the era of reconstruction through the turn of the century, it is important to remember that a large amount of their popularity is traceable to the parents who selected these books for their children. Because juvenile literature of the age was valued not merely as entertainment but also as good preparation of young readers for the adult world they were expected to enter, it has recently attracted a large academic audience proposing to study the prevailing social values of the era.[2] As a consequence, Alger's books, for example, are more frequently found in the history course than in the playroom. If *Little Women* and *Ragged Dick* particularly lend themselves to such an approach, one of the more fertile lines of inquiry, it seems to me, lies in seeking the nature of their respective successes. By addressing audiences composed almost exclusively of *either* boys or girls, these books mirror a society firmly committed to a sharp differentiation of the sexes. At the same time, both make a special effort to celebrate the sacred union of marriage—going even so far as to make it one of the basic indices of maturity. However, characterized in terms of those values, interests and attitudes which distinguish male from female, the protagonists created by both authors become aligned with positions which militate against marriage, thus unwittingly undermining the very institution these writers are consciously striving to recommend.

Ironically, both authors wrote these moral guidebooks to a successful, rewarding life as *oeuvres de compensation*, to alleviate the uneasiness which informed their decision to write them. Alger was the son of a stern domineering Unitarian minister who gave him his name and thereafter compelled him to follow in his footsteps. Submissive and too fearful to commit himself to the two love affairs in which he became involved, Alger was eventually ordained, only to find himself temperamentally unsuited to the responsibilities of the ministry.[3] Whether Alger resigned from his profession out of this sense of incompatibility or because of doubts concerning the nature of the profession itself remains unclear, but as an alternative he immediately undertook two projects which capitalized on the literary bent he had formerly displayed as an undergraduate. The discouraging response of his publisher A. K. Loring, to *Timothy Crump's Ward* and *Helen Ford* steered him away from the adults he proposed to address in the former and

*Reprinted from the *Journal of Popular Culture*, 9 (Winter 1975), 583–87, 591–92.

the girls in the latter to the subject of *Ragged Dick*, in which his hero's quest for reliable guidance presented a more fruitful challenge to his creative energies.

Although his impact was of a somewhat different nature, Louisa May Alcott's father exercised an equally strong influence on the course of her career. The idealistic goals Amos Bronson Alcott sought to attain in the radical innovations of his Temple School and the experimental community of Fruitlands won him abiding fame but left him perennially unable to support his large family, thereby firing in the ambitious Louisa a strong sense of responsibility for the needs of her mother and sisters. Putting aside whatever hopes of marriage she might have entertained, she determined to earn her way as a nurse and a serious writer. Due to setbacks she suffered on both counts,[4] she was eventually persuaded to try her hand at children's books, and in much the same way as Alger, she turned her disappointments into literary creations that inspired untold thousands of youthful readers.

After receiving several requests for a girls' book from Thomas Niles of the Roberts Brothers' publishing house, Louisa May approached him with a proposal for a fairy tale. Pressed by the financial needs of her family and the dim prospects for a serious book, she conceived of this undertaking as an easy diversion, perhaps even a happy alternative to her actual situation. However, Niles' tepid response to her suggestion prompted her to abandon such an escapist undertaking and return to the more familiar realm of her own childhood. According herself with the age's emerging concern for realism, she decided to substitute what she knew for what she might imagine. "Not a bit sensational," she was to say of the finished product, "but simple and true, for we really lived most of it."[5] Yet the impression of actual experience she sought to convey did not prevent her from allowing her innermost fears and wishes to enter into the story. Alienated by the conditions of her celibacy from the home life she sought to reconstruct, Louisa Alcott, like Horatio Alger, resisted the marital responsibilities essential to the familial happiness her book strives to project.

The opening pages of the book, which introduce the little women, constitute a sort of family portrait, since each of the characters is closely patterned after a member of the Alcott's family, yet there is a notable blank in the picture. The father is missing. It was Bronson Alcott who actually submitted Louisa's original proposal to Niles, and he seems to have met with the same fate as the fairy tale. Louisa had good reasons for depriving her Victorian family of its conventional head. In the first place, her very mixed feelings toward her admirable but impractical father made a satisfactory characterization extremely difficult. Moreover, Mr. March's participation in the war furnished an attractive alternative to Bronson's controversial involvements and a noble explanation for the poverty she made as central to the March household as it was to her own.[6] The reasons for this decision, however, are not nearly so important as the results. What the reader encounters is a world controlled by women where their concerns become the paramount issues. Marmee, Meg, Jo, Beth and Amy constitute a "jolly set,"[7] whose lively spirit derives from deeply shared ties of sex and family. Set against the background of the Civil War and its disruption of life in America, the book implies that the solidarity of the home is an equally critical test of the nation's health, the final result depending on the fortitude of the women who struggle to sustain it.[8]

Through the first chapter's emphasis upon the various dreams and frustrations of the March daughters, the family's pressing concern for money is attended by related worries about propriety. While the girls all complain about annoying duties and responsibilities, each retains a fundamental sense of commitment to them. The letter from the girls' father becomes the dramatic highlight of the chapter as it pointedly defines their moral obligations. Marmee quotes to her assembled children:

> I know they will remember all I said to them, that they will be loving children to you, will do their duty faithfully, fight their bosom enemies bravely, and conquer themselves so beautifully, that when I come back to them I may be fonder and prouder than ever of my little women. (28)

These words echoing Meg's initial reminder of "our little sacrifices" (19) are underlined by Marmee's reference to *Pilgrim's Progress* which she uses to explain that the girls are little pilgrims who must journey through life cheerfully bearing the burdens of their obligations. The pages and chapter headings which follow echo with allusions to this book which Bronson Alcott so favored in his teachings, in order to impress upon the reader the standards by which Jo and her sisters are to be judged, those of obedience, service, dependence and repression, the stereotypical profile of the Victorian woman. The girls are taught to consider the course of their lives as a tortuous path from the city of destruction to the celestial city. Initiated as a children's game running from cellar to attic (30), this trip never leaves the home in its journey from the wayward impulses of youth to the joyous fulfillment of motherhood. Marmee later explains:

> I want my daughters to be beautiful, accomplished, and good; to be admired, loved, and respected; to have a happy youth, to be well and wisely married, and to lead useful, pleasant lives, with as little care and sorrow to try them as God sees fit to send. To be loved and chosen by a good man is the best and sweetest thing which can happen to a woman; and I sincerely hope my girls may know this beautiful experience. (140–41)

This is not to say that *Little Women* is merely a hornbook in female propriety. Perhaps the greatest achievement of the work derives from its successes in presenting these "burdens" as neither an ordeal nor a tedious lesson in manners, but rather a colorful array of concerns and diversions, sorrows and joys, with which Alcott's audience could identify. Whereas Rollo, Peter Parley and Oliver Optic traveled to foreign lands and sought out the engaging events of history to provide interesting material for their readers, the March girls participate in activities and events which could easily have been part of their readers' own lives. The love of parties, their delight in games, their fear of alienation, their desire for recognition make the girls' experiences both exciting and familiar. However much Meg's vanity, Jo's temper, Beth's aestheticism or Amy's disobedience may appear ridiculously venial transgressions in comparison to the Bunyan vices with which they are associated, they are faults which their audience recognized and shared. The pronounced disparity between the sensational, romantic literature with which the girls are constantly involved (*The Witch's Curse, The Seven Castles of the Diamond Lake, The Wide, Wide World, Heir of Redclyffe, Ivanhoe,* etc.) and the very plausible, even plain lives they lead suggests that Alcott may have been signalling her departure from the prevailing literary standard of her audience and calling attention to the drama and impact that could attend the commonplace.

More probably, however, this contrast between the actual and the imaginary resulted from notable deficiencies that Alcott perceived in the very environment she strove to recommend. The challenges inherent to the normal expectations of her little women are sufficient to satisfy only a very dull mind. The various tasks and concerns in their normal range of experience are so frivolous and routine that they turn to literature as one of the few sanctioned outlets for their emotional and imaginative energies. Significantly, it is Jo, the character with whom Alcott most closely identifies, who possesses the greatest enthusiasm for literature, for it is she who most resists the role thrust upon her. Jo considers the library a "region of bliss" (64) in large measure because of the freedom it affords from the female preoccupations she is expected to cultivate.

However much Jo wishes to align herself with the example of her mother, whose disciplined temper, loving devotion to her children, and selfless commitment to her domestic responsibilities define her as an ideal Victorian woman, the daughter's attempts at being a "little woman" only show her to be a distinct nonconformist. Her willingness to wear a dress with scorch marks stems not only from a real lack of concern for her appearance and a realization that she would merely ruin a nice dress, but also from an underlying reluctance to assume a role she cannot play; whether or not her dress is marred, the strict social demands of a formal dance leave her much more comfortable behind a curtain with the ineffectual Laurie. In other words, the marred dress simply becomes an overt symbol of Jo's sense of disharmony with her outer role. She is at ease only in the "unfashionable" flop hat she wears to the picnic because it proclaims her uniqueness and visually anticipates the indecorous outbursts of "Christopher Columbus!" she cannot repress.

This impropriety in dress, manners and conversation gives her the reputation of being "boyish." Yet, for all her domination of Laurie and her croquet victory over Fred, Jo is no more masculine than she is childish. Her repeated wishes that she always remain the same age (21, 208), that she have an iron upon her head to keep her from growing up (273), like her reference to herself as "the man of the family," tell the reader not what she is, but rather her sense of deviance from what is conventionally expected of her. At the same time, both references reveal her essentially female nature, by virtue of her accord with the prevailing association of the woman with the home. Her wish to prolong her childhood stems from a desire to retain the intimacy she enjoys with her mother and sisters. Similarly, as "man of the family," she eagerly assumes the burden of responsibility for preserving this closely knit circle. However, these efforts to assume the responsibilities of the parent while preserving the security of the child leave Jo in the awkward position of opposing marriage, not only for herself but for her sisters. She makes a concerted effort to prevent the match between Mr. Brooke and Meg, not because of Mr. Brooke's lack of means, as she first insists (209), nor out of jealousy, but in order to preserve the integral intimacy of the family:

> I just wish I could marry Meg myself, and keep her safe in the family. . . . Brooke will scratch up a fortune somehow, carry her off, and make a hole in the family; and I shall break my heart, and everything will be abominably uncomfortable. Oh, dear me! why weren't we all boys, then there wouldn't be any bother. (271)

By way of extension, she insistently refuses to allow her involvement with Laurie to advance beyond that of a brother-sister relationship. Jo's determination to break up the Meg/Mr. Brooke match leads her to the expectation that Meg will marry Laurie "by and by" (273). Alcott herself resisted the pairing of Jo and Laurie to the extent that she would only agree to writing a sequel on the condition that they not be married; "I won't marry Jo to Laurie, to please anyone," she insisted.[9] However intrusive may be the Freudian overtones of this stance, Jo's reluctance to accept the responsibilities of marriage and motherhood is nonetheless a logical extension of her persistent rejection of the prevailing standards of womanhood. In the totally female world of the March household, Jo's strong personality has been allowed to flourish so that, despite her resolution to control her strong will, she still cannot abide the stifling constraints of the male-dominated society outside. Appropriately, Jo's story of "The Rival Painters," which wins her literary acclaim, financial reward and some consequent independence, is a tale of unrequited love ending with the death of both hero and heroine. Such a conclusion, as the narrator points out (211), eliminates any possibility of a sequel which would presumably cover the lives of the pair together. In trying to interest us in a rather similar depiction of Jo's development, Louisa May Alcott makes a concerted effort to win sympathy for a spirited heroine confronting the same plight she herself faced. Jo, indeed, has her faults, it is made clear, yet they are integral to her uniqueness as a passionate supporter of the Victorian home who rejects the debilitating role it imposed on the women who maintained it.

[Detailed discussion of Alger's *Ragged Dick* deleted.]

Notes

1. *Little Women* sold more than 2,000 copies during the first month of publication, and after six months, the figure had risen to 7,000. The sequel increased the popularity of Part I so that 30,000 had been sold after the first fourteen months in print. By 1885, sales had reached 175,000. Madeleine B. Stern, *Louisa May Alcott* (Norman, Okla.: University of Oklahoma Press, 1950), pp. 183, 191, 194, 313.

Sales figures for *Ragged Dick* remain unclear. Ralph D. Gardner, in the bibliographical supplement to *Horatio Alger* (Mendota, Ill.: Wayside Press, 1964) notes that Alger's total sales range somewhere between 100 and 400 million, but since Alger sold his stories for an outright sum, sales of his earliest works have remained a yet undisclosed secret of his wealthy publisher, A. K. Loring.

2. Some recent examples of such an approach to nineteenth-century American children's literature would include: John C. Crandall, "Patriotism and Humanitarian Reform in Children's Literature, 1825–1860," *American Quarterly*, 21 (Spring 1969) 3–22; Russel B. Nye, "For It Was Indeed He: Books for the Young," in *The Unembarrassed Muse: The Popular Arts in America* (New York: Dial Press, 1970), pp. 60–88; Michael Zuckerman, "The Nursery Tales of Horatio Alger," *American Quarterly*, 24 (May 1972), 191–210; John E. Boles, "Jacob Abbott and the Rollo Books," *Journal of Popular Culture*, 4 (Winter 1972), 507–29. For a fuller discussion of books and articles relevant to this area, see the collection of bibliographic essays in *American Literary Realism*, 6 (Spring 1973).

3. John Seelye, "Who was Horatio? The Alger Myth and American Scholarship," *American Quarterly*, 17 (Winter 1965), 749–56, has raised serious doubts concerning the validity of the sensational emphasis given to these affairs in the first and most influential biography of Alger, written by Herbert R. Mayes.

4. Louisa's tour as a nurse ended when she contracted typhoid and nearly died. Following her recovery, she wrote two serious works, *Hospital Sketches* (1863) and *Moods* (1865). Though they attracted favorable critical reviews, their commercial success was rather limited.

5. Louisa May Alcott, *Her Life, Letters and Journals* (Boston: Roberts Bros., 1889), p. 199.

6. Mr. March's participation in the war accounts only in part for the family's financial needs. The affluence the family is said to have once enjoyed was lost in a generous but unfortunate attempt to aid a friend in need.

7. Louisa May Alcott, *Little Women* (London: Penguin Books, 1953), p. 21. All further references to this text will be given in parentheses in the body of the article.

8. In order to give particular emphasis to this point, Alcott contrasts the cheery atmosphere of the March family with the Laurence mansion which is presented as "lonely" and "lifeless" (76) due to the absence of women, and proceeds to demonstrate the happy transformation the girls effect.

9. *Letters and Journals*, p. 201. In the sequel to the original *Little Women*, Alcott marries Jo to Professor Bhaer. This match satisfied few readers. Cornelia Meigs in her biography, *Invincible Louisa* (Boston: Little, Brown, 1935), pp. 216–17, calls Bhaer "less convincing than any of her other characters" and vividly illustrates the insurmountable problem Alcott faced in trying to invent a satisfactory marriage for the heroine she had created.

Money, Job, Little Women: Female Realism

Ellen Moers[*]

Of all the transcendentals no man made so much female literary history, in terms of sheer pages, as the philosopher of improvidence Bronson Alcott, for he had a daughter to support him named Louisa May, who to that end wrote forty books in about thirty years. Besides *Little Women*, she wrote dozens of "juveniles," many thrillers, and a few books intended in all seriousness for adult readers. In the last category, the one I have read that strikes me as most interesting is her first long fiction. Louisa May Alcott began to work on it only fifteen years after Charlotte Brontë wrote *The Professor*, but, for reasons similar to those that hindered publication of Brontë's first novel, it was not published till long afterward, in 1873. It is called *Work: A Story of Experience.*

Alcott's novel opens with a reference to American Independence very different from any to be found in *Walden:*

> "Aunt Betsey, there's going to be a new Declaration of Independence."
>
> "Bless and save us, what do you mean, child?"
>
> "I mean that, being of age, I'm going to take care of myself, and not be a burden any longer. . . . : I don't intend to wait . . . but, like the people in fairy tales, travel away into the world and seek my fortune. . . . I'm old enough to take care of myself; and if I'd been a boy, I should have been told to do it long ago."

Under the jaunty tone, which came naturally to Alcott (it is all over her journals as well as her juvenile fiction), she is quite in earnest. The fairy tale which underlies *Work* is actually *The Pilgrim's Progress*, most revered of Puritan fantasies, and it makes a structure far too solid for this unpretentious tale of a middle-class girl who waits on table, runs after children, and sews seams for her livelihood. Yet there is something impressive, too, about Alcott's attempt to make a latter-day Christian, a pilgrim on the dangerous journey to the desired country, out of the heroine she calls Christie, the working-girl.

Closely modeled after Alcott herself, Christie goes out into the world to make what turns out to be a very scanty fortune. Too poorly educated to be a governess, she goes to a Boston employment agency to apply for a job as housemaid. "I'll begin at the beginning, and work my way up. I'll put my pride in my pocket, and go out to service. Housework I like, and can do well. . . . I never thought it degradation to do it for [Aunt Betsey], so why should I mind doing it for others if they pay for it? It isn't what I want, but it's better than idleness, so I'll try it!" And a live-in housemaid she becomes,

[*]Reprinted from *Literary Women* (Garden City: Doubleday, 1976), pp. 86–89. "Money, Job, Little Women: Female Realism" © 1972 by American Jewish Committee from *Literary Women*, by Ellen Moers. Reprinted by permission of Doubleday & Company, Inc.

in cap and apron, at $2.50 a week, in an establishment where the cook, soon Christie's fast friend, is black.

All this is quite extraordinary for an American or English girl of Christie's type in the 1860s. Like everything else in *Work*—sewing for pay, or working as an actress—it was based on Alcott's real experience, but that did not make it less out of the run of normal American experience. Louisa May Alcott was of the "Brahmin" class, her father from a good if decayed old New England family, her mother a member of the distinguished, prosperous Boston clan of the Mays. The March girls in *Little Women* are presumably month-named for that reason.

A special gift Alcott had, accounting I think for much of her charm as a writer, was her ability to see her own experience—her weird father, her poverty-line childhood, the strange Concord ambiance, her unique working life—as the sunshiny norm, which it was not; and to so transform what she knew into a practical ideal. One result is the curious modernity of Alcott's fiction. It is hard to believe, when reading *Little Women*, that it was written in the 1860s, while Dickens and George Eliot were still writing; or that the War which conveniently abstracts the father from the female household of *Little Women* (and even more conveniently kills off Christie's husband in *Work*) is the contemporary Civil War. For the working girls in Alcott, Jo and Meg as well as Christie, seem more like the college girl of today, working at menial pickup jobs without loss of respectability or class status, than like the Lucy Snowes and Maggie Tullivers who were their near contemporaries.

Also oddly modern is the salute to a special kind of women's solidarity with which Alcott brings *Work* to a close. Widowed almost immediately after marriage, and the mother of a little girl, Christie at the end is forty and wealthy, but still occupied; she is an activist of working-class feminism. She goes among working women to shake their hands ("roughened by the needle, stained with printer's ink, or hard with humbler toil") and arouse their enthusiasm for "the new emancipation" with the sort of simple, earnest speech that only she among the feminists can make, "for I have been and mean to be a working-woman all my life." The novel ends with a scene of hand-clasping all around the table, charmingly illustrated in the Victorian edition I have at hand: Mrs. Wilkins the fat motherly laundress, Bella the elegant young society matron, Letty the fallen woman, Hepsey the black cook, Mrs. Powers the elderly Quaker lady, Christie, and her daughter Ruth—who "spread her chubby hand above the rest: a hopeful omen, seeming to promise that the coming generation of women will not only receive but deserve their liberty, by learning that the greatest of God's gifts to us is the privilege of sharing His great work."

The religion is Protestant, the voice that of nineteenth-century New England womanhood, but in the commitment to work as an act of faith, and in the insistence on humble work, there is a faint presage of the modern philosopher of work, Simone Weil—Jewish, French to the core, a Catholic thinker. Weil was of the first generation of women to have access to the best education and the most interesting work in France. In 1935 she left her normal career as *professeur agrégé* of philosophy to spend most of a year as an assembly-line worker in a factory—brutal and brutalizing work in those days, for which she was physically as well as mentally ill-adapted, and for which she received the lowest possible wages in the lowest status, that of woman worker. Manual work for Simone Weil was a willed martyrdom of disgust.

"What have I gained through this experience?" Weil asks in *La Condition ouvrière*, the collection of her powerful writings about the factory year, which many consider the most profound study of the working condition produced in this century. Comradeship is one of Simone Weil's answers; moral self-sufficiency another; and in the old tradition of women's realism, "direct contact with life." Finally, humiliation: "to live in this perpetual state of latent humiliation without being humiliated in my own eyes."

Humble work, lower in intellectual content and social prestige than the family ambiance from which her various little women come, is the kind of work that Louisa May Alcott describes with most spirit and conviction. Her first success, *Hospital Sketches*, deals with the unskilled, backbreaking work she herself did as a nurse in a Washington hospital during the Civil War. In *Little Women*, Meg works as a governess, Amy as a companion; Jo does child care and sewing for the mistress of a New York boardinghouse. All the girls are unfitted for the work they do, and dislike doing it as much as they dislike the housework—cooking, sewing, cleaning—that, just as much as games, romances, and dreams, makes up the texture of a girl's life in *Little Women*. Work is handled playfully by Louisa May Alcott, but it is not confused with play. It is something real, lasting, serious, necessary, and inescapable as Monday morning, to be shouldered manfully—by women, little and big.

Indeed, the importance of work in America's favorite girl-child's classic is worth pondering. A very different message, for boys, can be found in *Tom Sawyer*, published the following decade. There work is presented as something to be avoided at all costs and with all ingenuity, whether through the swindle, the ruse, or flight.

Little Women [and *Pride and Prejudice*]

Nina Auerbach*

> Publishers are very perverse & wont let authors have their way so my little women must grow up & be married off in a very stupid style.[1]

In *Pride and Prejudice* a world without men is empty of effects. Lacking in inheritance, the Bennet girls are only theoretically impecunious — unlike the March girls, they have nothing to do with the kitchen, and clothes available for any ball — but physically as well as psychically they live in an empty world. The world of the March girls is rich enough to complete itself, and in this richness lies the tension of *Little Women* and its two sequels.

" 'Christmas won't be Christmas without any presents,' grumble[s] Jo, lying on the rug" (*LW*, p. 2), to start the series off with a spiritual absurdity that will be contradicted by the almost immediate entrance of all-dispensing Marmee — unlike the mother-generated absurdity that opens *Pride and Prejudice*, which has no higher authority to contradict it. The Christmas gift Marmee seems tenderly to offer her girls is hunger. First, each decides to give up her one precious dollar to buy a Christmas gift for their mother instead of a loved item for herself; Marmee then enters with a letter from Father, who is nobly serving as a chaplain in the Civil War, admonishing the girls to "conquer themselves . . . beautifully" and making them all feel deliciously guilty. On Christmas Day, in response to their sacrificial gifts, she makes her climactic request that the girls give up their holiday breakfast to a starving family. They go trooping through the snow, with full hands and empty stomachs, "funny angels in hoods and mittens" who have learned that it is better to renounce than receive. And the book succeeds in making us believe that this hungry day is "A Merry Christmas."

When Ebenezer Scrooge gives Bob Cratchit a Christmas turkey as a token of fellowship, we easily but rather abstractly accept the bird as a metaphor of Scrooge's change of heart; but we know that Scrooge could buy a wilderness of turkeys for himself, had not his nephew Fred joyfully invited him to dinner. The March girls, whom no one invites, are made of sterner stuff. Their pilgrimage to the poor quarter of town is significant only because they themselves are hungry, and the food that Marmee gently requests they renounce is vividly appetizing. I surmise that their vanished buckwheat cakes, bread, cream, and muffins have been longed for by more female readers than the cold meat, cake, and pyramids "of the finest fruits in season" that Elizabeth Bennet was served when she finally entered Pemberley. The largesse is Darcy's; the renunciation is the March girls' own, and

---

*Reprinted from *Communities of Women: An Idea in Fiction* (Cambridge: Harvard Univ. Press, 1978), pp. 55–64, 68–73, 199–201. The notes have been renumbered because of deletions. Reprinted by permission of the publishers from *Communities of Women: An Idea in Fiction*, by Nina Auerbach. © 1978 by the President and Fellows of Harvard College.

their concert in performing it, *after* the narrative has established them as selfish and turbulent, wanting all sorts of things they won't be permitted to have, is the sisterhood the novel is about. Longbourn was a hungry world because an empty one; the hungry March cottage is full of things, each of which is both fact and spiritual emblem.

In the richness of that uneaten breakfast it is easy to forget that the March girls are rewarded for their generosity by masculine largesse. As Meg has said, "although [or because?] we do have to work, we make fun for ourselves" (p. 5), and that evening they put on a play Jo has written, which is described in extended detail. After it is over, all find waiting a splendid supper sent over by wealthy Mr. Laurence next door, in appreciation of their good deed. The supper is less important in itself than as a liaison established between the two houses that makes possible the friendship between the four girls and his grandson, rich, spirited Laurie. Laurie plays the role of Bingley in *Pride and Prejudice:* he is not only marriageable in himself, but the cause of marriage in other men. Introduction to him indirectly makes possible the marriages of all the girls: Meg marries his tutor; Jo goes to New York to escape his importunity and meets Professor Bhaer there; and he himself finally marries Amy. Like Darcy, Laurie has "good match" emblazoned all over him. The morning's renunciation ultimately aligns the March girls with the spirit of marriage, and Christmas is Christmas indeed.

The treatment of this simultaneous savior and intruder is quite different in the American story. In *Pride and Prejudice* the sisters acted in joyous concert only at Mr. Bennet's wry announcement that he had paid a formal call on Bingley. In *Little Women* the sisters act in concert with no reference to Laurie, and in deference to its beauty he solicits access to their harmony with only partial success. Instead of calculating the value of his establishment, Marmee perceives his need: "He looked so wistful as he went away, hearing the frolic, and evidently having none of his own" (p. 27). Her assessment turns out to be as compassionately knowing as Mrs. Bennet's was financially knowing:

> Laurie colored up, but answered frankly, "Why, you see, I often hear you calling to one another, and when I'm alone up here, I can't help looking over at your house, you always seem to be having such good times. I beg your pardon for being so rude, but sometimes you forget to put down the curtain at the window where the flowers are; and when the lamps are lighted, it's like looking at a picture to see the fire, and you all round the table with your mother; her face is right opposite, and it looks so sweet behind the flowers, I can't help watching it. I haven't got any mother, you know"; and Laurie poked the fire to hide a little twitching of the lips that he could not control.
>
> The solitary, hungry look in his eyes went straight to Jo's warm heart. She had been so simply taught that there was no nonsense in her head, and at fifteen she was as innocent and frank as any child. Laurie was sick and lonely; and, feeling how rich she was in home love and happiness, she gladly tried to share it with him. (p. 57)

The balance of *Pride and Prejudice* is inverted. The hero now peers wistfully in at the female family, "like looking at a picture," as Elizabeth did at Pemberley. Plenitude belongs to the community of women, hunger to the solitary man. When Elizabeth's family inadvertently exposed itself to Darcy by a parade of vulgarities at the Netherfield ball, he could only flee in horror with Bingley; but when the March family inadvertently exposes itself by leaving up the shade, Laurie glimpses a carefully poised fullness that draws him to its perfect self. He solicits entree to a sometimes reluctant circle in similar fashion throughout the first half of the novel, hiding in a closet while the girls debate his admission to their Pickwick Club, whose rituals and jokes are described in the same extensive detail as the Christmas play. He is even more importunate when he stumbles on their Busy Bee Society, which he again perceives as a carefully grouped and self-complete work of art:

> It *was* rather a pretty little picture, for the sisters sat together in the shady nook, with sun and shadow flickering over them, the aromatic wind lifting their hair and cooling their hot cheeks, and all the little wood people going on with their affairs as if these were no strangers but old friends. Meg sat upon her cushion, sewing daintily with her white hands, and looking as fresh and sweet as a rose, in her pink dress, among the green. Beth was sorting the cones that lay thick under the hemlock near by, for she made pretty things of them. Amy was sketching a group of ferns, and Jo was knitting as she read aloud. A shadow passed over the boy's face as he watched them, feeling that he ought to go away, because uninvited; yet lingering because home seemed very lonely, and this quiet party in the woods most attractive to his restless spirit. He stood so still that a squirrel, busy with its harvesting, ran down a pine close behind him, saw him suddenly and skipped back, scolding so shrilly that Beth looked up, espied the wistful face behind the birches, and beckoned with a reassuring smile.
> "May I come in, please? Or shall I be a bother?" he asked, advancing slowly. (pp. 155–156)

The March girls offer Laurie all the richness of interchange between art, taste, and nature that Pemberley held out to Elizabeth Bennet. Even when he is not present, the girls are almost always described as a balanced tableau. With characteristic abundance of detail, the author sees it as her artistic duty to give us, not the income, but the appearance of the March girls as soon as possible: "As young readers like to know 'how people look,' we will take this moment to give them a little sketch of the four sisters, who sat knitting away in the twilight, while the December snow fell quietly without, and the fire crackled cheerfully within" (p. 6). After an intimate survey of hair, coloring, carriage, and so on, the author archly concludes with a mystery which is no mystery at all: "What the characters of the four sisters were we will leave to be found out" (p. 7). We have already found their characters in their appearance; raised among disembodied sages in Transcendentalist Concord, Louisa May Alcott clings stubbornly throughout her novels to the primary reality of physical things.[2] In her world people can decipher character and mood instantly by subtle shifts in faces, bearing, eyebrows, clothes. Mr. Laurence's kindness speaks to Jo out of his portrait before they meet; when Jo becomes a writer her jaunty cap communicates instantly to the peeping family the degree to which genius is burning. When the physical body is so insistently alive and expressive there are no barriers to intimacy but time and death; this accessible and familial world, where character is a language all can read, contains no Austenian "intricate characters" who deceive by their appearance.

Alcott trusts what she can see, and nowhere is her reliance on the life in things more vividly apparent than in her delineation of the March haven: the expressive rattle of Jo's knitting needles; the high-heeled boots which crush Meg's feet; Beth's divine piano; Amy's plaster casts and the delicate "things" she dramatically sweeps off the bazaar table; Marmee's crooned-over slippers. Throughout the novel the March women are defined in their primary relationship to the "things" that display their characters. The physicality of their community is not bestowed, but inherent and overflowing. Clothes in *Pride and Prejudice* were vaguely mentioned, usually in terms of some inane question from Mrs. Bennet about "style" which was cut short by her contemptuous husband. But Alcott slips her views about dress reform into the novel by forcing the female reader to feel Meg's agony when she is pinched and squeezed in her attempts at elegance. Letters in *Pride and Prejudice* were sparsely used and significant; either they were severe tests of character, like those of Mr. Collins and Darcy, or they conveyed necessary information, like Jane's and Mr. Gardiner's about Lydia's elopement. But *Little Women* spills over with letters that are given to us simply for the purpose of relishing their writers: "As one of these packets contained characteristic notes from the party, we will rob an imaginary mail, and read them" (p. 186). We learn nothing from these letters but the fact that Meg is Meg, Jo, Jo, Beth, Beth, and Amy, Amy, which has already been amply demonstrated; but if we are engulfed in their lives as a fifth sister, it is enough. The abundance in which we perceive the life of the circle dramatizes its message of the richness of poverty when Marmee's and Alcott's moralizing makes us wince. Despite the girls' mechanical grumbling, it is difficult for the reader to believe in what they have given up when she finds herself surrounded with what they have.

In *Pride and Prejudice* the family fed itself to the omnipresent neighborhood, but in *Little Women* it is the heart of its world. Though Jo tells Laurie, "we have got acquainted with all our neighbors but you" (p. 58), Laurie and his grandfather are for most of the book the only neighbors we see, and they exist more as honorary family than as neighbors proper. When the girls get older, the Chesters and the Lambs and the rest exist for Jo and Amy to call on, but they function only as obstacles in the girls' perpetual Pilgrims' Progress game, as tests of character for the sisters rather than as an independent social context to which they must belong. The primacy of the female family, both as moral-emotional magnet and as work of art, is indicated by the quality of their appeal to Laurie: though he thinks he loves Jo best, his true role is that of son-brother-squire to the family unit as he is mulled over by each of the girls in turn. In the beginning of the book, the sophisticated Moffats and Jo herself link him to Meg, who is scornful about being matched to a mere "boy." Later comes Jo's rejection of him, which, despite Alcott's indifference to her obligatory marriage plots, remains the most talked-about part of the book from its day to ours;[3] and Jo's private hope that a match with Beth will soften him and cure her lingering illness. Beth amazedly disabuses her, her characteristic "trouble" being that she must die and leave the family circle, with never a thought of love or Laurie. So Jo brusquely and pragmatically consigns him to the match he does eventually make: " 'Why, Jo, how could I, when he was so fond of you?' asked Beth, as innocently as a child. 'I do love him dearly; he is so good to me, how can I help it? But he never could be anything to me but my brother. I hope he truly will be, sometime.' 'Not through me,' said Jo decidedly. 'Amy is left for him, and they would suit excellently; but I have no heart for such things, now' " (p. 416). Thus, before romance blooms for him, Laurie is rejected by each of the girls in turn. It is impossible to imagine romantic heroes like Darcy, or even Bingley, being so bandied around the Bennet circle before settling on the one sister who is "left for him." Even in designing his marriage to Amy, Alcott seems to smooth poor Laurie's path by making Amy shed her artistic ambitions in favor of being "an ornament to society" — as Louisa's singleminded sister May never did — and by Amy's homesick vulnerability abroad after learning that Beth has died without her. With all his winsomeness, love, and money, Laurie's attempts to enter the charmed circle are continually frustrated until death makes a place for him.

Amy's is not the only March marriage to take place under the shadow of death. Womanly Meg's love match to poor-but-honest John Brooke is colored for us by Jo's tragic sense that the wrench to the family it entails is more of an ending than a beginning: "I knew there was mischief brewing! I felt it; and now it's worse than I imagined. I just wish I could marry Meg myself, and keep her safe in the family" (p. 224). Though Jane Bennet was Elizabeth's only female companion in the family, as Meg is not Jo's, Elizabeth's desire to consign her to Netherfield and Bingley was wholehearted and intense: her rage at Darcy for attempting to separate them is at one with Jo's rage against Laurie for furthering her sister's love affair. Jo's equation of all life with the family circle echoes Louisa's own mournful love letter upon her older sister's wedding: "After the bridal train had departed, the mourners withdrew to their respective homes; and the bereaved family solaced their woe by washing dishes for two hours and bolting the remains of the funeral baked meats."[4]

Gawky, unawakened Jo is not alone in seeing Meg's marriage as a precious death; the structure of the novel reinforces this mournful tone. Even Marmee seems to view it with resigned acquiescence rather than joy, and their father's voice breaks as he performs the ceremony as it will at Beth and John's funerals. Despite the apparent severity of her regime,[5] Mrs. March allows her girls a great freedom that may explain why the book has been so unreasonably beloved for over a century: the freedom to remain children and, for a woman, the more precious freedom *not* to fall in love: "Right, Jo; better be happy old maids than unhappy wives, or unmaidenly girls running about to find husbands . . . One thing remember, my girls: mother is always ready to be your confidante, father to be your friend; and both of us trust and hope that our daughters, whether married or single, will be the pride and comfort of our lives" (p. 110). The solemnity of the moment when Mrs. March oracularly reveals her "plans" endows the sisters with an independent selfhood which is a rare dowry in any century, and draws the circle even more tightly together.

Meg's marriage is placed alongside a series of calamities that darken it irreparably: Mr. March's illness, Marmee's hurried departure for Washington, Beth's near-fatal illness, and father's return as a befuddledly noble center of reverence that deflects family intimacy.[6] The inclusion of young love among these upheavals implicitly defines it as more of a destroyer of sisterhood than an emotional progression beyond it; and the equation between the departures of marriage and of death continues in the last half of the book, where Beth's wasting illness and death run parallel to the marriages of the rest of the sisters. Both stress the loss of the childhood circle rather than the coming into an inheritance of fulfillment.

The intense bond between Jo and Beth is puzzling at first; the logical unit would seem to be Jo and Amy, the two most artistic and aspiring, whose relationship throughout is at best a tender truce. But in their desire for perpetual sisterhood Jo and Beth are at the heart of the novel. Jane Bennet's illness was a result of the exposure into which her mother flung her, precipitating herself and Elizabeth into success on the marriage market. Beth's long wasting is the waning of childhood and the collective death of the sisters; in a sense, she dies so that the others can marry. Beth is usually recalled as a tranquil domestic angel, but the intensity of her yearning for home recalls that of Emily Brontë's heretical Catherine Linton: "I'm not like the rest of you; I never made any plans about what I'd do when I grew up; I never thought of being married, as you all did.[7] I couldn't seem to imagine myself anything but stupid little Beth, trotting about at home, of no use anywhere but there. I never wanted to go away and the hard part now is the leaving you all. I'm not afraid, but it seems as if I should be homesick for you even in heaven" (p. 417). The spirit of home, Beth dies when it does. In her last illness Beth has a dying room into which are brought all the favored relics of the family. For as long as she can hold a needle she makes "little things for the school children passing to and fro," which she throws out the window like utilitarian manna from Heaven. She dies when she relinquishes her hold on these "things" that are the quintessence of the family; the necessity of the parting is the necessity of growing away from home completion and of living despite the splitting of the circle.

Alcott's other writing shows more directly what the circle of women meant to her than we can find in a moral tale for girls which she felt compelled by her publisher to write. Had she written the *Little Women* she envisioned, Beth might have survived to preside over a self-sustaining sisterhood: "Girls write to ask who the little women marry, as if that was the only end and aim of a woman's life. I *won't* marry Jo to Laurie to please any one," she wrote after the appearance of the first half.[8] In fact, she did write a piece about nondiminutive women, at the same time that she began the book we know. In her article "Happy Women"[9] she gratified her love of single life by describing the delightful spinsters of her acquaintance. Her sketches are all taken from life, and are not too highly colored. The Physician, the Artist, the Philanthropist, the Actress, the Lawyer, are easily recognizable. They were a 'glorious phalanx of old maids,' as Theodore Parker called the single women of his Society, which aided him so much in his work.[10] Here is the idyll lying behind Marmee's new wives' training school: a community of new women, whose sisterhood is not an apprenticeship making them worthy of appropriation by father-husbands, but a bond whose value is itself. Jane Austen may have been too close to Chawton to write about it, but for Alcott, the communal cottage itself, and not the roads out of it, was the palace of art that made her ideal subject.

[Discussion of *An Old-Fashioned Girl* and *Work* deleted.]

In the saga of the March family this militant vision of permanent sisterhood is a felt dream rather than a concrete possibility. Like all good art, Alcott's most famous trilogy represents a conscious compromise with her deepest fantasies. The most autobiographical of writers, she seems to have chosen the girls' name in deference to the maiden name of her mother, Abigail May: by naming her sisters after another month beginning with "M," she secretly makes them the mother's entirely, with nothing in them of the father—which would have warmed Lady Catherine's matriarchal heart. Along with its adherence to the mother, March also suggests militancy, as when Louisa departed for the Civil War more as soldier than as healer: "I was ready, and when my commander said 'March!' I marched."[11] But with all this, the month of March is an undeveloped anomaly, waiting for its consummation in summer: the suggestion is that the March girls will bloom only when they have lost their name in the warmth of a man's, as all but Beth eventually do. In the loss of this sisterhood, the three remaining girls establish a matriarchy under Jo's aegis at Plumfield.

Jo inherits Plumfield from her tyrannical Aunt March, who in *Little Women* plays the Lady Catherine role, even to precipitating Meg's marriage by her snobbish opposition to it. But while Lady Catherine existed to be escaped from, Aunt March is transmitted in the inheritance of her estate: unlike Elizabeth, Jo is delighted to inherit from a woman and promptly moves "her" movable professor there to teach "a wilderness of boys" and (rather improbably) farm the land. By the time we meet her *Little Men,* Jo has attained the position of Marmee, but her title is more formidable than that comfortable, clinging name: the power of Plumfield is known grandly as "Mother Bhaer," the Goldilocks-like joke containing a tinge of maternal threat. At times she is simple "Mrs. Jo," an image of self-sufficient maternal power; at other times she and her husband are raised Germanically to the status of cosmic powers: "the mother," "the father."[12] In the course of the sequel, all the sisters' children come to Plumfield to be educated; there will be no more cozy family enclaves like the one in which they grew up. Instead, Marmee's power is institutionalized and the lessons of their girlhood made into a "method" by which to form the little men who may become the men in power.

Only in the sequel does Jo's refusal to marry Laurie become comprehensible. (The reasons given in *Little Women* seem more rationalization than explanation.) True, Marmee has said both are too strong-willed and fond of freedom to be happy together; but as Jo has already reconciled Laurie to his authoritarian grandfather instead of running off to Washington with him, she obviously understands quite well her role as a "miserable girl" who softens men's wildness rather than sharing it. In the proposal scene itself, she blurts out desperately, "you'd hate my scribbling, and I couldn't get on without it" (p. 406). Though this is a good strong-minded reason, Laurie, far more than her sisters, has been Jo's ally in scribbling, the sharer of her secret when she publishes her first newspaper story and her collaborator in Plumfield theatricals. Throughout the series Laurie is excited about her writing; it is Bhaer's disapproval that makes her burn it. But while wealthy Laurie can make his comrade a lady, marriage to Professor Bhaer, an educator, makes her a cosmic mother — the greatest power available in her domestic world. Poor Laurie, pushed into the background as "Lord" to Amy's "Lady," spends the rest of the series compensating for his discontent in business by endowing all Jo's projects as her little empire spreads and spreads.[13]

Like that of *Work,* the real impetus of the saga focuses on the next generation. Planted and harvested at Plumfield like crops, according to principles of cooperation and mutual help, the children belong both to a "great family" and a "small world."[14] Raucous and cozy, conceived by women and on women's ground, Plumfield is the comic dream of Jo, though her portly husband brings to it a Teutonic intellectual weight. Yet as headmaster, he is an institutionalized denial of his own authority: when called upon to perform that great nineteenth-century ritual of flogging, so dear to boarding-school literature, Bhaer presents his big hand and orders the shocked, weeping boy to flog *him.* In presenting recreants with this token of his own vulnerability, Bhaer inflicts a greater punishment than the iron men of unshakable authority apotheosized in *Tom Brown's Schooldays* and its progeny, who are most cleanly defined in the poem that begins Kipling's *Stalky & Co.*:

> There we met with famous men
>   Set in office o'er us.
> And they beat us on with rods —
> Faithfully with many rods —
> Daily beat on us with rods —
>   For the love they bore us!

But Kipling's "famous men" were conscientiously training leaders of empire, who had to learn to obey in order to command. Bhaer, who is not famous and whose boys are not likely to rule, holds out his naked hand to a young liar; but Mrs. Jo, who will become famous in the third book, is fiendishly inventive in her punishments, the most Kiplingesque of which is to tie up hotheaded Nan like a dog for running away. For post-Abolitionist New England, this violation of liberty was a more radical affront than a flogging; but Nan, who may be a leader of women, needs severe discipline by wise Mrs. Jo, who sits laughing, unflogged and intact.

She rather than her husband assumes the authoritarian role of ingenious and judicious punisher of select students who may have battles to win. Beyond sisterhood, Mother Bhaer presides over a Utopian community of cooperation among and between the sexes, whose influence as it follows sailor Emil, musician Nat, and pioneer-jailbird Dan, spreads into the capitals and the wasteplaces of the world. Though stormy Jo now functions more as beacon than pilgrim — "I am not as aspiring as I once was" (*LM*, p. 367) — her influence penetrates the future. The school she shapes at Plumfield, which is also family, farm, and cosmos, bears a faint resemblance to the Shaker community which thrived in opposition to her father's own short-lived Fruitlands in Harvard, Massachusetts. Essentially matriarchal in its worship of its founder, Mother Ann Lee, the celibate Shakers lived according to principles of sexual equality and cooperation; like that of the March family and Plumfield, their greatest spiritual release was the ritual of confession. The Harvard society had an unusually large percentage of women who worked and governed equally with men, while in Bronson's neighboring Fruitlands, the men tended to do the thinking and the Alcott women, the work.[15] If Louisa could not desert her father in fact, she did in art; in her later works, she seems quite deliberately to shape her father's Utopian vision to the dimensions of her stoical mother, and of the rival paradise that destroyed his own.

In establishing Jo's matriarchal reign, Alcott has not forgotten her early dream of sisterhood. *Jo's Boys* sees a diminished reunion of the original circle, as Amy and Laurie and the widowed Meg move to the grounds of Plumfield, where the campus of Laurence College now stands in virtuous opposition to nearby Harvard, Jo's dumping ground for her "failures." If she can, Jo will train good sons rather than good governors. Hopes are higher for the female students, whom the sisters now direct in an institutionalized version of Marmee's old sewing circle: instead of repeating Marmee's lessons of suppression and self-conquest, hardly won out of her own experience, Mother Bhaer gives "little lessons on health, religion, politics, and the various questions in which all should be interested,"[16] reading copious extracts from the growing body of feminist literature and instilling in her pupils a greater respect for work and independence than for marriage.

This little school within the school seems a greater success even than Plumfield: among the girls whose lives we follow, only "poky" domestic Daisy marries in the course of the novel. Meg's Josie and Amy's Bess go on to attain artistic triumphs and "worthy mates," and "Naughty Nan" graduates under Jo's tutelage from hoyden to doctor: "Nan remained a busy, cheerful, independent spinster, and dedicated her life to her suffering sisters and their children, in which true woman's work she found abiding happiness" (*JB*, p. 338). Though the March girls themselves must compromise, they can at least create free women.

Though "Naughty Nan" grows up to create a healing sisterhood, only "A Firebrand" can institutionalize one: dangerous Dan, the black sheep of Jo's flock whom she loves most, the only one who might become a hero and leader. He grows up to rove the untamed West, and in *Jo's Boys* dreams briefly of founding "Dansville" there, a new town run along the cooperative lines of Plumfield which would accommodate and enfranchise all dispossessed social groups: "You shall vote as much as you like in our new town, Nan; be mayor and alderman, and run the whole concern. It's going to be free as air, or I can't live in it" (*JB*, p. 71). But the town that can be run by women never takes political shape: life tames Dan to self-sacrifice rather than self-perpetuation. He spends a year in prison for killing a rogue, has his legs crushed in a heroic mine rescue, falls hopelessly in love with Amy's daughter, a Hawthornesque snow maiden, and sacrifices his broken life defending the Indians. Jo's long relationship with him, half-envious and half-erotic, shows the irresolution behind the triumph of "the mother." The trilogy's final sight of her is of a wistful woman, "still clinging fast to her black sheep although a whole flock of white ones trotted happily before her" (*JB*, p. 337). She has achieved her position of matriarch, but the roads are closed to the offices of "mayor and alderman." The family has been stretched to its limit.

Notes

1. Letter to Sam May, quoted in Madeleine B. Stern, *Louisa May Alcott* (Norman: University of Oklahoma Press, 1950), pp. 189–190.

2. Ralph Waldo Emerson's 1856 *Journal* lauds Bronson Alcott's ability to escape the very world of things to which Louisa adheres: "The comfort of Alcott's mind is, the connection in

which he sees whatever he sees. He is never dazzled by a spot of colour, or a gleam of light, to value the thing by itself; but forever and ever is prepossessed by the individual one behind it and all." Quoted in *Bronson Alcott's Fruitlands*, compiled by Clara Endicott Sears (Boston: Houghton Mifflin Co., 1915), p. 5.

3. Patricia Meyer Spacks's students "resented the way Jo is finally disposed of" as clamorously as Alcott's first young readers did (Spacks, *The Female Imagination*, New York: Alfred A. Knopf, 1975), p. 100. See also p. 119 of *Critical Essays on LMA*. For them, and for Spacks as well, being denied the conventional romantic marriage is Jo's punishment for her aggression. But Elizabeth Janeway gives her a sweeping cheer for avoiding it, thus becoming "the one young woman in nineteenth-century fiction who maintains her individual independence." "It is worth noting that the two other adored nineteenth-century heroines who say No to the hero's proposal give way in the end, when circumstances and the hero have changed: Elizabeth Bennet and Jane Eyre. But Jo [like Melville's stubbornly American Bartleby] says No and does not shift." Elizabeth Janeway, *Between Myth and Morning: Women Awakening* (New York: William Morrow & Co., 1975), pp. 235, 237. Janeway was the first to make plain the high-spirited sedition behind the pieties of *Little Women*; but both critics still define Jo by her response to a proposal, which is not for Alcott a crucial area of definition.

4. Quoted in *Louisa May Alcott: Her Life, Letters, and Journals*, ed. Ednah D. Cheney (Boston: Roberts Brothers, 1890), p. 132.

5. In Spacks's grim view of the novel, "Discipline . . . is what women little and big require. They must be controlled or their passion for pickled limes and finery and freedom will precipitate chaos" (p. 101).

6. Mr. March's myopic detachment from female rituals and concerns recalls the more pernicious Dr. Blimber's intransigent erudition in the face of his boys' needs. "A warning from her mother checked any further remarks, and the whole family ate in heroic silence, till Mr. March mildly observed, 'Salad was one of the favorite dishes of the ancients, and Evelyn' — here a general explosion of laughter cut short the 'history of sallets,' to the great surprise of the learned gentleman" (*Little Women*, p. 194). Compare *Dombey and Son*, ch. 12, where Dr. Blimber intones over and over, "It is remarkable, Mr. Feeder, that the Romans" — while a boy is choking his throat out. At Amy's wedding party, at which Jo is finally falling in love, the good man discusses with ominous idiocy "the burial customs of the ancients" (p. 502).

7. In fact, as we see them in the first part, none of the girls thinks of being married; it seems to strike their aspirations unawares.

8. Journal entry, November 1, 1868. In Cheney, p. 201.

9. *The New York Ledger*, 24 (April 11, 1868).

10. Cheney, p. 187.

11. Journal entry, December 1862. Cheney, p. 140.

12. Compare with this plenitude of names the distant formality of Elizabeth Bennet's return home to the unshared family crisis: "And my mother—How is she? How are you all?" "My mother is tolerably well, I trust; though her spirits are greatly shaken" (p. 286).

13. Janeway, p. 237, makes a similar point. Both M-G-M versions of the novel (George Cukor, 1933; Mervyn LeRoy, 1949), soften Bhaer's role from censor to critic of Jo's scribbling: the wise professor presents her with the old chestnut young writers in movies seem never to have heard before, "Write about what you know." Jo obediently writes about Beth and the book is a masterpiece. But the teacher-lover Alcott created is never so constructive.

14. Louisa May Alcott, *Little Men* (1871; rpt. New York: Grosset & Dunlap, 1947), pp. 42, 369. Future references to this edition will appear in the text under the abbreviation LM.

15. For a description of the Shaker community, see Charles Nordhoff, *The Communistic Societies of the United States*, with a Prefatory Essay by Franklin H. Littell (1875; rpt. New York: Schocken Books, 1965), pp. 117–255. For an account of Bronson Alcott's nervous collapse

after Charles Lane deserted his community for that of the Shakers, see Sears, pp. 126–127, and Janeway, p. 236.

    16. Louisa May Alcott, *Jo's Boys* (1886; rpt. New York: Grosset & Dunlap, 1949), p. 263. Future references to this edition will appear in the text under the abbreviation JB.

Little Women: Alcott's Civil War

Judith Fetterley*

    When, toward the end of *Little Women*, Jo finds her "true style at last," her father blesses her with the prospect of inner peace and an end to all ambivalence: "You have had the bitter, now comes the sweet. Do your best and grow as happy as we are in your success." And Alcott adds her benediction: "So, taught by love and sorrow, Jo wrote her little stories and sent them away to make friends for themselves and her, finding it a very charitable world to such humble wanderers."[1] Finding her true style at last was not, however, such a peaceful arrival in safe waters for Alcott herself. She responded with alacrity to the opportunity afforded by the anonymous "No-Name Series" to write something not in her style, declaring that she was "tired of providing moral pap for the young" and enjoying the fun of hearing people say, " 'I know *you* didn't write it, for you can't hide your peculiar style.' "[2] She prayed more than once for time enough to write a "good" book and realized that without it she would do what was easiest and succumb to the pressure of the "dears" who "*will* cling to the 'Little Women' style."[3] And at the end of *Jo's Boys*, the last of her books on the March family, she longs to close with an "earthquake which should engulf Plumfield and its environs so deeply in the bowels of the earth that no youthful Schliemann could ever find a vestige of it."

    Alcott's commitment to her "true style" was evidently somewhat less a choice than a necessity, somewhat less generated from within than imposed from without. Her initial resistance to the proposal from Thomas Niles, a partner in Roberts Brothers Publishing Company, that she write a book for girls had its origins perhaps in an instinct for self-preservation; certainly the success of *Little Women* limited her artistic possibilities thereafter. Hard it was to deny the lucrative rewards attendant upon laying such golden eggs; hard to reconcile the authorial image inherent in *Little Women* with the personality capable of the sensational "Behind a Mask"; harder still to ignore the statement of what was acceptable from a woman writer implicit in the adulation accorded *Little Women*. Indeed, Alcott ceased to write sensation fiction after the publication of *Little Women*. In Madeleine Stern's analysis, "The author who had dispatched thrillers to Frank Leslie and James R. Elliott had presumably found her style. The niche she had walked into with *Little Women* was too comfortable to abandon."[4]

*Reprinted from *Feminist Studies*, 5 (Summer 1979), 369–70, 381–83.

The work of Stern in identifying and recovering Alcott's sensation fiction provides an important context for the reading of *Little Women* and for an understanding of the implications of its style. In these stories, written primarily between 1862 and 1867, there is no hint of the *Little Women* ethic or ambiance. Quite the contrary. In "Pauline's Passion and Punishment," for example, the heroine consecrates herself to the exacting of revenge on a man who has loved her but married an heiress. In this carefully planned and well-relished project, she is assisted by another man, younger than herself, who becomes her willing ally and almost slave. In "Behind a Mask," by far the most interesting of the materials which Stern has made available to us in her two volumes, *Behind a Mask* and *Plots and Counterplots*, the heroine, Jean Muir, uses the mask of femininity and the persona of a little woman to enact a devastatingly successful power struggle with a series of men who are clearly perceived as a single class and an enemy one at that. What these stories, taken as a group, make clear is the amount of rage and intelligence Alcott had to suppress in order to attain her "true style" and write *Little Women*. Alcott's sensation fiction provides an important gloss on the sexual politics involved in Jo's renunciation of the writing of such fiction and on the sexual politics of Jo's relation with Professor Bhaer under whose influence she gives it up.

Yet clearly both anger and political perception are present in *Little Women*, and, not surprisingly, there is evidence within *Little Women* of Alcott's ambivalence toward her true style. *Little Women* takes place during the Civil War and the first of Jo's many burdens on her pilgrim's progress toward little womanhood is her resentment at not being at the scene of action. Later, however, she reflects that "keeping her temper at home was a much harder task than facing a rebel or two down South" (p. 19). The Civil War is an obvious metaphor for internal conflict and its invocation as background to *Little Women* suggests the presence in the story of such conflict. There is tension in the book, attributable to the conflict between its overt messages and its covert messages. Set in subliminal counterpoint to the consciously intended messages is a series of alternate messages which provide evidence of Alcott's ambivalence. To a considerable extent, the continuing interest and power of *Little Women* is the result of this internal conflict. As Alcott got farther and farther away from the moment of discovery, as the true style became more and more the only style, this tension was lost and the result was the tedious sentimentality of *A Rose in Bloom* or the unrelieved flatness of *Under the Lilacs*. *Little Women* survives by subversion.

[Deletion of analysis of incidents in *Little Women*, and discussions of the book's concern for defining women's sphere, *Little Women* as a domestic drama, "the little woman character."]

Obviously, one of the major problems Alcott faced in writing *Little Women* was making up someone for Jo to marry since, as we have seen, marry she must. She cannot marry, as she cannot "love," Laurie, not, as Marmee claims, because they are too alike in temperament, but because they are too alike in status; they are too equal. If anything, Laurie is Jo's inferior, as her constant reference to him as "the dear boy" implies. Unfortunately, perhaps, for Jo and Laurie, little women can only love up, not across or down; they must marry their fathers, not their brothers or sons. Thus Laurie gets Amy who is a fitting child for him and Jo gets her Papa Bhaer who, as the Germanic and ursine connotations of his name suggest, is the heavy authority figure necessary to offset Jo's own considerable talent and vitality. His age, his foreignness, his status as a professor, his possession of moral and philosophic wisdom all conspire to put him on a different plane from Laurie and John Brooke and to make him an appropriate suitor for Jo whose relationship to him is clearly that of pupil to teacher, child to parent, little woman to big man. In exchange for German lessons, she will darn his socks; at their school he will do all the teaching and she will do the housework; he has saved her soul by a timely warning against the effects of sensational literature and later we are told of Jo's future that she "made queer mistakes; but the wise professor steered her safely into calmer waters" (p. 536). It is clear, however, that such an excessively heirarchical [sic] relationship is necessary to indicate Jo's ultimate acceptance of the doctrines of *Little Women*. In marrying Professor Bhaer, Jo's rebellion is neutralized, and she proves once and for all that she is a good little woman who wishes for nothing more than the chance to realize herself in the service of some superior male.[5] The process of getting her out of her boots and doublet and her misguided male-identification and into her role as a future Marmee is completed by placing her securely in the arms of Papa Bhaer.

We do not, of course, view this transformation with unqualified rejoicing. It is difficult not to see it as capitulation and difficult not to respond to it with regret. Our attitude, moreover, is not the result of feminist values imposed on Alcott's work but the result of ambivalence within the work on the subject of what it means to be a little woman. Certainly, this ambivalence is itself part of the message of *Little Women*. It accurately reflects the position of the woman writer in nineteenth-century America, confronted on all sides by forces pressuring her to compromise her vision. How conscious Alcott was of the conflict between the overt and covert messages of *Little Women*, how intentional on the one hand was her subversion of the book's "doctrine" and on the other hand her compromise with her culture's norms, it is impossible to say. What one can say, however, is that in failing to give Jo a fate other than that of the little woman, Alcott "altered her values in deference to the opinion of others" and obliterated her own identity as an economically independent single woman who much preferred to "paddle her own canoe" than to resign herself to the dependency of marriage.[6] Clearly, her true style is rather less than true. When Professor Bhaer excoriates sensation fiction in an effort to set Jo on the road to attaining her true style he exclaims, "They haf no right to put poison in the sugar plum, and let the small ones eat it" (p. 393). It is to Alcott's credit that at least covertly if not overtly she recognized the sugar plum was the poison.

Notes

1. Louisa May Alcott, *Little Women* (New York: Collier-Macmillan, 1962), pp. 481–82. I have chosen this edition as it is currently the most easily available, reputable edition. All subsequent references will be to this edition and will be included parenthetically within the text. *Little Women* was originally published in 1868/1869.

2. *Louisa May Alcott: Her Life, Letters, and Journals*, ed. Ednah D. Cheney (Boston: Roberts Brothers, 1890), pp. 296–97.

3. Ibid., p. 303.

4. Madeleine Stern, Introduction to *Behind A Mask: The Unknown Thrillers of Louisa May Alcott* (New York: William Morrow, 1975), p. xxvii.

5. It is hard for me to comprehend how Elizabeth Janeway can describe Jo as "the one young woman in nineteenth-century fiction who maintains her individual independence, who gives up no part of her autonomy as payment for being born a woman — and gets away with it. Jo is the tomboy dream come true, the dream of growing up into full humanity with all its potentialities instead of into limited femininity. . . ." Perhaps the answer lies in the fact that her concept of "full humanity with all its potentialities" reaches no further than the vision of a Jo who "marries and becomes, please note, not a sweet little wife but a matriarch: mistress of the *professor's* school, mother of healthy *sons* [while Amy and Laurie have only one sickly *daughter*] and a *cheerful*, active manager of events and *people*." (Italics mine.) It is doubtful that such a vision would be asserted as "full" if the character under consideration were male. Auerbach's analysis seems much more sensible and grounded in the facts of the novel. While giving more weight to the realm of matriarchal power which Jo enters on marrying Professor Bhaer than I am willing to do, she nevertheless recognizes that, even when "stretched to its limit," this power collides with and falters before "the history it tries to subdue. For . . . history remains where we found it at the beginning of *Little Women*: 'far away, where the fighting was.'" Indeed, Alcott's recognition that she must write not about the external world of male power embodied in the Civil War but about the internal world of Jo's struggle between resistance and capitulation to the doctrines of little womanhood indicates her understanding of Jo's exclusion from the real sources of power. See Elizabeth Janeway, *Between Myth and Morning: Women Awakening* (New York: William Morrow, 1975), pp. 234–37; and Nina Auerbach, *Communities of Women* (Cambridge: Harvard University Press, 1978), pp. 55–73.

6. Alcott, *Life, Letters, and Journals*, p. 122.

[Jo March: Male Model — Female Person]

Carolyn Heilbrun[*]

Oddly enough, one of the most revolutionary voices in American fiction about family roles and the expectations of girls in confronting them is to be found in one of the standard works of children's fiction. Early in *Little Women* Jo March tells us: "I hate affected, nimin-piminy chits. . . . I hate

---

[*]Reprinted from *Reinventing Womanhood* (New York: W. W. Norton & Co., 1979), pp. 190–91, 212. The notes have been renumbered.

to think I've got to grow up and be Miss March, and wear long gowns and look as prim as a China-aster. . . .I can't get over my disappointment in not being a boy." Jo is assured by Beth that she is a brother to them all; in her father's absence, she declares herself to be "the man of the family."

Jo plays the male parts in plays, she wears a "gentlemanly" collar and has a gentlemanly manner, she thinks of herself as a businessman and cherishes a pet rat. (The pet rat is male and has a son, "proud of his whiskers," who accompanies him along the rafters.) Jo finds it easier to risk her life for a person than to be pleasant when she doesn't want to, and she admires the "manly" way of shaking hands. The point is clear enough: men's manners speak of freedom, openness, camaraderie, physical abandon, the chance to escape passivity. Who would not prefer such a destiny, except those taught to be afraid?

A woman writer has here imagined, as she has lived, the truths of revolutionary girlhood. But as with so many women writers, Alcott could not sustain it.[1] She marries off Jo and allows her to devote herself to a school for boys (who would want to bother with girls?) and presents, in Meg's children, as perfect a description of stereotypical upbringing within a nuclear family as has ever been afforded us:

> At three, Daisy demanded a "needler," and actually made a bag with four stitches in it; she likewise set up housekeeping in the sideboard, and managed a microscopic cooking-stove with a skill that brought tears of pride to Hannah's eyes, while Demi learned his letters with his grandfather. . . . The boy early developed a mechanical genius. . . . Of course, Demi tyranized over Daisy, and gallantly defended her from every other aggressor; while Daisy made a galley-slave of herself, and adored her brother as the one perfect being in the world.

Etcetera, unfortunately. Perhaps only in America, with its worship of "manliness," could boy-girl twins, elsewhere universally a literary phenomenon characterized by their resemblance to one another, be so sharply defined and differentiated by sex roles. It is no wonder that Alcott never married; an all-girl family had not prepared her for service to the family's son: she *was* the family's "son."

[Passage deleted.]

But there is another way, the choice of Jo: to appropriate the male model without giving up the female person. The young woman must learn, as Jo did, to tell herself stories and to act in plays, in which she, a female, is the protagonist. Jo reinvented girlhood, but the task of reinventing womanhood was beyond her. Even so, while telling herself stories in which she was the protagonist, she remained in a community of women;[2] she did not desert or demean them, or look upon them as less worthy than herself.

Notes

1. There have been several recent, excellent studies of Alcott and her work: The essay on *Little Women* in Nina Auerbach, *Communities of Women: An Idea in Fiction* (Cambridge, Mass.: Harvard University Press, 1978); the Introduction to *Work*, by Sarah Elbert (New York: Schocken Books, 1977); the introduction to *Behind A Mask* and *Plots and Counterplots*, collections of the unknown thrillers of Alcott, by Madeleine Stern (New York: Bantam Books, 1978). *Louisa May: A Modern Biography of Louisa May Alcott*, by Martha Saxton (Boston: Houghton Mifflin, 1977) is conventional in its interpretation of the impulses to female action.

2. See Auerbach, *Communities of Women*, pp. 55–73.

Beneath the Surface: Power and Passion in *Little Women*   Madelon Bedell*

In F. Scott Fitzgerald's story "Bernice Bobs her Hair" one of the characters is advised to be virtuous in the manner of Louisa May Alcott's famous March sisters, Meg, Jo, Beth, and Amy.

> 'Oh please don't quote 'Little Women!' cried Marjorie impatiently. 'That's out of style.'
> 'You think so?'
> 'Heavens, yes! What modern girl could live like those inane females?'[1]

Fitzgerald's Marjorie is summing up a critical notion of *Little Women* that has prevailed for many years, from the time of its first publication when an anonymous reviewer for the *Nation* described the book as a "pleasant little story . . . just such a hearty, unaffected, and 'genial' description of family life as will appeal to the majority of average readers."[2] The implication is clear. No one of serious intent or sophisticated taste will be attracted to "pleasantness" or "geniality," especially when the latter word is encased in quotation marks. And beyond that, who would ever aspire to be labeled an "average reader"?

Thomas Wentworth Higginson, former editor of the *Atlantic Monthly* and putative male feminist, underlined the literary judgment of his times when he wrote after Alcott's death, "Her muse was sociable; the instinct of art she never had."[3] Helen Hunt Jackson's *Ramona*, he thought, was a better book and would last longer.

Ensuing generations of critics have tended to agree in the main. They have judged *Little Women* to be a sentimental "girl's book," not without charm, but on the whole, "empty of emotion,"[4] insultingly simplistic, hypocritical in the extreme, and devoid of both artistry and intelligence, its place

*Reprinted in part from the introduction to Louisa May Alcott, *Little Women* (New York: Random House, 1983), pp. ix–xi, xiv–xv, xxiii–xxv, xlvi–xlix.

in American culture akin to "taffy pulling and Flag Day."[5] The best that can be said for it is that its characters are realistic and vivid, its domestic details faithful to the period.

"Moral pap,"[6] said Louisa Alcott herself of her works, summing up all her critics, those past and those yet to come.

It is a truism that readers rarely agree with critics, but the polarization in this case is startling. *Little Women* is a popular book, one of the most popular ever written. It was published over one hundred years ago in the year 1868, became an instant best seller in its day, has never been out of print, and at this writing was available in seventeen different editions in the United States alone, plus an unknown number of foreign ones.

The story of a family of four girls seen in their crucial adolescent years, this female *bildungsroman* has survived the successive waves of both American feminism and antifeminism, able in some mysterious way to assume a protective coloration which blends with the prevailing ideological winds, emerging fresh, whole—and different—for the next generation of women. Its protagonist, Josephine March (who is also Louisa Alcott's persona), has survived as one of those few characters in literature so compellingly real that they transcend their times, their place, and their society to become for their readers, in the words of the writer Le Anne Schreiber, "a fixed point of reference for life."[7]

"The link between reader and writer forged by every popular book is a mystic one," says Helen Papashvily. "The writer may not know all he has said; the reader all he has heard; yet they understand each other perfectly."[8] This statement is particularly true of *Little Women*, a book which stretches or contracts its meanings, depending on the times when it is read and the person who reads it. In other words, it has the qualities of a myth or legend. Indeed it may be *the* American female myth, its subject the primordial one of the passage from childhood, from girl to woman.

It is this very quality of universality that the readers of the book appear to have understood with greater perception than either its critics or indeed its author.

[Comments on the surface narrative and characters of *Little Women* deleted.]

If we probe deeper beneath the surface story of *Little Women* in the manner of someone scraping off the surface texture of a painting, we find another picture underneath: the legend, which the story masks. The theme of the legend is also concerned with the sister's struggles, not against their faults—which are, after all, as depicted by the loving hand of the author, also their chief attractions—but against the inevitability of growing up, of leaving the delightful state of childhood for the restricted, narrow, and burdened condition of womanhood.

In the legend as opposed to the story, the plot focuses on the struggle of one sister, Jo, against the male intruder from the Palace Beautiful, Laurie's shy tutor, the poor but virtuous John Brooke. His successful courtship of Meg signals the eventual demise of the charmed circle of the female family.

There are other concerns beyond love and romance, however, in this many-layered tale. The themes of work, money, and social position, and the relation of these to female autonomy, are integral to the narrative. In the larger context of the legend, *Little Women* is not about "being good," nor even about growing up, but about the complexities of female power and the struggle to maintain it in a male-dominated society.

When viewed in this light, many of the surface events of the book take on wider dimensions, and the homely domestic scene which is the background for these events assumes deeper meanings, both social and psychological in nature.

[Deletion of details on conversation and characterization in *Little Women*, analysis of the Alcott gospel of work and "the capitalist rhetoric of the times," and of plot development in Part II of *Little Women*.]

Consider, for example, the ending of the book. In the surface tale everyone has been neatly disposed of, killed or married off as the case may be, the whole sanctified by Marmee's concluding words: "Oh, my girls, however long you may live, I never can wish you a greater happiness than this."

The conclusion of the legend, however, is not as tidy. The magic charmed circle has been completely destroyed. All of its members have yielded up their female exclusivity to male intruders, or, in Beth's case, to death. Even the Reverend March has returned for good, although to be sure, he is never more than a shadow father, nothing to compare with the incomparable, though fading, splendid Marmee. Both Jo and Amy have relinquished their artistic ambitions in favor of marriage and motherhood, although we are promised that they may take them up again—sometime in the future, exactly when we are not sure. And on this note—ambiguous, uncertain, and unsatisfactory—the legend draws to a close.

It is largely because of the fate allotted to Jo, the hero of the book, that we feel this sense of unease and dissatisfaction. If things are nicely tied up for her in the story, they are not so in the legend. In marrying this seemingly sexless, fusty middle-aged man, she seems to be abandoning, is it forever?, all her splendid ambitions—betraying herself, the reader, and the bright promise she showed at the beginning of the legend. She has sacrificed both romance *and* independence in taking for a husband a man who is her mentor, not her lover.

In the context of the book, however, no other ending except this flawed one would be appropriate. What other future is possible for Jo? Can one really imagine her as an independent artist living an adventurous life in some sort of Bohemian quarter of Boston, supposing such a place to have existed? That solution might be true to Jo's dreams, but not to Jo's character and certainly not to her time and place. She is no George Sand, and this is America, not France.

So if Jo must marry, what better choice than the professor? He may not be conventionally attractive in the manner of the young and lustful Laurie, but nonetheless he is intellectually far superior to this indolent youth, whose charm, as Alcott so perceptively suggests, is bound to fade with the years. The professor is warm, fatherly, but not intimate; for in intimacy lies the peril of surrender and dependence, with their consequences of rage and violence. It is no accident that he is a foreigner. Coming from a strange country, he is free of all associations, in Jo's and the reader's minds, with the confusing problems of intimacy, sex, and control in marriage that would arise with a fellow American. And further, is not the mentor-as-mate a special female literary fantasy of unusual power? Witness Austen's Emma and Knightly, Bronte's Lucy and her professor, or Hammett and Hellman in *Julia*.

Still, there is a haunting sense of incompleteness about the legend, as there is not to the tidy story. Like Cynthia Ozick, the writer who confesses to having read *Little Women* "a thousand, ten thousand"[9] times, we identify in the end not so much with the Jo of the book as with "some Jo of the future,"[10] the independent woman she failed to become.

In 1871, two years after the publication of Part II of *Little Women*, Alcott returned to the story of the March family with the publication of *Little Men*. In this book, quite an interesting change has taken place, which is forecast in the epilogue of *Little Women*. Jo and her professor are now the owners of a boys' school, Plumfield. At Plumfield, while Professor Bhaer teaches the boys, Jo runs their lives and is clearly in control of things at last. The magic matriarch Marmee has been retired and her daughter has taken her place. The all-female sanctuary has been replaced by an all-male retreat with a woman in charge. Jolly Aunt Jo tells the middle-aged, bland, benevolent Laurie: "I'm a faded old woman, but I'm a very happy one: so don't pity me."[11]

We are not convinced. We still yearn for "some independent Jo of the future." Is this imitation-Marmee really the Josephine March of *Little Women*? Or has that tempestuous character been transformed into the sullen, raging delinquent, the black-eyed vagrant Dan, who will not study, fights with the other boys, starts fires, and commits other acts of vandalism, but has a heart of gold underneath it all?

Only Aunt Jo understands this "untamed creature"[12] who reminds her of a wild hawk. She "seem(s) to know by instinct how he feels."[13] Someday he will calm down and turn into a responsible, law-abiding man, we are told. Love—family or parental love—conquers all. This is the message of *Little Men*. Once again, it satisfies the surface story but leaves the legend unfinished.

In 1886, two years before her death, Alcott published the final volume of the March family saga, *Jo's Boys*. More than any of her novels, this last one is sprinkled with heroines, all of whom are allotted varying fates. Some marry. Some take up careers. Some espouse feminism, some prefer to be old-fashioned ladies. Some are independent artists, some do-good reformers. There is something for everybody in *Jo's Boys*, including its central figure, Josephine Bhaer, who, having finally achieved literary fame, broods over her nest with a serenity that her creator Louisa Alcott never achieved.

We do not believe it. The real person of Josephine March — and of her creator — is not to be found in this aging matriarch. The legend is eternally unfinished, its author unwilling to resolve her conflicts of love, marriage, power, control, and independence, up to the very end.

But what of Josephine March's alter ego, wild Dan? He has returned all grown up in *Jo's Boys*, having survived a rough dangerous life and committed several crimes, including murder. Dan loves "Princess Bess," Amy's daughter, but can never marry her, for "light and darkness were not farther apart than snow-white Bess and sin-stained Dan."[14] He goes off to live with his "chosen people,"[15] the native American Indians who are, like him, exiles in their own land. He is finally killed defending them, at peace at last.

[Lengthy analysis of biographical background and its applications to *Little Women* and other Alcott stories deleted.]

In this symbol-laden conclusion to Dan's story can be found, finally, the hidden end of the *Little Women* legend. The fierce young woman who was Josephine March, with all her ambitions, passions, and excesses of character, has no place in the civilized world into which she was born. All the conventional stereotypes of home, love, marriage — career even — are too limiting for this "wild hawk" whom all the experiences of life had never succeeded in taming "down to docility." Only through wandering, exile, and eventual violent death could she fulfill herself.

Notes

1. Malcolm Cowley, ed., *The Stories of F. Scott Fitzgerald* (New York: Scribner's 1951), p. 47.

2. *The Nation*, December 14, 1875, reprinted in Virginia Havilland, ed., *Children and Literature* (New York: Lothrop Lee & Shepard, 1974), p. 64.

3. Thomas Wentworth Higginson, *Short Studies of American Authors* (New York: Longman's Green, 1906), pp. 66–67.

4. Katherine Fullerton Gerould, *Modes and Morals* (New York: Scribner's, 1920), pp. 182–198.

5. Martha Saxton, *Louisa May* (Boston: Houghton Mifflin, 1977), p. 4.

6. Louisa May Alcott, *Jo's Boys* (Boston: Little, Brown, 1930), p. 38.

7. Le Anne Schrieber, "Books of the Times," *New York Times*, May 24, 1982, p. C15.

8. Helen Papashvily, *All the Happy Endings* (New York: Harper & Row, 1956), p. xvii.

9. Cynthia Ozick, "The Making of a Writer," *New York Times Book Review*, January 31, 1982, p. 24.

10. Ibid.

11. Louisa May Alcott, *Works of Louisa May Alcott*, ed. Claire Boos (New York: Avenel, 1982), *Little Men*, p. 592.

12. Ibid., p. 446.

13. Ibid., p. 479.

14. Louisa May Alcott, *Jo's Boys* (Boston: Little, Brown, 1930), p. 300.

15. Ibid., p. 316.

THE LITTLE WOMEN SERIES

[Review of *An Old-Fashioned Girl*, 1870]

Anonymous*

. . . There is no country in the world, it is said, where children count for so much as in the United States, nor where so much is done for them; but, for some reason or other, we have not produced any thoroughly good writer for children. Possibly it may be true, as is charged against us by enemies, that it is only Young America that is born here, and that there are never any Americans who really are young. At all events, whether from want of an audience, or from whatever cause, it is easy to name all the American writers who at all skilfully address themselves to the childlike mind. Miss Louisa Alcott we take to be about as good as any, though one sort of the work that she does Mrs. [A. D. T.] Whitney perhaps does better. The young lady who is all but marriageable, but who has not yet quite finished her last year of boarding-school—the New England young lady who has still some months of school-life to finish, but who begins to have opinions in regard to the niceness of various young gentlemen; who, though she may play croquet, has "views of life;" who goes to the Thursday afternoon concerts in Boston, and to the Horticultural Hall lectures on Sundays; who has a cultivated taste in music and an eclectic turn in religions—this mingled young girl and young lady, produced in the vicinity of Boston and not elsewhere, Mrs. Whitney draws with what seems to the unlearned eye perfection. Miss Alcott draws her too; but, on the whole, Miss Alcott's sympathies seem to be rather with earlier stages of life than with this of which we speak, and there is—at least to the adult reader—something of a fresher sense of boyhood and girlhood to be got from her writing than from that of her cleverer contemporary. Miss Alcott, however, no more than Mrs. Whitney, is free from an influence which it appears to be agreed shall be called Bostonian, and which is, doubtless, of disadvantage to any one who proposes to make literature in which there shall be at once matter to interest children and, so to speak, the living figures of children themselves. Self-consciousness in not the worst sense of that term—a constant consciousness of the goodness and beauty and admirableness of one's good and beautiful

*Reprinted from the *Nation*, 11 (14 July 1870), 30–31.

and admirable acts and thoughts and behavior—a sort of patronizing and Jack-Horner-like practice of all excellent virtues and graces—would seem to be extremely common in that corner which knows itself to be the new and improved *umbilicus mundi.*

Then, too, it may be said of this "Old-Fashioned Girl" of Miss Alcott's that it is done from the outside, and that what is depicted is only partly the thing that was to be depicted, and is partly Miss Alcott's not perfectly intelligent and sympathetic conception of it. It is not boys, we should say, it must be women, who have acquaintance with any boy so persistently tously-headed as Miss Alcott's "Tom," and so extravagantly fond of pockets full of pea-nuts, and so sure to get into scrapes which prove nothing at all against the sinner's moral character, but merely bear witness to his superfluous animal spirits and energy. And, doubtless, our author's girls, also, are to some extent artificial, and persons of her drama rather than real persons—creatures of her will rather than beings with wills of their own. This is not always true, for every reader must recognize in Miss Alcott's stories many pictures that are strictly photographic—that are, indeed, strictly true to nature. But, speaking generally, her personages exist for their creator's purposes, not their own; they all are made that they may point a moral. The hero must preach a woman's notion of manliness—must be, violently, the nondescript known to women as The Boy; the heroine must be, out and out, the "old-fashioned girl"—that is to say, she must be unsophisticated to a degree which makes it too manifest that she was created in a world very familiarly acquainted with sophistication; the second heroine must be a "new-fashioned girl" of the most decided and fashionable type, and the doings and fortunes of these personages must be such as to teach us the value and beauty of simplicity and honesty, and the folly and badness and hollowness of pretension and display. Thus a wide door is opened to unnaturalness; and that a good deal of unnaturalness does not come in, few readers would say.

But—to stick to the quotation—if Miss Alcott's personages do rather too much and too regularly point a moral, they also in their way do adorn a tale; and the readers of her books are exceedingly few, discriminating and undiscriminating, who have not got from them pleasure. They are unfailingly good-hearted and kind-hearted; they have a great deal of fun in them, and a great deal of good sense; no one will learn from them to admire any moral qualities but those that are to be admired; they are, as stories, well enough constructed, and whether or not the author's "call to preach" she does well to answer, and whether or not her art of portraiture is defective, it is certain that she assists the reader to reproduce his youth, and to sympathize with the young and innocent and happy. Those who demand of each worker in literature an artistic success will be of another opinion, but to have produced, whether artistically and legitimately or otherwise, the effect with which we have credited Miss Alcott, seems to us not a small service to have rendered. Perhaps we might say more than this, and credit our author with having written books well adapted to the wishes of her ostensible audience, and likewise to its needs. Certainly her stories have been read by an immense number of girls and boys. But girls and boys read anything and everything, and are easily pleased; and, on the whole, one would set down Miss Alcott as being of that class of writers for children who write not so much for children as about them, and would not predict for her the true success of writers of "juveniles," as of other works—the pleasing of more generations than one.

[Review of *An Old-Fashioned Girl*, 1870]

C. L. P.*

Voltaire once said, "Would you be popular, startle your public—whether for good or evil, it matters not, but be startling at any price." This maxim, so venal in principle, appears to be regarded by a considerable number of modern novelists as one of the most important rules of literary composition. That the materialism of the present day should love to preserve the relics which it has inherited from the infidelity of the preceding century, is natural, and in conformity with that spirit of veneration with which a pupil is expected to cherish the precepts of a skillful and patient master. At all events, the vicious theories which found their practical realization in the excesses of the French Revolution have come down to us through the medium of a bad philosophy, and have finally succeeded in contaminating not only the aesthetic character, but also the moral tone of our popular literature. It is now understood that a book which appeals to the imagination must be sensational or it cannot be successful as a pecuniary speculation. In opposition to this verdict, few writers of romance, either here or in England, have lately attempted to address the public in a style entirely free from the influence of passion. A novel refined in thought, pure in morals, and yet sufficiently tender and exciting to touch the heart and to captivate the fancy, is now so great a rarity that the critic is disposed to hail such a volume with expressions of enthusiastic esteem. Still, it must not be supposed that legitimate fiction has ceased to elicit the attention of authors, or has wholly failed to attract the patronage of the public. On the contrary, it would be easy to name some honorable exceptions to the present literary degeneracy, and among these exceptions, which, to a great extent, owe their creation to female talent, a position must be accorded to *An Old-Fashioned Girl*.

Miss Alcott cannot indeed claim an extraordinary share of original genius, or a more diversified experience of human nature than has fallen to the lot of other conspicuous writers of the day. But every unbiased judge

*Reprinted from *Lippincott's Magazine*, 6 (August 1870), 230–32.

must admit that the work we are now considering is distinguished for delicate and faithful portraiture, a simple, graceful and modest style, a sensible appreciation of womanly character, a proper regard for the wants of real society, and, above all, a decided acknowledgment of the superior claims of mental and moral worth. These qualities in a modern work of fiction are surely uncommon enough to warrant particular eulogy.

It is true that Miss Alcott has not entirely escaped the materialistic influences which permeate the atmosphere of modern society; but she appears to have breathed this fatal miasma in a moderate degree, and her book has thus escaped any positive detriment. In fact, from the praises here accorded to her performance, it will be seen that her faults lie rather in her failure to give a complete impersonation of female virtues and instincts than in any visible departure from the model approved by reason and experience. Miss Alcott writes like an honest and fearless woman, and the effort she has so lately made to inspire her fellow-women of America, especially the younger portion of them, with a loftier and a worthier ambition, deserves acknowledgment. Any author who is sufficiently wise and determined to oppose with judgment the errors and follies of his age, even when they are indirectly countenanced by those who arrogate to themselves the title of philosophers, is certainly deserving of generous congratulation; but when to this exhibition of wisdom and determination are added the amenities of a wholesome literary style, we may fairly presume to rank the fortunate writer among the philanthropists of his times.

Miss Alcott has the modesty to admit that she does not propose her *Old-Fashioned Girl* as a faultless type of womanhood; but it is doubtful if she could, under existing circumstances, have produced a more elevated exemplar. The womanhood of America, though characterized by certain traits that are highly attractive, cannot, in a general way, be said to merit the encomiums with which our national pride would urge us to honor it. There are some American women as noble, as refined, as sensible and as sympathetic as any in the world; but many, nay, very many, of our daughters, our wives, and even our mothers, are still too frivolous in their mode of life, too material in their ambition, too selfish in their pursuits, to endure the scrutiny of an unprejudiced criticism. In making such a remark the critic may be accused of unreasonable attachment to those antique types of character which, it is said, have been rejected by the progressive temper of modern civilization. We should feel sorry to be thought either unpatriotic or ungallant, but we must confess that those older forms of social and domestic life have ever inspired us with a loftier admiration of female dignity and usefulness than have all the variable charms, the artificial graces, the irresponsible luxury and the pecuniary magnificence of what many are pleased to consider our native aristocracy.

When the cultured and traveled American gazes around him in quest of moral and aesthetic gratification, he misses that sense of mental calm, of delicate and expansive pleasure, of simple grandeur, of interior as well as exterior ease, of unbiased sympathy and of social equilibrium, which he has experienced in other lands and among other peoples than his own. If he be a man of a naturally elevated and analytical mind, the more he studies the manners and the aims of the wealthy and influential classes of his native land, the more apt is he to long for that brilliant repose and that quiet splendor, that richness of mental enjoyment and that profundity of Christian feeling, which yet subsist in the old provincial abodes of France. The nearer American womanhood approaches the standard which is there displayed, the greater reason Americans will have to feel proud of it, and the greater will be the good which it will be able to accomplish both for itself and for the sex upon which it depends, but which it is bound in duty to restrain, to elevate and to refine. That the majority of our maidens and matrons may one day reach this position of honorable distinction is a hope that all should cherish. How soon this wish may be realized it is difficult to tell. Certain it is that before so happy an event can be consummated, many an intermediate stage must be safely and patiently passed. But the necessary movement has been commenced; and its progress, if imperceptible to thoughtless observers, is still both regular and unyielding.

The little book which has elicited these reflections has already demonstrated, by the popularity which it has acquired, that in the rising generation of American girls there are thousands who are able to perceive and to appreciate the value of a social existence which is not entirely sacrificed to the puerilities of fashionable caprice and to the treacherous demands of a selfish philosophy. Let us trust that the good seed which Miss Alcott's book has sown, even if it be not the best which the hand of the social husbandman could have scattered, may fructify in youthful bosoms until it shall produce ample fruit; and may this harvest of more elevated thought and loftier morals form the substance of still higher and worthier efforts, until the work of regeneration has been happily accomplished.

[Review of *Little Men: Life at Plumfield with Jo's Boys*, 1871]   Anonymous*

It can hardly be asserted that *Little Men* by Miss Alcott (Roberts Brothers), is a natural story, or doubted that it is an entertaining one. The description of an actual boarding-school, with its humdrum life, would be as tedious as any thing that can well be conceived of, and that Miss Alcott is able to invest a story of boarding-school life with any interest must be taken as one of the evidences of her genius. There is hardly enough in the story itself to sustain the reader's interest in it; and despite the author's bright style and vivid descriptions, and, best of all, her hearty sympathy with

*Reprinted from *Harper's New Monthly Magazine*, 43 (August 1871), 458.

youth, the book drags a little if one attempts to read it directly through. It is more entertaining read as a series of sketches than as a single connected story. We beg leave to doubt whether, on the whole, it would be for the best interest of any well-ordered school for the boys to have unlimited liberty to slide down the balusters at the risk of broken heads, and every Saturday night, after their bath, to chase each other over the house in a sham battle with the pillows. We are inclined to think that Mr. Bhaer's original method of compelling the guilty boy to inflict the feruling on the teacher would lose its moral effect if it were generally adopted. We protest that for a boy to bring a lying accusation against himself to shield a friend is a very mistaken kind of heroism . . . [another incident of misguided kindness cited]. But, after all, the lesson which these improbable incidents are meant to teach, and do teach, is a good one—this, namely, that personal sympathy with children, in all their life, even their pranks and good-natured mischief, is the first condition of acquiring influence over them, and hence is the first condition of any true and good government in school or family. The children will be sure to read "Little Men" with interest, and the parents can read it with profit.

[Review of *Little Men: Life at Plumfield with Jo's Boys*, 1871] Anonymous[*]

Miss Alcott says, the unprejudiced criticism of children is not to be despised, and she has need to be gratified with the lavish praise offered her by her many youthful admirers. Though their flattering comments be not always couched in the most elegant phraseology, and a superabundance of adjectives—among which "awful nice" gains force by constant repetition—seems necessary to relieve their delighted hearts, yet are they none the less sincere and acceptable. Perhaps no book of the season has been so eagerly sought after as this, or has given such genuine satisfaction, which is saying a great deal, for *Little Women* raised expectations that we feared would not be realized. We are agreeably disappointed. We welcome *Little Men* heartily, and find them thoroughly enjoyable. Though "little men," they are full-grown, rollicking, hearty boys. Boys in the rough, but as such easily understood and appreciated by their many prototypes; boys to be admired for their frank good-heartedness, and boys to be envied for the "splendid times" they have. To less favored ones, what a haven of bliss does "Plumfield" appear, when they contemplate the "gorgeousness" of those "pillow-fights;" unrestricted flinging of pillows—of pillows with covers that would not tear! How the old-time glory pales in their light! How insignificant those engagements, where the final round and final *twist* invariably rent

[*]Reprinted from the *Overland Monthly*, 7 (September 1871), 293–94.

the dainty pillow-case asunder! No wonder even "Dan" was softened and subdued in an atmosphere where love held license in subjection, for what more convincing proof need we of the wonderful discipline of "Plumfield" than that the boys laid down their "arms" (or pillows) when the bell announced the "engagement" was over? "And nothing but an occasional giggle or a suppressed whisper broke the quiet which followed the Saturday-night frolic." Chief among the many pleasant things in this pleasant book, is the thorough insight displayed in the portrayal of children's characters, and the tender sympathy shown toward them. As we read of "Demi," "Nat," "Jack," "Ned," and the rest of "Jo's" boys, we take them to our hearts, and feel they are real, living children. And one who has ever been with, or known any thing of little folks, can not fail to be charmed with the naturalness of the scenes described. The "sackerryfice" of the "Naughty Kitty-Mouse" is a capital bit of fun, and a truthful illustration of the wonderful power of imagination in children.

The "Naughty Kitty-Mouse" is a terrible sprite, whose will is law, and whom "Demi" faithfully serves and "Daisy" fears; so that when "Demi," coming from school, solemnly whispers to "Daisy" that the "Kitty-Mouse" wants them, she, knowing there is no help for them, anxiously inquires, "What for?" With great gravity, "Demi" replies, "For a sackerryfice. There is to be a fire behind the big rock at two o'clock, and we are to bring the things we like best and burn them," with an awful emphasis on the last words. Poor little "Daisy" is terror-stricken, but the thought of denying the unseen tyrant any thing never occurring to her, she sorrowfully collects her treasures, and follows her brother. The sacrificial train sets forth, "Teddy" and others joining them — the whole having been suggested by "Uncle Fritz's" description of the customs of the Greeks. They reach the rock, a fire is kindled on a flat stone for an altar; they march around three times, and the ceremony begins. "I shall begin," says "Demi," "and as fast as my things are burned, you must bring yours." He solemnly lays a little picture-book on the flaming altar, then a boat, and, finally, one by one, a regiment of leaden soldiers. Not one faltered or hung back; from the splendid red and yellow captain to the small drummer, who had lost his legs, all vanished in the flames, and mingled in one common pool of melted lead. Then "Daisy's" turn comes; her little heart is rent in twain. "My dear dollies, how *can* I let you go?" she moans, hugging a promiscuous lot to her bosom; but the High Priest is inexorable. "You must," he says, and with a farewell kiss to each, she lays them upon the coals. "More, more," growls the "Kitty-Mouse," and a whole village is consumed, each successive offering adding excitement to the scene. The wildest sacrifices are made, until Annabella also falls a victim, and being kid, her death agonies are of the most startling character, which so terrify "Teddy," that he flies from the scene, refusing to be comforted. "Mrs. Bhaer" comes to the rescue, and after enjoying the fun, and laughing heartily at the solemn faces of the children, gives them some very sensible advice. There is genuine humor in this, as also in "Daisy's" Ball, where the boys are invited and bribed to good behavior by the promise of "nice things to eat," and where, after having eaten the good things, they so deport themselves as to leave their entertainers in tears; but they make up finally, and all goes well.

All things considered, "Aunt Jo" has a hard time of it; but she is happy, doing good, and we have no right to complain; our old friends have all turned out well. "Laurie," whom we all wanted "Jo" to marry, and she would not, is still her faithful friend and admirer, and "believes" in the "Plumfield" system; for the boys, though they learned less from books than boys at other schools, learned more of that wisdom which makes sterling men.

The Doll-Burners: D. H. Lawrence and Louisa Alcott
Grover Smith*

From the titles of books exchanged and discussed by D. H. Lawrence and Jessie Chambers, as enumerated in Miss Chambers' memoir, one may infer the catholicity of Lawrence's reading between 1901 and 1912. "The first book I recollect Lawrence bringing to me," says Miss Chambers, "was Louisa Alcott's *Little Women*. We thought the story delightful, and set about finding correspondences. I was Jo, there was no doubt about that, and Lawrence was Laurie. 'Only not quite so nice, do you think?' he said with a glance that asked to be contradicted."[1] It is not fully clear whether in 1901 Lawrence was just discovering Louisa Alcott or whether, under the influence of his new friend, the prototype of Miriam in his *Sons and Lovers*, he was reviving an old enthusiasm. It is fair to suspect that Lawrence, then sixteen years old, was much less delighted by *Little Women* than Jessie Chambers was. He may have introduced the girl to Miss Alcott's sequels, *Little Men* and *Jo's Boys;* from the occurrence of a parallel passage in *Sons and Lovers*, it would appear that he had read and remembered *Little Men*.

The episode that Lawrence seems to have converted to his use, perhaps divining in it certain "correspondences" undetected by Miss Chambers, is one of the most memorable in Miss Alcott's novels. It is one of those episodes, indeed not frequent, that give the adult reader a sensation of disgust, more because of the disparity between their actual content and their alleged moral meaning than because of any unhealthfulness in the content itself. Although it does not attain the uncomfortable moral pitch, for example, of Mr. Bhaer's story about the dear grandmother who, to discourage his infant falsehoods, snipped the end of his tongue with her sewing scissors, it does not lag far behind that.

*Reprinted from *Modern Language Quarterly*, 19 (March 1958), 28–32.

Little Men, the saga of "Professor" Bhaer's school-*cum*-orphanage, Plumfield, contains a catchall chapter entitled "Pranks and Plays," featuring an incident which Sir James Frazer might have brooded over. The nursery set at Plumfield — Daisy and Demi, Rob and Teddy — have been moved to perform ritual service to an imaginary local bogy, "the Naughty Kitty-mouse." Upon Demi, the eldest of the chits, devolves the task of interpreting the desire of this goblin for inconvenient rites and observances.

> One day after school Demi whispered to his sister, with an ominous wag of the head:
> "The Kitty-mouse wants us this afternoon."
> "What for?" asked Daisy, anxiously.
> "A *sackerryfice*," answered Demi, solemnly. "There must be a fire behind the big rock at two o'clock, and we must all bring the things we like best, and burn them!" he added, with an awful emphasis on the last words.

The intimidated votaries submit.

> At the appointed hour the sacrificial train set forth, each child bearing the treasures demanded by the insatiable Kitty-mouse. Teddy insisted on going also, and seeing that all the others had toys he tucked a squeaking lamb under one arm, and old Annabella under the other, little dreaming what anguish the latter idol was to give him.

Annabella, a venerable doll, awaits her turn. Meanwhile Demi, having started a fire on a flat stone, bids the children march three times around it to form a circle. The command executed, he burns in succession a small scrapbook, a toy boat, and a company of lead soldiers. Then he obliges Daisy to immolate a dozen paper dolls. When these are consumed, the children set up a miniature village of wood, which takes an entertaining interval to burn up but at length is charred to ashes. Finally comes the climax:

> The superb success of this last offering excited Teddy to such a degree, that he first threw his lamb into the conflagration, and before it had time even to roast, he planted poor, dear Annabella on the funeral pyre. Of course she did not like it, and expressed her anguish and resentment in a way that terrified her infant destroyer. Being covered with kid, she did not blaze, but did what was worse, she *squirmed*. First one leg curled up, then the other, in a very awful and lifelike manner; next she flung her arms over her head as if in great agony; her head itself turned on her shoulders, her glass eyes fell out, and with one final writhe of her whole body, she sank down a blackened mass on the ruins of the town. This unexpected demonstration startled everyone and frightened Teddy half out of his little wits. He looked, then screamed and fled toward the house, roaring "Marmar," at the top of his voice.

Having arrived at the scene of cremation (ghastly, after this account), and having learned what it means, "Aunt Jo" bursts into laughter — "the children were so solemn, and the play was so absurd." Demi explains that he invented the game in imitation of "the Greece people, who had altars and things, and so I wanted to be like them, only I hadn't any live creatures to sackerryfice, so we burned up our toys." This, the good lady finds, is funny too.[2] For her sake one can almost regret that Demi had no tractable puppy dog, or perhaps a tame black hen.

The moral drawn by Miss Alcott, namely that destructiveness is improper, possesses domestic importance of the first order. Unhappily the message was not original with her; and one fears that she missed the main chance in not adverting to the *Malleus Maleficarum*, to the New England witch trials, or even to the rites of Moloch, which might have left a more lasting mark on some of her young readers. Nor was the adventure itself necessarily original: at the beginning of her chapter the author confessed that most of the incidents related therein (expressly "the oddest") had been taken from real life.[3] Miss Alcott had a penchant for homely, and therefore wholesome, realism.

To guess what attraction this episode held for D. H. Lawrence, one would have to know both how consciously and how systematically he adapted it. His parallel passage is found near the start of Chapter 4 of *Sons and Lovers*, "The Young Life of Paul." In this context the victim is a doll belonging to Paul's sister, Annie Morel.

> She had a big doll of which she was fearfully proud, though not so fond. So she laid the doll on the sofa, and covered it with an antimacassar, to sleep. Then she forgot it. Meantime Paul must practise jumping off the sofa arm. So he jumped crash into the face of the hidden doll. Annie rushed up, uttered a loud wail, and sat down to weep a dirge. Paul remained quite still.
>
> "You couldn't tell it was there, mother; you couldn't tell it was there," he repeated over and over. So long as Annie wept for the doll he sat helpless with misery. Her grief wore itself out. She forgave her brother — he was so much upset. But a day or two afterwards she was shocked.
>
> "Let's make a sacrifice of Arabella," he said. "Let's burn her."
>
> She was horrified, yet rather fascinated. She wanted to see what the boy would do. He made an altar of bricks, pulled some of the shavings out of Arabella's body, put the waxen fragments into the hollow face, poured on a little paraffin, and set the whole thing alight. He watched with wicked satisfaction the drops of wax melt off the broken forehead of Arabella, and drop like sweat into the flame. So long as the stupid big doll burned he rejoiced in silence. At the end he poked among the embers with a stick, fished out the arms and legs, all blackened, and smashed them under stones.
>
> "That's the sacrifice of Missis Arabella," he said. "An' I'm glad there's nothing left of her."
>
> Which disturbed Annie inwardly, although she could say nothing. He seemed to hate the doll so intensely, because he had broken it.[4]

Now apart from the possibility that a similar event took place in Lawrence's childhood at Eastwood, in mimicry of the sacrifice in *Little Men*, it is obvious that the doll-burning captured his imagination. The idea of the sacrifice, moreover, rather than any simple moral based on the episode, must have been the fascinating thing. If one assumes that Lawrence used this incident of sacrifice and violence not merely to fill in his chronicle of Paul Morel's childhood and youth but, with full consciousness of the implications, to foreshadow Paul's crises with Miriam and his mother, one may make a conditional guess that Lawrence saw in the doll-burning a symbol of male retaliation against female domestic ascendancy. One must hedge in this way because, in *Sons and Lovers* particularly, Lawrence gives as actualities in the web of his plot many details that stand free from his explicit interpretations of character; such details are unconsciously "right" — which need not mean that he understood them.

By and large, violence in *Sons and Lovers* is a compensatory force. That is, Lawrence depicts it not as a virtue but as a necessary counterpoise of excess. Paul Morel, being smothered under the civilized refinements of Mrs. Morel, has a sufficient motive in battling crudely for his manhood. If his need for violence springs from masculine maladjustment, if it betrays want of certitude, his violence itself in fact only confirms that the feminine order, once established, cannot be toppled, for it triumphs in the very disorder of the male. Yet Lawrence, though often deferential to Mrs. Morel, justifies Paul's longing to escape the imperatives of sympathy and to vaunt himself free, dispossessed, of responsible and thus distressful emotions. Paul's breaking the doll is accidental, and this leads to bitter contrition; but his burning it is deliberate, an assertion of bravado. His effeminate shame gives way to masculine pride. The motive is childish; but Paul, a child here, is doomed to remain a child so long as his mother lives. Entrapped by her, he can only strike back like his father, Walter Morel, who once pitched a table drawer at Mrs. Morel and gashed her forehead.

When, at the end of the novel, Paul with Annie's connivance gives Mrs. Morel an overdose of morphia as she lies dying of cancer, he might almost be trying, though now unconsciously, to retaliate against her long tyranny over him. But Paul there sees his act only as a merciful one; he is still in bondage to her ethic of responsibility.[5] Neither he nor Lawrence himself perceives that the victory is won, and for this reason it is perhaps not won; Lawrence, in a famous letter to Edward Garnett, described Paul as "left in the end naked to everything, with the drift towards death."[6] Yet, better artist than critic, Lawrence, in the last paragraph of *Sons and Lovers*, gave Paul the victory anyhow, without confessing the efficacy of violence in making it possible.

The doll-burning in its sacrificial aspect relates, of course, to Paul's affair with Miriam. The masculine right of self-assertiveness, exercised in the arena of sex, demands a submissive victim, a sacrifice. But Paul, having been reared in delicacy by Mrs. Morel, is bedeviled with conscience. In wooing Miriam, he is unable to enjoy power either during or after its imposition. Nevertheless, when he burned Annie's doll, he has rehearsed the drama of Miriam's oblation. And Miriam in due course accepts her role: "Now it was spring, and there was battle between him and Miriam. This year he had a good deal against her. She was vaguely aware of it. The old feeling that she was to be a sacrifice to this love, which she had had when she prayed, was mingled in all her emotions. . . . She saw tragedy, sorrow, and sacrifice ahead. And in sacrifice she was proud, in renunciation she was strong. . . ."[7] Miriam offers up her virginity, but Paul is not content. He cannot officiate at this sacrifice essential to his ego without pitying his victim and afterwards blaming her for his failure:

> she lay as if she had given herself up to sacrifice: there was her body for him; but the look at the back of her eyes, like a creature awaiting immolation, arrested him, and all his blood fell back.
>
> . . . .
>
> She lay to be sacrificed for him because she loved him so much. And he had to sacrifice her. For a second, he wished he were sexless or dead. Then she shut his eyes again to her, and his blood beat back again.
>
> . . . .
>
> He had always, almost wilfully, to put her out of count, and act from the brute strength of his own feelings. And he could not do it often, and there remained afterwards always the sense of failure and of death. If he were really with her, he had to put aside himself and his desire. If he would have her, he had to put her aside.
>
> "When I come to you," he asked her, his eyes dark with pain and shame, "you don't really want me, do you?"[8]

He can possess her in detachment, but he cannot sustain a passion that requires him to feel sacrificed to, and hence guilty. "He seemed to hate the doll so intensely, because he had broken it"; only now, it is as if he were breaking and burning the doll in one act, incurring blame and wreaking vengeance all at once. Miriam, like the doll Arabella, is but too surely a substitute for Mrs. Morel.

The significance of the doll-burning in *Sons and Lovers* appears, in the last analysis, to be a horrible one. Whether by design or instinct, Lawrence included in his novel a symbolic incident recapitulating the central theme of a son's effort to fight against the spiritual vampirism of his mother. Yet few would disagree, however perversely, that this incident was less horrible than the one recounted by Louisa Alcott in fanning the balefire of her jolly moral tale.

Notes

1. E. T., *D. H. Lawrence: A Personal Record* (London, 1935), p. 92.
2. Louisa May Alcott, *Little Men: Life at Plumfield with Jo's Boys* (Philadelphia, 1928), pp. 116–21.
3. *Little Men*, p. 116.
4. D. H. Lawrence, *Sons and Lovers* (New York, 1913 and 1922), pp. 70–71.

5. Cf. the comment of Graham Hough on the passage, in *The Dark Sun: A Study of D. H. Lawrence* (New York, 1957), p. 52: "Realistically considered, it is simply an act of despairing mercy. Symbolically, it has another significance. Here, where the regression of Paul's character has reached its farthest point, there is still something within him which is capable of decisive action—capable even of killing the mother to whom he is bound, to liberate both of them and to end her agony and his." Lawrence, I think, must have been unaware of the symbolic meaning; nevertheless, in accepting that meaning, I should wish to push it even further than Hough does in his admirable study.

6. Quoted, *ibid.*, p. 36.
7. Lawrence, *Sons and Lovers*, p. 254.
8. *Ibid.*, pp. 340–41.

[Review of *Eight Cousins; or, The Aunt-Hill*, 1875]

Henry James*

It is sometimes affirmed by the observant foreigner, on visiting these shores, and indeed by the venturesome native, when experience has given him the power of invidious comparison, that American children are without a certain charm usually possessed by the youngsters of the Old World. The little girls are apt to be pert and shrill, the little boys to be aggressive and knowing; both the girls and boys are accused of lacking, or of having lost, the sweet, shy bloom of ideal infancy. If this is so, the philosophic mind desires to know the reason of it, and when in the course of its enquiry the philosophic mind encounters the tales of Miss Alcott, we think it will feel a momentary impulse to cry Eureka! Miss Alcott is the novelist of children— the Thackeray, the Trollope, of the nursery and the school-room. She deals with the social questions of the child-world, and, like Thackeray and Trollope, she is a satirist. She is extremely clever, and, we believe, vastly popular with infant readers. In this, her latest volume, she gives us an account of a little girl named Rose, who has seven boisterous boy-cousins, several grotesque aunts, and a big burly uncle, an honest seaman, addicted to riding a tilt at the shams of life. He finds his little niece encompassed with a great many of these, and Miss Alcott's tale is chiefly devoted to relating how he plucked them successively away. We find it hard to describe our impression of it without appearing to do injustice to the author's motives. It is evidently written in very good faith, but it strikes us as a very ill-chosen sort of entertainment to set before children. It is unfortunate not only in its details, but in its general tone, in the constant ring of the style. The smart satirical tone is the last one in the world to be used in describing to children their elders and betters and the social mysteries that surround them. Miss Alcott seems to have a private understanding with the youngsters she depicts, at the expense of their pastors and masters; and her idea of friendliness to the infant

*Reprinted from the *Nation*, 21 (14 October 1875), 250–51.

generation seems to be, at the same time, to initiate them into the humorous view of them taken by their elders when the children are out of the room. In this last point Miss Alcott does not perhaps go so far as some of her fellow-chroniclers of the nursery (in whom the tendency may be called nothing less than depraved), but she goes too far, in our opinion, for childish simplicity or parental equanimity. All this is both poor entertainment and poor instruction. What children want is the objective, as the philosophers say; it is good for them to feel that the people and things around them that appeal to their respect are beautiful and powerful specimens of that they seem to be. Miss Alcott's heroine is evidently a very subjective little girl; and certainly her history will deepen the subjective tendency in the little girls who read it. She "observes in a pensive tone" that her health is considered bad. She charms her uncle by telling him, when he intimates that she may be vain, that "she don't think she is repulsive." She is sure, when she has left the room, that people are talking about her; when her birthday arrives she "feels delicate about mentioning it." Her conversation is salted with the feminine humor of the period. When she falls from her horse, she announces that "her feelings are hurt, but her bones are all safe." She certainly reads the magazines, and perhaps even writes for them. Her uncle Alec, with his crusade against the conventionalities, is like a young lady's hero of the "Rochester" school astray in the nursery. When he comes to see his niece he descends from her room by the water-spout; why not by a rope-ladder at once? When her aunts give her medicine, he surreptitiously replaces the pills with pellets of brown-bread, and Miss Alcott winks at the juvenile reader at the thought of how the aunts are being humbugged. Very likely many children are overdosed; but this is a poor matter to tell children stories about. When the little girl makes a long, pert, snubbing speech to one of her aunts, who has been enquiring into her studies, and this poor lady has been driven from the room, he is so tickled by what would be vulgarly called her "cheek" that he dances a polka with her in jubilation. This episode has quite spoiled, for our fancy, both the uncle and the niece. What have become of the "Rollo" books of our infancy and the delightful "Franconia" tales? If they are out of print, we strongly urge that they be republished, as an antidote to this unhappy amalgam of the novel and the story-book. These charming tales had, relatively speaking, an almost Homeric simplicity and "objectivity." The aunts in "Rollo" were all wise and comfortable, and the nephews and nieces were never put under the necessity of teaching them their place. The child-world was not a world of questions, but of things, and though the things were common and accessible to all children, they seemed to have the glow of fairy-land upon them. But in 'Eight Cousins' there is no glow and no fairies; it is all prose, and to our sense rather vulgar prose.

[Review of *Eight Cousins; or, The Aunt-Hill*, 1875]

Anonymous*

Miss Alcott is always welcome, not only to the boys and girls she has taken under her special patronage, but also to their elders, whom she does not seem to love nearly so much; indeed, she inverts the old nursery traditions of infallibility, and most openly and audaciously gives her verdict that children are generally in the right! This, we suppose, inclines the hearts of young readers to her. They know that in her they have a friend who understands and sympathizes with their difficulties. It is true that in her hands even naughty, tiresome children are amenable to reason and good example; but then she has the making of her own pattern parents and guardians, who seem to understand, as by some magic, how to throw light into the dark corners and crooked windings of the children's hearts, and to find out the best way to put them to rights. Elder readers, who have to take things as they find them, and make the best of their own unwritten difficulties and unsolved problems, can at least profit by studying the spirit in which Miss Alcott works in the little allotment she has appropriated in the morning-land of childhood; and they will rejoice in the bright and cheerful view of life and its duties with which she always closes her stories, even when she has been obliged to inflict the sorrows and perplexities of its harder lessons upon her beloved little men and women as they grow up. Miss Alcott's stories are thoroughly healthy, full of racy fun and humour, even when she is teaching some extra hard task which must be learned and accomplished. *The Eight Cousins* consist of a clan of seven boys, all of different ages and dispositions, and in different stages of what maiden aunts and old servants designate as "being rampageous." The eighth cousin is a charming little girl, an orphan, who plays the part of fairy princess and good angel to the boys, who worship her, wonder at her, teaze her, and obey her, whilst she, in her turn, under the wise guidance of "Uncle Alec," her guardian, grows out of a puny, sickly, over-taught little girl at a boarding-school, into a healthy, happy, sensible, and well-educated little maiden, able to hold her own and enforce respect, as well as hearty love, upon her unruly subjects. The influence for good of a gentle little mortal girl upon the rough and not by any means perfect specimens of the "superior sex" is true to life, and Miss Alcott works out the problem of woman's real mission in its elementary state not only with tact and skill, but with advantage to the story, which is exceedingly entertaining. The boys are American boys, though they call themselves the "Clan Campbell," and wear kilts, and dance the Highland Fling; but boy nature is much the same at the bottom all the world over. Miss Alcott's "Uncle Alec" preaches his doctrines about female upbringing, and raises his voice and his example against the specially American defects in the education and training of girls; but the good sense can bear tranfusion into

*Reprinted from the *Athenæum* (London), 66 (23 October 1875), 539.

English homes, for though in England we may avoid some of the errors into which America falls as regards the education of girls, we have faults enough of our own to make it possible that we may profit by Uncle Alec's precepts and practice in matters of health and dress and useful feminine accomplishments. There is another excellence in this book. Although there are seven boy cousins, one or two of whom are quite *men* in their own eyes, and although there is a lovely fascinating little girl, who grows up to be a charming young lady, there is not one breath of precocious sentiment, and the frank healthy cousinly element is not disturbed by a single hint of love or lovers to come hereafter, and this we take to be an example which might be followed with great advantage in many of our own stories for the young, which are neither more nor less than diminutive and diluted novels. We can recommend *The Eight Cousins* as an entertaining and healthy story.

[Review of *Eight Cousins; or, The Aunt-Hill*, 1875]

Anonymous*

Miss Alcott has fairly won the title of "The Children's Friend," and she will lose nothing of former prestige in the chatty-volume before us, dedicated "To the many boys and girls whose letters it has been impossible to answer," and to whom she would now make a peace-offering. The fact of the work having first appeared serially will not decrease its popularity, for, like the author's previous works, it carries its own recommendation with it. There are the same vigor, discrimination, character-portraiture, and racy dialogue that characterize all her writings. It is no mean artist who can group with consummate skill a score or more of prominent figures, and still bring his hero or heroine into bold relief, at the same time preserving the distinct individuality of every leading character. This Miss Alcott achieves with rare genius and ability. She marshals her battalion of uncles, aunts, cousins, nephews, and nieces with the dexterity of a commanding general, and every one of them steps forth with military precision at the word of command. It would be quite impossible to mistake the beautiful and meek Aunt Peace, with hair as white as snow and cheeks that never bloomed, but ever cheerful, busy, and full of interest in all that went on in the family, especially the joys and sorrows of the young girls growing up about her, to whom she was adviser, *confidante*, and friend in all their tender trials and delights. Equally impossible would it be to fail to discern instantly the striking individuality of Aunt Plenty—the stout brisk old lady, with a sharp eye, a lively tongue, and a face like a winter-apple, always trotting, chatting, and bustling amid a great commotion of "stiff loops of purple ribbon that bristled all over her cap, like crocus-buds."

*Reprinted from the *Overland Monthly*, 15 (November 1875), 493–94.

In character analysis, Miss Alcott shows herself the true artist. She is also most skillful in the construction of her plot, if, indeed, she can be said to lay out a plot; for plots too often have a well-rounded completeness that suggests unreality, whereas Miss Alcott's stories are too life-like to have smooth sailing throughout the voyage; nor must the reader expect everything to come out "just right," as the world would have it.

The heroine of the story before us, little Rose — a delicate, sensitive, fastidious child, with much good common-sense and generous gifts of mind and heart — is left an orphan at an early age, and turned over to the tender mercies of a bevy of aunts, uncles, and cousins, who pass critical judgment upon the "morbid, spoilt girl, so plainly marked for the tomb." But Rose herself has no predisposition in favor of early death, and with keen womanly instinct betakes herself to the sheltering fondness of sensible Uncle Alec, and on the wings of his gentle counsel she mounts toward sunnier skies. Uncle Alec is in strong contrast with Uncle Enos, to whose tender mercies Christie was consigned, in Miss Alcott's wholesome and able story, *Work*. Whether Rose is to develop any of those fine qualities of womanly character evinced by Christie in the manifold vicissitudes through which she passed before she found her David only to lose him again, the ingenious authoress leaves us to guess, only promising to divulge the secret in a forthcoming volume, whose advent will be hailed with ill-concealed curiosity and interest.

We catch a momentary glimpse of some of the strong points of Rose's character in her occasional outbursts toward some pet aversion in the way of a playmate, as, for instance, Ariadne Blish, who was picked out as the model child of the neighborhood to come and play with her, but whom Rose declared to be so perfectly horrid that she could not bear the sight of her, and said "she was so like a wax doll that she longed to give her a pinch and see if she would squeak."

Phebe, the girl from the poor-house, evokes the keenest interest, and the real character of the heroine Rose is best displayed by her treatment of and interest in this hapless but happy child, "whose heart was so full of content that it overflowed in music, and the sweet voice singing all about the house gave thanks so blithely that no other words were needed. Her willing feet were never tired of taking steps for those who had smoothed her way; her skillful hands were always busy in some labor of love for them, and on the face fast growing in comeliness, there was an almost womanly expression of devotion, which proved how well Phebe had already learned one of life's great lessons — gratitude."

The sequel to this interesting and delicious little story will be eagerly looked for by the many admirers of this gifted author, who is always welcomed not only by the children in short-clothes, but by the "children of a larger growth" as well.

[Review of *Rose in Bloom: A Sequel to "Eight Cousins,"* 1876]

Anonymous*

Miss Alcott's *Rose in Bloom* (Roberts Bros.), being a sequel to her *Eight Cousins*, requires a previous acquaintance with her latter work. Rose, who returns from Europe, is engaged as the story ends; but as the line between what is juvenile reading and what is not must be drawn somewhere, we suppose childish curiosity in regard to her married life will not be gratified. Her lover seeks to give a direction to her blooming and unfolding, and hands her Emerson's *Essays* with marked passages and leaves turned down; tells her that Emerson "has done more to set young men and women thinking than any man in this century at least"; quotes "my Thoreau" at her, by way of "poetical reproof"; and easily beguiles her into correspondence on the subject of her reading. Mac's declaration and subsequent courtship take us to the utmost verge of fiction for minors.

[Review of *Under the Lilacs* and *Jack and Jill,* 1905 reprints]

Anonymous*

Two . . . old friends, revived and newly dressed, are Miss Alcott's *Under the Lilacs* and *Jack and Jill* (Little, Brown & Co.), both illustrated prettily in black and white, the former by Alice Barber Stephens, the latter by Harriet Roosevelt Richards. The renascence of former acquaintances like these gives something to think of in relation to the then and now of children's books. There have been critics who, while delighting in the generally bracing atmosphere of Miss Alcott's books, have found somewhat to object to in the slang, the untidy English, and even more strongly in the amateur lovemaking. Upon the charge of slang it must be owned that wonder-working Time has had an effect. Whether because the slang of yesterday is often the usage of to-day, or because every succeeding period has bettered the instruction of the original villainy — who shall say? An enormous amount of cruelty to children has been perpetuated in this way. Certainly the Alcott books read less offendingly than they once did in this respect. As to the lovemaking in them, it remains a distinct blot on girl and boy literature. Not that it ever monopolises the scene or takes any but a natural turn. The plea that "things are so" is irrelevant. This, the crux of so much of the whole dispute in art matters, may well be waived for our children. They will not be hurt by exaggeration in what a modern writer calls "the hoary bugbear of retributive justice"; but a good many "things" that

*Reprinted from the *Nation*, 23 (21 December 1876), 373.
*Reprinted from the *Nation*, 81 (16 November 1905), 406.

are "so" should be postponed to a later day. It is fair to say that *Under the Lilacs* is an exception in this matter so far as the boys and girls go. But why need the leading lady read letters with a far-away look?

[Review of *Jack and Jill: A Village Story*, 1880]

Anonymous*

Miss Alcott's *Jack and Jill* has the merits of her writing more conspicuously than the faults. There is the generous confidence in children which she always shows, the rosy light in which she looks upon the hobbledehoy period, and the persistent lesson of kindness, charity, and amiable sacrifice. The scenes are lively, the incidents varied, and a cheerfulness predominates which is justified by the unfailing success of every character in the book. Yet there is nothing like real character drawing, and the air of life in the book is secured not by an endowment of the persons represented, but by the animation and cheeriness of the author. Nor can we altogether find satisfaction in the suppressed love-making of these young people. The author protests that she is only drawing the picture of a natural society of boys and girls who are soon to be young men and young women, but there is a self-consciousness about the book on this side which impairs its simplicity. We are, no doubt, unreasonable readers; we object to the blood-and-thunder literature, and when in place of it we have the milk-and-sugar we object again. What do we want?

[Review of *Jo's Boys and How They Turned Out: A Sequel to "Little Men,"* 1886]

Anonymous*

It has been some years since the best of our story writers for children has written anything, and the many early admirers of Miss Alcott, the fathers and mothers of to-day, will be delighted to meet once more their former acquaintances, those bright boys and girls who peopled her pages. In *Jo's Boys* the lads have grown older, as have the girls. But they are all as pleasing as of yore. Miss Alcott, whose books have made her famous, tells humorously how such *kudo* brings with it penalties. Anybody who has read *Little Men* seems to think he has a perfect right to call on Miss Alcott, to tramp over her grounds, and to insist on having her autograph. Bevies of

*Reprinted from the *Atlantic Monthly*, 47 (January 1881), 123–24.
*Reprinted from the *New York Times*, 26 October 1886, p. 10.

schoolgirls on their vacation demand recognition. This is a charming bit, which we do not think is imaginative on Miss Alcott's part, for it sounds true. The servant says: "A queer kind of lady wants to know if she can catch a grasshopper in the garden." "A what?" . . . "A grasshopper, ma'am. I said you were busy, and asked what she wanted, and says she, 'I've got grasshoppers from the grounds of several famous folks, and I want one from Plumfield to add to my collection.' Did you ever!" The authoress, Mrs. Bhaer, gives her consent, and presently her maid returns. "She's much obliged, ma'am, and she'd like an old gown or a pair of stockings of yours to put in a rug she's making. Got a vest of Emerson's she says, and a pair of Mr. Holmes's trousers and a dress of Mrs. Stowe's." *Jo's Boys* gives the last, the very, very last appearance of all the characters. When they have grown to be men and women Nan remains a spinster, Stuffy becomes an Alderman, Dolly a tailor, Rob a Professor, and Teddy a clergyman, and so the curtain falls on the Marsh [sic] family.

The New Woman Revisited [in *Jo's Boys*]

Carolyn Forrey*

[Discussion of concept of New Woman in literature deleted.]

Among the earliest of American novelists to champion the ideal of the New Woman was Louisa May Alcott, who is more apt to be identified with sentimentality and domestic virtues than with a crusading feminist spirit. Yet while she upheld a domestic ideal in her novels and drew as well as anyone portraits of old-fashioned femininity, she was very sympathetic to the emancipation of women. She was an advocate of higher education for women; she favored woman's suffrage; and she appears to have believed that any woman who wanted a career should have one, even if it meant rejecting marriage and motherhood. A reader who knows Louisa May Alcott only as the author of *Little Women* might do well to look at *Jo's Boys* (1886), a later novel in which her sympathies for the New Woman are quite evident.

Jo's Boys shows us the little women grown to middle age. Jo and her professor husband run a co-educational college, Plumfield. Jo also has her own career as a novelist. Amy, another of the original little women, is an artist happily married: "she was one of those who prove that women can be faithful wives and mothers without sacrificing the special gift bestowed upon them for their own development and the good of others."[1] By setting her story at a co-educational college, Alcott gave herself a vehicle for dis-

---

*Reprinted from *Women's Studies*, 2 (1974), 40–42. Reprinted by permission of Gordon & Breach Science Publishers, Inc., London.

cussing the issues of woman's emancipation. Her young women scholars all ponder over and compare their talents and ambitions in life, and argue with their male counterparts about woman's abilities and role. These young women have been taken out of their own homes, and albeit Plumfield is a peculiarly domestic institution, here they are free to prove what they can do.

One young woman, Daisy, is a thoroughly old-fashioned girl, a dutiful and docile daughter with an enormous reverence for her mother. Daisy longs only for "a nice little home and family to take care of" (p. 12). She promptly falls in love and at the end of the novel is married in conventional style. However, Alcott showed little enthusiasm for her angelic Daisy. Daisy is described as "a dear" but also as "an old fogie" by other characters in the novel, and the author takes no pains to contradict the latter epithet. Her most evident sympathy is with two other characters in the novel—Josie and Nan.

Josie is introduced as a little "romp," leaping over hedges, climbing trees and tearing her skirts in her spirited play. She is anything but prim, and no one wants her to change. Her good-natured mischievousness provides a measure of comic relief in a novel full of serious-minded characters. Josie is a fiercely competitive and self-assertive girl. She is hotly indignant at the suggestion that women ought to obey men and look up to them as wiser beings. She declares that her brain is just as good as a boy's, and struggles to beat the boys at tennis with no thought of preserving masculine pride or the illusion of feminine frailty. Josie has a great ambition to be an actress, despite the fact that the stage is looked upon as an unwholesome atmosphere for a decent young woman. She works hard at her drama and in the end wins everyone over to her plans. We are told that she will win honors on the stage and find a worthy mate besides.

The strongest New Woman figure in the novel is Nan, formerly "Naughty Nan" the romp, now "the pride of the community." Nan is a young doctor who finds so much satisfaction in her work that nothing can turn her from it. A model of the educated woman, she holds advanced views on all reforms, especially woman's rights, and is a staunch advocate of woman's suffrage. Nan is plagued by a young suitor, Tom, who constantly follows her around begging her to marry him. A good wife and a nice little home, he tells her, are "what a fellow needs to keep him steady; and it's the duty of nice girls to marry as soon as possible" (p. 22). Alcott did believe in the steadying power of marriage and home, but she apparently did not believe that it was any girl's duty to sacrifice her own plans for marriage. Jo, who is Alcott's surrogate in the novel, supports Nan in her desire for independence, declaring: "That girl shall *not* be hampered by a foolish boy's fancy. In a moment of weariness she may give in, and then it's all over. Wiser women have done so and regretted it all their lives. Nan shall earn her place first, and prove that she can fill it; then she may marry if she likes, and can find a man worthy of her" (p. 150). There is no danger, however, of

Nan's sacrificing her career for marriage. She is determined to be a "useful, happy, and independent spinster," which is exactly what she does become. She dedicates her life to relieving suffering, "in which true woman's work," Alcott assures us, "she found abiding happiness" (p. 365). Apparently there is no man worthy of her.

There are plenty of weddings in the novel; indeed, Alcott seems to have thought it her duty to the expectations of her readers to provide them. There is much domestic sentiment and an inordinate amount of reverence for motherhood. Alcott fulfilled all the demands of the sentimental domestic novel and did not reject the old feminine virtues, but she thoroughly admired the New Woman. She saw more than one path to woman's self-fulfillment: old-style marriage and motherhood, marriage and motherhood combined with a career, or a career alone with no strings attached. The philosophy of her novel is that each girl should be free to choose her own mode of life and her own kind of happiness. Woman's sphere is not necessarily the home; woman's sphere is wherever she finds it.

[Analysis of New Woman theme in works by other authors deleted.]

Notes

1. Louisa May Alcott, *Jo's Boy's, and How They turned Out* (1886; rpt. Boston, 1898), 27. Additional page references are to this edition.

SCRAP-BAGS AND COLLECTIONS

[Review of *Aunt Jo's Scrap-Bag*, I, 1872]

Anonymous*

We brought home Miss Alcott's last book, and left it unintentionally on our library table. Our home *sanctum* is not so sacred but that after tea the children have the liberty of it; and we were scarcely engaged in a social conversation in the parlor adjoining before the shouts of laughter from the library became so loud and long as to threaten serious consequences, and invoke visions of bursting blood-vessels. This was our introduction to *Aunt Jo's Scap-Bag* (Roberts Brothers). We afterward read the mirth-provoking scrap, "the children's joke." We are afraid that serious-minded parents who think that children in this age are too "fast" would hardly approve this chapter, if, indeed, they did any other in the book; but we know more than one household where we wish it could be perpetrated, and the parents could wear for twenty-four hours the strait-jacket in which they ordinarily keep their children.

[Review of *Aunt Jo's Scrap-Bag*, II, 1872]

Anonymous*

One hardly knows whether to class *Shawl-Straps* (Roberts Brothers) with fiction or with books of travel. It is the latter under the guise of the former. The travelers are three girls, and their perpetual conversation, which sometimes becomes a chatter, gives to the tour a dramatic form if not a truly dramatic interest. Miss Alcott's style is so well known that we can not better characterize this little volume than by simply saying that it is her last book. It is always vivacious, but not always natural and simple. It contains a good deal of fresh information and but little that is stale, and on the whole affords a decidedly agreeable method of visiting the places it describes— Brittany, France, Switzerland, Italy, and Sweden.

*Reprinted from *Harper's New Monthly Magazine*, 44 (February 1872), 463.
*Reprinted from *Harper's New Monthly Magazine*, 46 (March 1873), 616.

[Review of *Aunt Jo's Scrap-Bag*, III, 1874]

Anonymous*

Miss Alcott's little stories are written in that peculiar vein which interests alike children and those of older growth. For the little ones, there is plenty of incident and adventure, for the elders, a thoughtful portraiture of character; and a verisimilitude that appeals to both—"Nelly's Hospital" and "Cupid and Chow-Chow," are each a finished story, and impress themselves upon the childish memory. One of the best of holiday series is *Aunt Jo's Scrap-Bag.*

["Transcendental Wild Oats," 1873]

William Henry Harrison*

Louisa May Alcott's "Transcendental Wild Oats" is a fictionalized account of her father Bronson Alcott's utopian venture, the Fruitlands community. Louisa was only a child of ten when she came to Fruitlands; she became eleven on November 29, 1843. Thirty years after the abandonment of the idealistic venture, her story of the experiment was published.

Considering it a wild, harebrained scheme, Louisa pokes mild fun at Fruitlands' slightly madcap follies. She never grasped her father's ideology, a mystic and speculative philosophy; she made that clear when asked by Professor William Torrey Harris to write a biography of her father. "His philosophy I have never understood," she replied, "and biography is not in my line . . . . He has seen several of his ideals become facts and that is more than most of us ever do . . . ." [from a letter in the Fruitlands Museums Library]

Can "Transcendental Wild Oats" be taken as a reliable history of the Fruitlands community? Only in part. There is no question that absurdities such as Louisa recounts took place. This community (or "commune," as it would be known today) had its zany side; it attracted some freaks, cranks, and near lunatics. But there were also those who could be taken very seriously. In this story, the ludicrous obscures the serious intentions of the founders, Bronson Alcott and Charles Lane. One is reminded of Emerson's remark concerning some dubious, radical reform literature Alcott had sent him from England in 1842, the year before Fruitlands was established. "They speak to the conscience," Emerson commented, "and have that su-

---

*Reprinted from *Godey's Lady's Book*, 88 (February 1874), 186.

*Reprinted from *Transcendental Wild Oats and excerpts from the Fruitlands diary*, by Louisa May Alcott, introduction by William Henry Harrison (Boston: Harvard Common Press, 1981), pp. 1–2, 8. Reprinted with permission of the publisher.

periority over the crowd of their contemporaries, which belongs to men who entertain a good hope."

The final episode in Louisa's story, where Alcott takes to his bed in despair, was probably fabricated for a reading public with an insatiable appetite for the sentimental and melodramatic. The Victorian deathbed scene was popular, and Louisa presents it in full and mournful measure; but the present-day reader is tempted to smile instead of cry. That Bronson Alcott was depressed by the turn of events at Fruitlands is only natural. But we find no mention of this incident elsewhere, and the conduct described in this story does seem uncharacteristic of the ever-hopeful Alcott.

[Discussion of Fruitlands background and characters deleted.]

The transition from "Fruitlands" to "Apple Slump" was not as dramatic an event as Louisa describes it.

[Review of *Silver Pitchers: And Independence, A Centennial Love Story,* 1876]

Anonymous*

"Silver Pitchers," the first story in Miss Alcott's volume is a pretty temperance tale, much pleasanter than temperance moralities have the gift of being in general. It tells how three beautiful young girls made a league together to induce the young men of their acquaintance to forswear the use of wine or stimulants. The young ladies in Miss Alcott's tale are American, and the conditions of American society are somewhat different from our own, so that English girls, whilst adopting the spirit, must carry out the details according to their own sense of ingenuity and propriety. It is, however, a certain fact that if women choose they can do more for the cause of temperance than all the "Permissive Bills" and speeches in Parliament or elsewhere put together. The other stories in this volume are not temperance tales, but pretty, graceful sketches, such as Miss Alcott well knows how to write. "Letty's Tramp" is the best, but we wish there had been some further intelligence about the "Little Men and Women," and above all some tidings about that darling of our heart, the Old-fashioned Girl, who, we heartily hope, is still alive and well.

*Reprinted from the *Athenæum* (London), 68 (12 August 1876), 206.

[Review of *Proverb Stories*, 1882]

Anonymous*

We are a little puzzled as to the class of readers for which Miss Alcott's *Proverb Stories* are intended. Not for children, at least not for English children; for there is a great deal of love-making, while the tales are hardly of sufficient weight to satisfy the demands of later and more exacting years. "Kitty's Class Day" is a sketch of the typical American damsel (of fiction) who contrives to make an elegant toilet out of the commonest materials, and is rewarded somewhat unkindly by discovering that she would have had more real happiness had she appeared among her brilliant companions in a much-washed muslin. We doubt whether the moral is true to human nature, least of all to American human nature. Miss Alcott has, however, a bright picturesque way of telling things, which is particularly exemplified in "A Country Christmas."

[Review of *Lulu's Library*, I, 1886]

Anonymous*

Miss Louisa Alcott has made her specialty of those years in a girl's life that come between the time of the doll and the time of the lover. She has written of all the phases of youth—of bridals and of schools and of "little men" and of young mothers. But her own subject is the girl proper. In *Lulu's Library*, however, she writes of little children for little children, and does it charmingly. Best, perhaps, of the stories is that which tells of Lily's journey into Candy Country, Cake Land, and Bread Land. Excursionists of this kind have followed now for some twenty years the footsteps of Alice into Wonderland; but Miss Alcott shows a fresh inventiveness, and takes her little readers so realistically through the sticky and indigestible countries of sweets and cakes that they will enjoy the plain loaf at the end in perfect sympathy with the heroine. Names of good things are generally international enough, we find, for English readers, though some of the candies and "cookies" may need translation, and there is more maize meal in the wholesome country than our little ones are accustomed to. The book is very prettily illustrated.

---

*Reprinted from the *Saturday Review of Politics, Literature, Science, and Art*, 54 (9 December 1882), 774.

*Reprinted from the *Saturday Review of Politics, Literature, Science, and Art*, 62 (3 July 1886), 27.

The Promise of Destiny [in *Aunt Jo's Scrap-Bags*]

Joy A. Marsella*

. . . Her stories pleased the editors of the children's periodicals which published them. . . . Most of the editors looked for "well-devised plots" that showed characters engaged in "healthy thinking" and "brave action." Because Louisa May Alcott's stories so clearly formed minds, prepared hearts, and molded characters, these editors were overjoyed to have her among their contributors.

. . . the sixty stories in the five volumes of the *Scrap-Bag* [Volume II of the series, *Shawl-Straps*, a travelogue, is not considered] fulfill and complement the goals of the editors of these children's periodicals. The characterizations and conflicts in her stories are defined by a moral code. . . . the basic tenets of the code—labor, love, and hope—fulfilled the moral requirements the editors set.

. . . Alcott's stories reflect the cultural traditions of domesticity that made up the world of mid-nineteenth century children and women. . . . Alcott truly believed both children and young women were meant to fulfill a higher destiny than the previous generation had; her stories showed us examples of children and women who, in her terms, "lead the way."

. . . Alcott brings to the tradition of the children's story several gifts: a strong narrative voice and the use of imaginative insights that grow out of her sense of an essential underlying spirit—certainly a transcendental touch inherited from her father and his friends—which imparts a kind of power or magic to what she says. . . . The stories are . . . primarily . . . cultural documents and secondarily . . . works of art. . . . Alcott intended that they be interpreted as teaching stories. As did other female writers of the nineteenth century, Alcott wanted her readers to take away a lesson that would help them in their lives.

---

*Reprinted from *The Promise of Destiny: Children and Women in the Short Stories of Louisa May Alcott* (Westport, Conn.: Greenwood Press, 1983), pp. xxi–xxiii.

DEVIATIONS FROM THE PATTERN

Work

[Review of *Work: A Story of Experience*, 1873]
Anonymous*

These two books [*The Other Girls*, by Mrs. A. D. T. Whitney (Low & Co.) and *Work* by Louisa May Alcott] deal with the same topics: what women can do, what women may do, and what women ought to do. In both there are clever sketches of life and character under various aspects. The difficulties and obstacles that make working for a living so hard to women are described with truth and reality. Above all, there is plenty of wise and understanding sympathy with the temptations that specially beset the path of women, dazzling their eyes and wounding their hearts, until the right way seems to be even harder to find than to pursue. . . . [comparison with *The Other Girls* deleted].

Work: A Story of Experience, is full of good and excellent passages; but we miss the cheery energy there was in the *Old-Fashioned Girl*, *Little Women*, *Good Wives*, and other works, too numerous to specify, for which we have to thank Miss Alcott. She uses her present heroine, Christie Devon, worse than ever the traditional step-mother in fairy-tales used the neglected child: — much worse; for she does not even leave her to be "happy ever after," when her tasks are finished and the rightful Prince has come! Poor Christie Devon, after turning her hand to everything that a woman's hand can find to do, and doing it heartily, though she is bruised, and battered, and all but beaten in her battle with the world, has just attained a comfortable haven, and married a good man whom she loves, when the authoress swoops down upon her once more, with "the uses of adversity," and heaps upon her more sorrow, bent on distilling the very coldest, purest, and dreadfully precious elixir from it all. The reader feels that a little bit of happiness would have been much better for everybody, and much more like the real "Providence that shapes our ends." The story of *Work* is too restless; and the result is so fatiguing, that we should not be surprised if the reader, after finishing it, gives up, and refuses to do anything whatever for the rest of the day.

*Reprinted from the *Athenæum* (London), 62 (26 July 1873), 111.

[Review of *Work: A Story of Experience*, 1873]

Anonymous*

. . . Miss Alcott's first real novel, *Work* (Roberts Brothers), is perhaps the most noteworthy [of recently published novels], as it certainly is the most noted. Miss Alcott's name will give to this pleasant story a circulation and a celebrity which otherwise it would not attain. The book would not have made her reputation, but her reputation will make the book. The first thing that strikes the reader after he gets fairly under way is that the novel is not a novel at all, but a serious didactic essay on the subject of woman's work. Not, indeed, that Miss Alcott has loaded it with instruction, or put on any unwomanly vestments and taken to preaching in the guise of a storyteller; but the bee on the cover, the motto on the title-page, the title itself, and the current and course of the story, all point in the same direction. Miss Alcott wished to exhibit the various phases of woman's work, and the story was the instrument she chose for that purpose. Christie starts out in the opening chapter to take care of herself. She tries various avocations, and her hardships in each are graphically described. She is successively servant, actress, governess, companion, seamstress, assistant, and finally nurse in a soldiers' hospital.

The first half of the story is without even the semblance of a plot. Miss Alcott appears to have sat down to write the first chapter without knowing what the next chapter would be, and to have drifted along in the current of her own thoughts till she found a novel growing under her hands. Then, under a sense that a novel needs design, she conceived a simple one, and finished off her series of sketches in a very simply constructed story. But despite this defect, and it is a serious one, she has written what is both an interesting and an entertaining narrative. Some of her pictures are exceedingly pretty; some of her characters are exceedingly well drawn. The best bit of painting in the book is Mrs. Wilkins and her home; and the contrast between the tireless energy of the wife and the nerveless quiet of the husband gives vividness to both. In Mrs. Wilkins's home the unmanageable children play a principal part; and with them Miss Alcott is unmistakably in her element. Mr. Power may be a portrait, as some of the critics have thought it, of Theodore Parker; if so, it is a portrait drawn by a feminine admirer, and clothed with traits that woman's admiring imagination easily attributes to her heroes. A pleasant humor sparkles in the book, and a cheerful good nature imparts to it a singularly pleasant flavor. It is this sunny cheerfulness infused through all its pages by the glow of a woman's bright, trusting, and loving heart, and which imbitters even the death of David "Sunrise," which gives to the book its peculiar charm, and will make it acceptable to hundreds of readers, who will rise from its perusal stronger for the battle of life because of its inspiration, and who will hardly recognize,

*Reprinted from *Harper's New Monthly Magazine*, 47 (September 1873), 618–19.

though they may vaguely feel, the defects which impair it as a work of art. In brief, passing by the externals of this story, which are not above criticism, and getting at its heart, we may say of it what Mrs. Wilkins said of Mr. Powers's preaching: "Ain't it fillin'? Don't it give you a kind of spiritual h'ist, and make things wuth more, somehow?"

[Review of *Work: A Story of Experience*, 1873] Anonymous*

This novel has been very highly praised, and in some quarters where favorable verdicts are usually delivered with some circumspection. The standard of its merit, then, has been lifted pretty high. With this reflection disappears whatever may have collected itself on a lower plane for commendation; and the applause with which we might have testified Miss Alcott's success in several of the minor colloquies—for example, that in which the heroine consults Cinthy Wilkins about accepting Philip Fletcher's second offer—is dumb before the demand for a suffrage for or against the effort as a whole. True, the title and plan of the book solicit from the reader a discriminating judgment. But it is stern to take a novelist too strictly at his word; for if the work is engaging, and not too obtrusively faulty, it may deserve praise enough to justify its publication. Here, however, the author's admirers, by approving her execution of the undertaking, constrain us to examine touching the validity of their praise.

In the first place, the undertaking itself is a questionable one. We would not light down on the very cover of the book with its single word "Work," and its symbolic bee, if we could not concede the fidelity with which the idea of work is adhered to throughout. Work is the real religion, the idea, the action of the piece, from end to end. We dare consent that work is an eminent excellence, essentially, attributively, instrumentally. The work of nature's meteorology and chemistry, the work of steam engines, the work of formulating ideas, realizing designs, chopping trees, or washing soiled clothes—all is excellent, because it is healthful in nature and man; it is useful, and, for the most part, indispensably requisite. More than any one thing, work brings happiness, and work secures against misery.

Such are the powerful motives to induce us all to go to work. And, in fact, we do so. But now is there not just about enough of this apotheosis of Madam Work? Is it not a frightful evil to the contemplation of our scientific teachers, that in this country we *over*work? In getting foremost, the strong are weakened, and the weak are destroyed. It has come to pass that he that works moderately lags, and must fail, if he does not perish. But is immoderate work less destructive than immoderate drink? Whether this morbid and

*Reprinted from the *Lakeside Monthly*, 10 (September 1873), 246–49.

ruinous industry is chargeable to at least fifty years' unchallenged supremacy of Work over every other god in New England, or to the mere intensity of competing ambition and avarice, it is certain that the practice is absolutely baleful of glorifying aught that has even the name of vice confessedly tending to general madness. In the South Sea, work is virtuous; in the United States, it is more than half vicious. Were a novel, under the title "Laziness," and with a moral distinctly in favor of a life of utter inconsequence, to circulate extensively, we put it to candor if, where it would unstring one worthy resolution, it would not redress a thousand senseless and criminal overtasks? The sober and wholesome *cui bono?* is perfectly unanswerable by those the state of whose nervous centres qualifies them to applaud everything that is exhaustively laborious; for the concluding phrase of this story is about as sensible an answer as the case admits of. The heroine, then a comfortable widow of forty, with a daughter to train, and poor people—the weak, the sick, the ignorant, or the vicious—immediately about her, to help, to strengthen, to instruct or to moderate, for any ten hours, any day, in any community, but—it must be admitted—with no field for gratifying her desire to be publicly distinguished above men and women generally, resolves to mount the rostrum for a public career. This "work" is characterized thus: "The greatest of God's gifts to us is the privilege of sharing His great work." Of course, it is the privilege of any person to sanctify his labors—even his vices—by the claim that he is "sharing God's work;" not that anybody in his senses believes that God needs his help in any way but perhaps by attending to his business without harming others, either by assaulting, oppressing, defrauding, or neglecting them, or, most culpably, by exciting their emulation for an unnatural and inevitably unrighteous scramble for some common object, in the hope of beating them, and calling it assistance rendered to God in his work; but that if he professes to believe it, nobody under the sun can gainsay him. In Western phrase, this is "too thin." There is a kind of intellectual nausea excited by the spectacle of a disguise at once so beggarly and so hardy, for motives so vulgar.

We therefore condemn as mischievous, in proportion to its success, any publication tending to increase the already unnatural ardor of effort by inculcating the glory of a life of work. But of this production we may contemplate the issue with limited anxiety.

Of numerous and variegated, rather than contrasted characters, there is not one whose make-up includes the ingredient—thought to be so necessary somewhere in every novel—of sentiment. There is not even religion, except in those decent, well-worn stage properties, not to be spared without awkward blanks from certain extremities, even in novels. Nothing ideal, poetical, or even finely meditative is suffered to expose the writer to the suspicion of sentimentalism. But the sentimentalism itself, which might at least have been caricatured and proscribed for symmetry sake, is ignored altogether. Some of the characters are foolish, some violent, some sordid, some generous, some strong, some weak; but amongst them all, nobody represents the sad, spiritual, beautiful nobody, who may be picked up any day, to make a necessary contrast to Christie, the heroine. Indeed, there is not a workless character in the whole plot, except Mrs. Saltonstall, a downright noodle.

The story is one of the most extraordinary assemblages of incredible events ever reconciled with a general air of verisimilitude. This is apparent upon the least scrutiny; though less so upon a careless perusal. A lady, whose only active solicitude is for her social position — which turns out to really be what was first signified by her liveried servants — employs a self-sufficient, nubile young stranger as a governess for her children, immediately on her presenting herself in answer to an advertisement, without even the form of a curiosity as to who she was; and her brother, an experienced man of the world, readily consents, still more improbably — he having just this much knowledge, that he secretly recognizes in her a person he had seen on the stage, a fact which she reserves. A family is introduced, in whom a known tendency to insanity — no very uncommon thing — remains entirely unsuspected by a younger sister, until she is a woman, when it is dramatically communicated, like a hitherto most practicable secret, by an older sister, who, while she is supposed to be still sane, though sick, in a manner the most strangely unfilial, with the sympathy of her brothers, too, declares war on her mother, not as a peevish ebullition, but as the result of solemn convictions of duty, for marrying their father with a knowledge of the malady in her relatives. That this conduct of a sane daughter did not set the mother crazy on the spot, she having — as yet potential, only — the whole stock of the dreaded insanity in her own head, is a separate and sufficiently absurd improbability; to which may be added the most improbably unsophisticated moral treatment — of course, he was a competent physician — of good Dr. Shirley. But no part of the narrative bears the least analysis. It is not a "Story of Experience," since, to befit that name, the situations should be uncommonly credible.

But the undeniable insufficiency of imagination, thought, and sentiment, giving the story a sort of jobbed appearance, is unerringly shown by — at this late day — introducing the once indispensable "nigger," with the cant of the subject in that coarseness of texture that refined abolitionists could indulge only during the delirium of the war; and which comes, in a book of this date, like that sometimes belated shriek, which would not have been rowdyish if it had come time enough to be tumultuous, in the general cheer. Slavery is abolished — let us have peace. For example, the husband of the heroine, entitled at least to die for his country in open battle, perishes in a despicable skirmish about a wench, who preferred an adventure in the Union camp to awaiting at home her certain deliverance from slavery. But this was preceded by an exploit, as whimsical as the occasion of it is inconceivable. All manner of white people conversant with negroes are acquainted with the practice of negresses toward their dead children. The Chinese, superior as they are, and, like negroes, making the funeral of adolescents or adults the occasions of ostentatious and clamorous grief, cast away the corpses of young children with indifference. Officials of the Freedmen's Bureau early discovered, what all Southern people had told them, that the average negro mother was not reliable for the nurture of her own living child, if found irksome. But the female contraband, in this case, in no respect presented as an exceptional person, in making her escape from slavery into a military camp, had, in a spirit assumed to be common to negro women, brought along a dead baby, which she said was hers. This she delivered to an officer of judgment and intelligence, of near two years' service thereabouts, who, in the most affecting manner, buries it with his own hands. There was no tie of acquaintance, reciprocity of favor, or even association of ideas, connecting the parties, to redeem the extreme poverty of this contrivance for aggrandizing the hero of a story. It would insult the author herself to ask what probably became of the wretched negress, after this supposed sacrifice of a valiant and useful citizen. It is the most natural thing in the world, that this species of enthusiastic, all embracing humanity, should elsewhere in the book confess utter intolerance for Irish.

The heroine herself is not a very distinct character. The publisher has been good enough to help the author by a portrait of Christie, at the head of the first chapter, of whom we are bound to say no phrenologist is needed to reveal her character—and it is a good one, too—even great. The girl in the picture is full of "work," of every kind, of ambition, of pride, generosity, passion, and affection. As long as she was not in love, she would have a strong prepossession for a "mission," a "self-relying career," and a "determined independence." But our word for it, when she found a man she deeply loved, she would reverence him with something the Christie whose story is told never so much as dreamed of—womanly selflessness. Then would come out a miraculous softness not possible to the self-defending, which, of course, is the same thing as the self-depending state. The girl in the picture would repulse with rash disgust and contempt the offer of a suitor that she did not respect. She could not possibly make up her mind to accept a man whose barren egotism she perfectly knew, and then, before she had time to say yes, refuse him irrevocably on the spot for making an inopportune manifestation of it. In actual life, this would betray a spirit meanly mercenary, willing to take a selfish invalid as a rich husband, provided he did not, by flagrantly exposing himself before marriage, compel her to admit that she knew what she was doing.

Again, the girl in the picture would never have loved—and, for that matter, neither would any superior girl—the David Sterling for whom the author has reserved her. The author says he was so and so pious and noble, and it is therefore to be so; but there is little enough to show it by. On the other hand, that impossible character—at least a trinity of persons in one—Philip Fletcher, by his devotion, shown in his lifting himself out of all the sloughs of petty egotism, indolence, and elegant debility, into comparative great-heartedness, all in order to please and win her, had claims on which no woman in the world would have turned her back in favor of the ready-made David, who, for aught we can see, was at least equally selfish, with that uncompromising kind of imperiousness which must be served implicitly, without even the joke of antagonism, because the moral excellence of the man, including perfect meekness, must be asserted for him by implications of plenary sanctity.

In a word, if the woman in the picture is the one in question, she never loved; or if that was love which made Christie nurse and serve David, even more faithfully than the other patients and soldiers amongst whom her well-done duties lay, it was the affection—ardent enough it may be, even intense to morbidness—of a woman, not gifted with the susceptibility of her sex, which makes the love of the right man, to none so much as to a strong and self-reliant woman, a transmuting spell—utterly transmuting, because her character had so distinct a pole to change, and joyfully did change it.

This book is the story of a female who was not a woman, married to her choice who was not a man, taking these plain old words differentially in the range of those deeper and grander phases of life, where instinct, intuition, or inspiration—call it what you will—prescribes the unwitnessed *work*, and listens neither for yea or nay. If that range is in the heart, this book has not a heart. We trust the author has.

Introduction to *Work: A Story of Experience* Sarah Elbert[*]

[Biographical information and discussions of other Alcott works have been deleted throughout.]

. . . *Work* is an expression of Alcott's feminist principles and a major effort toward synthesizing in popular, readable form the broad set of beliefs encompassing family, education, suffrage, labor and the moral reform of social life that defined feminist ideology in the nineteenth century. In addressing these concerns, she broadened the scope of her fiction from the domestic relations she excelled in portraying, to an urgent, passionate portrait of the female life cycle in all its complexity.

For modern readers, an understanding of *Work* is enhanced by the analysis of events, problems, and characters drawn from Alcott's own life and times. The novel develops a definition of womanhood shaped by the

---

[*]Reprinted from Louisa May Alcott, *Work*, edited by Sarah Elbert (New York: Schocken Books, 1977), pp. x, xxii–xxxvii, xl–xliii. Deletions necessitated the renumbering of notes. Reprinted by permission of Schocken Books Inc. from *Work*, by Louisa May Alcott. © 1977 by Schocken Books Inc.

changes and the continuity of woman's experience from 1833 through 1873. In that time, women's lives were marked by an awareness of the democratic potential liberated through the rise of individualism. But they also felt deeply about the loss of harmony and balance in a world divided into separate male and female spheres, social classes, ethnic and racial groups. The proper relationship of the individual to society was being questioned by Transcendentalists, who believed in the principle of individual self-reliance but also in the need to maintain a balanced and harmonious society. The search for answers to the problems of a fragmented and divided society defined Alcott's personal history and *Work*. The integrity of her writing reaches across a hundred years to readers who will find the search to be their own.

[Passage deleted.]

In *Work: A Story of Experience* Louisa May Alcott created her most complex and sustained heroine, Christie Devon, "one of that large class of women, who moderately endowed with talents, earnest and true-hearted, are driven by necessity, temperament, or principle out into the world to find support, happiness, and homes for themselves." In the ante-bellum period, Harriet Martineau, a British social critic and traveler in America, had listed governess, seamstress, and teacher as genteel female employments in America. Out of her own experiences and those of her contemporaries Alcott added domestic service, factory-workshop labor, nursing, and the stage as possibilities. The portraits of single and married women forced to work under circumstances of limited skills, education, and experience soon become familiar to Alcott's readers in *Work*. Women who knew their worth in terms of domestic responsibilities and skills found out that their experience was worthless in terms of jobs. Women's secondary job status reflected the pervasive notion that their primary status was as unwaged housewives and mothers.

The years between 1861, when Louisa began *Success*, and 1873, when the novel was finally completed as *Work*, included her most productive literary efforts and also her liveliest involvement in active social reforms.

[Passage deleted.]

Alcott's first task was to find a satisfactory definition of the status and role of women, one which would lend itself to the heroine's story as a personal search for meaning, and one that could make that meaning universal to readers. She was inspired by Theodore Parker's sermon, "The Public Function of Woman."[1] Ednah Cheney, Alcott's friend and the editor of letters and diaries, recalled that Louisa once said, "Christie's adventures are many of them my own; Mr. Power is Mr. Parker."[2] Parker assumed that the function of women "begins at home, then, like charity, goes everywhere."

Women were not to abandon homemaking for waged labor but were to have the home work transformed through the "progress of mankind, and the application of masculine science to what was once only feminine work."[3] If a woman could buy her flour ready-ground and her cloth ready-woven, she could cut her housework in half and spend the other half of her time in a combination of philanthropy and waged labor as her class position allowed. There was, he noted, a sorry historical transition period in his lifetime in which spinsterhood was on the rise, but it would pass if only men would recognize that women were their equals mentally and morally. Marriage, he felt, must be based upon sexual equality even though he hardly envisioned the sharing of domestic tasks in the home.

Christie Devon is an orphan and so is freed from her natural obligations as the daughter of a farm household to seek her fortune in the broader experience of the waged world. In fact, she uses the language of the Seneca Falls Convention to claim her rights. "There's going to be a new Declaration of Independence," and "emphasized her speech by energetic demonstration in the bread trough, kneading dough as if it was her destiny, and she was shaping it to suit herself." The conversation is, naturally enough, carried on in the large farm kitchen, her Aunt Betsey replying in the form of a recipe. Though humorously done, the scene is really a farewell to rural life with its timeless pattern and prescribed stages of women's work and life. The Civil War had given many women the opportunity to participate in voluntary nursing and social service through the Sanitary Commission; it had disrupted family life sufficiently to turn housewives into heads of households temporarily. Secondary schools for girls were beginning to be commonplace at least in New England, and Christie's longing for the larger world was reflected in her desire to explain to Aunt Betsey that it was now possible to choose a pattern of life different from her aunt's. Christie's farewell statements are an indictment of the conventional choices for women.

Her experience has been a domestic one; all of her skills have been learned either at a village school or at home where she has received a thorough training in housewifery. She goes off knowing that "work was always to be found in the city." The wage-system, then, is initially seen by Christie in mid-nineteenth century as the means to independence. At first the boarding house where she begins her round of job hunting frees her from the endless round of tasks that define domesticity and dependence. Abba Alcott had opened an employment office when her city missionary experience dramatized the need to find places for "good girls." Christie goes to just such an office, "the purgatory of the poor." But the combination of skills she associates with housewifery does not seem to be what is wanted. She must define herself by one particular skill and, unable to do so, she goes out into service as a maid, just as Louisa Alcott did.

When her fashionable employer denies her the use of her own name, Christie is beset by her first experience with the anonymity of the waged world. Her new employer is pleased that, unlike the Irish servant girls previously employed, Christie does not object to working with a black cook. It is the cook, Hepsey, who gives Christie a lesson in humility, kindness and patience. Directed to pull off her master's boots and clean them, Christie is horrified, regarding the order as a direct humiliation. In fact, Louisa, in the ordeal of her own few weeks in domestic service, was asked to perform just such a task, and her humiliation led her to quit the job. Hepsey, however, offers to perform the bootblacking for Christie: "Dere's more 'gradin works dan dat, chile, and dem dat's bin bliged to do 'em find dis sort bery easy. You's paid for it, honey . . . I's shore I'd never ask it of any woman if I was a man, 'less I was sick or ole. But folks don't seem to 'member dat we've got feelins."

Domesticity produced a consciousness of work not only as "craft" but also as a process quite apart from a wage and hours definition of service. This awareness made domestic service alienating and exploitative, and many servant "girls" openly preferred waged, factory work to the long hours and endless tasks set by household employers. Lucy Maynard Salmon, in discussing the "social disadvantages of domestic service," found the lack of "home privileges" to be a serious source of distress to female servants. "Board and lodging do not constitute a home, and the domestic can never be a part of the family whose external life she shares." As one girl reported, "One must remember that there is a difference between a house, a place of shelter, and a home, a place where all our affections are centered."[4] Domesticity was quite different from domestic service, and it was the substitution of a wage for affection and interdependency that made the one a house and the other a home. This consciousness of work as distinct from job was to cause some confusion in Alcott's heroine and in her own life. In her first twenty-four hours of domestic service Christie learns that she is expected to do the tasks asked of her with the devotion of a family member but with none of the kindness or even closeness of a family relationship to reward her. Actually, it is the pretensions of upwardly mobile social climbers that get Christie fired within a few months; for her elegant mistress, forgetting genteel pretensions, screams at her servant like a fishwife and, having lost her refined manner, is too embarrassed to keep the servant "Jane," who has, of course, seen through the "lady" long ago.

Christie is on her own once again, though she retains both the friendship of Hepsey Johnson and the commitment to abolition and racial integration. Hepsey's loyalty to her enslaved family, whom she hopes to free with her wages, had its real counterpart in many black families, and we know that such evidence in the form of slave narrative later reached Louisa Alcott. Winnie Beale, a freed slave, gratefully acknowledged the receipt of Abba Alcott's clothing and sent a message through Sally Holley to Louisa. "I wish I had something to send the lady. Why! She is a mammy to me. I shall be warm now."[5] Winnie did send something more valuable than clothes to the Alcotts—the long and sad tale of her struggles to reunite her family. Holley promised, "I will not forget to write out more stories as our colored folks tell us—and send you." Louisa had wanted to teach in Port Royal before her illness forced her retirement as a nurse in the Civil War. Hepsey is the first link in the chain of sisterhood that Christie Devon, like Alcott, forges as she discovers that jobs do not fulfill the promise of independence for women, though wages might buy freedom from chattel slavery.

Female friendship in her boarding house brings Christie the opportunity to try Alcott's own long cherished dream of a stage career. The work was tempting, exciting, and romantic enough to fulfill some of the farm girl's dreams; but the life offered unwholesome temptations too, and Christie found that an actress could rarely be a true woman. Sexual familiarities were commonplace, rivalries between actresses prevented real companionship, and Christie left this form of employment of her own volition. Having been warned that the stage was an impediment to "genteel" employment, she refrained from mentioning her experience and went off to the seashore with a mother, two children, and the bachelor brother of her employer.

The bachelor, Philip Fletcher, is a wealthy, snobbish invalid, hardly attractive to novelist or reader. But it is plain that Alcott knew enough of the world of fashion to make him a "catch" to husband-hunting maidens at the resort. The observation is clear; the alternative to waged work or slavery is "to marry for a living." Christie believes, as any true woman does, that marriage must be for love alone, yet she is briefly tempted not only by the prospect of luxury but also by the promise of ending her lonely struggle for independence. Family security with Fletcher, however, can only mean subordination and dependency. Christie, recalling that she left the stage of her own will and that honest work of any sort is honorable, refuses the offer of marriage.

At the end of three jobs it is clear to Christie that personal service occupations are humiliating not for the tasks done, or the wages paid, but for the social relations prescribed. Later on in the novel, a mature Christie sums up this experience. "Even in democratic America, the hand that earns its daily bread must wear some talent, name, or honor as an ornament before it is very cordially shaken by those who wear white gloves."

A pervasive social malaise is evidenced in the homes served by Christie and her working sisters. The homes are troubled, insecure, part of an endless round of upward striving for social status. Individualism, which requires the home as a refuge in "a cruel and heartless world," prevents the ideal from being realized. There are no true women in these scenes of genteel family life; for as husbands and fathers participated in the "freedom" of a competitive, speculative marketplace, they needed wives and daughters who could maneuver in the social marketplace to the advantage of their menfolk's businesses and careers. Philip Fletcher's sister was a parody of the fashionable woman; her husband traveled abroad on business and she only wrote to him for spending money.

Christie's experience as the companion of a young, mad woman indicated that even inherited insanity could have its link to the drive for social status. Mrs. Carroll married and bore children knowing of her husband's fatal flaw because she came from a poor, humble home, and marriage offered a wealthy and socially prominent one. So these women were not really outside or even elevated from their husbands' world, and, unable to achieve independence, they were similarly unable to achieve true womanhood, as ordinary women, waged and unwaged, understood it.

There are no faithful family retainers among the female servants in *Work*, even though their labor gives integrity to their lives, because the workers' insecurity is part and parcel of their employers' insecure status and anxiety. Theodore Parker remarked that it was not work which crushed the spirit of the laboring people but rather: "the tacit confession on the part of the employer, that he has wronged and subjugated the person who serves him; for when these same actions are performed by the mother for her child, or the son for his father, they are done for love and not money; they are counted not as low but rather ennobling." The gulf between Christie and her employers is never bridged by love, but warmth and sympathy develop between the workers, especially when the domestic world of women's relationships makes communication and shared tasks possible. Hepsey cooks because she is saving to buy her aged mother's freedom. As an illiterate, runaway slave, Hepsey's job opportunities are doubly limited by sex and race. Still, she makes very clear to Christie and to the reader that a wage is a very definite gain over slavery. The job brings wages, and wages buy freedom from slavery. Further, the status of a free wage earner gives Hepsey the opportunity to become literate and so to progress further along the continuum to independence. Knowledge is power of a real sort in *Work*, and not only Hepsey but Christie and all of her sisters hunger for it, strive to acquire it and understand it to lead to some sort of control over their lives. The genteel ladies, on the other hand, carry velvet covered Bibles and only pretend to "culture."

The turning point of the novel is Christie's employment as a seamstress in a factory-like workroom. The details of Louisa Alcott's life in the 1860s and 1870s were enough like Christie Devon's to make the cautionary tale of the seamstress one of the best and most touching episodes in *Work*. Louisa had a momentary impulse to suicide during a period of unemployment and family mourning over the death of Elizabeth Alcott. She heard Parker's sermon on "Laborious Young Women" and pronounced it "just what I needed; for it said: Trust your fellow beings, and let them help you. Don't be too proud to ask, and accept the humblest work till you can find the task you want."[6] Just as she was about to sew ten hours a day at the Girl's Reform School at Lancaster, her old place as a governess came open and she took it. "Fixed for the winter . . . thank the Lord."

She had already experienced what it meant to be a part of the "putting out" system when she sewed for a Mr. G "a dozen pillow cases, six fine cambric neckties, and two dozen handkerchiefs, at which I had to work all one night to get them done. . . . I got only four dollars."[7] There were other times when genteel customers "forgot" or delayed payments that meant a humiliation for Alcott she never forgot.

Christie held herself aloof from all but one quiet, romantic girl, Rachel. Rachel is clearly fallen gentry and is hired as a trimmer because her taste is "superior" (or more precisely her taste is more like that of the prospective customers) despite the forewoman's lack of information about her personal background. It is almost a case of "how did a nice girl like you wind up in a place like this?" The respectable workshop manager must be intent not only on production but also on maintaining the legitimacy of such a system by hiring only girls of good character. In a dramatic confrontation between the necessities of production and the maintenance of social order, Rachel is fired as an undesirable influence on the workers, and the contradictions between true womanhood and waged work are made explicit.

Rachel is the first real friend in Christie's long search, a true heart's companion. Louisa met Rebecca Harding, author of a widely read novel about a fallen woman, *Margaret Howth*, in 1861 and commented, "She never had any troubles though she writes about woes. I told her I had lots of troubles, so I write jolly tales; and we wondered why each did so."[8] The importance of Rachel and Christie's affection for one another involves the difficult problem of woman's status in nineteenth century American society, a status that made marriage the most serious event in a woman's life. Such a conventional truth meant that for those women who chose to remain single, like Louisa Alcott, the means of gaining subsistence, love, and recognition were very limited. Female friendships were doubly important for spinsters. Although married women retained their female friends, they had prior commitments that could not easily be laid aside. Alcott also observes that "a brief but most sincere affection between two women was a viable experience which could open the heart to happiness that was its right." It makes perfect sense that, given all the shared experiences of women in that "large class," relationships could and did develop that aroused a female consciousness of the heart's potential. We may have assumed that young women's experience of romantic love was limited to novels unless we pause to notice the possibilities of direct and affectionate experience between female friends. The power of friendship was strong enough in *Work* to redeem a fallen woman, and this conviction foreshadows Harriet Beecher Stowe's similar belief in *We and Our Neighbors*, published in 1875. Since *Work* was serially published in Beecher's *The Christian Union* during 1872 and 1873, it was certain that Mrs. Stowe read it.[9] Rachel's plight, like that of Stowe's heroine, points to the inadequacy of the conventional institutions for fallen women; the Christian's duty is to stretch out the hand of friendship directly to the unfortunate. Rachel's dismissal heralds the beginning of Christie's conscious search for religious faith as a means of joining with others to directly affect the organization of a society that promised opportunity and delivered oppression to that large class of women defined at the beginning of *Work*.

The full contradiction of individualism is now evidenced in the betrayal of all that ideology had promised to Christie. The waged job invalidates the principles of true women. Profit supersedes moral responsibility and charity must be measured by its price. Even the manager of the factory is not a free woman but must choose only what the laws of supply and demand allow. The solution of an extended sphere for women when "charity goes everywhere" are blown apart in this scene. Private, personalized solutions to the injustices of developing industrialism are now presented as impossible.

Still, a personal, moral witness is called for, and Christie must maintain her humanity at the cost of leaving her job. Alone, ill, and reduced to piecework, she finds herself in debt. The contradictions between job and work have collapsed before a new spectre — the experience of unemployment. In the first half of *Work* the only alternative to the family was a job for Christie, the promise of independence held out by the age of individualism. But if her independence was based upon either family support or job, how could she survive when confronted with absence of both? Her Aunt Betsey was dead, and she was unemployed. It is the lowest point in the heroine's life and also the amazing beginning of Alcott's alternative proposal to the dominant society's values. Individualism and women's acceptance of it either by entrance into the waged world or by acceptance of the compensatory separate sphere are part of the development of an ideology that sought hegemony in the nineteenth century. But that hegemony was complete, or nearly so, *only* if women consented to it. To the extent that they became aware, as Christie did, that patriarchy prevented independence for women and that unchecked competitive, private enterprise prevented true womanhood, the personal problems of women in the nineteenth century became social problems. As a reformer, Alcott finally accepted the responsibility to her female readers of presenting a feminist consciousness that implied a new relationship between men and women. She speaks of it quite openly throughout the rest of the book.

This new, open relationship between the sexes is ushered into the novel by Rachel. She sends Christie to stay with Cynthie Wilkins, a humble laundress, whose greatness of heart resembles Peggotty in *David Copperfield*. Cynthie is the voice of the working woman who manages to preserve complete dedication to the family as she raises a brood of children and props up a husband whose wages cannot support them. Cynthie's awareness of true womanhood is the result of a natural disaster that transformed her from a runaway wife-mother to a paragon of domestic social relations. But this personal transformation is not enough; she joins a band of reformers, led by the Reverend Mr. Power and assisted by David Sterling, in order to extend her domestic compassion to the entire society.

Cynthie plays the part of the mother Christie scarcely knew. She advertises her services by a sign, "Cynthie Wilkins, Clear Starcher," and her vision of the world is as clear as her starching: social change will come through liberal Christianity in which Christ washes whitest of all. Alcott's favorite childhood book was *The Pilgrim's Progress*,[10] and she used it for many of the chapter headings in *Little Women* and much of the moral message of *Work*. Cynthie, David Sterling, and Reverend Power together embody the path through which nineteenth century Christians could find salvation. As Cynthie describes Power, "He starts the dirt and gits the stains out, and leaves em ready for other folks to finish off." His sermons give heart to his battered congregation, and he does not stop at exhortation but goes on to criticize the institutions and social relations that damage the souls and bodies in his charge. He spends much of his time listening to the problems of his congregation and finding companions to help them on their way, much as the pilgrims in Bunyan's morality tale are helped by the band of angels.

Christie's own feet are set on the path to redemption by her experiences in the households of Cynthie Wilkins and later of David Sterling. In Cynthie's kitchen she helps with the laundry and the cooking, but the real easing of her heart's pain comes when Cynthie sets her infant daughter in Christie's lap. Transcendentalism expressed the conviction that material reality was the expression of the ideal: divinity lay within each human being, and the spirit could transcend the prison of the flesh through an original relationship with Nature. Nature was the symbol of the spirit, and insofar as women cherished children they were closer to nature and closer to the spirit, the essence of life that transcended material appearances. Christie was battered in body but more seriously damaged spiritually by her combat with the waged world. It was her spirit that was restored in Cynthie's kitchen, and the domestic relations of that woman's world gave her a model to extend the process of individual salvation to social reform.

Christie's relationship to David Sterling, who runs a greenhouse and a half-way shelter for wayward pilgrims, is informed by Thoreau's essay on "Friendship."[11] It is not too presumptuous to say that David Sterling is Alcott's idealized portrait of Henry David Thoreau. "Friendship," said Thoreau, "is evanescent in every man's experience and remembered like heat lightning in past summers."[12] It is through friendship, and the growing recognition of equality, mutuality, and commitment to a democratic society that Christie and David fall in love. But, like Thoreau's description of summer lightning, the incandescent relationship between Christie and David is brief; while culminating in a new sort of companionate marriage based upon equality, it is ended by David's death. As a fallen hero in the Civil War, his spirit both vitalizes Christie's commitment to carry on his reform efforts and, paradoxically, frees her to return to the world of women's work and companionship.

It had been safe to speculate on Thoreau as a mate since he was dead by the time Louisa created David Sterling, and she had already written a lovely poem "Thoreau's Flute" for *Altantic Monthly*, reminding friends that Thoreau's music could be heard in Concord long after his death.[13] Thoreau himself had said that "the only danger in friendship is that it will end," and in compensation "even the death of friends will inspire us as much as their lives." The nineteenth century feminists, including Thoreau and the Alcotts, believed that harmony in marriage depended upon sexual equality and, most importantly, on openness and truth in relationships; where inequality made males dominant over females, tyranny and fear could destroy open communication. "Between whom there is hearty truth there is love; and in proportion to our truthfulness and confidence in one another, our lives are divine and miraculous, and answer to our ideal," said Thoreau.[14] But Alcott's own spinsterhood and the examples of her friends and associates may have led to a certain amount of skepticism as to the possibilities of perfect equality in nineteenth century marriage. She felt surer of women's work and companionship or at least of her own ability to write about it.

Christie's daughter, Pansy, becomes the center of her hopes and expectations for a new generation of women, but Christie does not retire on her widow's pension to do good works. She takes over her husband's greenhouse business, runs it not only efficiently but collectively, and proposes a new set of property relations. To her Uncle Enos, financial success is the only real measure of achievement, and when he questions the "bargain" in which Christie does the major work and receives the minor share of profits, she replies, "Ah, but we don't make bargains, sir: we work for one another and share every thing together." "So like women," grumbled Uncle Enos.

In joining an association of working women and making her first public speech, Christie's vision of the new women's movement after the Civil War is not only exciting but informative in its recognition of the problems evidenced by the gaps between their specific, personal experiences and their common experiences as women. The meeting is marked by familiar difficulties. "There were speeches of course, and of the most unparliamentary sort, for the meeting was composed almost entirely of women, each eager to tell her special grievance or theory . . . how difficult it was for the two classes to meet and help one another in spite of the utmost need on the one side and the sincerest good will on the other."

Finally, when Christie stops at the bottom step of the speaker's platform and says, "I am better here, thank you; for I have been and mean to be a working woman all my life," she joins forces with her creator. Louisa May Alcott, like Christie Devon, was a working woman all her life, moving through the experiences of domesticity, jobs, and unemployment. Her awareness of these experiences as shaping women's responses to the expectations raised by the dominant ideology of individualism enabled her to write more vividly and with a greater sense of urgency in *Work* than in any of her more commercially successful novels.[15] Her accomplishment is the more remarkable because she was able to present both the common sensibility of women and their individual experiences in a way that exhibited the conflict of interests manifest in their lives.

Work, then, describes Alcott's sense of the formation of women's consciousness in the nineteenth century; true womanhood clearly meant different things to women than to men. Excluded from direct social power, women found it difficult to affect a society that attempted to destroy their experience of true womanhood. Alcott's heroine moved through a period of adolescent struggle, demanding that the principles of the American Revolution be applied to women and naively assuming that her domestic virtues could remain intact and were not in conflict with the promise of individualism. But here awareness did not remain limited by a passive acceptance of ideology. The ideological promise had to be fulfilled in terms of real material rewards in order to be accepted by women. For many women, then, the choices presented were lonely, impoverished spinsterhood or "marrying for a living." True womanhood, as Christie defined it and as it was struggled out in the Working Womens Association, transcended the individualist sensibility.[16]

[Passage deleted.]

Work was not, as Harper's supposed, Alcott's first real novel, but it was a substantial attempt to break through conventional plot lines to inform her audience that the real lives of women were more complex and more deserving of attention than the idealization of woman as the spiritual helpmate of man could portray. A modern reading of Alcott's Work is substantively different from either the interpretation of her contemporary audience or the literary critics' appreciation. "It is well to remember that although literature reflects an age it also illuminates it."[17] Alcott was a faithful social secretary, and she did shed light on what she saw and felt; the development of her own consciousness was interwoven with the process she located in the lives of other women. The strength of her vision is revealed in the authenticity of Work; the facts of women's lives in mid-nineteenth century, as well as we can reconstruct them, are vivid and true in Alcott's novel. And women still struggle today with the contradictions between the promise of individuality and the restrictions of individualism, between commitment to family and the impersonality of the wage system. The contradictions have taken new historical forms that often obscure their roots. Work deserves a modern audience, not only as an historical document and a minor literary achievement, but also as a key to understanding the commonality of our daily struggles with those of our mothers and grandmothers.

Notes

1. Theodore Parker, "The Public Function of Woman," reprinted in Theodore Parker, *Sins and Safeguards of Society* (Boston: American Unitarian Association, 1907), 9: 178–206.

2. Alcott, *Life, Letters, Journals*, p. 265.

3. Parker, pp. 178–206.

4. Lucy Maynard Salmon, *Domestic Service* (New York: Macmillan Co., 1911), pp. 141–150.

5. Letter to Louisa May Alcott from Sally Holley, Alcott Family Papers, Houghton Library, Harvard University, Cambridge, Mass., January 1882.

6. Alcott, *Life, Letters, Journals*, p. 102–103.

7. *Ibid.*

8. Alcott, *Life, Letters, Journals*, p. 131.

9. "Work: Or Christie's Experiment," *The Christian Union*, December 1872–June 1873. The first chapter was reprinted in *The Independent*, January 1873, and *Hearth and Home*, 18 January 1873.

Madeleine B. Stern's biography *Louisa May Alcott* contains the most reliable and comprehensive bibliography, and I have relied on it for dates of publication.

10. John Bunyan, *The Pilgrim's Progress.*

11. Henry David Thoreau, *Friendship* (New York: Thomas Y. Crowell & Co. 1906), excerpted from "A Week on the Concord & Merrimack Rivers." For more details on the Thoreau-Alcott friendship see Madeleine B. Stern, *Louisa May Alcott.*

12. *Ibid.*

13. Louisa May Alcott, "Thoreau's Flute," *Atlantic Monthly* 12, (September 1863).

14. Thoreau, *Friendship.*

15. In 1881 in a letter to Thomas Niles, her publisher, she said, "I can remember when antislavery was in just the same state that suffrage is now, and take more pride in the very small help we Alcotts could give than in all the books I ever wrote or ever shall write." Quoted in Alcott, *Life, Letters, Journals*, p. 341.

16. Louisa Alcott attended the Women's Congress at Syracuse, N.Y., in October 1873 where Antoinette Brown Blackwell spoke on the rights of married women to combine domestic life and waged work.

17. F. O. Matthiessen, *American Renaissance* (New York: Oxford University Press, 1941), p. x.

A Modern Mephistopheles

Review of *A Modern Mephistopheles*, 1877] Anonymous*

    We have not much doubt that Julian Hawthorne is the author of *A Modern Mephistopheles*;[1] and the belief should be understood as implying a compliment to his powers, for the book is certainly a remarkable one and instinct with ability. The parallel with Goethe's *Faust* which its title at once challenges is not very close or continuous, but it is as much so as it need be. Indeed the author, whoever he or she, male or female, may be, has managed this variation on the master's theme with much good sense. We do not think Helwyze, who takes the Mephistophelian part, is supplied with a sufficient motive. He is, to be sure, created in a vacuum from which all real human nature has been previously withdrawn, and cannot, therefore, be expected to have very rational motives. With this we have no quarrel; but even after making such allowance, we fancy that he begins operations too much as if he were moved by a crank. Still, when once he has started on his career of inhuman mischief, he works with entire consistency, and his relations with the other characters, Olivia, Canaris, and Gladys, are harmonious and probable. Probable, that is, when we take into account the figurative and hyperbolical atmosphere which the author has chosen. It is a question whether the *outré* effect gained by such a choice is worth while, measured by any profound truth enforced in the present case. The whole drama seems like a movement of shadows thrown from a *porte-lumière* upon a curtain of rather lurid mist; and we cannot see how the heart is to be touched by it. But granting that the lesson will be ardently received by most readers, it amounts only to this, that wanton exercise of the intellect and a suppression of the better forces in the heart are very dangerous and devilish. It is not always the case that this kind of work involves high qualities of imagination; not infrequently "cold performs the effect of fire," and invention aided by talent may put on the likeness of genuine creative ability. But define and qualify as we may, it remains none the less true that there is signal force of some sort in this peculiar production. The turns in the plot, the changes, the surprises, the mystery for some time not even remotely de-

*Reprinted from the *Atlantic Monthly*, 40 (July 1877), 109.

cipherable, all this is well done. The character of Gladys is shaped with dignity and some sweetness; and the chapter in which Canaris undergoes the temptation to murder fastens one's attention with the gradual and conclusive pressure of a vise. The language is vigorous and clear, having a sculpturesque effect, and the succession of periods and paragraphs is often so admirable that many pages together seem to be set to solemn rhythm.

Notes

1. *No Name Series. A Modern Mephistopheles.* Boston: Roberts Brothers, 1877.

[Review of *A Modern Mephistopheles*, 1877]

Anonymous*

We should judge, after reading a hundred pages of this book, that it was written by a young person, probably a girl, with much literary facility and fluency, and an excellent grasp of plot, but with little experience of life. The characters remind us of no one, and would be, indeed, in real life impossible; but they move in an atmosphere of their own, in which their actions and words seem consistent enough, till we turn from the world of fancy to that of reality. The language is stilted and dramatic sometimes, but never degenerates into slang or vulgarity. With advancing years and a larger experience the author may make her mark.

[Review of *A Modern Mephistopheles*, 1877]

Edward R. Burlingame*

A Modern Mephistopheles is an imaginative sketch, — more than half an allegory, — written with considerable grace of fancy, and with fair success in carrying out the spirit in which it was conceived. The unknown author — who, of whichever sex, writes in this instance with both the defects and merits of a woman's pen — has given a new, fantastic dress to a world-old story, — a story that will suggest to its readers, as it does to its writer (so clearly that he feels, as it were, in duty bound to mention it), Retzsch's familiar picture of *The Game of Life.*

Jasper Helwyze (whose name, by the way, is meant to fit him after the most approved models of the "Pilgrim's Progress") is seized by a sudden

*Reprinted from *Godey's Lady's Book*, 95 (July 1877), 86.
*Reprinted from the *North American Review*, 125 (September 1877), 316–18.

fancy to rescue and aid, for the ultimate purpose of a psychological experiment, a young author of whom he hears by accident, whom failure and privation have made desperate, and whom he interrupts in the midst of an attempt at suicide. The youth, Felix Canaris, accepts his new life eagerly, and in Helwyze's luxurious home—such a "dream of luxury," of course, as every writer has a prescriptive right to introduce into a story of this order, albeit architecture and the possibilities are thereby outraged—he blossoms into the beauty and vigor nature had meant him to possess, and want had hitherto kept from him. Full of all the possibilities of young manhood, he forms an admirable subject for the Mephistophelian designs of his protector; whose first desire, of course, is to gain over him a power from which he cannot well escape. The keen ambition of Canaris offers him a way. He offers to help the young author with the volume of poems he has dreamed of, yet failed to finish or to find success for. For a while Canaris labors on alone; but the inspiration will not come. Led by the stronger mind, he consents to the secret substitution of some poems by Helwyze for his own; the book comes out under Canaris's name and makes him famous. From that day he is the slave of the "modern Mephistopheles."

Naturally, we have not space or inclination to trace here the course of Helwyze's experiments, whether on the mind of his chief victim, or on the minds of the only other two characters who enter into the fantastic little story. These two are women,—and the types of women necessary to make up what may be called the psychologic quadrilateral. One is Olivia, the "sumptuous beauty," attracting all the sensuous part of Canaris's nature, but herself absorbed in a devoted worship of the master-spirit, Helwyze. The other is called Gladys, the best-drawn character the book contains, whose appeal is to the young man's better, more ideal side; the watching angel in his game.

The story is too lightly drawn to be judged by stern standards; and the delicacy of its execution entitles it to praise. Its little faults, and even a few absurdities, are of a kind to make it seem absurdly hypercritical to comment on them harshly. If Helwyze's eyes are a little too intensely black and magnetic, if Olivia is a trifle too "sumptuous," and "the villa," as we intimated, magnificent beyond the power of all upholstery, why should we quarrel with the too liberal fancy that created them? *A Modern Mephistopheles* remains a fresh and dainty fantasy; and this was all its author offered.

[Review of *A Modern Mephistopheles*, 1877]

Anonymous*

All criticism of fiction must be, to a certain extent, an averaging of results. The "novel of the season" may be, through strict comparison, forced the succeeding year to give place to a half-dozen finer creations out of the ranks of which, in turn, another superior work will be chosen supreme favorite for a time. That novel-readers are yearly growing more appreciative, more critical, is an acknowledged fact; and it is a question deserving of some consideration, whether the tendency of certain publishing firms to embody all the works of fiction issued by them, in one or more series — that is, in similar size and binding, with some attractive general title — is not a movement having for its root an increasing and more dainty appetite for the best light literature. Of course, the desire of publishers to reduce to a minimum the cost of production, must be taken into consideration; but given an increased demand for a superior article, such a demand will give rise to a corresponding attempt to reduce to the lowest possible figures the cost of production, in order that the increased percentage on the raw material — which in this case is the brain-work of the author — may be met, and yet leave the largest possible margin of profit. In these pretty uniform volumes this end is attained, while the artistic designs of the cover, and the similarity of size and color, which, though objectionable to the epicurean bibliophile, is apt to appeal pleasurably to the taste of the many, is, or should be in itself, a guarantee that the contents must be above the average to be worthy of a *debut* in so dainty a form.

One of the most consistent and appreciative efforts in this line is the No Name Series of Messrs. Roberts Brothers; consistent, because the tacit agreement that each issue should be of the best literary merit, has, in this instance, and thus far been faithfully adhered to; it is not as yet numerically strong; it numbers but eight volumes, but among the eight there is not one that has not deserved and received its meed of praise. And that there has not been lacking among them sufficient variety of style and diversity of talent, the three volumes which have served to give subject to this article, and which are the latest issues of this series, will sufficiently attest; three novels more dissimilar in method and in treatment, it would be difficult to cite.

One effect produced upon the reader of *A Modern Mephistopheles* causes him involuntarily to compare the first and larger portion of the volume with the final chapters. At the outset, the tone is cold, the language narrative, Goethe's conception is well paraphrased, the description of the characters is so analytic as to border upon irony; gradually the tone changes; the language is glowing, earnest, eloquent; the situations grow intensely dramatic, the similarity to the Faust of Goethe is less striking, and the end comes with a pathos so intense that the final pages seem almost to

*Reprinted from the *Library Table*, 3 (27 September 1877), 185.

resolve themselves into a sob of pain. It is as though the author were struck at first simply with the fertility of his subject, but grew as he wrote into unconscious sympathy with it, and allowed his pages to become colored with the slow gradations of his changing mood. We cannot at the moment recollect anything more exquisite than the slow ripening of character in Gladys—the "woman-soul" dormant in the maiden; in the wife, roused to a sweet helpfulness and an intense capacity to love; in the mother, attaining its perfection—supreme in comprehension, in forgiveness, in unselfishness, in the completeness of the sacrifice of self. A study, rather than a novel, there is, nevertheless, enough of humanity to give it strength, enough of pathos to win it interest, enough of sin and of misery to make it life, enough of joy to relieve the darkness with little rifts of light.

APPRAISALS AND REAPPRAISALS

["Her Works Are a Revelation of Herself"]

Ednah D. Cheney*

Louisa May Alcott is universally recognized as the greatest and most popular story-teller for children in her generation. She has known the way to the hearts of young people, not only in her own class, or even country, but in every condition of life, and in many foreign lands. Plato says, "Beware of those who teach fables to children;" and it is impossible to estimate the influence which the popular writer of fiction has over the audience he wins to listen to his tales. The preacher, the teacher, the didactic writer find their audience in hours of strength, with critical faculties all alive, to question their propositions and refute their arguments. The novelist comes to us in the intervals of recreation and relaxation, and by his seductive powers of imagination and sentiment takes possession of the fancy and the heart before judgment and reason are aroused to defend the citadel. It well becomes us, then, who would guard young minds from subtle temptations, to study the character of those works which charm and delight the children.

Of no author can it be more truly said than of Louisa Alcott that her works are a revelation of herself. She rarely sought for the material of her stories in old chronicles, or foreign adventures. Her capital was her own life and experiences and those of others directly about her; and her own well-remembered girlish frolics and fancies were sure to find responsive enjoyment in the minds of other girls.

It is therefore impossible to understand Miss Alcott's works fully without a knowledge of her own life and experiences.

[Comments on Alcott journals and letters deleted.]

---

*Reprinted from *Louisa May Alcott: Her Life, Letters, and Journals*, edited by Ednah D. Cheney (Boston: Roberts Brothers, 1889), pp. [iii]–iv.

Books That Separate Parents from Their Children
Anonymous*

[A discussion of the deplorable consequences of the vast quantities of juvenile books contains the statement] Not many months ago, in a symposium of mothers, a gentlewoman was brave enough to say: "I am sorry to be obliged to be sorry that Miss Alcott ever wrote." It seemed a hard saying, but it was a wise one.

Louisa Alcott
G. K. Chesterton*

It is very good for a man to talk about what he does not understand; as long as he understands that he does not understand it. Agnosticism (which has, I am sorry to say, almost entirely disappeared from the modern world) is always an admirable thing, so long as it admits that the thing which it does not understand may be much superior to the mind which does not understand it. Thus if you say that the cosmos is incomprehensible, and really mean (as most moderns do) that it is not worth comprehending; then it would be much better for your Greek agnosticism if it were called by its Latin name of ignorance. But there is one thing that any man can fairly consider incomprehensible, and yet in some ways superior. There is one thing that any man may worry about, and still respect; I mean any woman. The deadly and divine cleavage between the sexes has compelled every woman and every man, age after age, to believe without understanding; to have faith without any knowledge.

Upon the same principle it is a good thing for any man to have to review a book which he cannot review. It is a good thing for his agnosticism and his humility to consider a book which may be much better than he can ever understand. It is good for a man who has seen many books which he could not review because they were so silly, to review one book which he cannot review because it is so wise. For wisdom, first and last, is the characteristic of women. They are often silly, they are always wise. Commonsense is uncommon among men; but commonsense is really and literally a common sense among women. And the sagacity of women, like the sagacity of saints, or that of donkeys, is something outside all questions of ordinary cleverness and ambition. The whole truth of the matter was revealed to Mr. Rudyard Kipling when the spirit of truth suddenly descended on him and

*Reprinted from the *New York Times Saturday Review of Books and Art*, 8 January 1898, p. 18.

*Reprinted from *A Handful of Authors: Essays on Books & Writers*, ed. Dorothy Collins (New York: Sheed & Ward, 1953), pp. 163–67. The chapter on Alcott appeared originally in the *Nation* in 1907. Copyright 1907, 1953 *Nation* magazine, The Nation Associates, Inc.

he said: "Any woman can manage a clever man; but it requires a rather clever woman to manage a fool."

The wisdom of women is different; and this alone makes the review of such books by a man difficult. But the case is stronger. I for one will willingly confess that the only thing on earth I am frightfully afraid of is a little girl. Female children, she babies, girls up to the age of five are perfectly reasonable; but then all babies are reasonable. Grown girls and women give us at least glimpses of their meaning. But the whole of the period between a girl who is six years old and a girl who is sixteen is to me an abyss not only of mystery, but of terror. If the Prussians were invading England, and I were holding a solitary outpost, the best thing they could do would be to send a long rank or regiment of Prussian girls of twelve, from which I should fly, screaming.

Now the famous books of Miss Alcott are all about little girls. Therefore, my first impulse was to fly screaming. But I resisted this impulse, and I read the books; and I discovered, to my immeasurable astonishment, that they were extremely good. *Little Women* was written by a woman for women—for little women. Consequently it anticipated realism by twenty or thirty years; just as Jane Austen anticipated it by at least a hundred years. For women are the only realists; their whole object in life is to pit their realism against the extravagant, excessive, and occasionally drunken idealism of men. I do not hesitate. I am not ashamed to name Miss Alcott and Miss Austen. There is, indeed, a vast division in the matter of literature (an unimportant matter), but there is the same silent and unexplained assumption of the feminine point of view. There is no pretence, as most unfortunately occurred in the case of another woman of genius, George Eliot, that the writer is anything else but a woman, writing to amuse other women, with her awful womanly irony. Jane Austen did not call herself George Austen; nor Louisa Alcott call herself George Alcott. These women refrained from that abject submission to the male sex which we have since been distressed to see; the weak demand for masculine names and for a part in merely masculine frivolities; parliaments, for instance. These were strong women; they classed parliament with the public-house. But for another and better reason, I do not hesitate to name Miss Alcott by the side of Jane Austen; because her talent, though doubtless inferior, was of exactly the same kind. There is an unmistakable material truth about the thing; if that material truth were not the chief female characteristic, we should most of us find our houses burnt down when we went back to them. To take but one instance out of many, and an instance that a man can understand, because a man was involved, the account of the quite sudden and quite blundering proposal, acceptance, and engagement between Jo and the German professor under the umbrella, with parcels falling off them, so to speak, every minute, is one of the really human things in human literature; when you read it you feel sure that human beings have experienced it often; you almost feel that you have experienced it yourself. There is something true to all our own private diaries in the fact that our happiest moments have happened in the rain, or under some absurd impediment of absurd luggage. The same is true of a hundred other elements in the story. The whole affair of the children acting the different parts in *Pickwick*, forming a childish club under strict restrictions, in order to do so; all that is really life, even where it is not literature. And as a final touch of human truth, nothing could be better than the way in which Miss Alcott suggests the borders and the sensitive privacy of such an experiment. All the little girls have become interested, as they would in real life, in the lonely little boy next door; but when one of them introduces him into their private club in imitation of *Pickwick*, there is a general stir of resistance; these family fictions do not endure being considered from the outside.

All that is profoundly true; and something more than that is profoundly true. For just as the boy was an intruder in that club of girls, so any masculine reader is really an intruder among this pile of books. There runs through the whole series a certain moral philosophy, which a man can never really get the hang of. For instance, the girls are always doing something, pleasant or unpleasant. In fact, when they have not to do something unpleasant, they deliberately do something else. A great part, perhaps the more godlike part, of a boy's life, is passed in doing nothing at all. Real selfishness, which is the simplest thing in the world to a boy or man, is practically left out of the calculation. The girls may conceivably oppress and torture each other; but they will not indulge or even enjoy themselves — not, at least, as men understand indulgence or enjoyment. The strangest things are taken for granted; as that it is wrong in itself to drink champagne. But two things are quite certain; first, that even from a masculine standpoint, the books are very good; and second, that from a feminine standpoint they are so good that their admirers have really lost sight even of their goodness. I have never known, or hardly ever known, a really admirable woman who did not confess to having read these books. Haughty ladies confessed (under torture) that they liked them still. Stately Suffragettes rose rustling from the sofa and dropped *Little Women* on the floor, covering them with public shame. At learned ladies' colleges, it is, I firmly believe, handed about secretly, like a dangerous drug. I cannot understand this strange and simple world, in which unselfishness is natural, in which spite is easier than self-indulgence. I am the male intruder, like poor Mr. Laurence and I withdraw. I back out hastily, bowing. But I am sure that I leave a very interesting world behind me.

Reminiscences of Louisa M. Alcott

F. B. Sanborn*

The representation of Miss Alcott's *Little Women* as a drama, in theaters from Buffalo westward, amid applause and appreciation, is a long-deferred tribute to the dramatic element in her gifted nature. This tendency to the melodramatic, which she began to manifest as a child, and which almost placed her on the stage as an actress in the mimic scenes that had attracted her so forcibly in the plain country landscape amid which she grew up, is worth dwelling on for a moment, altho it never took effect so as to make of her a prima donna of the exalted and attractive class. For that role she was qualified by nature, had the circumstances been a little more propitious.

The actual qualification by nature for an effective actress is varied and diverse. Beauty is an element, but a superficial one; except for light comedy, mere beauty is insufficient in an actress; tragedy, and even melodrama, demand a serious and profound vein of feeling. This Louisa Alcott, as I first saw her at her father's Boston house in Pinckney street, in the autumn of 1852, seemed to have in her well-endowed nature; and it was exprest in her energetic but represt manner. I made a half hour's call while I was in Harvard College, for the purpose of being introduced to her father, Bronson Alcott, whose attached friend and final biographer I became. Mrs. Ednah Littlehale Cheney was my introducer, while she still bore her maiden name, tho affianced to Seth Cheney, the graceful artist, whom she married the next year. All thru that ceremonious call Louisa sat silent in the background of the family circle, her expressive face and earnest, almost melancholy eyes were fixt on the visitors; but slight appeal was made to her interest in the conversation, which turned on the philosophic themes that Alcott had made his own long before 1852. He had been one of the leaders in the spiritual movement that began twenty years before, about the time of Louisa's birth — November 29, 1832 — the very day of the month and year with her father, who was thirty-three years old the day this daughter was born.

[Biographical details and remarks on Concord deleted.]

I suppose Louisa's first dramatic appearance was on her third birthday (November 28, 1835), when Mr. Alcott's pupils in his Boston school, at the Temple, on Tremont street, celebrated the joint advent of father and daughter the day before, because it was Saturday, and it would not have been decorous to have the ceremony on Sunday, the actual anniversary. In his diary Alcott gave this account of the festival:

> This morning my pupils celebrated my birthday at the schoolroom. They assembled at the usual hour, nine. At ten o'clock they crowned me

*Reprinted from the *Independent*, 72 (7 March 1912), 496–98.

with laurel, and also Louisa, my little girl being three years old. An address was then given in the name of the school by one of the pupils, and they presented me with a fine edition of 'Paradise Lost.' I then gave them a short account of my life, and an ode was pronounced by one of the little girls. We then partook of some refreshment.

The beginning of the ode was this:

> This hour in love we come
>   With hearts of happy mirth, —
> We've sallied forth from home
>   To celebrate a birth.
>
> *Chorus.*
>
> A time for joy, — for joy!
>   Let joy then swell around!
> From every girl and boy
>   Let joy's full tones resound.

The laurel was prophetic on Louisa's head, and the tones of joy were those which naturally she used. But the gift of "Paradise Lost" to the father was no less prophetic, since from that day forward he was exiled from one Eden after another, till this laurel-crowned daughter restored him to the "Paradise Regained" of Concord, as he reached the age of three score and ten.

Books for Children

Amy Lowell[*]

Miss Alcott I was forbidden to read for many years, as she was supposed to use very bad English and to be untrue to life, both of which criticisms I now thoroughly endorse. I did read the books after a while, since all my friends were reading them and parental authority, as it always does, had in the end to bow to public opinion. As I look back upon them I do not think they were valuable in any way, nor did they really give me very much pleasure, and I do not at all recommend them.

[*]Reprinted from the *Literary Digest*, 63 (29 November 1919), 31.

Miss Alcott's New England
Katharine Fullerton Gerould*

I remember being very much impressed—and not a little shocked—when a friend of mine told me that she had never, in her childhood, been able to get any real pleasure out of Louisa Alcott's stories. It had never occurred to me that being brought up in New York instead of in New England, or even being of Southern instead of Pilgrim stock, could make all that difference. Miss Alcott seemed the safe inheritance, the absolutely inevitable delight, of childhood. *Little Women* was as universal as *Hamlet*. I remembered perfectly that French playmates of mine in Paris had loved *Les Quatre Filles du Docteur March* (though the French version was probably somewhat expurgated). If children of a Latin—moreover, of a Royalist and Catholic—tradition could find no flaw in Miss Alcott's presentment of young life, I could not see why any free-born American child should fail to find it sympathetic.

I questioned my friend more closely. Her answer set me thinking; and it is probably to her that I owe my later appreciation of Miss Alcott's special quality and special documentary value. For what my friend said was simply that the people in the books were too underbred for her to get any pleasure out of reading about them. My friend was not, when I knew her, a snob; and I took it that she had made the criticism originally at a much earlier age. All children are as snobbish as they know how to be; and I fancy that the child's perennial delight in fairy-tales is not due solely to the epic instinct. One is interested in princes and princesses, when one is eight, simply because they are princes and princesses.

[Comments on children's thoughts about royalty deleted.]

The astounding result of re-reading Miss Alcott at a mature age is a conviction that she probably gives a better impression of mid-century New England than any of the more laborious reconstructions, either in fiction or in essay. The youth of her characters does not hinder her in this; for childhood, supremely, takes life ready-made. Mr. Howells's range is wider, and he is at once more serious and more detached. Technically, he and Miss Alcott can be compared as little as *Madame Bovary* and the *Bibliothèque Rose*. Yet, although their testimonies often agree, his world does not "compose" as hers does. It may be his very realism—his wealth of differentiating detail, his fidelity to the passing moment—that makes his early descriptions of New England so out of date, so unrecognizable. Miss Alcott is content to be typical. All her people have the same background, live in the same atmosphere, profess the same ideals. Moreover, they were ideals and an atmo-

*Reprinted from Katharine Fullerton Gerould, "Miss Alcott's New England," in *Modes and Morals* (New York: Charles Scribner's Sons, 1920), pp. 182-95, 197-98. Copyright 1920 Charles Scribner's Sons: copyright renewed 1948 Katharine F. Gerould. Reprinted with the permission of Charles Scribner's Sons.

sphere that imposed themselves widely during their period. Mr. Howells gives us modern instances in plenty, but nowhere does he give us clearly the quintessential New England village. It is precisely the familiar experiences of life in that quintessential village that Miss Alcott gives us, with careless accuracy, without *arrière-pensée*.

[Comments on New England village life deleted.]

The village that Miss Alcott knew best was Concord; and if, for our present purpose, we find it convenient to call Concord typical of New England, we shall certainly not be doing New England any injustice.

As I say, what strikes one on first re-reading her, is the extraordinary success with which she has given us our typical New England. Some of her books, obviously, are less successful in this way than others— *Under the Lilacs*, for example, or *Jack and Jill*, where (one cannot but agree with her severer critics) there is an inexcusable amount of love-making. There is an equally inexcusable amount of love-making, it is interesting to remember, in much of the earlier Howells. But for contemporary record of manners and morals, you will go far before you match her masterpiece, *Little Women*. What Meg, Jo, Beth, Amy, and Laurie do not teach us about life in New England at a certain time, we shall never learn from any collected edition of the letters of Emerson, Thoreau, or Hawthorne.

The next—and equally astounding—result of re-reading Miss Alcott was, for me, the unexpected and not wholly pleasant corroboration of what my friend had said about her characters. They were, in some ways, underbred. Bronson Alcott (or shall we say Mr. March?) quotes Plato in his family circle; but his family uses inveterately bad grammar.

[Examples of bad grammar deleted.]

The bad grammar, in all the books, is constant. And yet, I know of no other young people's stories, anywhere, wherein the background is so unbrokenly and sincerely "literary." Cheap literature is unsparingly satirized; Plato and Goethe are quoted quite as everyday matters; and "a metaphysical streak had unconsciously got into" Jo's first novel. In *The Rose in Bloom*, Miss Alcott misquotes Swinburne, to be sure, but she does it in the interest of morality; and elsewhere Mac quotes other lines from the same poet correctly. Of course, we all remember that Emerson's *Essays* helped on, largely, Mac's wooing—if, indeed, they did not do the whole trick. And has there ever been an "abode of learning"—to slip, for a moment, into the very style of *Jo's Boys*—like unto Plumfield, crowned by "Parnassus"? After all, too, we must remember how familiarly even those madcaps, Ted and Josie, bandied about the names of Greek gods. The boys and girls who scoff at the simple amusements of Miss Alcott's young heroes and heroines are, alack! not so much at home with classical mythology as the young people they despise. Yet, as I say, the bad grammar is everywhere — even in the mouths of the educators.

Breeding is, of course, not merely a matter of speech; and I fancy that my friend referred even more specifically to their manners — their morals being unimpeachable. Miss Alcott's people are, as the author herself says of them, unworldly. They are even magnificently so; and they score the worldly at every turn. You remember Mrs. March's strictures on the Moffats? and Polly's justifiable criticisms of Fanny Shaw's friends? and Rose's utter lack of snobbishness about Phoebe, the little scullery-maid, who eventually was brought up with her? Of course, Archie's mother objects, at first, to his marrying Phoebe, but she is soon reconciled — and apologetic.

Granted their unworldliness, their high scale of moral values, where, then, is the trace of vulgarity that is needed to make breeding bad? They pride themselves on their separation from all vulgarity. "My mother is a lady," Polly reflects, "even if" — even if she is not rich, like the Shaws. The March girls are always consoling themselves for their vicissitudes by the fact that their parents are gentlefolk. Well, they are underbred in precisely the way in which, one fancies, the contemporaries of Emerson in Concord may well have been underbred. It is the "plain-living" side of the "high thinking." They despised externals, and, in the end, externals had their revenge. Breeding, as such, is simply not a product of the independent village.

[Remarks on "the gift of civilized contacts" deleted.]

According to the older tradition, a totally unchaperoned youth would mean lack of breeding. Here, on the contrary, all the heroines are unchaperoned, while the match-making mamma is anathema. We did not cut off King Charles's head for nothing. The reward of the unchaperoned daughter is to make a good match. In that rigid school, conventions are judged — and nobly enough, Heaven knows! — from the point of view of morals alone (of absolute, not of historic or evolutionary morals) and many conventions are thereby damned. The result is a little like what one has heard of contemporary Norway. "Underbred" is very likely too strong a word; yet one does see how the social state described in *Little Women* might easily shock any one brought up in a less provincial tradition. There is too much love-making, for example. Though sweethearting between five-year-olds is frowned on, sweethearting between fifteen-year-olds is quite the thing. In real life, it would not always be safe to marry, very young, your first playmate. Any one who has lived in the more modern New England village knows perfectly well that people still marry, very young, their first playmates, and that disaster often results. Nor can Una always depend on the protection of a lion that is necessarily invisible. Granted that Jo's precocious sense was right, and that it would have been a mistake for her to marry Laurie; which of us believes that, in real life, she would not have made the mistake? You cannot depend on young things in their teens to foresee the future of their temperaments accurately. One cannot but feel that if Mrs. March really saw the complete unfitness of those two for each other, it was her duty to put a few conventional obstacles in their path.

Perhaps all this was part of what my friend meant by lack of breeding in the traditional sense: the social *laissez-aller* in extraordinary (and perhaps not eternally maintainable?) combination with moral purity. But I suspect that she referred, as well, to another aspect of Miss Alcott's environment: to the unmistakable lack of the greater and lesser amenities of life. The plain living is quite as prominent as the high thinking. The whole tissue of the March girls' lives is a very commonplace fabric. You know that their furniture was bad — and that they did not know it; that their aesthetic sense was untrained and crude — and that they did not care; that the simplicity of their meals, their household service, their dress, their every day manners (in spite of the myth about Amy) was simplicity of the common, not of the intelligent, kind. You really would not want to spend a week in the house of any one of them. Nor had their simplicity in any wise the quality of austerity. Remember the pies that the older March girls carried for muffs (the management whereof was one of the ever unsolved riddles of my childhood).

No: in so far as breeding is a matter of externals, one must admit that there is some sense in calling Miss Alcott's people underbred. Perhaps we do not choose to call breeding a matter of externals. In that, we should perfectly agree with Miss Alcott's people themselves; and to that we shall presently come. For what is incontrovertible is that Miss Alcott's work is a genuine document.

I have spoken of the unimpeachable morality of Miss Alcott's world. Charlie lost Rose for having drunk one glass of champagne too much. That is the worst sin committed in any of the books, so far as I remember. Of course, the black sheep, Dan, had been in prison; but he had killed his man inevitably, almost helplessly, in self-defence; and besides, the treatment of Dan is purely snobbish, from start to finish. Even Mrs. Jo, while she stands by him, is acutely conscious of the social difference between him and her own kin. The moment he lifts his eyes to Bess—! No: the books are quite snobbish enough, in their way. Nat, foundling and fiddler, is permitted to marry Daisy in the end (though, really, anybody might have married Daisy!). But Nat, though a *parvenu*, is a milksop, and is quite able to say that he has never done anything really disgraceful. The fact is that their social distinctions, while they operate socially, are yet all moral in origin. And this is a very "special" note: the bequest, it may well be, of Calvin.

[Verses deleted.]

Another point is perhaps even more interesting. There are not, I believe, any other books in the world so blatantly full of morality — of moral issues, and moral tests, and morals passionately abided by — and at the same time so empty of religion. The Bible is never quoted; almost no one goes to church; and they pray only when very young and in extreme cases. The only religious allusion, so far as I know, in *Little Women*, is the patronizing mention of the Madonna provided for Amy by Aunt March's Catholic maid. And even then, you can see how broad-minded Mrs. March considers herself, to permit Amy the quasi-oratory; and Amy does not attempt to disguise the fact that she admires the picture chiefly for its artistic quality. Yet it is only fair to remember that, in Miss Alcott's day, people were reading, without so much as one grain of salt, the confessions of "escaped" nuns, and the novels of Mrs. Julia McNair Wright — and that Elsie Dinsmore developed brain fever when her father threatened to send her to a convent school. Perhaps Mrs. March had a right to flatter herself. Again, as I say, these are documents.

There are many other straws to show which way the wind blows. Would any one but Miss Alcott, for example, have allowed her chief heroine to marry a Professor Bhaer? No modern child ever quite recovers from the shock of it. But we must remember that, in Miss Alcott's time, German metaphysicians were not without honor in Concord. The breath of reform, too, is hot upon the pages. "Temperance"— remember Charlie's unlucky glass of champagne, and Laurie's promise to Meg on her wedding-day; the festivals of the virtuous are a perpetual bath of lemonade. "Woman Suffrage"— recall the discussions alluded to in "The Pickwick Portfolio," and the fate of the few scoffers in co-educational Plumfield. The children are all passionate little Abolitionists; and the youths are patriotic with a fervid, unfamiliar patriotism, which touches, at its dim source, emotions that to us are almost more prehistoric than historic.

In the minds of Miss Alcott's world, there is still a lively distrust of the British. They are wont to oppress their colonies, and they cheat at croquet. Indeed, Miss Alcott's characters look a little askance at all foreigners — except German professors. There is no prophecy of the Celtic Revival in their condescending charity to poor Irishwomen. The only people, not themselves, whom they wholly respect, are the negroes. The rich men are nearly all East India merchants, and their money goes eventually to endow educational institutions. The young heroes have a precocious antipathy to acquiring wealth for its own sake. Demi would rather, he says, sweep door-mats in a publishing-house than go into business, like "Stuffy" and his kind. "I would rather be a door-keeper in the house of the Lord"— it would hardly over-emphasize Demi's so typical feeling for the sanctity of the printed page; for the utter desirability of the publisher's own office, where, as he says, great men go in and out, with respect. And — to complete the evidence — the books do not lack the note of New English austerity, though they come by it indirectly enough. The New English literary tradition seems to be fairly clear: either passion must be public, or, if it is private, it must be thwarted. There is a good deal of public passion — for philanthropy, for education, and what-not — in the books, after all. There is no private passion at all: though the books brim with sentiment, Miss Alcott writes as one who had never loved. It would be difficult to find, anywhere, stories so full of love-making and so empty of emotion.

Straws show which way the wind blows; and these straws are all borne in the same direction. Is not this the New England on which, if not in which, we were all brought up?

[Remarks on New England social life and thought deleted.]

I have not done more than indicate Miss Alcott's exceeding fidelity. Begin recalling her for yourself, and you will agree that she gives us social life as New Englanders, for decades, have, on the whole, known it. The relations of parent and child, brother and sister, community and individual, of playmates, of lovers, of citizens, are all such as we know them. They are familiar to us, if not positively in our own experience. Life has grown more complicated everywhere. Yet I doubt if, even now, any New English child would instinctively call Miss Alcott's people underbred. We still understand their code, if we do not practise it. New England is still something more than a convenient term for map-makers. These be our own villages.

Subversive Miss Alcott   Elizabeth Vincent[*]

It is a humorous reflection that Louisa M. Alcott did not like girls. When her publishers asked her to write a book for girls she complied reluctantly, with more of an eye to the price than the pleasure, though of course she did not slight her duty to be a wholesome influence. "I plod away, though I don't like this sort of thing. I never liked girls or knew many," she wrote. Whereupon *Little Women* became a best seller before it was a week off the press, and a classic before its second half was written. When the second half did come out, and it appeared that Jo had turned down Laurie, and that the minx Amy had caught him on the rebound, there was such great excitement that several young persons are said to have gone to bed with a fever. Miss Alcott feared at one time that her book contained too much "lovering," but this the young folks denied, and even their elders did not feel called upon to disapprove. "No mother fears," wrote a feminine critic, "that Miss Alcott's books will brush the bloom of modesty from the faces of her young men or maidens," — an assertion anyone will support who has read Professor Bhaer's proposal to Jo under the umbrella, or Laurie's to Amy in the rowboat.

" 'How well we pull together, don't we?' said Amy . . .

[*]Reprinted from the *New Republic*, 40 (22 October 1924), 204.

" 'So well, that I wish we might always pull in the same boat. Will you, Amy?' very tenderly.

" 'Yes, Laurie!' very low.

"Then they both stopped rowing, and unconsciously added a pretty little tableau of human love and happiness to the dissolving views reflected in the lake."

Now there is a young girl — I might almost say a young woman — of thirteen among my acquaintance, who is not by any means old-fashioned. She dances whatever is latest and talks the fashionable divorce and likes to get sermons over the radio because they sound so silly. Yet I found her once sunk in a chair, her long legs bridging the gap to a table, with an ancient battered *Little Women* in her lap.

"I read it every year," she said.

There you are. Miss Alcott didn't like girls, but she wrote a book that was immediately read — laughed and cried over is the proper way of saying it, I believe — by every little girl in America. Our insurgent age has discarded nineteenth century New England with a great fanfare, yet here is our hopeful youth addicted to the double distilled essence of New England, to the very thing we were at such great pains to get rid of for their sakes. The fact is that *Little Women* and *Little Men*, those late classics, are classics still. "They touch," Miss Cheney says, "the universal heart deeply." And so it would appear, for here are Little, Brown and Company bringing out a brand-new edition.[1]

The question is Why? Why do people republish these books? Why do small girls with the freedom of Sheik fiction and the films read them? Take *Little Women*. The characters are perfectly categorical — each patterned on a simple formula like this: Mr. March, father, philosopher and friend; Mrs. March, Mother and All That Stands For; Meg, fastidious womanliness; Amy, a perfect little lady; Beth, angel in the house. Even Jo is not the person to cut much ice with the current 'teens. At least you'd not think so. She is a tom-boy according to her lights:

" 'We are a pretty jolly set, as Jo would say,' said Meg.

" 'Jo does use such slang words!' observed Amy . . . Jo immediately sat up, put her hands in her pockets and began to whistle," — not such a tomboy as would take the breath of a first-team forward. And look at Meg married to her steadfast John and safely on the shelf, — "the sort of shelf on which young wives and mothers may consent to be laid, safe from the restless fret and fever of the world . . . and learning, as Meg learned, that a woman's happiest kingdom is her home, her highest honor the art of ruling it," — a fine popular doctrine for the age of equality and economic independence.

The so-called plot holds few apparent thrills for a generation raised on Fairbanks. Miss Alcott herself admitted it was not "sensational," and at that she exaggerated. Except for the uncomplicated chronicle of their loves and marriages the Marches have really nothing to offer in the way of plot at all.

The structure of the book is largely segmental, each chapter a neatly rounded episode, loaded with its lesson, and capped with repentance and tears and a few words of comfort from Mrs. March.

And yet — and yet: one does have to admit that these impossible Marches are real people. The children who get so absorbed in them are not wrong in finding them alive and true. The only wonder is that any child raised this side of 1900 has been able to put up with the things they do and the things they say, these all too real people. Of course the Marches *were* real people. Except for the trussing up of episodes and the simplification of character which passes for Miss Alcott's art, she has merely reported her own family. The searching of consciences and amateur theatricals and domestic trials which went on in the March family all happened to the Alcotts. It is not the people in the book who are unreal, but the people who lived. The Alcotts flourished on transcendental truth. But the truth of their day, the simple faith of our fathers, we have seen thinned and worn, until it has become the bandwagon drool and pulpit hypocrisy of ours. Can this be what our modern small daughters like?

The sort of thing that used to be said was that Miss Alcott's books have been a greater force for good among the girls and boys of this country than any other one etc., etc. Then rose a Modern — from New England, too — who cried out that Miss Alcott's books have done incalculable harm in all the nurseries of the land by implanting in young minds a false and priggish picture. I think Miss Alcott, with her conscientious little morals, turned over in her grave at that point. But I confess that that statement holds the best explanation I can see of why little girls still read her books. They are bad for them of course. Could any but pernicious influence hold such a fascination for so long? The fact is that little girls have a natural depraved taste for moralizing. They like to see virtue rewarded and evil punished. They like good resolutions. They like tears and quarrels and loving reconciliations. They believe in the ultimate triumph of good, in moral justice, and honeymoons in Valarosa. And Miss Alcott panders to these passions!

Let modern mothers bob their hair and talk the neopsychic talk. Let children spell by drawing rabbits; let them study the city water works. Yet it will not avail. For unless we take to censorship to protect them against the subversions of the past, little girls will read Little Women still.

Notes

1. *Little Women; Little Men*, by Louisa M. Alcott, in the Beacon Hill Bookshelf series. $2.00 each volume.

[The Influence of Louisa Alcott] Thomas Beer*

[Details of biographical background deleted.]

. . . Then her publisher wanted a book for girls. She didn't much like girls. Girls, it is possible, had always been rather shy of the Alcott sisters with their bad gowns and their curious papa. But she could write of herself and her family, so she wrote that first part of *Little Women* — and there it is, simple and as effortless as though she had spilled bright rags of silk from her lap on sunlit grass beneath a blowing lilac-tree.

[Further details of biographical background deleted.]

All this while the fat volumes of Louisa May Alcott had gone swarming in ugly covers across America from the press of Roberts Brothers, spreading the voice not of Bronson Alcott but of Abba May, his wife, a Puritan lady born in 1799. Her biographer admits that Louisa was unfitted by nature to comprehend Bronson Alcott. In the journal he is "my handsome old philosopher" but it isn't evident that his child cared for transcendentalism. In *Little Women*, *Little Men* and *Jo's Boys*, Pa is the merest shadow, and the heroic males of the long series are either handsome lads or brisk, successful bearded doctors, men who would hardly lug a delirious lady four hundred miles in railway coaches and who always have cash in pocket. Such philosophy as the books hold is just what Abba May had taught her children, and when the young folk of the tales have flared into a moment of wilful hedonism, it is a firm, kind lady, middle-aged, who steps forward and puts them right. Louisa was writing "moral pap." She couldn't conceive an unmoral book for children, and her own morality hadn't shifted since it was pressed into her by Ma, who had Louisa analyse her small self in a diary for inspection. Pa's lessons, such as "Apollo eats no meat and has no beard . . ." seem to have faded from her completely. God's ministrant is always female, sometimes abetted in virtue by one of the bearded doctors, and always a success. The children wriggle for a breath and then are towed meekly in the cool tide of rectitude. One learns a deal of Abba May Alcott in the progress. She was charmed with *Eight Cousins*, in which her representative rebukes current books for boys, the nonsense of Horatio Alger and Oliver Optic, with a fleet slap for *Innocents Abroad*, and comments: "It gives them such wrong ideas of life and business; shows them so much evil and vulgarity that they need not know about. . . . It does seem to me that someone should write stories that should be lively, natural and helpful — tales in which the

---

*Reprinted from *The Mauve Decade: American Life at the End of the Nineteenth Century* (Garden City: Garden City Publishing Co., 1926), pp. 20–21, 23–27. From *The Mauve Decade*, by Thomas Beer. Copyright 1926 by Alfred A. Knopf, Inc. and renewed 1954 by Alice Beer. Reprinted by permission of the publisher.

English should be good, the morals pure and the characters such as we can love in spite of the faults that all may have. . . ." She must have been delighted with *Rose in Bloom*, in which Rose Campbell gives talks on conduct to other girls in the dressing-rooms of balls, throws over her lover when he comes in a state of champagne to wish her a happy New Year, and waltzes only with her male cousins. She did not live to read *Jo's Boys*, which decides that men who have been, no matter how forgivably, in prison may not woo pure young girls. Righteous diversion? A jolly picnic on the river or a set of patriotic tableaux; a romp on the sands at Nonquit; red apples and a plate of gingerbread after sledding in winters; tennis and rootbeer under the elms in summer.

It is a voice of that fading generation which crowned William Dean Howells and shuddered with pleasure as it dabbled its hands in strong Russian waters, for Miss Alcott found *Anna Karenina* most exciting and liked *Kings in Exile* with its pictures of a dissolute Europe. She would even recommend *Le Père Goriot* as suitable reading for a girl of eighteen, but as for *Huckleberry Finn*, why, "if Mr. Clemens cannot think of something better to tell our pure-minded lads and lasses, he had best stop writing for them." . . . But she went on writing moral pap for the young and it sold prodigiously. The critics paid no particular attention. Miss Alcott wrote admirably for our little folk. It seems to have struck nobody that Miss Alcott's first audience, the girls who had wept over *Little Women* in the latter '60's, were now rearing their daughters in an expanded world on the same diet. In 1882 Joseph Choate turned on a witness in one of his cross-examinations with the cry, "Good God, madame! Did you think that your husband was one of Miss Alcott's boys?" but the lawyer was a profane fellow, given to whist and long dinners. There was no discussion of Miss Alcott's morality, and certainly nobody talked of her art: she wrote for the young.

[Details of Alcott's death deleted.]

The journals observed that she had been an admirable writer for the young. Mayo Hazeltine stated casually that "Miss Alcott has found imitators among writers who aspired to something more than the entertainment of nurseries." The gentle, forgotten Constance Woolson exclaimed on paper: "How she has been imitated!" and resumed the imitation of Henry James, a habit in which she so far progressed that *A Transplanted Boy* might have been written and destroyed by James himself. It was plain, to be sure, that a cooing legion was now busy in devising tales on the Alcottian formula, and one follower, Margaret Sidney, was simply a vulgar duplicate of Miss Alcott. But the reviewers generally had little to say of an influence, loosed and active for a quarter of a century, embedded in grown women from the nursery, familiar as a corset.

Dear Louisa

Eleanor Perényi*

In the 1886 edition of *Jo's Boys*, with a foreword written two years before her death, appears the engraved rendering of a profile of the best-loved children's writer this side of the Atlantic. The physical appearance of authors is always interesting and it is instructive to compare her with portraits of her contemporary female Victorians. Sand, of course, had the luck, or the taste, to be painted by a major artist. She is noble, cat-faced, elegant, and massive by turns as Delacroix saw her. E. B. B., even in the hands of a minor portraitist, is an irresistible cross between a poetess and a spaniel. George Eliot's hideousness is the authentic face of genius, as Lincoln's was.

Louisa May Alcott resembles none of them. Nothing in her face suggests genius or, it must be said, charm, but rather effort, discipline, and a kind of untidy gentility. With her rather large nose, hair in a bun, and tightly drawn mouth, she looks like an overworked English teacher. One is not surprised to learn that she did, indeed, die of overwork, at the age of fifty-six, and in the same year as her father, who did so much, in his simplehearted way, to kill her off. One remembers a phrase she often used—"early old"—to describe her prototype, Jo. Yet in her way she also had genius and, one may believe, charm.

It is curious how few children's classics were, in fact, written for children. Children tend to take over the adult immortals of the generation just past, and they remain faithful to the *démodé*. Louisa was not alone but somewhat exceptional in that she always knew her audience. And that audience she has not lost. Her publishers still sell some six thousand copies a year of her books to today's children and there is no telling how many people (myself included) reread her faithfully in spite of every killing change of fashion. She is astonishingly out-of-date. Sermons in stones are endless and the clichés fall like hail. One wonders that young stomachs ever digested it all, why they still do, and—as one reads unwillingly on and on—why one is oneself moving along with so much pleasure on the well-worn tracks. What is her fascination?

Apart from fantasy—*Alice in Wonderland* and sundry classics of our own day, in which Thurber's children's stories must be included—perhaps the most solid appeal to children's taste can be found in regionalism. Stevenson, *Uncle Remus*, and every cowboy story ever written make this appeal, and no one was more regional than Louisa Alcott. Though, like other prophets, she was not born in her soul's country but in Germantown, Pennsylvania, she eventually found her way to the geographic spot she belonged in. New England became her own. Concord is in every sense close to Walden Pond, and we are not surprised to learn that she prattled at Thoreau's knee, or that her father made his own Transcendental Utopia within

*Reprinted from *Harper's Magazine*, 211 (October 1955), 69–72.

the confines of that sacred circle which can be drawn by stabbing one branch of the compass into Beacon Street and sweeping the other in a fifty-mile radius.

Plain living and high thinking flourished within this circle as nowhere else in America and in Louisa's books the principle is rampant. Her liberalism is real, there is no doubt about it, but it takes some surprising forms to today's readers, surprising but, I think, very regional too.

Consider her attitude toward money. Nearly everyone in her books has it, or, as in the case of the Marches, has had it. And solid money it is, mostly we gather derived from ships and the China trade. Laurie's grandfather, the uncles in *Eight Cousins*, Tom Shaw's father, all are engaged in this business. (One astonishing little passage in *Eight Cousins* has a tiny Chinese kissing Aunt Plenty. He is a business associate of the uncles and presumably from that sink of iniquity, Macao, to which so many New England merchants and sailormen retired, though not in Louisa Alcott's books, with unuttered sighs of relief.)

There are, however, two very different ways of being well off. In all her works, we are shown the vulgar—only hinted at as Irish, and this in their names only—who are coming up. They are ostentatious, they have no breeding, they most mistakenly snub the simply dressed heroine. They are in complete contrast to the "good rich"—who are easily identifiable by simplicity, and even more by charitableness. Charity and breeding are intimately connected and this charity is curious in that no one seems to have found it offensive. To our minds, it is profoundly so. The solemn decisions to feed or clothe or employ the underprivileged radiate patronage, and sometimes foolishness. Beth, after all, got scarlet fever from her series of unnecessary visits to the poor German family next door. The Rose of *Rose in Bloom*, transparently modeled on Jane Austen's Emma but lacking, alas, all wit, is nothing short of insufferable to her protégée, the maid of all work, Phoebe.

Yet when all this is said, it must also be said that the moral is a sound one. It *is* nobler not to grind the faces of the poor, to assume responsibility for one's fellow creature. The capitalistic conscience, like other forms of conscience, first made itself felt in New England and Louisa could hardly help portraying it. In her world, everyone not only *seemed* to be on the side of the angels. In the 1860s, they really were. Bronson Alcott was, among other things, a Garrisonian Abolitionist. So, it can be assumed, was his daughter. No one suffered more than she from his improvident idealism. No one can have seen more clearly than he was something of a fool. But he was the right sort and she must have known this too.

As with slavery and economic responsibility, Louisa is also the liberal in her attitude toward women's rights and the dignity of labor. She wrote of ballot boxes and careers for women in 1869. This was not extraordinary in itself. The subject was not new. Frances Wright was lecturing on sexual equality thirty years earlier and my own grandfather, Robert Dale Owen, writing the first shattering tract on birth control for women as long ago as 1830. Louisa never ventured into such dangerous areas, naturally, but she was for women's rights all the same and not only because the achievement of independence is a reliable variant of the Cinderella theme. Herself forced to make her own way by hard work, she knew what she was talking about, and it is perhaps for this reason that her Jos and her Pollys, her hard-working girls, are her most successful characters.

So far, it is easy enough to analyze her personal version of New England liberalism. More difficult to sift is her point of view toward New England religion. To be sure, God is constantly mentioned. There is a most embarrassing scene in which Professor Bhaer, that shaggy philosopher devoted to the Socratic method, breaks into what we can guess (and she has real genius in that she is able to suggest more than she tells) to be a conversation among learned agnostics. At any rate they are questioning the existence of God and the Professor interrupts to defend the "good old beliefs" (Socrates? The New Testament? We are not told) and assert his faith. This makes Jo proud of him and even makes her love him.

Yet going to church is literally never mentioned in *Little Women*. Not even on Christmas Day, after the family has given their breakfasts to the exceptionally dreary Germans next door, do the Marches go to church. None of the girls is married in church. Mr. March is fleetingly depicted as some sort of minister, but again with no church, no parish, no religious duties. What is he supposed to be? One can only suspect that he is the rather curious shade of Ralph Waldo Emerson, whom Louisa knew and admired all her life. He wrote: "A man contains all that is needful for government within himself . . . the highest revelation of God is in himself." This was in his diary and she cannot have read it, but it is the essence of the institutional philosophy in which her father believed, and in which we must assume she believed also. It explains the flatness of the religious precepts, which appear everywhere but which seem to exist without a frame, and very nearly without truth. It saved her from some of the more tiresome forms of Puritan bigotry (which might also have bored or irritated her readers in other parts of the country), though not from all. In, for example, her attitude to foreign things, it is hard to say whether she is animated by bigotry or simple chauvinism.

Her New Englanders, like the real New Englanders, are traveled people. Their Europe, however, is a rather special continent. In Rome, the paintings — not the murals — of Raphael and the Forum are the important things. The idea of gaudily painted Greek temples was as hard for Louisa to bear as for the rest of the Victorians, and hers are the standard white. There is England — London is comfortably like Boston — sugar-coated Swiss Alps, and lastly, there is France.

France has ever been a tricky problem for the Anglo-Saxon of Louisa's temperament. Whether they have viewed it with horror or admiration, they have never conquered the idea that it isn't quite nice. Paris, to Louisa, was a place to indulge in harmless girlish vanities like kid gloves. Apart from Napoleonic relics, there is little to see. The real capital is Nice, which is full of light-minded, overdressed French, and many equally unreal other foreigners. It is pretty in a vulgar sort of way but on the whole it only makes one long to go back to Concord. By and large, her French are like her underbred rich, not the thing. The position of the "good rich" is occupied, astonishingly, by the Germans, who were, besides the English, the only respectable Europeans. Consider that mysteriously wicked affair known as "the French novel." A lifted eyebrow goes with the phrase, but what can it have referred to? Balzac? Flaubert? More probably Eugene Sue or the younger Dumas. No nice girl could afford to be found dead with one, though we may wonder if Louisa herself was. She was surely too good a craftsman not to be curious as to what others were up to. At any rate, from her special Emerson-Carlyle-Bronson Alcott bias, she rejected them, along with most of European civilization.

This rejection is interesting in another way, which appears in her views on education. It is a subject frequently dealt with in her books — there is Jo's school for boys, Laurie's college, etc. The system described as in use in these schools seems to be firmly anti-classical. It is, in fact, progressive. The pupils learn by doing (as Mr. March teaches his grandson the alphabet by forming the letters with his arms and legs), not by stuffing their little heads with dry facts, *i.e.* Latin grammar and English composition. The girls take the Victorian equivalent of home-economics courses. Now, there has always been something appealing to all Americans in this view of education's function, and we have been increasingly unable to make the European distinction between trade schools and schools. It is not the purpose here to go into this subject, except to say that in her attitude to it, Louisa Alcott was perhaps less New England than simply American. She hated the thought of the young subjected to any pressure other than that imposed by a healthy poverty, and had she lived another fifty years, would no doubt have come to hate that also.

In other words, for all the old-fashionedness of her technique and point of view, she is still modern in a number of surprising ways, of which the most striking is her mixture of high principle with immaturity. She was never quite grown-up, but then neither was her audience, and it has been her lasting legacy to mirror for young Americans certain more or less permanent attitudes inherent everywhere in American culture, but most particularly in New England culture. I believe it is this even more than the charm of her four immortal young women which has kept her going all these years. For children do not, strangely enough, merely demand a good story. There are many magnificent good stories which bore them to death. Hawthorne and Melville, for example, are today rarely sought outside the classroom. They are, as it were, too original, too full of creative risk. She was not.

Under the portrait spoken of before is Louisa's signature. For a creative writer, a woman who had labored as prodigiously as only the children of improvident idealists know how to labor, the handwriting is a strange one. It is a round, back-sloping hand of the kind associated a hundred years later with fashionable finishing schools for young women. It is also, if graphologists are to be believed, extremely inhibited. Here, one would say, was someone who never had her full chance, in life or as an artist. This we can believe was the case. Yet she succeeded brilliantly and in this was true to herself as well as to the peculiar tradition which bred her.

Mysteries of Louisa May Alcott

Ann Douglas*

I

When she published the phenomenally popular *Little Women* in 1868, and began her career as America's best-loved author for the young, Louisa May Alcott was thirty-five years old. An intensely private person, she disliked the lion-hunters who soon came in frightening numbers to the Alcotts' Concord home. She could not always avoid them, however, and the ensuing encounters were usually painful to her, and sometimes to her visitors. She recorded how a little girl wept violently and could not be comforted that this sharp-featured, grim, middle-aged woman was the author of *Little Women*. The anecdote is not so predictable and slight as it at first seems. Most of Alcott's critics have been less perceptive or less open than the little girl who so frankly registered her shock at the discrepancy between the literary persona and the reality of Louisa May Alcott.

Yet it is in part our growing awareness of this discrepancy that helps to restore Alcott's interest for us today. Martha Saxton's recent biography, *Louisa May*, is a major step in the process of reassessment. Her book follows logically upon Madeleine Stern's critical discovery and republication of Alcott's lost "thrillers" written before *Little Women*.[1] Saxton offers a psychological and cultural study of Alcott and her milieu, emphasizing the darker sides of her life and career. Although Alcott is diverse enough to provide material for books very different from Saxton's,[2] Saxton has powerfully delineated what has too long been ignored: the compulsions and fears that both inspired and limited the "children's friend." "Duty's faithful child," as her father, the transcendental philosopher Bronson Alcott called her, Alcott is for Saxton a haunting example of the consequences of unwilling adherence to Victorian literary and personal conventions.

---

*Reprinted from the *New York Review of Books*, 25 (28 September 1978), 60–63. Reprinted with permission from the *New York Review of Books*. © 1978 Nyrev, Inc.

"Shall never lead my own life," Alcott wrote in one of her many unhappy late journal entries, and she was partly right. A vehement, adventurous person with a dread of boredom, she played with boys as a girl, remained single all her life, at thirty enlisted briefly as a nurse in the Civil War, supported women's rights and other activist causes in middle age, and wrote prolifically always. Despite intermittent feverish travel, however, Alcott lived most of her life with her family in or near Concord. Her mentors were, of course, her father and his friends, Emerson, Thoreau, and other luminaries of Concord's Transcendental group. She increasingly disliked the place as high-talking and small-minded, yet never managed to escape it.

There is also an evident paradox in her career. She rose to fame as the author of cheery, nearly plotless books like *Little Women*, *An Old-Fashioned Girl* (1870), and *Eight Cousins* (1875), which she herself found of little interest. Yet she earlier published pseudonymously at least a dozen dazzling, highly plotted, sensational "thrillers" on which she worked with the utmost absorption. She had in fact a gift for melodramatic plot and the working out of deception and discovery which such a plot entails. How are we to understand the two very different sides of her work and character? Saxton offers a partial, but convincing, clue.

Louisa May Alcott was born in 1832, the second child of Bronson and Abba Alcott. Of farming stock, Bronson became a brilliant and improvident educator, unemployed for the better part of thirty years. Abba was a talented member of the well-bred, reform-minded Sewall and May families. The couple had four daughters and no son. From the start, Bronson and Abba considered Louisa difficult, even violent. Abba, a strong-minded, willful woman devoted to her husband but anxious for a little more of the worldly goods Bronson's high-mindedness bypassed, saw her second-born as cast in her own mold. She sensed in Louisa's moodiness, and the tenacious loyalty the girl increasingly used as the only means of controlling it, both a source of affection and some hint of future success in the world.

Until after the Civil War, Abba did more to support the Alcott family than her husband. An amateur pioneer in social work, a tireless laborer in her own home, she everywhere saw—her trenchant phrase—"woman under the yoke," and she impressed upon Louisa early that there would be "few to understand" her. Abba Alcott's matriarchal feminism and the largely patriarchal arrangements it kept afloat were to be, Saxton argues, an uneasy source of inspiration for Louisa all her life.

Abba is of course the model for "Marmee" in *Little Women*. Her energy, passion, and determination also lie behind the damned, struggling heroines of Louisa's early thrillers. But it was Louisa's father, as Saxton, I think rightly, stresses, whose precepts and personality guided, and perhaps damaged, Louisa's development most seriously.

Abba felt Louisa was her ally. Bronson, despite all the pride he eventually took in her, often considered her his opposition. He felt, not incorrectly, that Louisa was a creature of will, able to learn only through conflict. Hence, he noted in the journal he devoted to her early development, she experienced the world largely as intractable *materialia;* she would not discover the unchanging Platonic unity behind appearances in which he believed. And since Bronson was Louisa's teacher as well as father, it was difficult for her to elude or modify his definitions of her.

Bronson Alcott, a radical and unpopular pioneer in children's education, experimented largely perforce on his own offspring. His technique was deliberately to merge the extremes of introspection with the extremes of sublimation. His little daughters and the young students at the famous Temple School he ran for a few years in Boston in the mid-1830s were encouraged in unconventional ways to plummet the deepest reaches of their spirit in earnest discussions of everything from conscience to conception; but in the process they subjected their findings to inspection and judgment by their elders. Bronson once asked his pupils to "give me some emblems on birth." Most of them were well under ten years of age, and responded with answers such as birth is "like rain," or birth is "a small stream coming from a great sea," or birth is "the rising light." Alcott then simply closed the discussion: "I should like to have all your emblems, but have not time. There is no adequate sign of birth in the outward world, except the physiological facts that attend it, with which you are not acquainted." He had asked his students to think of things they could not fully realize.

Everywhere, there was little separation between private experience and public life in Louisa's education. She kept a journal from early childhood on. For some of us, keeping a journal as children is the first strike for secrecy, for having our own lives. Louisa's journal, her fledgling authorial effort, was written for her parents, who read it and penned commentaries for her edification. Louisa was by nature a complicated and perhaps difficult person; she might well have short-circuited herself under any conditions. But it is true, as Saxton argues, that she never even began to map out her inner self as she might have done if she had rebelled against a more conventionally pious and repressive family.

Saxton's analysis, if deterministic, is shrewd, but there are complexities in her own interpretation which she overlooks. Louisa, as Saxton notes, never wrote as extensively about her father as she did about the other members of her claustrophobically tight-knit family. She did not understand, much less sympathize with, his ideas, or with the poverty they entailed for his family. But Saxton, who sometimes casts Bronson simplistically as the villain in the piece, misses much that was interesting about him.

Many of his friends concurred with Emerson that, despite Bronson's inability to write, laugh, or "vary" himself (considerable defects), he might well be the "highest genius of his age." And Louisa herself not infrequently voiced the widespread if frequently contested view that her father was a "saint." Abba supported Bronson, if at times grudgingly, somewhat in the spirit that people supported anchorite recluses in the Middle Ages. Emerson felt the Commonwealth of Massachusetts owed Alcott a subsistence, and personally donated thousands of dollars to what Abba called her husband's "experiment in living." Bronson was convinced that he was called; like a medieval saint, he saw his life as a laboratory in which to explore the higher possibilities of his kind.

An early abolitionist, a full supporter of feminine rights, the founder of a short-lived but impressive Utopian community at Harvard, Massachusetts, Bronson rightly described himself as a "prophet" and a "hoper," and he put his hope in a future that might or might not be similar to the present. He restored old buildings. He was fascinated by gardens, and he planted and ably tended dozens of them. He is the only prominent American of the Victorian age who appears to have been almost consistently at peace with himself. He was complacent, yet he did not stagnate. Success as a writer and thinker came to him in his sixties and seventies; at eighty he opened a summer school for philosophic minds.

I stress my own view of Bronson Alcott, which is much more positive than Saxton's, because it both supports and modifies her analysis of Louisa's career. Saxton sees, rightly, that Louisa May Alcott's later work shows a steady decline. She dates the start of that decline with the publication of *Little Women*, because, she believes, Louisa was subject in that work to Bronson's influence, or her sense of it. This view seems too simple.

Bronson Alcott wrote that Louisa's favorite activity when she was a little girl was moving all her playthings back and forth between her father's study and her mother's realm, the nursery. He was recording a vignette that may be crucial to understanding Louisa, divided as she seems to have been between the different influences of her parents. Abba possessed a passion, a will that Louisa shared but mistrusted as perhaps wrong and certainly painful. Bronson was calm, serene in ways that seemed admirable, enviable, and yet perhaps deadening to his tense and troubled daughter.

In the few strong works of literature she wrote, we can, I think, see her drawing on these two very different sides of her nature. But we can also suspect that she was too torn between them to continue serious work for long in either the sensational or the domestic vein. She found herself blocked — and the impasse became itself the subject of her most interesting work.

Louisa May Alcott's achievement was both inspired and limited, as Bronson observed, by her obsessive need to objectify experience. In her work, emotions are best understood as purposes, and purposes almost literally as objects. Louisa always emphasized her "brains," by which she meant less her intellect than her will and ability to exploit it. She constantly talked of her mind in terms of physical entities, often mechanistic, technological, military ones: "Spinning brains," using brains as a "battering ram" against the world or as a "thinking machine" — these were her phrases in discussing her ambition. Always she disavowed "inspiration" and "genius" in favor of "necessity" to explain her motive for writing. Bronson never thought of himself as poor: for Louisa, as for Abba, poverty was her means of self-identification. It helped to explain her radical materialism. Louisa trusted only the concrete, and yet she was not, as her father sometimes thought, unimaginative. Far from it. It was rather that in contrast to—perhaps in impatient reaction to—Bronson's mystical inner life, Louisa's imagination was literal-minded: gravity was the law of her artistic impulse.

Louisa told part of the story of her creative career in the rather episodic novel *Work* (1873), written five years after *Little Women*, now finely re-edited by Sarah Elbert. Christie Devon, the heroine, sets out at twenty-one to find her fortune. Christie is an orphan, but she is also warm, talented, emotional, and giving. She marries happily, and has a child, only to be conveniently widowed so that she may head a little matriarchal community. Here as elsewhere in Alcott's work, what Elbert calls "domestic feminism" is the doctrine of the book; but it is not, as Elbert seems to think, its great strength. Louisa May Alcott's reformist themes were serious yet, for an Alcott, safe, and it was not in safety that Louisa's chief interest or her gifts lay.

What makes *Work* powerful is its description of Christie's quest for a career that will represent, stabilize, and even substitute for her inner life. *Work* is the saga of an unsuccessful search for objective, tangible self-realization. Christie, resembling here Louisa, tries in turn being an actress, a maid, a nurse, a companion, a hero-worshipper. The most haunting, truest material in the book is Christie's intermittent loneliness, her drift toward death — there are four suicide attempts in *Work* including Christie's own — and her constant fight, with the help of other women, against depression. Louisa almost drew in Christie a portrait of exhaustion; we catch glimpses of a woman determined to fight but drained by the struggle with a reality whose rigidity is the product both of her poverty and of the workings of her psyche. But only glimpses. By 1873, Louisa was stopping short of the demands of her subject. She had not always done so.

II

It is in her first novel *Moods* (1865) and the subsequent anonymous or pseudonymous "thrillers" she wrote for the popular periodical press during the 1860s, in the years immediately preceding *Little Women*, and now republished by Madeleine Stern, that we find some of Alcott's most powerful and revealing insights. On these Saxton rightly bases her critical re-evaluation of Louisa May Alcott.

During this period, Alcott was following the English masters of the so-called "sensation" novel. Dickens's *Great Expectations* and *Little Dorrit*, Mrs. Henry Wood's *East Lynne*, Wilkie Collins's *Woman in White*, and

M. E. Braddon's *Lady Audley's Secret* were enormous best-sellers of the early 1860s. These are all tales of premeditated crimes. The plots are characterized by incest, bigamy, confusions of identity, disguised returns from the grave—in short, by any violation of Victorian norms which involved deception and double identities.

Indebted as she was to her English contemporaries, however, Louisa May Alcott made this genre her own. She spent almost no time on the detective figures who intrigued Dickens, Collins, and Braddon. At her best, she did not let her *femmes fatales* even pretend to be helplessly sweet or feminine, nor did she waste time on the traditional "good" heroine who in the work of her peers opposed the bad one. She kept few secrets from her readers. She was more interested in the criminal mentality than in the process of comparing or unmasking it. Like Poe before her, Louisa May Alcott ignored the intricacies which other authors more interested in exposing the workings of society created; for her, deception, the essential plot of the sensation story, was material enough.

"Behind a Mask," written in 1866, is Alcott's masterpiece in this genre. The story concerns a governess called Jean Muir, who poses as a nineteen-year-old victim of fortune. In actuality (we know this from the start), she is an embittered thirty-year-old ex-actress, whose selfish ambition has condensed down to a desire to outwit the world once and for all and retire from her exhausting career of deceiving everyone all the time. Calculated step by calculated step, she wins the obsessive attention and love of the members of the well-born affluent family in which she is working. But her success is short-lived, and soon it seems her various deceptions will be publicly exposed. In a race against time, however, Jean secures the affection and hand of the elderly chivalric uncle of the house. She sweeps out of her fictive kingdom in triumph, leaving her detractors permanently silenced by her new status—a victory, one notes, seldom granted her English counterparts. She has proved herself a heroine—if only of deception.

For Louisa May Alcott, deception can be a means for women to infiltrate a closed world and get some of what they want from it. And, if nothing else, deception allows women to manipulate and make excitingly perilous their one culturally sanctioned area of expertise: the creation and display of emotion. Boredom is the ultimate nightmare in the sensationalist mode. Yet I do not agree with Saxton that the only source of Louisa May Alcott's artistic fascination with lies was her dilemma as a woman, closely linked as the two are. For Alcott, as for many of her literary contemporaries, deception was most compelling when used in cold pursuit of an object; a kind of literary calisthenics of the will.

Deception as the narrative focal point undermines the narrator's moral and reflective commentary on the plot, no matter how elaborate the plot itself. The novelist undertaking such a plot must have, first, as Wilkie Collins wrote, an "idea"; he must, almost perversely, work backward from the end, not forward from the start. We are back with Alcott's obsession with her "brains." Thinking backward, like counting backward, is abstract, an effort of the will. Jean Muir can promise a hostile young man who mocks her histrionic skill at the opening of the action that her "last act will be better" than her first. And it is, as she cruelly reminds him in the story's last line.

Deception requires an intense effort of the will, a constant vigilante hunt mounted against the emotions. Mark Twain once remarked that the pleasure of telling the truth is that one doesn't have to remember what one says. But the memory enforced by deception, memory as relentless attention, a persistent hangover of the most aggrandizing curiosity, a constant lashing of the mind to the objects it perceives, is exactly what Jean Muir and her creator are after. The plot of the sensation story provides an uncanny parallel to the way the mind desperately strives for some conscious hold on essentially unconscious material. Deception as a theme provides a way to psychologize a plot.

Deception, moreover, suggests a paralyzed tension between the desire for omnipotence and the fear of rejection, the twin fueling process of the will. Jean Muir makes everyone fall in love with her, at least for a while, and she does so by her ability to be all things to all people. Jean, using every charm in the book, proves that she can possess any gift which can be translated from a resource into a weapon. As long as she can conceive of a hostile purpose for any skill or feeling, it is within her command. She does not want to love; we know from other of Alcott's sensationalist stories like "V. V." that to love, for this kind of woman, is to die. Jean does not even want to be loved; she wants the exemption from scrutiny granted the loved object. She is buying time to avoid confronting the fissures of her self. Her ability to deceive depends on her belief that if she is herself fully known, the contradiction of her psyche will be literally explosive; she will not only be rejected, she will come apart. As Jean nails down the infatuation of various people in her world, she deals with each person more or less in isolation from the others. She is building up, objectifying in more and more extensive and concrete ways, the different facets of herself. The impending nemesis, from which Alcott rescues her, is one in which Jean would be left in a psychic graveyard full of the monuments of her fragmented personality.

It is a finale which her author could not altogether avoid. Louisa May Alcott could not sustain the inner strain of such fiction. In 1868, she turned more or less permanently from sensationalist novels to the even more lucrative and certainly safer juvenile market. We should not be surprised by the financial success of someone so aware of the difference material reward can make. Her first book for children, however, *Little Women*, despite Alcott's expressed lack of interest and belief in it, is an important book, even aside from its legendary popularity. Saxton reads it largely as a story of repression: Jo denies herself and becomes a woman, i.e., a diminished creature. I see it somewhat differently. A kind of Alcott family autobiography, *Little Women* seems an examination of the moral effort which a nature like Alcott's makes to bridge the distance between its own turmoil and the serenity represented by her father. To put it in literary terms, Alcott hoped to let sensational and domestic fiction educate each other.

Little Women is of course the story of four sisters, Meg, Jo, Amy, and Beth, and their strong and kindly mother, "Marmee." Although the women have seen better days, they are true gentlefolk who win the love and regard of their rich neighbors, Mr. Lawrence and his dashing, difficult grandson, Laurie. Mr. March, the father, clearly based on Bronson Alcott, is away for most of the action, serving as a chaplain in the Civil War. But he is not excluded simply as too difficult, or even too uninteresting, to handle; he is also an unattainable ideal for the conflict-laden Jo and her equally strong-tempered mother. He has the active life permitted men and the serenity legislated for women.

Jo's remarks, reflecting those of Alcott's early journals, are dotted with resolves to be good, dutiful, calm, in general "better." As she is well aware, she breaks most of her resolves daily. Jo, like other Victorians, like her author, hoped by resolution, especially by failed resolutions, to mount the will to change to crisis proportions and, in the process, to turn it in a complex campaign against itself. *Little Women* is about this incessant stimulating of the moral will; events, Marmee, Father, and her own conscience continually intensify Jo's struggle to subdue herself. She turns down the charming Laurie so like herself and accepts the poor, scholarly, awkward, warm-hearted German emigre, Professor Bhaer, so like her father, not just out of self-denial—as Saxton believes—but out of a genuine sense of herself. Jo, like Louisa, may confuse peace with repression, but that does not mean she does not want peace.

Jo is never entirely successful in her efforts at change. This is why we like her, and why she is real to us. We understand her desire to be steadier, less agitated. After all, her capacity for anger, unlike Jean Muir's, is, in this realistic setting, frightening: she almost kills Amy, her selfishness hastens Beth's death. And her partial success in modifying behavior is also convincing: this is the way it is, we think, this is what we can expect. The very fact that Jo does not marry above her social or financial station guarantees an ongoing life of work for her, and that is what she needs.

Beth of course is Jo's alter ego, and very similar to Mr. March. Jo is strong, although she is often frustrated and in turmoil. Beth has serenity, although she is very limited. We believe in Beth too—because we know from the start she is going to die. The trouble with the work that followed *Little Women* is that Jo's female successors bypass or overcome their wills, as Jo could not, and yet survive, even flourish, as Beth did not.

Under the Lilacs (1878), perhaps Alcott's worst book, concerns two sisters, the sweet, rather dull Bette, a Beth figure, and the warm-hearted but impetuous Bab, a Jo figure. At the story's close, Bab, a crack little archer—no one needs a knowledge of Freud or of classical mythology to sense the implications of her skill—deliberately throws an archery contest to a boy. Presumably, Bab thus becomes a true girl and at last earns the same affection Bette effortlessly attracts. Bab's conflict is Jo's, but her answer is not. Jo tried to cope with her nature, not cancel it. Bab's story is a fantasy, not a representation, of moral effort. Something has gone wrong.

Everything Louisa May Alcott wrote after 1869 was read. She gained an approval at home and abroad that never ceased to amaze and disturb her. She clearly felt, and with reason, that the acclaim showered on her was unearned. In her later children's books, such as *An Old-Fashioned Girl* (1870), *Little Men* (1871), *Eight Cousins* (1875), *Rose in Bloom* (1876), *Jack and Jill* (1880), and *Jo's Boys* (1886), Alcott simply reversed the patterns she had developed in her "lurid" writing, instead of testing them as she did in *Little Women*. In the early sensational writing, characters exploit and destroy "love" to gain their objects. In the late juvenile stories, children are taught to abandon the objects of their will to win love and approval: "taming" is the word repeatedly used to describe this breaking-in process. The sensational characters exist in a painful and creative solitude; their only real links to society are conspiratorial. In the later work, Alcott's little folks are seldom alone. They can never free themselves from what feels like a claustrophobically communal atmosphere: the orphan Rose meeting her "cousins," not to speak of half a dozen aunts and uncles, in a single week is a case in point. In a real sense, the later characters, for all the learning they ostensibly do, are just plain outnumbered.

The most enduring children's literature, Lewis Carroll's, Mark Twain's, E. Nesbit's, or Frances Hodgson Burnett's, shows children creating an autonomous world separate from the adult realm; childhood serves the author as a means to explore a less trammeled consciousness. In contrast, Alcott's later young people are under the constant and unquestioned guidance and surveillance of their Uncle Alecs and Mother Bhaers. "Queer" was a word Alcott often used in childhood about herself in the journals she wrote for parental inspection. The word does not appear in her sensational fiction, but it crops up again and again in her domestic tales. It serves Alcott as a catchbag for unexplored areas of psychic life.

Flippancy, even slyness, as Henry James noted in his hostile review of *Eight Cousins*, are the hallmarks of Alcott's later books for children. These works are often almost insultingly careless: Alcott's very real professionalism as a writer functions as a license to be slipshod. Whereas she entirely rewrote *Moods* (1865) at least three times, *Little Women* and all the books which succeeded it were sent off to be published more or less as rough drafts. Alcott's sincere avowals about the literary merits of unpretentiousness do not quite cover the case, or excuse the self-conscious use of slang, the acknowledged rambling and episodic nature of the narratives, the slighting references to major historical events, the willingness to reshuffle the prospects and fates of her characters to suit her little readers. These stories have no plots because the only permissible ending they offer is self-betterment. And if Alcott could not plot, she could not think, or perhaps even feel.

Yet the little girls of Alcott's later work have something in common with the *femmes fatales* of her early books: they too undergo metamorphosis, not growth. In a sense, murder pervades the worlds of both. The most interesting young figure in the last two March books, *Little Men* (1871) and *Jo's Boys* (1886), is Dan; he is an inadvertent murderer, a semi-sensational character, and Jo's favorite adopted "boy." But Jo has little more real contact with him than with her Bronson-like husband, Professor Bhaer. Dan has gone to the bad, as surely as Bhaer has gone to the good. Jo is in the middle, and the middle increasingly became the place for Alcott where extremes could not meet.

Notes

1. *Behind a Mask* (William Morrow, 1975) and *Plots and Counterplots* (William Morrow, 1976).

2. Note particularly Nina Auerbach's brilliant and subtle reading of Alcott in *Female Communities* (Harvard, 1978) and Sarah Elbert's forthcoming *Louisa May Alcott* (Little, Brown, 1978).

A Writers' Progress: Louisa May Alcott at 150   Madeleine B. Stern*

On 29 November 1832, Bronson Alcott, teacher and philosopher, wrote the following letter from Germantown, Pennsylvania, to his father-in-law Col. Joseph May: "It is with great pleasure that I announce to you the *birth of a second daughter*. She was born at half-past 12 this morning, on my birthday (33), and is a very fine healthful child, much more so than Anna was at birth, — has a fine foundation for health and energy of character. . . . Abba [Bronson's wife] inclines to call the babe *Louisa May*, — a name to her full of every association connected with amiable benevolence and exalted worth. I hope *its present possessor* may rise to equal attainment, and deserve a place in the estimation of society."[1]

While Louisa May Alcott could never be characterized as a woman of "amiable benevolence," her "place in the estimation of society" 150 years after that letter was written is indeed secure. She is recognized the world

*Reprinted from *AB Bookman's Weekly*, 70 (22 November 1982), 3579, 3582, 3584, 3586, 3590, 3592, 3594–97. The notes have been renumbered.

over as "a natural source of stories . . . the poet of children" who "knows their angels."[2]

Her books, especially the most famous of all — *Little Women* — and the so-called Little Women Series, have been translated into French and German, Italian and Spanish, Swedish and Norwegian, Polish and Portuguese, Finnish and Hungarian, Czech and Japanese. By 1947, when Frank Luther Mott compiled his *Golden Multitudes*, *Little Women* had sold "some two million copies . . . in America," and was thus entitled to a place among his "Over-All Best Sellers in the United States."[3]

As early as 1885, the Indianapolis Public Library showed considerable prophetic acumen by classifying all her books as "adult fiction,"[4] and now Ph.D. dissertations are being written on such subjects as "Concepts of Childrearing and Schooling in the March Novels of Louisa May Alcott" and "An Examination of Louisa May Alcott as 'New Woman.'"[5]

NOT ONLY FOR CHILDREN

Today her books are no longer regarded simply as primers for childhood but as works that crystallize the New England family in compassionate versions of the domestic novel genre. As she moves from the nursery to the study, Louisa Alcott is at last attaining a niche in American literary history long owing to her.

Louisa Alcott's extraordinary skill in creating a family portrait did not materialize overnight. It was, as most masterly writing is, the result of experimentation in diverse literary fields. Here was a writer who wove her fictional fabric not only from the threads of her own life but from the exercises of her experimenting pen. In the case of Louisa May Alcott, the stages by which she elevated herself to mastery and professionalism have long been overlooked, so intent has been the interest in the work of her literary maturity. Yet those stages are, to the critical explorer, transparent and revealing. More than most writers, Alcott essayed a variety of genres and tried her ink-stained fingers upon many techniques. To trace her development . . . is to trace the development of a writer from feeble beginnings through a labyrinth of failures and successes, to professional mastery. The stages in her writer's progress can be followed, step by step, in an adventure story of their own.

Louisa May Alcott was not always "The Children's Friend." Indeed, she began her writing career as many writers do, as child herself. Little Louy Alcott, age 8, penned four couplets addressed "To the First Robin."[6] Her childhood years were shaped by her extraordinary, perceptive, imperturbable and exasperating father Bronson Alcott, whose ultra-modern pedagogical theories were tried out on Louy and her three sisters; by her understanding, progressive, long-suffering and beloved mother Abba; by the radical tenets applied in father's Temple School in Boston where the pioneer kindergartner Elizabeth Peabody was a teacher as well as the redoubtable feminist Margaret Fuller.

Louisa Alcott's childhood was molded also by her experiences — by that unique sojourn in the community of Fruitlands in Harvard, Massachusetts, where her father and his associates proposed to establish a New Eden but where cold baths, linen tunics and solar diet were not compatible with a New England winter. As Emerson had put it after a summer visit to this consociate family in Paradise: "In July they looked well. He would see them in December." Then too little Louy Alcott's childhood was fashioned, after the family move to Hillside Cottage in Concord, Massachusetts, by father's neighbors, especially Emerson whom she worshiped, becoming the Bettine to his Goethe. For him and other neighbors, the Channings and the Hosmers, the Hillside barn was converted into a theater, and Louisa and her sisters enacted original scripts of melodramas, among them "Norna; or, The Witch's Curse," "The Unloved Wife," "The Captive of Castile," plays that invariably included desertions, suicides, and several elaborate speeches, not to mention daggers, love potions and death phials.

Louisa's childhood was enriched by excursions to the woods with neighbor Henry David Thoreau and by much reading in Charles Dickens. By the time she reached her teens the author was scribbling fairy stories for Emerson's daughter Ellen — those *Flower Fables* would become her first published book in 1855 — and filling her scrapbook with lines from Goethe and Wordsworth. Her mother wrote: "I am sure your life has many fine passages well worth recording. . . . Do write a little each day, . . . if but a line, to show me how bravely you begin the battle, how patiently you wait for the rewards sure to come when the victory is nobly won."

Still another influence was exerted upon the 19-year-old Louisa, a far less beneficent influence than any she had thus far experienced, but one that would also prove grist for her literary mill. At the mid-century, the family poverty was extreme. Mrs. Alcott opened an intelligence office or employment agency in Boston, and when the Hon. James Richardson of Dedham, Massachusetts applied for a companion for his sister, Louisa decided to take the position herself. Mr. Richardson proved somewhat less honorable than his title indicated, and Louisa Alcott as domestic servant was expected not only to dig paths through the snow, fetch water from the well, split kindling and sift ashes, but to play audience to her employer who invited her into his study for oral readings and metaphysical discussions. At the end of seven weeks of drudgery, the 19-year-old Miss Alcott was paid $4.00. Eventually she would write a bowdlerized account of "How I Went Out to Service," and eventually too she would find in the Hon. James Richardson a prototype for certain of her fictional villains.

The year of the humiliating experience at Dedham — 1851 — was also the year of Louisa Alcott's first appearance in print. Her poem "Sunlight" was published in *Peterson's Magazine* in September, and it was signed "Flora Fairfield."[7] This was the first but by no means the last of the Alcott pseudonyms. "Sunlight" was followed by bolder attempts at narrative, among them "The Rival Painters. A Tale of Rome," which adorned the pages of the *Olive Branch* in May 1852, and "The Rival Prima Donnas," a tale of vengeance by a stagestruck author in which one singer crushes her competitor to death by means of an iron ring placed upon her head. Again under the name of "Flora Fairfield," this exuberant piece of prose illuminated the pages of the *Saturday Evening Gazette* in 1854. Louisa Alcott, who was writing now both from experience and from imagination, was also crafting her narratives to suit a particular audience and was thus taking the first step toward professionalism. As a result, she soon became the mainstay of the *Saturday Evening Gazette* in which her contributions in verse and prose appeared until 1859.

The following year, a different type of work by the young author was published in the pages of an altogether different type of periodical. "With a Rose, That Bloomed on the Day of John Brown's Martyrdrom" was printed in *The Liberator* and would subsequently be reprinted in James Redpath's *Echoes of Harper's Ferry*. With the outbreak of the Civil War, Louisa Alcott entered upon yet another phase in her progress as a writer, and for that phase she assumed still another name half amusing, half pathetic. Her experience as nurse in the Union Hotel Hospital, Georgetown, D.C., transformed "Flora Fairfield" into "Nurse Tribulation Periwinkle."

[Details of the writing and publication of *Hospital Sketches* deleted.]

In return for five cents on each copy sold of the 1,000 printed, Redpath published "Tribulation Periwinkle's" *Hospital Sketches* in August. Louisa Alcott's first truly successful book, *Hospital Sketches* reaped praise from the press as a work "graphically drawn," "fluent and sparkling," with "touches of quiet humor." The writer who had at last tried her hand at realism was aware that truth might well be the fountainhead from which the best of her stories would one day flow.

Blood-and-Thunder Tales

She was still, however, experimenting. She had attempted both the roses of fairyland and the realism of hospital scenes. Now, under the compulsion not merely of her own desires but of publishers' demands, she was dipping her pen into a gall-like brew. Louisa Alcott's blood-and-thunder stories, published between January 1863 and February 1869, appeared for the most part either anonymously or under the pseudonym, not of "Flora Fairfield" or "Tribulation Periwinkle," but of "A. M. Barnard."[8]

[Details of the discovery of the Alcott thrillers by Leona Rostenberg deleted.]

The study of those extraordinary narratives seemed to indicate that their author knew as much about the macabre attractions of opium and hashish as she did about the wholesome pleasures of apples and ginger cookies. She had experimented with the fairy tale, with realistic war scenes, and with the gory and the gruesome. After *Hospital Sketches*, Redpath had published *The Rose Family* in 1864, Loring had published *Moods* in 1865, and her shockers had punctuated the late 1860s. Louisa Alcott had tried her hand at fiction and at fact. The time had come for her to combine the two in a tale that would "live in the memory" and win the reader forever.

Louisa Alcott's journal entry of September 1867 reads as follows: "Niles, partner of Roberts, asked me to write a girls' book. Said I'd try. F. [Horace Fuller] asked me to be the editor of 'Merry's Museum.' Said I'd try."[9] The author did indeed try both suggestions in reverse order. Having edited and written numerous contributions including the animal stories *Will's Wonder Book* for the juvenile monthly *Merry's Museum*, she began her girls' story for Niles of Roberts Brothers in May 1868, sending him 12 chapters the next month.

Her girls' story turned out to be a domestic novel set in 19th-century New England. In it she recovered her recollections of childhood and found in the biography of a single family the miniature paraphrase of the hundred volumes of the universal history. Her characters were her own family—her sisters, Anna, transformed into Meg, beautiful of course, for there must be one beauty in the book; artistic May, transmuted into Amy, afflicted with a nose not quite Grecian enough, and struggling in laborious attempts at elegance; Lizzie, metamorphosed into Beth, glorified a bit, the cricket on the hearth who sat in corners and lived for others. Beth was Jo's conscience. And Jo of course was Louisa—"Flora Fairfield," "Tribulation Periwinkle," "A. M. Barnard" all in one, tall and thin, with sharp gray eyes and long thick hair, odd blunt ways and a fiery spirit. Her father, addicted as he was to fads and reforms, was softly adumbrated, a mere shadow, but her mother shone forth as Marmee, whose gray cloak and unfashionable bonnet adorned a staunch defender of human rights.

Now in her mid-30s Louisa Alcott assembled the experiences and observations of her life and reproduced them in a book as vibrant and fresh today as it was in 1868. Louisa took up her pen, but the Marches wrote her story. Its background was the Concord, Massachusetts where her family lived. Its episodes included a composite melodrama entitled "The Witch's Curse, an Operatic Tragedy," alarmingly like the plays of the Hillside barnstorming days. The American home was here, reanimated in these pages, the good times, the tableaux, the sleigh rides, the skating frolics. By mid-July the author had finished what would become Part One of *Little Women*. Toward the end of August she read the proofs, writing in her journal: "It reads better than I expected. Not a bit sensational, but simple and true, for we really lived most of it; and if it succeeds that will be the reason of it."[10]

The reception was favorable, notices and letters indicated much interest in the four little women, and the publisher demanded a sequel or second volume for the spring. It was Part Two of *Little Women* that sealed its destiny. There, the sisters, three years older, were brought into young womanhood, Meg marrying John, Amy making a plaster cast of her own foot, Jo March reenacting Louisa's checkered literary career even to the inclusion of the *Blarneystone Banner* and the *Weekly Volcano*. The American countryside of the mid-19th century was unfolded here, historic notes of life and letters in New England were written, and under the roof of a single New England home could be discovered all the homes of America. A tale embodying the simple facts and persons of the family had been written. As one reader would observe: "She unlatches the door to one house, and . . . all find it is their own house which they enter." At the time of her death *The Boston Herald* would declare: "When the family history, out of which this remarkable authorship grew, shall be told to the public, it will be apparent that few New England homes have ever had closer converse with the great things of human destiny than that of the Alcotts."[11]

The publication of Part Two of *Little Women* in 1869 divided Louisa Alcott's life and profoundly influenced the course of her writer's progress. While its tremendous success relieved her from economic anxiety, it placed upon her the onus of persisting in the genre she had so enriched. "Flora Fairfield," "Tribulation Periwinkle," "A. M. Barnard" were discarded, and in their place emerged the world-famous author of *Little Women*, the "Children's Friend," who must place upon the altar of her reputation the literary sacrifices of sequel after sequel.

The first of them—*An Old-Fashioned Girl*, published in 1870—was not literally a sequel except that it adapted the style of *Little Women* to a different concept. Here Louisa Alcott simply inverted her household portrait of *Little Women* and created a domestic drama in reverse. The Shaw home, unlike the March home, provided glaring examples of the fashionable follies and absurdities against which the "Children's Friend" crusaded: the wad on top of Fanny's head, the fringe of fuzz around her forehead, her huge sashes and little panniers. From prevalent attacks of "nerves" to Grecian bends, from the giddy lives of 14-year-olds to the silly orthography that placed an *ie* after a jumble of *Netties*, *Nellies* and *Sallies*, she sent the stab of satire. And, set against this erring family shone the Old-Fashioned Girl Polly, who hailed from a home similar to the Marches', whose hearty good will and honest realism saved her from the fate of becoming a prig in a storybook.

Despite her own failing health, the author of *Little Women* completed her new book for Roberts Brothers. With her left hand in a sling, one foot up, head aching and no voice, she continued her crusade against the absurdities of a time when doctors flourished and everyone was ill, when switches and waterfalls adorned the hair of the fashionable, and when the fear of what people would think dominated polite society. It is in *An Old-*

Fashioned Girl that the author reveals the reasons for her adoption of a mannerless manner, a styleless style: "I deeply regret," she wrote, "being obliged to shock the eyes and ears of such of my readers as have a prejudice in favor of pure English, . . . but, having rashly undertaken to write a little story about Young America, for Young America, I feel bound to depict my honored patrons as faithfully as my limited powers permit; otherwise, I must expect the crushing criticism, 'Well, I dare say it's all very prim and proper, but it isn't a bit like us,' and never hope to arrive at the distinction of finding the covers of 'An Old-Fashioned Girl' the dirtiest in the library."

That ambition was filled not only for *An Old-Fashioned Girl* but for the stories about Young America and for Young America that followed. From memories of her father's Temple School in Boston she portrayed the Plumfield School of *Little Men*. The book was written while the world-famous author was touring Rome, and it was written to provide funds for her sister Anna whose husband had died. Since the story was told for Anna's two boys, she called it after them, *Little Men*. Louisa selected her "little men" carefully, choosing boys ripe for the methods of Plumfield where Latin and Greek were considered all very well but self-knowledge, self-help and self-control far better. To each of her characters she gave some fault awaiting help and, as she sat on a balcony overlooking the Piazza Barberini, she wove from her memories of Bronson Alcott's methods and Dio Lewis' musical gymnastics, from lessons at Fruitlands and the Hillside theatricals, from recollections of Dickens and neighbor Thoreau, from Walden woods and Tremont Temple the delightful episodes of *Little Men*. It was published on the day of her return home. Bronson Alcott and Louisa's publisher, Thomas Niles of Roberts Brothers, appeared at the wharf, and a great red placard announcing the new book—50,000 copies of which had been sold in advance of publication—was pinned in the carriage.

The attitudes of *An Old-Fashioned Girl* and of *Little Men* reappeared in the next volume of the so-called Little Women Series—*Eight Cousins: or, The Aunt-Hill*. Here the author's gospel on the education of American children was proclaimed, a gospel that included the discarding of medicine and the use of brown bread pills instead, the substitution of new milk for strong coffee, and brown bread for hot biscuit. Dress reform that loosened tight belts and suggested freedom suits was championed, along with the three great remedies of sun, air and water. As at Plumfield, less Greek and Latin, and more knowledge of the laws of health were recommended. As usual, Alcott was able to depict her dramatis personae with the broad strokes used in her thrillers and so she made not merely palatable but exciting her advocacy of the new enlightenment in food, clothing, and schooling. As Henry James remarked of her protagonist Uncle Alec, she had ridden atilt at the shams of life.

That crusader's ride was continued in the sequel to *Eight Cousins*, *Rose in Bloom*. So too was the author's skill in extracting from the mine of memory the beads to string upon a thin thread of plot. The two themes—autobiography and reform—were combined. Touches reminiscent of *Little Women*—the gifts four sisters had given one another, May's casts and easels, Lizzie's fever—reappeared in a new guise, along with gems from Thoreau's *Week on the Concord and Merrimack Rivers*, Emerson's *Self-Reliance*, and Dickens' *Nicholas Nickleby*. Upon her thread the author also strung the beads of temperance, woman's rights, and philanthropy, and, since her characters were strong and credible, her message reached its target. In 1876 *Rose in Bloom*, the fifth of the Alcott full-length juveniles, joined its predecessors on the bookshelf.

Between 1877 and 1886 only three more would follow. Like *Eight Cousins*, *Under the Lilacs* was serialized before book publication in the pages of *St. Nicholas*, and there a new type of Alcott hero made his appearance—a performing poodle, Sancho, who wore a tassel at the end of his tail and ruffles around his ankles. Research for her leading character was carried on at Van Amburgh's Menagerie, and once again, partly to forget the anxieties of her mother's illness and partly to embellish her story, Louisa plumbed the depths of the past. The result was a waltzing, parading poodle who, with a whisk of his tasseled tail, leapt straight into the hearts of all readers of *Under the Lilacs*.

In a sense, *Jack and Jill*, which appeared over the Roberts Brothers imprint in 1880, was an expansion of *Little Women*. Here, not a single family, but an entire village takes the stage. A boy and girl in an upset sled are discovered at the rise of the curtain, and from then on Concord, Massachusetts, transmuted into Harmony Village, is spotlighted. The clubs and skating excursions, the Milldam stores, the hemlocks, the river are all here, the fairground and yearly apple picking, the school festival in Town Hall, the performances of the Dramatic Club—the whole quiet life of a New England village is reanimated in these pages. So too are the children, for they are life studies of the children the author had known in Concord. Here indeed Louisa Alcott produced another domestic novel, not of a single family but rather of a village whose geography was New England's, whose history was Concord's.

The last of the Little Women Series was not published until 1886. A sequel to *Little Men*, *Jo's Boys, and How They Turned Out* catches a thread dropped more than a decade before and follows the little men to maturity. Here again was a dramatis personae from the past—an Aunt Jo in a vortex, an Amy whose proteges included ambitious young painters and sculptors, a Mr. March who discussed Greek comedy in the study for the edification of the Plumfield Parnassus. Partly because of her ill health, partly perhaps because she sensed the book would bring down the final curtain on the Marches, Louisa Alcott tarried over its writing. Working only one or two hours a day, she once again drew the threads of her life into the fabric of a book. The Plumfield plays were the theatricals of her youth; a scene depicting a ward in an army hospital was modeled directly upon Georgetown; again the trumpet of reform sounded clarion calls for women's rights, temperance and the freedom dress. If some of those calls sounded like echoes, and if certain of the incidents were stereotyped, there were still enough simple domestic scenes left to touch the hearts of readers. The weary historian was strongly tempted to close her tale with an earthquake that would engulf all of Plumfield. Instead, having, as she put it, endeavored to suit her readers with many weddings, few deaths, and as much prosperity as the eternal fitness of things would permit, she simply let the music stop, the lights die out, and the curtain fall forever on the March family.

If none of the books that followed *Little Women* quite attained the stature of that masterpiece, the eight books that comprise the Series form a composite picture of life in 19th-century New England. The March family and the families in companion volumes are, however, also touched with universality. In a simple and enduring way, Louisa Alcott created a saga of 19th-century America that is unbounded by time or place. The door she unlatched to one home unlatched the doors of every home.

During the almost 20 years when those books were written, the author, "a natural source of stories," composed an abundance of minor works. Hundreds of her tales appeared in periodicals and were reprinted in collections—the six volumes of *Aunt Jo's Scrap Bag, Spinning-Wheel Stories*, the three volumes of *Lulu's Library* named for May's daughter after May's tragic death. Unequal as these stories may be, they all reflect the facile skill of the professional writer who, after diverse experimentations, had learned the art of painting character to the life and the art of extracting from the exigencies of installment demands the triumph of suspense.

Experimenter that she was, Louisa Alcott understandably wearied of the task of supplying the books expected by her avid public.

[Comments on the Alcott interest in "lurid style" deleted.]

Upon a few occasions she deviated from the pattern set in her Little Women Series and wrote to please herself and indulge her "natural ambition . . . for the lurid style." One of the most interesting of those deviations is *A Modern Mephistopheles*.

Opportunity to give vent to her "gorgeous fancies" came to her when her publishers, Roberts Brothers, launched a No Name Series to which well-known authors were to contribute anonymously. Louisa Alcott's anonymous contribution was a novel in which she analyzed the "psychological curiosity" that penetrates and violates "the mysterious mechanism of human nature." Interspersed through *A Modern Mephistopheles* are metaphysical borrowings from Goethe and Hawthorne, as well as themes dredged up from the days of her thrillers: mind control and the lure of drugs.

When it was published in 1877, reviewers gratifyingly asked: "Who wrote this story? Whose hand painted these marvellous pictures of the angel and the demon striving for the mastery in every human soul?"[12] As for the author, she commented in her journal: " 'M.M.' appears and causes much guessing. It is praised and criticised, and I enjoy the fun, especially when friends say, 'I know *you* didn't write it, for you can't hide your peculiar style.' "[13]

Yet Louisa Alcott's style was far less limited in its applications than her friends believed. That she is indeed entitled to a high place in the hierarchy of American writers is only recently becoming apparent. The bowdlerized and uncritical work of her first biographer Ednah D. Cheney did nothing to advance such a conviction. The delightful picture of *Invincible Louisa* by Cornelia Meigs was painted for a juvenile market, while the *Louisa May Alcott* drawn by Katharine Anthony in 1938 suffered from the limitations of the genre known as psychological biography. My own biography of Alcott which was first published in 1950 was an attempt to provide a full-length portrait with extensive documentation, and it has been described as marking "the beginning of serious modern study of the subject." So-called modern studies have included two recent biographies—one by Martha Saxton who, inspired by publication of the Alcott blood-and-thunder stories, viewed their author "through a glass darkly," suggesting that she was the guilt-ridden victim who hailed from a house of horrors. Madelon Bedell's *The Alcotts*, scholarly and authoritative, is rather the biography of an entire family than of any one of its members.

As for Louisa Alcott bibliography, at least three useful works are available:[14] the first by Lucile Gulliver, which is limited to the writer's publications in book form; my own which includes 291 numbered items of books and contributions to periodicals; and a recent reference guide by Alma J. Payne which is particularly useful for its secondary bibliography of writings about Alcott.

A careful study of that secondary bibliography indicates that gradually Louisa May Alcott is coming into her own. *Little Women* has been compared with *Pride and Prejudice*, and Alcott's educational concepts, her attitudes toward feminism, her relations with her father, her novels as commentary on the American family, are all being analyzed. The few unpublished stories still available in manuscript form—such as *A Free Bed* which was acquired by Brigham Young University Library—and the letters that occasionally appear on the market . . . are the object of avid collection and eager study. . . .

Although Louisa Alcott was indeed the "Children's Friend," she was far more. As "Flora Fairfield," "Tribulation Periwinkle," "A. M. Barnard" and author of *Little Women*, she made her writer's progress. The multi-faceted career of this experimenting author may at last be traced in all its fascinating phases, and the mastery to which it led may now be recognized.

Notes

   1. Richard L. Herrnstadt, ed., *The Letters of A. Bronson Alcott* (Ames: Iowa State University Press, 1969) pp. 19 f.

   2. The description, by Emerson, is quoted in Madeleine B. Stern, *Louisa May Alcott* (Norman: University of Oklahoma Press, 1971) preliminary page.

   3. Frank Luther Mott, *Golden Multitudes: The Story of Best Sellers in the United States* (New York: Macmillan Company, 1947) pp. 102, 309.

   4. John Tebbel, *A History of Book Publishing in the United States* (New York and London: R. R. Bowker, 1975) II, 600 f.

   5. Alma J. Payne, *Louisa May Alcott: a reference guide* (Boston: G. K. Hall & Co., 1980) pp. 73, 75.

   6. Ednah D. Cheney, ed. *Louisa May Alcott: Her Life, Letters, and Journals* (Boston: Roberts Brothers, 1889) p. 16 [Hereinafter Cheney]. For biographical references to Louisa May Alcott throughout, see Cheney and Stern, *Louisa May Alcott*.

   7. For this and further bibliographical Alcott references, see Madeleine B. Stern, ed., *Louisa's Wonder Book — An Unknown Alcott Juvenile* (Mount Pleasant: Central Michigan University, 1975) pp. 25–52.

   8. For the Alcott blood-and-thunder stories, see Leona Rostenberg, "Some Anonymous and Pseudonymous Thrillers of Louisa M. Alcott," *Papers of the Bibliographical Society of America* XXXVII:2 (1943); Madeleine B. Stern, ed., *Behind A Mask: The Unknown Thrillers of Louisa May Alcott* (New York: William Morrow, 1975); Madeleine B. Stern, ed., *Plots and Counterplots: More Unknown Thrillers of Louisa May Alcott* (New York: William Morrow, 1976).

   9. Cheney, p. 186.

   10. *Ibid.*, p. 199.

   11. These comments, the first by Cyrus Bartol, the second from *The Boston Herald* (7 March 1888) are quoted in Stern, *Louisa May Alcott*, preliminary page.

   12. Louisa May Alcott, *A Modern Mephistopheles and A Whisper in the Dark* (Boston: Roberts Brothers, 1889) advertisement at end, quoting from review in *The New Age*.

   13. Cheney, p. 297.

   14. Lucile Gulliver, *Louisa May Alcott: A Bibliography* (Boston: Little, Brown, and Company, 1932); Alma J. Payne, *Louisa May Alcott: a reference guide* (Boston: G. K. Hall & Co., 1980); Madeleine B. Stern, *Louisa's Wonder Book*, pp. 25–52.

The Scarlet Strand: Reform Motifs in the Writings of Louisa May Alcott

Freda Baum[*]

In *Jo's Boys*, by Louisa May Alcott, there is a scene in which Jo counsels her nephew as he prepares to go to the sea. There is, she tells him, a strand of red in every inch of rope used by the British navy so that wherever a bit of

---

[*]This essay was written for this volume and appears here for the first time by permission of the author.

it is found, it can be identified. Similarly, virtue — by which is meant honor, honesty, courage, and "all that makes character" — marks a good man wherever he is.[1]

As the scarlet strand appears throughout the rope, so do espousals of those values and ideals favored by Alcott appear throughout her writings. Louisa May Alcott was not satisfied that the world was as true or as just as it could be, and she repeatedly used her pen as a weapon against injustice.

In order to understand Alcott's commitment to reform, it is necessary to consider her perception of individual worth. Alcott was raised in the midst of a group of intellectuals which included Ralph Waldo Emerson, Henry David Thoreau, and, of course, her father, Bronson Alcott. These men believed that all individuals, regardless of race or sex, were part of an "oversoul" and were therefore divine. The potential of human beings was stressed, not the limitations upon them. It is natural that the thinking of the young Louisa was molded by this community. In addition, Louisa knew and was influenced by many reformers and philosophers of the day, including Theodore Parker, William Lloyd Garrison, Elizabeth Peabody, Margaret Fuller, Frederick Douglass, and her uncle, Samuel J. May. Acquaintance with such personalities early convinced Alcott of the worth of the individual self, and anything which threatened the development of human potential was fuel for her ire.

The journals of Louisa May Alcott reveal that the greatest concern of her early life seems to have been the abolition of slavery and the greatest concern of her later years, women's rights. These interests are reflected in her writings, along with defenses of temperance and the rights of blacks, Indians, and the poor.

In the evil of slavery Alcott recognized a class of persons who had been deprived of the opportunity to develop their individual worth. Alcott was raised in an abolitionist household. Her home in Concord was a station on the underground railroad, and the Alcott family consciously attempted to boycott goods produced by slave labor.[2] Slavery was believed to be an unholy subjection of worthy individuals and was among the greatest of all wrongs.

Alcott's first antislavery story, "M. L.," was written as early as 1860 but was not published for three years. As Alcott wrote in an 1860 journal entry, "Mr. — — — won't have 'M. L.' as it is antislavery, and the dear South must not be offended."[3] The hero of "M. L." is Paul, the son of a Cuban planter and a slave. After much hardship, Paul escapes his slavery and comes to the United States, where his good character wins the love of a worthy woman and the respect of those able to see beyond his race.[4]

Alcott's second antislavery tale, "The Brothers," was published in 1863. In this story, a mulatto contraband is assigned to help a Civil War nurse in caring for a wounded Confederate. Upon first seeing her assistant, the nurse is impressed with his noble appearance. The instant the black becomes aware of the white woman's presence, however, "the man vanished and the slave appeared. Freedom was too new a boon to have wrought its blessed changes yet. . . ."[5] Treated respectfully by the nurse, the former slave eventually gains self-respect and becomes the man God intended him to be.

These two stories, although overly sentimental, are striking in their uncompromising antislavery sentiment. They are also striking in that the heroes of both tales are noble characters. Alcott makes no assumption of black inferiority. Both characters are degraded because of their slavery, not because of their race. Once the shackles of slavery have been abandoned, Alcott implies, the Negro can reach his potential as a human being. In 1881, when Alcott was a famous and successful author, she wrote about the abolitionist movement, saying, "[I] take more pride in the very small help we Alcotts could give than in all the books I ever wrote or ever shall write."[6]

Louisa Alcott did not simply look back to the abolitionist movement. Her fiction reveals a continued concern with the rights of blacks. In *Work*, published in 1873, the character Hepsey is a noble and self-sacrificing freedwoman who needs only friendship and an education, both of which are provided by Alcott's heroine, to erase "the tragedy of her race written in her face."[7] When the "little women" grow up, the school operated by Jo and her husband accepts a Negro pupil, "though some people predicted that his admission would ruin the school."[8] In *Jo's Boys*, a college is established which so believes "in the right of all sexes, colors, creeds, and ranks to education" that those welcomed include "the awkward freedman or woman from the South."[9]

Blacks were not the only worthy individuals powerless in a white man's world. The worth of women was also largely unrecognized. Alcott's anger at the subjection of women is reflected in her fiction, which presents a powerful, and sometimes angry, picture of the role of women in nineteenth-century America. A great contribution of Louisa May Alcott to literature is her insistence that women are capable beings who should be allowed a choice of life-styles. Whether she chooses to be a wife and mother or a career woman, she should prepare for her vocation. Mrs. Shaw, in *An Old-Fashioned Girl*, falls into her role as a mother and fails miserably. Marmee, whose nature suits her for the home, has developed those qualities which enable her to wisely guide her daughters. Alcott never suggests that it is better to be a professional than a homemaker, nor does she suggest that it is better to be a wife and mother than to follow a career. Both types of lifestyle are noble as long as each has its roots in the nature of the individual.

Louisa Alcott's heroines vary in talent and temperament, and they find fulfillment in various ways. Marmee and Meg achieve useful, self-satisfying lives in the home, while Nan finds happiness as a physician and Josie as an actress. Jo successfully combines her role as wife and mother with her writing career. Polly, Fanny, and Rose achieve a sense of personal worth by helping others. Each contributes to society in a way that Mrs. Shaw or

Rose's stylish Aunt Clara cannot because each has achieved her potential as a human being.

If women were to be able to achieve their potential, they needed access to adequate educations. Alcott's writings are sprinkled with remarks concerning the education of both boys and girls, which is perhaps to be expected from the daughter of Bronson Alcott. The daughter agreed with the father that education should be based not on sex but on interest and ability. Young minds should not be tasked with long, hard lessons "parrot learned" but should be made to unfold as naturally as a blooming rose. Exercise and play were as important as lessons in educating the whole child.

Alcott urged women and men to get to know one another so that men could realize that women were not decorative, mindless dolls but capable, intelligent individuals who could help their brothers with the work of the world. She insisted that boys and girls should play and attend school together so that they could know each other as human beings, not merely as potential mates. Such a system is in operation at Plumfield, which is in effect a microcosm of a better world in which women are accepted as man's equals. The world is operated jointly by man and woman, as Jo and Professor Bhaer each uses his talents to contribute to the school. At Plumfield, boys and girls play and learn together, gaining in knowledge and respect for each other. Each child is encouraged to discover, develop, and use his inherent capabilities, and each achieves a sense of identity and fulfillment. The males of Plumfield never relegate the females to a sphere; each individual, male or female, is accepted on the basis of his nature. Plumfield is no utopia; Alcott was too aware of human frailties to create a vision of perfection. It is, however, a glimpse of the better world which she was sure would come one day when women achieved full citizenship and recognition.

If women were to function and to contribute to the world, they needed health and comfort unimpaired by the uncomfortable and ungainly garments designed for them. The adoption of clothing which is loose and comfortable enough to allow women to work and exercise is repeatedly advocated by Alcott, most notably in *Eight Cousins* when Rose is given a new outfit by her Aunt Clara. Rose rejects the outfit which, though fashionable, impairs her step, exposes her neck and feet to the cold, veils her eyes, and encases her in a corset, in favor of Uncle Alex's warm, loose-fitting suit which allows her to run and breathe freely.

With her abilities, her education, and her health, the new woman should be allowed to support herself. Alcott was, however, sensitive to the plight of working women. Christie's employment experiences in *Work* are similar to Alcott's own, leaving no doubt that Alcott was aware that hard work and low pay were the norm, rather than the exception, for working women. When, in *An Old-Fashioned Girl*, Jane, who is not gifted like Polly or Jo or wealthy like Rose or Nan, attempts to commit suicide rather than face the temptation of turning to prostitution in order to support herself, Alcott makes it clear that such women deserve a better chance at life. For the benefit of women like Jane, Fanny's wealthy sewing circle is urged not to be tightfisted with their seamstresses, Rose operates an apartment house for poor but respectable women, and an education is offered to dozens of girls at Laurence College.

Her acquaintance with intelligent women and her concern with social issues led Alcott to support the organized battle for women's rights. She advocated the adoption of suffrage as acknowledgment of woman's worth and because the issues voted upon were of importance to both sexes. When Concord's female residents were granted the right to vote for members of the school committee, she was the first woman to register her name as a voter. Alcott prized her voting privileges, meager as they were, saying, "I, for one, don't want to be ranked among idiots, felons, and minors any longer, for I am none of the three."[10] Her writings in the *Woman's Journal*, for which she was an "unpaid contributor," are not widely known yet include lively descriptions of her voting experiences and her largely unsuccessful efforts to encourage other townswomen to vote.

The issue of suffrage is not ignored in Alcott's fiction but is presented as a desired recognition of woman's worth. The women of Plumfield, like those of Concord, are granted limited enfranchisement, and they take full advantage of their new right. Similarly, when Becky in *An Old-Fashioned Girl* decides to sculpt the "coming woman," a ballot box is placed at the feet of the statue as an indication that the new woman has earned the right to use it.

Along with her belief that women were worthy individuals, Alcott felt that women were fully capable of doing some of the work needed to make the world a better place, and she labored to give women a voice in society. Alcott thought it ridiculous to remain silent in the face of injustice or social wrong simply because female involvement was not considered proper. Even the wife and mother should be concerned about social issues because, as Marmee says, "Don't shut yourself up in a bandbox because you are a woman, but understand what is going on, and educate yourself to take your part in the world's work, for it all affects you and yours."[11]

Among the reforms that Alcott, via her characters, advocated was temperance. The author helped to start a temperance society in Concord because it was "much needed in C. A great deal of drinking, not among the Irish, but young American gentlemen, as well as farmers and mill hands."[12] Charlie, in *Rose in Bloom*, serves as a sad example of an individual so consumed by alcohol that he never becomes the man he might have been. In Alcott's temperance story, "Silver Pitchers," the three heroines decide to discourage drinking among their fathers, brothers, and beaux. The girls realize that they are being unladylike by the standards of the day, but they cannot justify turning "virtuously away from the poor soul we might perhaps have saved if we had dared."[13]

Alcott, and her characters, also spoke out for those she perceived as the downtrodden. She felt that Indians, like blacks, had been mistreated. In *Jo's Boys*, Dan refers to the Montana Indians as a much wronged people who had been "cheated out of everything, and [were] waiting patiently, after being driven from their own land to places where nothing will grow."[14]

In *Little Women,* Jo and Amy have a conversation in which Amy expresses her dislike of reformers. The character of Jo is modeled after Louisa, and her response to Amy's statement is characteristically Alcott. Jo says, "I do like them, and I shall be one if I can, for in spite of the laughing the world would never get on without them. We can't agree about that, for you belong to the old set, and I to the new: you will get on the best, but I shall have the liveliest time of it. I should rather enjoy the brickbats and hooting, I think."[15] Throughout her life, Alcott demonstrated concern for those who by accident of race or sex or circumstance were not allowed to develop their full potential as human beings. Alcott's novels and stories are not mere adventure tales written to amuse young readers. They constitute a whole catalog of nineteenth-century social concerns. The scarlet strand of reform makes Alcott's works important cultural artifacts and provides ever-constant reminders of her dissatisfaction with an imperfect world.

Notes

1. Louisa May Alcott, *Jo's Boys and How They Turned Out* (Boston: Little, Brown, 1905), p. 116.

2. Amos Bronson Alcott, *The Journals of Bronson Alcott*, ed. Odell Shepard (Boston: Little, Brown, 1938), p. 188.

3. *Louisa May Alcott: Her Life, Letters, and Journals*, ed. Ednah D. Cheney (Boston: Roberts Brothers, 1889), p. 120.

4. Louisa May Alcott, "M. L.," *Journal of Negro History*, 14 (1929), 493–522.

5. Louisa May Alcott, "The Brothers," *Atlantic Monthly*, 12 (1863), 585.

6. L. M. Alcott, *Journals*, p. 342.

7. Louisa May Alcott, *Work* (Boston: Roberts Brothers, 1893), pp. 20–21.

8. Louisa May Alcott, *Little Women* (New York: Collier, 1976), p. 537.

9. Alcott, *Jo's Boys*, p. 282.

10. L. M. Alcott, *Journals*, p. 342.

11. Louisa May Alcott, *Little Women*, p. 432.

12. L. M.Alcott, *Journals*, pp. 342–44.

13. Louisa May Alcott, "Silver Pitchers," in *Silver Pitchers and Independence: A Centennial Love Story* (Boston: Little, Brown, 1908), p. 40.

14. Alcott, *Jo's Boys*, pp. 75–76.

15. Alcott, *Little Women*, p. 331.

The Secret Imaginings of
Louisa Alcott   Martha Saxton*

Jo March, taking a critical look at the "sensation stories" she was writing said, "They *are* trash, and will soon be worse than trash if I go on; for each is more sensational than the last. I've gone blindly on; hurting myself and other people, for the sake of money; I know it's so, for I can't read this stuff in sober earnest without being horribly ashamed of it; and what should I do if they were seen at home, or Mr. Bhaer got hold of them."[1] With that, Jo quit writing thrillers.

Just like Jo, Louisa Alcott wrote what she called "lurid" stories. And, just like Jo, in 1867, after five years, she swore off them. These tales, written under the pseudonym A. M. Barnard for a pair of weekly newspapers, disappeared, and only in 1943 did Leona Rostenberg recover them.[2] They were edited and published in two volumes by Madeleine Stern.[3]

The stories, which deal with revenge, murder, incest, insanity, thwarted love, and drugs represent, of course, an almost unbelievable departure in subject matter for the author whose fame rests on *Little Women*. Madeleine Stern in her introduction to the first volume, *Behind a Mask*, supplies answers to the provocative question, how did the author of *Under the Lilacs* know about madness, deceit, vengeance, hashish, and homicide? She also suggests a theme on which I would like to enlarge, namely, the emotional release these stories offered Louisa Alcott and the liberating effect a pseudonym had on her imagination.

The strength of these stories is directly proportional to the degree to which Alcott felt them. Her style remains fluid from the best to the worst, but the most successful stories are differentiated by the involvement and the depth of understanding the author displays for her characters, especially her heroines, and the consequent intensity of emotion these characters elicit.

Using this criterion, "Behind a Mask"[4] is among the most engaging and reveals much about the author. Jean Muir is probably the most complex and human of the A. M. Barnard heroines — a thirty-year-old actress with a disreputable past who seduces her way through an entire family before marrying an elderly lord. Jean is two people, one who performs her governess and companion duties perfectly while turning the heads of all the household males by her apparent frankness, youth, and charm. The other, the real Jean, is dangerous, vengeful, unscrupulous, and bent on getting her own way. She is, above all, hidden, keeping every true feeling inside and displaying only those which will forward her cause.

Like every character truly felt by its author, Jean Muir represents aspects of Alcott's imagination of herself. So, in this case, she represents Al-

---
*This essay was written for this volume and appears here for the first time by permission of the author. © 1984 by Martha Saxton.

cott's view of herself as good on the surface, but bad, angry, and unforgiving underneath. One of the beauties of this story, in terms of both writing and psychology, is that the reader understands and forgives Jean. Alcott has made her "bad" heroine attractive to us. Technically, she does it by keeping the "good" Jean on stage most of the time, while we only experience the "bad" Jean in letters and secondhand reports. She also makes Jean's judgments of people accurate whether they are informed by sympathy or detestation. Thus, we always agree with Jean's view of what is going on even if we do not approve of her methods and goals.

A major emotional satisfaction of this story is that Louisa Alcott manages to integrate good and bad Jean by the end. Jean makes off with her prize, the no-longer-young Lord Coventry, one of Alcott's many fictional father-husbands. That he marries her in spite of revelations about her ugly past says that he accepts both Jeans and will love them as one woman.

Another satisfying aspect of the story is that Jean's industry, right or wrong, triumphs over aristocratic lethargy. She shakes up a dull, inward-looking family of the spoiled upper class. Like any good Alcott heroine, she teaches all of them little moral lessons in the process of getting what she wants. The fact that she has a scandalous past is morally balanced out by the Coventrys' tendency to self-indulgence and arrogance.

This compelling narrative was deeply rooted in Alcott's life and feelings. For one thing, she had just returned from a long journey abroad as companion to an invalid, Anna Weld. Alcott considered her charge self-absorbed and lazy. She spent much of the trip fretting that she could not travel about energetically as she wanted instead of spending her time trying to lure her ward out of her room with little tricks and bribes. She hated being patronized and despised dependency, so it was with full sympathy that she wrote of Jean's anger at her employer's unconscious slights and condescension. In addition, when she returned from her European trip she had to take care of her sickly mother, support her family as a stand-in for her vague, unemployed father, and look after the household affairs. She felt proud to do all these things, but angry and trapped at the same time. As a result, her inner voice criticized the people and circumstances around her, while she tried to maintain a cheery, selfless exterior.

A long-term factor predisposing Alcott to feel like a bad person masquerading as a good one was her relationship with her father. She had, as a child, suffered at her father's lack of comprehension and sympathy with her active, moody character. He preferred her older, quieter, more passive sister Anna, and found Louisa on occasion "demonic" and often in need of stern discipline. Since all the Alcotts defined him as the "good" one, despite his egocentrism and selfishness, Louisa had, therefore, to be the "bad" one. His disapproval of Louisa as well as his antipathy and distance toward her made her anxious about herself. It also provoked in her both a great desire to please as well as a great resentment at having to strive so hard to achieve the love that seemed to flow so easily to her older sister. For Alcott, the psychological beauty of Jean Muir was that Lord Coventry, who was old enough to be her father, by marrying her forgave her for what she was. In so doing, he promised her a happy, anger-free future. By loving her, as Alcott's real father had not, he would remove the cause of her unhappiness and, therefore, the source of her scandalous behavior.

This story reflects another aspect of Alcott's psychological makeup, that is, her general assessment of men as unobservant and vain. All three Coventry men fall in love with Jean, each influenced by Jean's presentation of her feelings for them. She mirrors back to each what he wants to see and hear. None of them possesses the interest or skill to study her character in return. This was true to Alcott's experience of her father, who only loved her when she was behind her "good" mask. It also reflected his relation to her mother whom he loved, he wrote, because she was good and "because she loves me."[5]

"A Marble Woman"[6] is another psychologically important A. M. Barnard story, exploring other aspects of Alcott's feelings about the relations between men and women. The young orphaned girl Cecil is made the ward of Bazil Yorke, a misanthropic and misogynist artist who attempts to keep her from becoming a woman capable of inflicting emotional pain on anyone. Cecil does not realize that her mother caused Bazil's misogyny by rejecting his love. He isolates the young girl, teaching her to sculpt in silence beside him in his studio. Cecil grows up like many A. M. Barnard heroines, unable to show her real feelings to men. In the process of her education, she becomes detached from her emotions to the extent that she, like Jean Muir, can imitate whatever sentiment will suit her purpose. At first she deadens herself to please her guardian. She goes so far as to eat opium to paralyze her expressive nature, only ceasing when her addiction is discovered. Later, when Bazil marries her (in name only), she tries to awaken her cold husband to his affection for her, a task requiring patience, concealment, and subterfuge. (Unlike most of the A. M. Barnard heroines, Cecil is a victim of unrequited love and, therefore, morally "better"—and less fascinating—than, for example, Jean Muir. She is "good" because she chooses to damage herself rather than others.)

This story underscores the father theme. Here, the man whom the heroine marries really is, in a sense, her cold, unresponsive, self-absorbed father. Alcott then has Cecil's biological father appear as the girl's lover, in the guise of Bazil's handsome, mysterious friend. At the very end, Cecil discovers who this lover is, just as he dies. In the same scene Bazil reveals his love for her as well. So, Alcott rewards her heroine with the love of not just one but two fathers.

Waking up the cold father was an old theme with Alcott. The first story in her volume of *Flower Fables*, fairy stories she had written at sixteen for Ellen Emerson and published in 1855, concerned Violet, a fairy who has to try to persuade the Frost King to allow flowers to live during the winter. His heart is as "hard as his own icy land; no love can melt, no kindness bring it back to sunlight and joy."[7] The little fairy, however, after suffering patiently and enduring much hardship, manages to thaw out the chilly ruler. She teaches him the lesson that "love is mightier than Fear,"[8] the same message Cecil takes Bazil.

In "Pauline's Passion and Punishment,"[9] a somewhat silly story but characterized by genuine vitality and some psychological truth, the central figure is beyond waking up her unresponsive man, and wants merely to reduce him to remorse. Pauline was too wicked for Alcott to identify with wholeheartedly, but the author understood and shared her single-mindedness. She also understood the power of rejection and resentment which animated Pauline.

This is another example of the notion that women cannot reveal themselves to the men they really love. When they do feel comfortable with men, it tends to be with old ones like Lord Coventry or Dr. Bhaer or very young ones like Manuel, Pauline's boy-husband, whom she marries to revenge herself on her real love, Gilbert. Much is made of Manuel's Southern temperament, which bestows upon him some traditionally female traits like sensitivity and emotionalism. He is, therefore, a safe confidant, but excites sisterly love, unlike the distant, cold, and "lovable" heroes like Bazil and Gilbert.

Some of the A. M. Barnard stories lack emotional truth. The plot machinations become everything and, lacking real characters, seem extravagant and gimmicky. On the other hand, the richer, more complex tales with complicated heroines who embodied strong elements of good and bad gave Alcott an outlet for her appreciation of the many-sidedness of human nature.

And yet, sadly, just like Jo March, Alcott felt that she had to abandon her secret pastime. She wrote that she was too hampered by her Concord upbringing, her admiration for Mr. Emerson, and, most of all, her idea of what her father expected of her, to acknowledge these stories. It seems that she was most afraid of owning up to her strong angry women. As Stern points out, she did put her name to *The Mysterious Key*, a story about unwitting bigamy and mistaken inheritance, which lacked a vengeful heroine.

Alcott regretted giving up this kind of fiction for which she correctly asserted that she had a flair. It was remunerative, emotionally liberating, and less mechanical than what she described as her "moral pap for the young" mode. It is significant that in *Little Women* she had Jo give up writing the stories because Dr. Bhaer, her fatherly husband-to-be, asks her to. He assures her they are harmful and compares them ethically to selling liquor. Jo decides to stop because she sees through Dr. Bhaer's "moral spectacles" and understands that writing more stories will interfere with her efforts to become, as Alcott expressed it at seventeen, a "truly good and useful woman."[10] Indeed, Alcott described Jo as living "in bad society, and, imaginary though it was, its influence affected her, for she was feeding heart and fancy on dangerous and unsubstantial food, and was fast brushing the innocent bloom from her nature by a premature acquaintance with the darker side of life, which comes soon enough to all of us."[11] By making Bhaer responsible for Jo's decision to quit, Alcott gave us a view of the immense power her father's moral scheme had over her life and how she imagined that in marrying someone like him she would have to sacrifice all of the outlets for her tumultuous emotional life. His influence contributed to her exaggerated assessment of her own (and Jo's) badness in composing these stories. In a duet between Louisa Alcott and Jo March, they summed up their ambivalence about their moral standards as well as acknowledging their infinite strength.

" 'I almost wish I hadn't any conscience, it's so inconvenient,' " says Jo. " 'If I didn't care about doing right, and didn't feel uncomfortable when doing wrong, I should get on capitally. I can't help wishing sometimes that father and mother hadn't been so particular about such things.' 'Ah, Jo,' apostrophizes Alcott, 'Instead of wishing that, thank God that "father and mother *were particular*; and pity from your heart those who have no such guardians to hedge them round with principles which may seem like prison-walls to impatient youth, but which will prove sure foundations to build character upon in womanhood.' "[12] We are fortunate that, at least for five years, Alcott felt free enough to experiment with a kind of fiction that was not steeped in the rigid morality of her family. The results were always entertaining and occasionally remarkable.

Notes

1. Louisa May Alcott, *Little Women* (Boston: Little, Brown, 1915), pp. 379–80.

2. Leona Rostenberg, "Some Anonymous and Pseudonymous Thrillers of Louisa M. Alcott," *Papers of the Bibliographical Society of America*, 37 (2nd Quarter 1943), 131–40.

3. Madeleine B. Stern, ed., *Behind a Mask: The Unknown Thrillers of Louisa May Alcott* (New York: Morrow, 1975); Madeleine B. Stern, ed., *Plots and Counterplots: More Unknown Thrillers of Louisa May Alcott* (New York: Morrow, 1976).

4. A. M. Barnard, "Behind a Mask: or, A Woman's Power," *Flag of Our Union*, 21 (13 October–3 November 1866).

5. Martha Saxton, *Louisa May* (Boston: Houghton Mifflin, 1977), p. 40.

6. A. M. Barnard, "A Marble Woman: or, The Mysterious Model," *Flag of Our Union*, 20 (20 May–10 June 1865).

7. Saxton, p. 199.

8. Saxton, p. 199.

9. "Pauline's Passion and Punishment," *Frank Leslie's Illustrated Newspaper*, 15 (3, 10 January 1863).

10. Saxton, p. 182.

11. Alcott, p. 372.

12. Alcott, p. 380.

"Our Children Are Our Best Works": Bronson and Louisa May Alcott

Joel Myerson*

Of Bronson Alcott's importance to the personal and literary development of Louisa May Alcott there can be no doubt. His educational philosophy helped to form her personality, and his life with his family provided the basis for many of Louisa's literary works. But what of Louisa's importance to Bronson, particularly when she became a famous author? Most critics who address this question provide a simple answer: Louisa's success as an author brought in much-needed cash and the Alcott family found itself, for the first time, in a reasonably secure financial position.[1] However, an examination of Bronson Alcott's journals and letters shows that his response to Louisa's success was more complicated than has usually been supposed.[2]

Louisa had earned money as a professional author for over a decade before achieving her finest literary and monetary success with the first part of *Little Women* in 1868. Over the next three years, she responded to her public's desire to read more works from her pen by publishing the second part of *Little Women* (1869), an expanded edition of *Hospital Sketches* (1869), *An Old-Fashioned Girl* (1870), and *Little Men* (1871). I would therefore like to concentrate on Bronson's reaction to Louisa's works during this period, for it was between 1868 and 1871 that Louisa firmly established herself as a major author.

One thing that strikes the reader of Alcott's journals and letters is that their author's interest in the world around him is in inverse relation to the world's interest in him. That is, when Bronson is riding high, as when he first opened his Temple School in Boston, he is the center of his narration, but when things go badly, as when the Temple School is forced to close, he takes more interest in the lives of those around him. A similar pattern emerges from his journals and letters of the 1868–71 period, for Louisa was not the only Alcott enjoying a literary success.

Bronson's career as an author had been cut short when the publication of Elizabeth Peabody's account of the *Record of a School* (1835) and his own *Conversations with Children on the Gospels* (1836–37) drew down the wrath of conservative Boston. Scattered periodical contributions, a few school reports for the town of Concord, and the privately printed *Emerson* (1865) were all the publications that Bronson could show for the next thirty years of his life. Then, suddenly, as Louisa achieved her public fame, Bronson experienced a renascence. Roberts Brothers, coincidentally Louisa's publisher, came out with *Tablets* in 1868 and *Concord Days* in 1872. Both books were widely and positively reviewed.[3] At the same time, Bronson's

---

*This essay was written for this volume and appears here for the first time by permission of the author.

lecture tours in the West had brought him a modicum of renown. In short, for the first time in a long while, Bronson was in the limelight, and this is reflected in his comments on Louisa.

Because Thomas Niles of Roberts Brothers encouraged both father and daughter in their literary pursuits, part of Bronson's attitude toward Louisa's fame is that of one author sharing in the success of another author. As he wrote Louisa in early 1868, Niles "obviously wishes to become *your* publisher and *mine*" (19 February: *L*, 427). Over the next three years Bronson chronicles the sales figures for Louisa's books in his journal. With mounting pride he watches *Little Women* go from "an edition of 1500 copies . . . almost disposed of" on 9 October 1868 (299) to a "second edition" on 1 December (435) and a "fifth" on 22 December (467), and then, as sales really take off, from "the 19th 000" on 10 July 1869 (535) to "the 48th 000" on 14 April 1870 (204). In a similar fashion, he notes on 2 June 1870 that 30,000 copies of *An Old-Fashioned Girl* have been printed in just two months (326). And on 28 June 1870 he writes in his journal that Louisa has so far received from Roberts Brothers for her books the sum of $12,292.50 (401).

Bronson's comments on Louisa are as often those of a proud father as they are of a fellow author. When Thomas Wentworth Higginson and his wife write Louisa a letter of praise, Bronson hopes this will "encourage her to estimate, as I fear she has not properly, her superior gifts as writer" (14 October 1868; 391). Indeed, a constant theme of Bronson's is how Louisa is unable to accept her fame. On 30 April 1869, Bronson comments that Louisa "takes her growing repute modestly, being unwilling to believe her books have all the merit ascribed to them by the public" (343–44), and a few months later he again stresses her "modesty" in having "won so wide a celebrity," for she is "unwilling to believe that there is not something unreal in it all" (4 September 1869; 654). Not only is Louisa "slow to accept" her reputation, she "cannot even comprehend" it (2 December 1869; 830). Bronson, however, takes Louisa's fame in stride, writing to a friend that the praise for Louisa is "not as her mother and father think undeserved" (25 February 1869; *L*, 462), and commenting in his journal that "A father may take pride in [Louisa's] talent and growing good name" (5 April 1870; 174).[4]

Bronson also comments directly on the quality of Louisa's literary works. When *Moods*, which Louisa had reluctantly cut in order to get it published in 1865,[5] was reprinted in 1870, Bronson notes that "Had the story been printed as she wrote it, with the supports given to the questionable characters as it now stands, it would have been less objectionable, and found favor with over-nice readers" (23 July 1870; 453). About Louisa's "The Cost of an Idea," a novel dealing with Fruitlands which she never completed,[6] Bronson says that "It surprises one by the boldness and truthfulness of the strokes, and if other parts of her tale are told in this dramatic and sprightly way, her success in this, as in former efforts of the pen, is assured" (30 August 1872; 462). In general, he sums up his opinion of Louisa's writings by saying

> She is among the first to draw her characters from New England life and scenes, and is more successful, in my judgement, in holding fast to nature, intermingling less of foreign sentiment, than any of our novelists. Her culture has been left to nature, and the bias of temperament, and she comes to her pen, taught simply by an experience that few of her age have had the good fortune to enjoy — freedom from the trammels of school and sects — help that her predecessors in fiction, Hawthorne, [Sylvester] Judd, and Mrs. Stowe, had not. (30 April 1869; 344)

Because Bronson's own life is filled with success at this time, he handles Louisa's success very well. He notes, "I am introduced as the father of 'Little Women,' and am riding in her chariot of glory, wherever I go" (1 December 1869; 829), but this does not concern him, for he believes "Our children are our best works" (4 September 1869; 654). Accordingly, he tells Louisa's story at a woman's suffrage convention in 1870 "as an example of what an American girl can do" (8 April; 195), and he adds her to the roll of New England authors on whom he regularly holds conversations during his Western travels.[7]

Bronson also looks favorably upon Louisa's success because it resulted in *Record of a School* being republished in a revised edition, one which now bore the title *Record of Mr. Alcott's School*.[8] As Bronson wrote to his friend William Torrey Harris in St. Louis, " 'The *Plumfield* school' described in 'Little Men' has prompted Roberts Brothers to reprint 'the Record of a School,' as an answer to readers who question whether such a school as Louisa has drawn were possible" (4 July 1871; *L*, 535).[9] Moreover, Louisa agreed to write an "advertisement" for the new edition of the *Record of a School*, which Bronson copied into his journal:

> As many people have done me the honor to inquire if there ever was or could be a school like Plumfield, I am glad to reply by giving them a record of the real school which suggested some of the scenes described in Little Men.
>
> The methods of education so successfully tried at the Temple long ago, are so kindly welcomed now, even the very imperfect hints in the story, that I cannot consent to receive the thanks and commendations due to another.
>
> Not only is it a duty and a pleasure, but there is a certain fitness in making the childish fiction of the daughter play the grateful part of herald to the wise and beautiful truths of the father: truths which for thirty years have been silently, hopefully living in the hearts and memories of the pupils who never have forgotten the influences of that time and teacher.[10]

To have his own life and its values appreciated by his family was nothing new to Bronson Alcott, but when Louisa achieved fame it naturally seemed to him to validate his own career, especially since so much of her work was a fictional portrayal of his own life and that of his family. So when Bronson wrote his old friend, the English Transcendentalist William Oldham, that "Louisa has grown into something of a popular author" (26 April 1869; *L*, 469), one can say that Bronson was at least subconsciously applying that statement to himself. Small wonder, then, that the father not only approved of his daughter's success, but that he eagerly shared in it himself.

Notes

1. For a summary of these views, see Carol Gay, "The Philosopher and His Daughter: Amos Bronson Alcott and Louisa," *Essays in Literature*, 2 (Fall 1975), 181–91, which also criticizes Louisa's inability to appreciate or understand her father.

2. Material from Bronson Alcott's manuscript journals is used by permission of the Houghton Library of Harvard University, and is cited by date and page number in the text. Some of the passages used were first printed in *The Journals of Bronson Alcott*, ed. Odell Shepard (Boston: Little, Brown, 1938), but since Shepard's transcriptions were polished for a general audience, I have chosen to quote from the manuscripts. Material from *The Letters of A. Bronson Alcott*, ed. Richard L. Herrnstadt (Ames: Iowa State Univ. Press, 1969), is noted in the text by *L* and cited there by date and page number.

3. See Carol McIntyre Gay, "Bronson Alcott and 'His Little Critics': A Study in Reputation," Diss. Kent State, 1972.

4. Bronson helped keep track of that "good name" by pasting reviews of Louisa's works into his journal and scrapbooks, even correcting them, as when he deleted the line "and sometimes willful in disposition" from a biographical sketch of her (1 June 1870; 419–20).

5. See Madeleine B. Stern, *Louisa May Alcott* (Norman: Univ. of Oklahoma Press, 1950), pp. 140–41.

6. The only parts of the work that were published were "Transcendental Wild Oats" (1873) and "Eli's Education" (1884).

7. For example, when M. Louise Thayer, acting on behalf of the Ladies' Library Association of Flint, Michigan, wrote inviting Bronson to lecture on "American Authors," she said: "If you come we shall endeavor to make your stay agreeable & show you how we appreciate the works of your gifted daughter, whose works are loaned very much from the shelves of our infant library" (27 November 1870; Houghton Library).

8. Although Niles first broached this idea in 1871, Elizabeth Peabody's delays in writing a new preface and her insistence on promoting Froebel instead of Alcott put off publication until 1874.

9. On his part, Harris found that *Little Women* had kept him "quivering with laughter," not the response one would expect from a Hegelian philosopher (letter to Bronson Alcott, 28 June 1871; Houghton Library).

10. 2 July 1870; 375. This "advertisement" was apparently not published, but sent in a letter to Peabody, who printed the second and third paragraphs in her preface, dated August 1873 (*Record of Mr. Alcott's School*, 3rd ed., rev. [Boston: Roberts Brothers, 1874], pp. 3–4).

A Literary Youth and a Little Woman: Henry James Reviews Louisa Alcott

Adeline R. Tintner*

Although the conjunction of Louisa Alcott, "the Thackeray — the Trollope of the nursery and the school-room," and Henry James (who called her that), the recorder of adult consciousness in its most complex states, seems at first glance somewhat ridiculous, actually it is not, for when the twenty-two-year-old James reproved Miss Alcott, nine years his senior, in his 1865 review of *Moods*, he did so as one member of a literary community to another. His father had close relations with Louisa's father, although their famous contretemps did not take place until after Henry Jr. had written his two reviews ten years apart. Louisa has recorded meeting the family, including Henry Jr. himself after he had written his review of *Moods*, when Henry's father attended one of Bronson Alcott's lectures in Boston. She "met Henry James, Sr., there, and he asked me to come and dine, also called upon me with Mrs. James. I went, and was treated like the Queen of Sheba. Henry Jr. wrote a notice of 'Moods' for the 'North American,' and was very friendly. Being a literary youth he gave me advice, as if he had been eighty and I a girl. My curly crop made me look young, though thirty-one."[1]

What had Henry Jr. done to justify his impertinent stance to the more seasoned writer of fifty-four publications, including *Hospital Sketches* (1863) Henry James, Sr., had read and liked,[2] as well as *Moods*? Surely Henry Jr.'s six publications at this time put him in a minor league, especially since he had published his first signed tale, "The Story of A Year" (March 1865), in which certain details indicate that he may have been reading *Hospital Sketches*. "The Story of A Year" is based on the reality of the Civil War, which James missed because of his "obscure hurt," and the atmosphere of wounded and dying soldiers visited by their mothers is similar to that found in Louisa's record of her war experiences. James's early tales contain many borrowings from literature and in his own words show "an admirable commerce of borrowing and lending, . . . not to say stealing and keeping."[3] Louisa's fairy tale, "A Modern Cinderella" (1860), may have given James the notion of using a classic fairy tale as an analogue. James was much later to write his own Cinderella tale in "Mrs. Temperley" (1887), the year he wrote his essay on Emerson in which he considered Fruitlands, Bronson Alcott's experiment, a "Puritan Carnival."[4]

Perhaps the most amusing comment in James's review of *Moods* is "we are utterly weary of stories about precocious little girls," considering how his own were to appear in "The Turn of the Screw" thirty years later (1898) and *What Maisie Knew* (1897). His youthful priggishness emerges when he accuses Sylvia of "impropriety" in camping "in company with three gentle-

---
*This essay was written for this volume and appears here for the first time by permission of the author.

men" even though dressed as a boy. James is not ready for the "new" girl who made a precocious appearance in Louisa's novel. He will face up to her in *The Bostonians* twenty years later and again as late as 1909 in "Mora Montravers" whose heroine goes further than Sylvia in defying conventions. But they are basically of different stuff from the very American tomboy whom Louisa was the first to record, her Jo becoming the classic example and Katharine Hepburn her contemporary embodiment.

James begins his review with "Under the above title, Miss Alcott has given us her version of the old story of the husband, the wife and the lover." He had just reviewed Mrs. Seemuller's *Emily Chester* (1864), where the situation was the same, as Louisa herself knew, for she wrote in her *Journal* for October 1864, "Read 'Emily Chester' and thought it an unnatural story, yet just enough like 'Moods' in a few things to make me sorry that it came out now."[5] James uses this same adjective, yet in spite of the fact that *Moods* becomes "more and more unnatural . . . it becomes considerably more dramatic," and "if it were not so essentially false, we should call it very fine."

This twenty-two-year-old dares to tell an experienced writer who has actually been to the front and saved her family from starvation, that he is struck by her "ignorance of human nature and her self-confidence in spite of this ignorance." That is because he does not understand Louisa's material. The problem that Sylvia's "moods" creates for her is resolved by her choosing to be a friend rather than a wife. Since the novel is one in which the problem of marriage, of deep concern to Louisa, is threshed out in an original manner (marriage should be "out" for "odd" women) we can understand why Henry James was not at all impressed by the novel's dilemma. James makes the mistake of confusing a very American novel with the typical French novel; the heroine's wishful disguise as a boy is the Yankee mode of the tomboy. Miss Alcott's view of marriage is closer to modern mores than to James's.

When ten years later James reviewed *Eight Cousins* his position in the literary world had changed. He was the author of *A Passionate Pilgrim* (a collection of tales), *Transatlantic Sketches* (a group of travel pieces), and *Roderick Hudson*, a novel serialized during the year and published one month after his review. During 1875 James published seventy-one articles, the fruit of two trips to Europe. After finishing *Roderick Hudson* he decided to go to Europe for good. Three days before he left for London on 17 October his review of Louisa's book appeared in the *Nation*. For Louisa he would no longer be "a literary youth" but an example of the "young men . . . growing up here of high promise" whom Emerson wrote about to Carlyle in 1883.[6] She would pay attention to his comments.

James's second literary judgment about Louisa's work had to take into consideration two things: first, her new position as the leading writer in America *about* young people, but not necessarily *for* them, a role R. L. Stevenson would also play for the English a decade later; second, his own Europeanization. His opening sentence confirms these two changes. His is now a European attitude which notes that American children have lost "the sweet, shy bloom of ideal infancy." He sees Louisa as "the reason of it" — for she "is the novelist of children. . . . She is extremely clever and, we believe, vastly popular with infant readers." Louisa may have recorded the loss of bloom but how could she be the cause of it? James still is priggish, for while admiring her as a "satirist" he thinks the book "a very ill-chosen sort of entertainment to set before children. . . . The smart satirical tone is the last one in the world to be used in describing to children their elders and betters and the social mysteries that surround them."

In finding this anomaly in her work, James has put his finger on Louisa's peculiar straddling of the two worlds of childhood and adulthood. It had created the problem in *Moods* for Sylvia, who felt happier in a pal-like relation to men, rather than a sexual one, and it no doubt reflected Louisa's permanent role as a successful child to her parents and as the tomboy in a family of girls. She had distressed generations of girls who cannot forgive her for not letting Jo marry Laurie ("I *won't* marry Jo to Laurie to please anyone"),[7] but rather a middle-aged professor. Today one can understand that Jo was happier as a friend to Laurie, and if she had to marry to become the heroine of *Jo's Boys*, her husband would have to be some father symbol, based on Bronson Alcott, probably the only man she could relate to. It is this androgynous characteristic a hundred years before its time that disturbed the young James. Twenty years later his Maisie and Mrs. Wix would repeat some aspects of the conspiracy between an adult and a child against the "others" that Rose and her Uncle Alec engage in and that annoyed James. But in 1875 he yearns for the " 'Rollo' books of our infancy . . . as an antidote to this unhappy amalgam of the novel and the storybook." He failed to recognize in this "amalgam" a new genre of American literature because his eye was turned eastward; he was troubled by the need to choose between America and Europe. To placate his uneasiness he now wrote many adult fairy tales, one, "Benvolio" (1875), just a few weeks before his review. Careful to include "the glow of fairy-land" he was to miss in *Eight Cousins*, he nevertheless had no happy endings. When he wrote that there were "no fairies" in Louisa's novel—"it is all prose"—he should have remembered that the therapeutic value of the classic fairy tales resided in their archetypal structures of sibling rivalry and incest. Louisa's imagination caught the imperatives for her in the Cinderella tale in which the depressed sister wins, just as Sleeping Beauty, living in an unawakened state, represented the period of suspended action in which James existed before he made his choice for Europe. Because of his irritation at the precocious children he found annoying even in *Moods*, a novel for adults, he failed to see the fairy-tale underpinnings in *Eight Cousins*, the seven boy cousins obvious equivalents for the Seven Dwarfs, and Rose, a modern Snow-White. Each boy is individualized as the dwarfs are and all fall in love with their cousin in the sequel, *Rose in Bloom*. The ideal family structure for a girl with three sisters like Louisa would be to have many brothers or male cousins, as does Rose, happily surrounded by sexually harmless males. *Eight Cousins* thus shows a fantasy world in which marriage has no place. Uncle Alec who had given up marriage and his medical practice to care for Rose is put into a half-paternal, half-fraternal (and somewhat incestuous) relation to Rose who is also an heiress. Cinderella continues to operate as a metaphor.

In 1865 James had predicted that Louisa could someday "write a very good novel, provided she will be satisfied to describe only that which she has seen." In *Eight Cousins* she has described certain true aspects of family life, yet James deplores her "private understanding with the youngsters she depicts, at the expense of their pastors and masters." The knowingness of the little heroine shows that she "reads the magazines, and perhaps even writes for them." He objects to the fact that Louisa has transposed the romanticism of *Jane Eyre* to present-day conditions and to her Rochester using the water-spout to descend from her room: "why not by a rope-ladder at once?" Here it amuses the reader of James to remember that while he criticizes Uncle Alec for dancing a polka with Rose for getting the best of her aunt, Sir Claude in *What Maisie Knew* had even more deeply conspired with Maisie against the adult women involved with him.

Louisa seems to have taken to heart some of James's criticism of *Eight Cousins*, so that in *Rose in Bloom* (1876), in which the heroine grows to marriageable age, she tries to magnify the fairy-tale glow by multiplying fairy-tale metaphors. Mac, who was the Ugly Duckling, turns into a Swan; Phoebe is a Cinderella who has "turned out a princess."[8] Louisa seems to be correcting what James had criticized in her treatment of Rose's aunts who were not "beautiful and powerful specimens of what they seem to be." Now Rose takes Aunt Jessie seriously in a discussion of marriage: "I shall follow Aunt Jessie's advice, and try to keep my atmosphere as pure as I can; for she says every woman has her own little circle, and in it can use her influence for good, if she will."[9]

In his turn James's strong feelings about Louisa's novel seem to have affected his own fiction. The "knowing" air of Randolph Miller, Daisy's younger brother, might be a reflection on American children not so much observed as read about in Louisa's novel. In 1878 he was not sympathetic to this kind of child, and we are not in any way to love or admire little Randolph. We are simply to recognize the truth of his portrait, which may depend on James's initiation into the psychology of children in America through Louisa's novel. Randolph Miller can be seen as a tribute from James to Louisa for providing him with seven variations of the type among Rose's cousins.

In spite of the immeasurable difference between the consciousnesses of Louisa's and Henry's characters, the two writers may have given each other useful hints in constructing their fiction. Their interaction was probably more important when the young James was learning to write. Louisa's prototypes may have served as a source for the young Americans James needed in his first international tales. And even in his fin de siècle stories about English children it is possible he fell back on his earlier impressions of Louisa's family groups. But in Louisa's books the adults are never evil in relation to the youngsters; in James's fiction they almost always are, and the few adults who protest "the plasticity" of youth, like Mrs. Wix and Mr. Longdon, are outnumbered by such equivocal guardians as the oppressive governess in "The Turn of the Screw" and Mrs. Brookenham's corrupting circle, so different from Rose's.

Notes

    1. Louisa May Alcott, *Her Life, Letters, and Journals*, ed. Ednah D. Cheney (Boston: Little, Brown, 1911), p. 165.

    2. Madeleine B. Stern, *Louisa May Alcott* (Norman: Univ. of Oklahoma Press, 1950), p. 133.

    3. Henry James, *Autobiography* (New York: Criterion, 1956), p. 495.

    4. Henry James, *Partial Portraits*, ed. Leon Edel (Ann Arbor: Univ. of Michigan Press, 1970), p. 27.

    5. Alcott, p. 162.

    6. Leon Edel, *Henry James: The Conquest of London* (Philadelphia: Lippincott, 1962), p. 31.

    7. Alcott, p. 201.

    8. Louisa May Alcott, *Rose in Bloom* (Boston: Little, Brown, 1950), p. 51.

    9. Alcott, *Rose in Bloom*, pp. 208–09.

Thoreau in the Writing of Louisa May Alcott

Marie Olesen Urbanski[*]

As all writers have done, Louisa May Alcott used her experiences with people she knew in her fiction. An interesting subject of speculation is why writers include certain people they know and leave others out. Due to her extraordinary father, Alcott encountered many unusual men, especially in the constellation of transcendentalists who clustered with Bronson Alcott around their star, Ralph Waldo Emerson. One of the most eccentric in the transcendentalist group was Henry David Thoreau, whose genius was recognized more fully in the twentieth century than in his own time. Perhaps due to his idiosyncratic personality, Alcott chose Thoreau from the Concord passionate seekers of truth, but emotionally distant men, to transform with her literary art into Adam Warwick, Mr. Hyde, David Sterling, and Mac Campbell.

    The Alcott family first moved to Concord in 1840 when Louisa was

[*]This essay was written for this volume and appears here for the first time by permission of the author.

seven and Henry David Thoreau, twenty-two. Except for the Alcott family's sojourn for some months at Fruitlands and Still River in 1843–44, they remained in Concord until Louisa was almost sixteen. Moving back to Concord some ten years later, when Alcott was a grown woman, her parents finally managed to purchase Orchard House. For the rest of her life, Alcott stayed in Concord recurrently, but preferred to live in Boston.

A man admired by Bronson Alcott, Thoreau was his close friend, and Louisa was exposed to his influence when she was in Concord, most intimately as a child. Thoreau was comfortable around the children and men who accepted him on his terms, but ill at ease with women. With a group of children, Louisa followed Thoreau on nature walks through the fields and woods. As he picked up arrowheads, he reminded them of the Indians who had walked the land before them and of the fairies visible to those who could see them. He taught the children how to look closely at trees and their parasites, at birds and insects, of the symbiotic characteristics of nature. On berry hunts, he revealed the secret places where huckleberries grew profusely. The wild creatures accepted Thoreau and did not flee his approach. When the Alcott family visited Thoreau at Walden, he rowed the girls on the pond, as he had earlier in his boat *Musketaquid* on the Concord River. In much of her fiction, then, Alcott showed that communion with nature could help the troubled spirit as she had experienced healing while with Thoreau and another naturalist, Sophia Foord.

After briefly attending the Thoreau brothers school, the Alcott girls later studied under Sophia Foord, a teacher and naturalist, who lived with the Alcott family. Foord purportedly proposed marriage to Thoreau, who in his words rejected his "foe" with a "hollow shot, after it had struck and buried itself and made itself felt there." Apparently aware of Foord's unreciprocated feelings for Thoreau, Alcott kept up with her for many years, and wrote her a letter describing his death and funeral.

As a grown woman, Alcott saw much less of Thoreau than she had as a child. Still, as a family friend he accepted dinner invitations, acted as a pallbearer at Beth's funeral, and attended Anna's wedding. A shy person herself, she understood the timidity which was veiled by Thoreau's gruff manners. Also, growing up in a family of social activists, she respected Thoreau's values, his defense of John Brown, and his unconventional life-style. In her letter to Sophia Foord, written in 1862, two days after Thoreau's funeral, Alcott wrote that Nature seemed to welcome her "loving son" with a lovely day: "As we entered the churchyard birds were singing, early violets blooming in the grass & the pines singing their softest lullaby. . . ." In death perhaps their friendship with him could be closer.[1] Some months later, while nursing dying soldiers at night in a Union Hospital during the Civil War, Alcott composed a poem in Thoreau's memory, celebrating him as Pan, "the Genius of the wood." After his death, Alcott began to metamorphose Thoreau into a character with idealized, almost mythic qualities.

Although she began work on her mature novels *Moods* (1865) and

Work (1873) shortly before Thoreau's death, she spent much more time revising them than was her custom. *Work*, in fact, took twelve years of evolution, its title having changed from *Success*. Both novels feature a love triangle, with two men seeking to marry the same woman. The major women characters of the novels, Sylvia Yule and Christie Devon, are manifestations of the archetypal heroine, Jo March. Sylvia is a tomboy with money, and Christie, an older, chastened Jo March. Independent and stubborn, they have problems conforming to the restricted role for ladies defined by Victorian society. In both novels, the great temptation is a loveless marriage. In *Moods*, Sylvia succumbs, and like Isabel Archer in *The Portrait of a Lady*, decides to make the best of her decision: but in *Work*, Christie, although living in poverty, resists this temptation. In both novels, however, the man the heroine loves is the Thoreau-prototype, Adam Warwick (*Moods*) and David Sterling (*Work*). In both instances, this character is slow to declare his intentions, which complicates the action and adds suspense.

As is generally known, Thoreau was not good looking. A short man with a prominent nose and interesting, gray-blue eyes revealed only on the rare occasions he made eye-contact, he was described by Hawthorne as "ugly as sin, long-nosed, queer-mouthed."[2] In *Moods* Adam Warwick is very tall, physically powerful, broad-shouldered and bronzed. His head is "massive" and, like Thoreau's, his nose, "eminent"; and his gray eyes "seemed to pierce through all disguises."[3] Although her creation of David Sterling is less attractive—his face with "no striking comeliness or color"—he has Thoreau's brown beard which to Christie is "becoming." His "broad arch of a benevolent brow added nobility to features otherwise not beautiful" (242). On the other hand, Warwick has Heathcliffian, Adamic qualities; he dominates the landscape. Alcott suggests he is a natural force, identifying him with the ocean, the wind, and the mountains: he looked "down at Sylvia much as the tall cliffs looked at the little pimpernel close shut in its pink curtains among the stones at their feet" (56). Marriage with him would be like a wood bird mating an eagle. When the exhausted Sylvia climbs a rugged mountain and tells Adam that she knows an easier path, he replies: "I always take the shortest way, no matter how rough it is" (55). He literally pulls her up the face of the cliff. Alcott's depiction of her two Thoreau-like characters shows the earlier one, Adam Warwick, to be a projection of a youthful dream of love, whereas the later one, David Sterling, exhibits the quiet virtues many women come in time to believe are preferable in a husband.

Their physiques mirror their personalities. Like Hawthorne's guilt-ridden Arthur Dimmesdale, David harbors a secret sin; his expression reveals a "vigilant look as if some hidden pain or passion lay in wait to surprise and conquer the sober cheefulness that softened the lines of the firm-set lips, and warmed the glance of the thoughtful eyes."[4] David is a chastened man; instead of being a wilderness man like Thoreau and Adam, he is a florist who cultivates flowers. Like Thoreau, he lives with his mother and is reluctant to travel. Adam's domain, however, was the world. "Violently virtuous," a good way of characterizing Thoreau, Adam is "a masterful soul, bent on living out his aspirations and beliefs at any cost; much given to denunciation of wrong-doing everywhere, and eager to execute justice upon all offenders high or low" (60). As if following Thoreau's famous dictum, "Simplify," he has few wants. Both characters possess Thoreau's blunt, tactless, taciturn, uncompromising, unworldly, self-reliant personality. At first, Christie is disturbed by David's lack of ambition. However, as Alcott evidently divined in her contact with Thoreau, David has a rich and troubled inner life: "under this composed, commonplace existence another life went on . . . a word, a look, a gesture, betrayed an unexpected power and passion, a secret unrest, a bitter memory that would not be ignored" (246). Both of Alcott's heroes, then, have personalities remarkably similar to Thoreau's.

Consistent with the Byronic tradition of romanticism, Adam saves Sylvia's life twice, once from the sea, once from fire. Later, during a revolution in Italy, he single-handedly saves a village from marauding Croatian soldiers about to pillage a town and despoil a convent. The villagers believe him to be superhuman, the convent's patron saint. Wounded in the fray, true to the stoical martial tradition, he acts as if his wound were a mere scratch. Later, returning home with his best friend, now married to Sylvia, he gives him the only available seat on a life boat in a shipwreck scene reminiscent of Margaret Fuller's death at sea. Like Sydney Carton, he sacrifices himself for the woman he loves so that her husband would return home to her. In *Work* David Sterling is a hero, too, but on a diminished scale. Alcott specifically repudiates heroics: "although he made no brilliant charge . . . his comrades felt his brave example kept them steady till a forlorn hope turned into a victory . . ." (387). From a Quaker background, David makes a point of treating his Confederate enemies with respect. His death is not in a battle, but as a sacrifice helping female slaves with children to escape. Obviously, by portraying her protagonists in heroic action, Alcott was conforming to a melodramatic novel tradition rather than to Thoreau's life.

One salient episode in *Moods* which Alcott must have derived from Thoreau's writing is the three-day river excursion that figures so prominently in the novel. As Ednah Dow Cheney observed, the "picnic-voyage" of a young girl with her brother and two young men was "contrary to common ideas of decorum."[5] Alcott's idea must have come from Thoreau's *A Week on the Concord and Merrimack Rivers*, a travel book describing his boat trip with his brother, John. Thoreau's *A Week* describes people the brothers met, camping, fish, flora, and Indian lore, blended with philosophical speculation and poetry quotations. In fiction form, Alcott uses a river trip as the occasion on which Christie insists upon doing her share of the rowing and displays such disingenuous charm that Adam and his rival fall in love with her. On this camping trip, there is even an echo from *Wal-*

den, a battle between black and red ants. *Work*, on the other hand, is episodic, with structure and theme influenced by *Pilgrim's Progress*. There is less focus on love and more on the temptations "Every Woman," especially the working girl, meets in the person of men as seducers or suitors.

Like Thoreau, Alcott was troubled by the opposite sex, but, unlike Thoreau, Alcott could not exclude the opposite sex from her writing, since women were dependent on men for their survival. Her comments in a letter she wrote to Miss Lawrence, 3 February 1865, shortly after *Moods* was published, are revealing of her attitude toward love: "Moods wont [sic] suit you so well I suspect, for in it I've freed my mind upon a subject that always makes trouble, namely, Love. But being founded upon fact, & the characters drawn from life it may be of use as all experiences are & serve as a warning at least."[6] Her admission that her characters were "drawn from life" further suggests her use of Thoreau as her model for Adam Warwick, but instead of simply awakening her audience as he did with his Chanticleer, she expects her novel to serve as a warning.

Both Adam and David differ radically from their prototype when they express their indignation at the injustices women encounter in society. Ignoring Thoreau's misogyny, Alcott creatively fused much of herself into Adam and David. Always wishing to be "a lord of creation," as she referred to males, Alcott has Sylvia say wistfully, "men go where they like" (27). Adam's globe-trotting was a projection of her dreams. Nevertheless, so imbued was she with the idea of self-sacrifice, that both her heroes sacrificed their lives to save others. In an eloquent passage she has Adam, as did Thoreau, make an "onslaught upon established customs, creeds, and constitutions," but she includes in his iconoclasm her own concern for women, "the false public opinion that grants all suffrages to man and none to woman yet judges both alike . . ." (148). She posits David's feminist concerns as a part of her novel's theme of sisterhood. In *Work*, in the romantic tradition of the "broken heart," Christie thinks David is suffering from betrayed love. It turns out that he is suffering because he was unforgiving when he learned his sister was a "fallen woman." In expiation he has vowed to pity and protect women. With his mother he operates a kind of halfway house, a place of refuge for desperately needy women. Alcott's development of these characters, then, took them beyond the concerns of Thoreau.

In *Rose in Bloom* (1876), a sequel to *Eight Cousins*, Alcott's Mac is another male character sympathetic to the heroine's support of gender and class equality. In an almost formulaic triangle, Mac and Charlie vie for Rose. Reminiscent of Thoreau, Mac has a sterling character but is socially maladroit. His rival, handsome "Prince" Charlie, is charming but an alcoholic. Rose is attracted to Charlie but repelled by his drinking. Mac, who quotes Thoreau and Emerson, is inspired by his love for Rose to write poetry. Whether or not Mac would continue writing poetry is uncertain. Alcott makes this clear by using a famous analogy, directly connecting Mac with Thoreau: "Having proved that he *could* write poetry, he might drop it for some new world to conquer, quoting his favorite Thoreau, who, having made a perfect pencil, gave up the business, and took to writing books with the sort of indelible ink which grows clearer with time."[7] His poems have served their purpose. They have been the catalyst for Rose's love to bloom. Mac and Rose vow to work together to make a better world.

Alcott's Thoreau reappeared again briefly in *Little Men*, as Mr. Hyde. No longer a major figure, but an inspiration to the juvenile delinquent Dan to mend his ways and become a naturalist, Mr. Hyde lives in the woods studying. He "could make birds come to him, and rabbits and squirrels didn't mind him any more than if he was a tree," Dan observes in admiration. Just as the themes of nature as healer and nature as teacher appeared recurrently in Alcott's juvenile works, so, too, did Thoreau's flute. Professor Bhaer keeps an old flute on his mantelpiece, and, in *Little Men*, Franz plays the flute.

Her memory of Thoreau stayed with Alcott all of her life. As a child, Alcott must have responded to him as Sylvia did to Adam, feeling "rebuked and comforted at the same time" (55). Living at a time when there was great social pressure to marry, she knew her father pitied Thoreau for not having a wife. Perhaps prompted by Sophia Foord, she tried to envision Thoreau as a husband. As Alcott's character Sylvia realized, Adam would never have married her: "He clings to principles; persons are but animated facts or ideas; he seizes, searches, uses them, and when they have no more for him, drops them like the husk, whose kernel he has secured" (306–7). At the same time, Alcott was inspired by Thoreau; with Sylvia she "felt the fire of a noble emulation kindled in her from the spark he left behind" (312). Alcott understood the essence of the man, and metamorphosed him for her own artistic purposes. Her vision of Thoreau was pristine.

Notes

1. *"A Sprig of Andromeda": A Letter from Louisa May Alcott on the Death of Henry David Thoreau* (New York: Pierpont Morgan Library, 1962), p. 10.

2. Thomas Blanding and Walter Harding, *A Thoreau Iconography* (Geneseo, N.Y.: Thoreau Society, 1980), p. 1.

3. Louisa May Alcott, *Moods* (Boston: Roberts Brothers, 1887), p. 59; hereafter page references are cited in the text.

4. Louisa May Alcott, *Work* (Boston: Roberts Brothers, 1886), p. 242; hereafter page references are cited in the text.

5. Ednah Dow Cheney, *Louisa May Alcott: Her Life, Letters, and Journals* (Boston: Roberts Brothers, 1889), p. 117.

6. Annie M. L. Clark, *The Alcotts in Harvard* (Lancaster, Mass.: J. C. L. Clark, 1902).

7. Louisa May Alcott, *Rose in Bloom: A Sequel to "Eight Cousins"* (Boston: Little, Brown, 1927), pp. 318–19.

"Sweet, If Somewhat Tomboyish": The British Response to Louisa May Alcott

Mary Cadogan*

The novels of Louisa May Alcott, particularly those featuring the March family, have long been favorites with British readers. The more ambivalent response of critics and reviewers, however, is suggested by the title of this article, which is a quotation from Edward Salmon's essay, "Should Children Have a Special Literature?"[1] Salmon concentrates mainly upon English writers, but Alcott is listed as an author with whose "printed thoughts" Salmon has spent "many pleasant" and "not unprofitable" hours. He goes to some length to stress the profound and positive influence of characters from children's fiction upon young readers, and concludes that "the best defence which can be made of boys' and girls' literature in general is to assert . . . that it is peopled chiefly with boys not far removed in their chivalrous rectitude of character from Tom Brown, and with girls as worthy to be loved as the sweet, if somewhat tomboyish central figure of *Little Women*."

The practice of entangling social comment with literary criticism is, of course, not confined to any period. Some of today's reviewers make profligate use of potent words like "chauvinism" and "racism" as sticks for beating authors. The Victorians applied different but equally daunting social strictures, and many critics were deeply suspicious of tomboyism and — by extension — the more radical trait of "hoydenism" in books written for girls. And Josephine March was not only a tomboy but an archetypal one who embodied a beautiful balance of robustness and charm, of wit and warmth, and who, through Alcott's skillful writing, was to extend the frontiers of girls' fiction on both sides of the Atlantic and to give readers new and liberating real-life aspirations.

Alcott's *Little Women* stories, despite the domesticity of their settings, were revolutionary in the England of the 1860s; they were the proverbial breath of fresh air that began the process of blowing away the mustiness of sermonizing and repression that had hung for decades over previous tales of hearth and home. It is interesting that *Alice's Adventures in Wonderland* by Lewis Carroll, published just two years before *Little Women*, had a similarly revolutionary effect upon fiction at the younger, nursery level. In some ways Alcott's impact upon British authors and readers has been masked by the tremendous and continuing literary influence of what *Aunt Judy's Magazine* in 1866 called "the exquisitely wild, fantastic, impossible, yet most natural history of *Alice in Wonderland*."[2] This fact is underlined by the differing responses in Britain to the recent sesquicentenary of these two authors, both born in 1832. For Carroll, there were numerous new and

---
*This essay was written for this volume and appears here for the first time by permission of the author.

sumptuous editions, dramatized events all over the country, many local and national radio and television tributes, and the culminating glory of the unveiling of a memorial stone in the Poets' Corner of Westminster Abbey. For Alcott there were no special reissues of her books; there were three short national radio and television tributes and, if there were any more local celebrations, they were not widely publicized. Nevertheless, most British women and girls would acknowledge that Alcott's influence upon their lives has been significant.

Without wishing to strike an aggressively feminist note, one has to comment that Alcott has not always received her deserved acclaim from male reviewers in England. Many histories of children's fiction have been written by men, and it is obvious from their remarks on Alcott (and indeed on several other writers for girls) that they have not always read the books thoroughly. Sometimes Alcott has received the worst of both worlds — the Victorian and our own. Certain nineteenth-century critics had reservations about the *Little Women* books because these made tomboyism attractive, and modern reviewers occasionally condemn them for promoting the opposite qualities of sentimentality and mawkishness, and for passive, antifeminist acceptance of the social status quo!

In his detailed and persuasively presented *Written for Children*,[3] John Rowe Townsend confidently but erroneously says that there are half a dozen books dealing with the March family in addition to *Little Women* and *Good Wives*.[4] He outlines how Alcott came to write *Little Women* and its sequels, of which he writes: "I have not read all the later books, and what I have read failed to hold me."[5] This eminent literary historian's patchy knowledge of Alcott's work is astounding, but to an extent typical of that of so many male writers. Nevertheless, Townsend concedes that *Little Women* was a new kind of book for the mid-Victorian period, leading away from the didactic style. He also sees the book "as the first great example" of the family story, with increased truth to life, and a relaxation of the stiff and authoritarian stereotypes previously accepted in the domestic tale. And, rightly, he regards Jo as "the obvious inspiration of many a later heroine."[6]

In *The Victorian Child*,[7] F. Gordon Roe, himself of late nineteenth-century vintage, discusses the "enlarging influences" of certain American stories upon English literature. He rates Alcott in this respect second only to Harriet Beecher Stowe, referring to *Little Women*'s and *Good Wives*' "obstinate success" with British girls. Why, one wonders, does the word "success" have to be prefixed so grudgingly?

In his extremely comprehensive *Children's Books in England*,[8] F. J. Harvey Darton allocates a paragraph to Alcott but fails to appreciate the original nature of her work: "Louisa May Alcott was fortunate in coming . . . when domestic fiction, unpretentious and not aggressively moral, had already got a footing which her own work made sure." He goes on to refer to the "quiet, even dull, simplicity" which he sees as "the staple of *Little Women*." For him apparently the book's only "enticingly exotic" quality is to be found in its descriptions of American food, especially waffles! "Miss Alcott never became, so to speak, naturalized; but she was and has remained a permanent and well-loved guest."

A more recent male critic is far less gracious. In *Catching Them Young: Sex, Race and Class in Children's Fiction*,[9] Bob Dixon gives Alcott four pages in his chapter, "Sexism: Birds in Gilded Cages." By extremely selective quotations he suggests that Alcott's books reinforce female images of passivity by making the social restrictions imposed upon girls appear attractive. He sees this as a "process, by which the oppressed takes on—internalises—the attitudes of the oppressor." Dixon sums up as follows: "These books are competently written and skilfully constructed. The values and attitudes so untiringly put forward in them, however, leave a lot to be desired. I can never see much in the argument which 'makes allowance' for the period when a book was written. If books are read now—and these are certainly very widely read indeed—then surely we have to apply contemporary standards in evaluating them. It would, in any case, be difficult to make any allowances for the kind of indoctrination examined here. There are too many sly digs at feminism, scattered throughout the books, for us to excuse Alcott of unawareness. She knew what she was doing."[10] After this diatribe one wonders if Bob Dixon knows what *he* is doing! Admirers of Alcott can take comfort from the fact that she is in excellent company in being condemned by Mr. Dixon—in the company of many popular writers influential in children's literature.

It is refreshing after dipping into Dixon to turn to a male writer of greater style and perception. Brian Doyle in *The Who's Who of Children's Literature*[11] comments warmly on *Little Women*'s "universal appeal," its charm, humor, and sentiment. "It was an immediate success and to this day is probably the most popular and widely-read book ever written for girls."

Whatever reservations Harvey Darton or Dixon might have about local and period limitations in Louisa Alcott's stories, these are not generally shared by women critics. They seem better to recognize the quintessential universality not only of the March family books but of many of Alcott's other works. A browse through some of the most popular British magazines for girls and young women over several decades provides evidence of Alcott's wide-ranging appeal. In late Victorian magazines she seemed to share the illustrious pinnacle of English heroines like Florence Nightingale or the queen herself.

Coming forward in time to a periodical for younger girls, the *Schoolgirl*, we find the editor enthusiastic about "the wonderful new serial" about to start in May 1934. This was *Little Women*, "set in America, yet a firm favourite with girls all over the world for many years. Just ask your mummy how she liked it. Her enthusiasm will be unbounded . . . and so will yours be."[12] To serialize a Victorian story, and one written by a woman, in this paper was unprecedented; the emphasis was upon modernity and stories of school and sport rather than domesticity; in addition, the publisher, Lord

Northcliffe, believing that female writers in trying to protect young girls wrote unadventurous stories, nearly always used for his girls' magazines male authors who concealed their identities behind feminine pen names.

It is significant that the robustness of *Little Women*, almost seventy years after its first appearance, was still able to break down barriers, in this case Northcliffe's rigid editorial policy. In *You're a Brick, Angela! A New Look at Girls' Fiction from 1839 to 1975*, by Patricia Craig and Mary Cadogan,[13] the liberalism of Alcott's books is considered, and Jo is seen to epitomize "the desire of many girls for participation in intellectual life."

Gillian Avery remarks on Alcott's influence upon Victorian readers in *Childhood's Pattern: A Study of the Heroes and Heroines of Children's Fiction 1770–1950*:[14] "There was no English equivalent of Louisa Alcott's *Little Women* which endeared itself to so many millions by the warmth and informality of its family life." She finds Alcott's (and Susan Coolidge's) ability to convey goodness without sermonizing far more effective than the serious and lofty idealizations of Charlotte M. Yonge, for example.

The last words on the British response to Louisa May Alcott can aptly be left to Margery Fisher, a leading authority in children's literature for over two decades. She gives considerable space to Alcott in her excellent *Who's Who in Children's Books*,[15] and suggests that her novels are "most skilfully written and planned, as well as being among the most warmly human, entertaining and absorbing of all family stories." She comments that the experiences of Jo March undoubtedly "transcend the barriers of time and fashion"—something that Alcott's works will long continue to do.

Notes

1. Edward Salmon, "Should Children Have a Special Literature?" *Parent's Review*, 1890, p. 344.

2. "Reviews," *Aunt Judy's Magazine*, 1 (June 1866), 123.

3. John Rowe Townsend, *Written for Children* (London: Garnet Miller, 1965, London: Kestrel, 1974), pp. 78–80.

4. *Little Women*, Part II, has always been known in Britain as *Good Wives*.

5. Townsend, *Written for Children*, p. 79.

6. *Townsend*, p. 79.

7. F. Gordon Roe, *The Victorian Child* (London: Phoenix House, 1959), p. 98.

8. F. J. Harvey Darton, *Children's Books in England* (Cambridge: Cambridge Univ. Press, 1932), pp. 230–31.

9. Bob Dixon, *Catching Them Young: Sex, Race and Class in Children's Fiction* (London: Pluto Press, 1977), pp. 7–10.

10. Dixon, p. 10.

11. Brian Doyle, *The Who's Who of Children's Literature* (London: Hugh Evelyn, 1968), pp. 4–5.

12. "Whispers from the Den," *Schoolgirl*, 10 (May 1934), 11.

13. Patricia Craig and Mary Cadogan, *You're a Brick, Angela! A New Look at Girls' Fiction from 1839 to 1975* (London: Gollancz, 1976), p. 37.

14. Gillian Avery, *Childhood's Pattern: A Study of the Heroes and Heroines of Children's Fiction 1770-1950* (London: Hodder & Stoughton, 1975), p. 123.

15. Margery Fisher, *Who's Who in Children's Books* (London: Weidenfeld & Nicolson, 1975), pp. 166, 197-98.

Louisa May Alcott: A Bibliographical Essay on Secondary Sources

Alma J. Payne*

Bibliographical study offers a twofold value to the scholar: it provides those sources which treat the subject and it offers a portrait of the changing national self revealed in the emphases inherent in the treatments by the critics. In the *New England Magazine* of March 1892, Maria S. Porter described the "simple, but most impressive" funeral services for Louisa May Alcott. Among those participating was Ednah D. Cheney, who "read the sonnet written by Mr. Alcott, which refers to her [L. M. A.] as 'Duty's faithful child . . .' " ("Recollections of Louisa May Alcott," *New England Magazine*, 6 [March 1892], 2-19). Thus, at the end of her life one of the dominant critical images of Alcott was established by the woman whose influence is still observable.

Cheney's first published tribute, *Louisa May Alcott: The Children's Friend* (Boston: L. Prang, 1888) stressed Alcott's interest in and influence upon children readers, an influence still present. However, it lacked the important primary material found in *Life, Letters, and Journals* (Boston: Roberts, 1889). This volume, with its introduction, inclusions and omissions, structure, and stress upon the autobiographical nature of Alcott's "best work," shaped critical interpretation until the 1940s. Cheney portrayed Alcott as "Duty's Child," strongly influenced by her family and family friends such as Thoreau and Emerson. There were overtones of personal and artistic rebellion, attitudes noted but not stressed. Given the paucity of Alcott letters, many of which had been destroyed at the author's request, Cheney's position as observant family friend gave authenticity and foundation for the "Alcott myth."

For the next twenty years, the Alcott image established in the Cheney work underwent some additions and variations but little basic change. A careful reading of Porter's "Recollections of Louisa May Alcott" reveals Alcott as an often caustic yet humorous critic of her society, an unenchanted viewer of her father's philosophical concepts and of his Fruitlands debacle, and an outspoken advocate of woman suffrage and college education for women. However, the predominant theme was that of "Duty."

---
*This essay was written for this volume and appears here for the first time by permission of the author.

Reminiscent treatments were numerous. The two-volume edition of *Amos Bronson Alcott: His Life and Philosophy*, by Frank B. Sanborn and W. T. Harris (Boston: Roberts Bros., 1893), added a few diary excerpts and stressed the influence of Bronson Alcott (and Sanborn) upon Louisa's career. In 1902 Annie M. L. Clark recalled *The Alcotts in Harvard* (Lancaster, Mass.: J. C. L. Clark), while Clara Gowing shared her memories of *The Alcotts as I Knew Them* (Boston: C. M. Clark, 1909).

Despite Louisa's wish to have all of her letters destroyed, Alfred Whitman published parts of twelve letters to him in "Letters to her Laurie" (*Ladies' Home Journal*, 18 [16 September 1901], 5-6, 18 [11 October], 6). The most interesting revelation was that the character of Laurie in *Little Women* combined Whitman and Louisa's Polish boy, Ladisilas. Whitman interpreted Alcott as "caught in the web of fame," trying "to find her own soul, while easing the life of her beloved family." The tension between duty and rebellion was again apparent.

Seth Curtis Beach included Alcott among his *Daughters of the Puritans* (Boston: American Unitarian Association, 1905). Highly derivative of the *Journals* and regarding Alcott as the "most popular storyteller for children, in her generation," he recognized Alcott's *Work* as deserving of critical attention. In the midst of reminiscent accounts, he was one of the first to emphasize her contribution to woman's suffrage.

The first noteworthy attempt at a biography was *Louisa May Alcott, Dreamer and Worker: A Story of Achievement* (New York: D. Appleton, 1909). Its author, Belle Moses, built upon Cheney's *Life, Letters, and Journals* but included selected contemporary comments by Dr. Edward Emerson, Nathaniel Hawthorne, and others. She examined the majority of Alcott's works and included known details of publication, thus departing from the purely reminiscent.

Between 1910 and the centenary year of 1932 the reminiscent tone remained strong in Alcott criticism, but there were hints of critical emphases to come. Katharine F. Gerould, as strongly anti-Victorian as her time, examined Alcott's work as a cultural mirror of her time and place ("Miss Alcott's New England," *Atlantic Monthly*, 108 [August 1911], 180–86; expanded under the same title in *Modes and Morals* [New York: Scribner's, 1920], pp. 182–98). Gerould regarded *Little Women* as a valuable contemporary record of manners and morals. The relatively new instrument of sociology was used to analyze relationships within Alcott's families and between her characters and their fictional communities.

For the first time Alcott was specifically recognized in a Negro periodical for her contribution to abolitionism. Cheney's work had contained clear evidence of Louisa's emotional support of John Brown and others, but little attention had been paid to her treatment of the subject in literary works. Lorenzo Dow Turner analyzed "Louisa May Alcott's 'M. L.'" in the *Journal of Negro History* (14 [October 1929], 495–522) and provided a reprint of the story as it had appeared in the *Boston Commonwealth* (1 [January–February 1863]). He found that the tale, despite the sentimentality of the story of the love and marriage of a white girl and a mulatto, was "definite in its stand against prejudice."

In 1914-15 appeared evidence of increased interest in locating and analyzing primary sources. *Little Women: Letters from the House of Alcott*, collected by Jessie Bonstelle and Marian DeForest (Boston: Little, Brown, 1914), provided material which proved valuable for later biographies. The awareness that such sources must be preserved was demonstrated by *Alcott Memoirs Posthumously Compiled from Papers, Journals, and Memoranda of the Late Dr. Frederick L. H. Willis*, edited by Edith Willis Linn and Henry Bazin (Boston: Badger, 1915).

The decade of the 1920s was marked by numerous short reminiscent treatments. Julian Hawthorne's "Woman Who Wrote *Little Women*" (*Ladies Home Journal*, 39 [October 1922], 25, 120-24), and Mary Hosmer Brown's *Memories of Concord* (Boston: Four Seas, 1926), along with *Classic Concord* by Caroline Ticknor (Boston: Houghton Mifflin, 1926), reveal aspects of Alcott's personality and work within the frame of her contemporary Concord. A varied approach was provided by studies of other members of the Alcott family such as Honoré Willsie Morrow's *The Father of Little Women* (Boston: Little, Brown, 1927) and Caroline Ticknor's *May Alcott: A Memoir* (Boston: Little, Brown, 1929). In 1928, Cheney's *Louisa May Alcott: Her Life, Letters, and Journals* was reprinted (Boston: Little, Brown). Its reception did little to indicate that the next decade would be one of the two most important periods in Alcott scholarship, for its Victorianism was not in tune with the "Roaring Twenties."

Among the numerous publications marking the century of Alcott's birth was the important bibliographical study, *Louisa May Alcott: A Bibliography*, compiled by Lucile Gulliver, with an "Appreciation" by Cornelia Meigs (Boston: Little, Brown, 1932). For the first time all known editions were annotated—a useful tool for subsequent critics and bibliographers.

A year later Cornelia Meigs won the Newbery Medal for *The Story of the Author of Little Women: Invincible Louisa* (Boston: Little, Brown, 1933). Although not strictly critical, the study established Alcott in relationship to her family and friends, her various homes, and her personal attitude toward her often-difficult life. It provided background valuable for an in-depth understanding of Alcott's works.

The importance of the familial and literary relationships of Louisa and her father was reinforced by the careful, scholarly, one-volume selection from the wealth of Amos Bronson Alcott's handwritten journals by Odell Shepard (*The Journals of Bronson Alcott* [Boston: Little, Brown, 1938]).

Katharine S. Anthony's "The Happiest Years" in *North American Review* (241 [June 1936], 297-310) began a psychoanalytical study that was expanded in *Louisa May Alcott* (New York: Knopf, 1938), a highly controversial biography. Among the favorable reviews was an important and typical statement by Maxwell Geismar whose "Duty's Faithful Child" (*Nation*,

146 [19 February 1938], 216) was less praise of Anthony's "first mature biography" than severe criticism of the Victorian age in which Alcott lived.

One of the first challenges to the "myth" established by Cheney and reinforced by Anthony and Geismar appeared in the same year, written by one of Alcott's few surviving contemporaries. In "Glimpses of the Real Louisa May Alcott" (*New England Quarterly*, 11 [December 1938], 731–38) Marion Talbot denied that Alcott lived a life thwarted by "duty." She presented strong evidence, taken from personal letters, that Louisa May Alcott was actively involved in educational reform, suffrage, and labor reform. The emphasis was upon the modern applicability of Alcott's life, not the Victorianism.

The criticism of the decade 1940–50 was dominated by two women, Leona Rostenberg and Madeleine B. Stern, who added a new dimension to the Alcott image. Although contemporaries were aware of Alcott's anonymous and pseudonymous productions, they had been concealed by the "myths" of "Duty's Child" and "Mother of *Little Women*." Leona Rostenberg's "Some Anonymous and Pseudonymous Thrillers of Louisa May Alcott" (*Bibliographical Society of America Papers*, 37 [2nd Quarter, 1943], 131–40) gave the first detailed account of Alcott's "pot-boilers" under such pseudonyms as A. M. Barnard and Flora Fairfield in *Frank Leslie's Illustrated Newspaper* and the *Flag of Our Union*. (See also Stern's survey of "Louisa M. Alcott's Contributions to Periodicals, 1868–1888," *More Books*, 18 [1943], 411–20.) These disclosures were supplemented by a number of articles by Stern that expanded on Alcott's theatrical experiences, travels, nursing experiences, and long years of literary experimentation prior to the writing of *Little Women*. The climax of the decade was Stern's *Louisa May Alcott* (Norman: Univ. of Oklahoma Press, 1950). This was a sound critical biography, readable but important for its bibliography and notes on sources which provided valuable scholarly tools.

The University of Oklahoma Press also provided a new facet of Alcott study. Sandford Salyer's *Marmee: The Mother of Little Women* (Norman, 1949) emphasized the influence of Mrs. Alcott on Louisa May, personally and literally.

For the scholar, Jacob N. Blanck provided a wealth of material in his *Bibliography of American Literature* (vol. 1 [New Haven: Yale Univ. Press, 1955], pp. 27–45). "Louisa May Alcott" listed all first editions chronologically, briefly described books that contained the first appearances of prose (except letters) or poetry, and cited variant issues or states of first editions. The door for comparative examination of the texts was opened wider.

Correspondence holds a universal fascination, and Elizabeth Bancroft Schlesinger, in "The Alcotts through Thirty Years: Letters to Alfred Whitman" (*Harvard Library Bulletin*, 5 [11 August 1957], 363–85), permitted the reader to share letters between Louisa May, Anna, and Abby May Alcott and Whitman from March 1858 to 29 May 1891. These glimpses of the Alcotts' daily life concluded with Schlesinger's judgment: "Louisa, caught in the web of fame, tries in vain to find her own soul, while easing the life of her beloved family." Thus another variation on the theme of "duty."

Marjorie Worthington's *Miss Alcott of Concord: A Biography* (New York: Doubleday, 1958) generally reworked material from Cheney's edition, with the addition of some personal experience and one previously unpublished letter containing comments on the Hawthornes.

The only Alcott entry in 1959 was indeed provocative, although disappointingly brief. Agatha Young made a penetrating comparison between Alcott's *Hospital Sketches* and Whitman's *The Wound Dresser* (*The Women and the Crisis: Women of the North in the Civil War* [New York: McDowell Obolensky], pp. 228–32). Unfortunately, Young did not pursue the comparison, being content to emphasize the effect of the hospital experience upon Alcott's writing. It gave "richer maturity" and changed the tone of her entire life.

Two women opened the gates for the literary deluge of the *Little Women* centennial. Brigid Brophy explored the mystery of why *Little Women* still lived and in the process moved the work from juvenile level to true craftsmanship ("Sentimentality and Louisa May Alcott," *Sunday Times Magazine*, December 1964; see also *New York Times Book Review*, 17 January 1965, pp. 1, 44).

In 1956, Helen Waite Papashvily briefly examined Alcott's heroines except for those in the early sensational tales (*All the Happy Endings* [New York: Harper]). In 1965, her *Louisa May Alcott* (Boston: Houghton Mifflin) expanded the earlier material into a biography by making use of letters, diaries, and other primary materials. Her most important contribution was her emphasis upon Alcott's "deep, tempestuous character," an interpretation far from "Duty's Daughter."

Another point-of-view character was featured in *We Alcotts: The Story of Louisa May Alcott's Family As Seen Through the Eyes of "Marmee," Mother of Little Women*, by Aileen Fisher and Olive Rabe (New York: Atheneum, 1968). There were many reviews and editorial treatments during this centennial period, but there was little that was new — most of the themes had been repeatedly explored.

The decade closed with an annotated selected bibliography, *Louisa May Alcott: A Centennial for "Little Women,"* compiled by Judith C. Ullom and prepared by the Rare Book Division of the Library of Congress (Washington, 1969) in celebration of the centennial. This bibliography did much to elevate Alcott to "respectability" in the history of the domestic novel yet did not insist upon lowering her position in children's literature.

The "variations" upon the theme of Louisa May Alcott in the period 1970–82 provided a concordance to social, political, and cultural stances as well as a continuation of traditional literary approaches. Sensitivity to racial tensions was apparent in analyses of Alcott's participation in and literary treatments of abolition and miscegenation. In 1970 Jan Cohn studied the survival of stereotypes of Northern abolitionists and Southern slaveholders in early stories by Louisa May Alcott ("The Negro Character in Northern Magazine Fiction of the 1860's," *New England Quarterly*, 43 [1970], 572-92). David W. Levy also examined such stereotypes in *Phylon* ("Racial Stereotypes in Anti-Slavery Fiction," 31 [Fall 1970], 265-79). Abigail A. Hamblen not only examined stories but traced Alcott's journal entries on race ("Louisa May Alcott and the Racial Question," *University Review* [Kansas City], 37 [1971], 307-13).

While the "Duty's Child" refrain had always highlighted the father-daughter relationship, there was increased emphasis upon Louisa's dramatization of her father's educational concepts. The important *Letters of A. Bronson Alcott* by Richard L. Herrnstadt (Ames: Iowa State Univ., 1969); Frederick L. H. Willis's *Alcott Memoirs* (Americanist, 1970); Taylor Stoehr's *Nay-Saying in Concord* (Hamden, Conn: Archon-Shoestring, 1979); and Charles Strickland's "Alcott, A Transcendentalist Father" (*History of Childhood Quarterly*, 1 [1973-74], 4-51) — all explored other areas of this parent-child relationship.

The influence of the entire Alcott family upon Louisa May was evident in the reprint of the 1909 edition of Clara Gowing's *Alcotts As I Knew Them* (Norwood, Pa., 1980). *The Alcotts, Biography of a Family*, by Madelon Bedell (New York: C. N. Potter, Crown, 1980), absorbed "the spirit of the Alcotts" in her interview with "Little Lulu"—Louisa May Nieriker Rasim. This introduction to the biography provides an immediacy through its physical and personal tie to the past. Bedell also used Herrnstadt's *Letters* to integrate Bronson Alcott's "infant diaries" and his psychology of childrearing into such chapters as "Power Struggle in the Nursery" and "Interlude: The Philosopher as a Young Man," with its implications of a possible romantic attachment of Bronson to that "diluted Margaret Fuller," Ednah Littlehale Cheney, who was largely responsible for establishing the "myth of Duty's Child."

It was not accidental that in 1981 Harvard Common Press produced *Transcendental Wild Oats; and Excerpts from the Fruitlands Diary*, with an introduction by William Henry Harrison, for nowhere else were the basic tensions between daughter and father more evident. It was perhaps these basic differences which led Carol Gay to suggest that Louisa never fully understood or respected her "controversial father," with all of his "potential humbug" ("The Philosopher and His Daughter: Amos Bronson Alcott and Louisa," *Essays in Literature*, 2 [1974], 181-91).

Sarah Elbert (Diamont), whose Cornell dissertation in 1974 stressed Alcott's commitment to domestic reforms and women's rights, analyzed the relationship of Louisa May and her sister May through her editing of previously unpublished materials dealing with Louisa's reactions to May's artistic profession and marriage (*Diana and Persis* [Arno, 1977]).

One of Alcott's personally favorite volumes, largely unknown to the twentieth century, was *Work: A Story of Experience*, which was reprinted with an insightful introduction by Sarah Elbert (New York: Schocken,

1977). In the same year, Arno Press reprinted the 1873 edition of *Work* in its "rediscovered fiction by American women series." The introduction was written by Elizabeth Hardwick.

Other largely unknown material was introduced in two volumes that were edited and introduced by Madeleine B. Stern: *Behind A Mask: the Unknown Thrillers of Louisa May Alcott* (New York: William Morrow, 1975) and *Plots and Counterplots: More Unknown Thrillers of Louisa May Alcott* (New York: William Morrow, 1976). In keeping with the attitudes of the mid-seventies, most reviewers stressed the "testy feminism" of these Gothic tales by Alcott, which Stern called "superb rubbish." Stern also introduced *Louisa's Wonder Book: An Unknown Alcott Juvenile* (Mount Pleasant: Central Michigan Univ. Press, 1975) and printed "Louisa M. Alcott in Periodicals" (*Studies in the American Renaissance*, 1 [1977], 369-86). In *Studies in the American Renaissance* (2 [1978], 429-52) appeared Stern's "Louisa May Alcott's Feminist Letters."

Other articles treating Alcott's "feminism" were so numerous that the whole must be represented by a few. As early as 1973 in "Duty's Child: Louisa May Alcott" (*American Literary Realism*, 6, No. 3 [Summer], 260-61) Alma J. Payne expanded Alcott's "Duty" to include her image as a liberated woman and her individualized artistic integrity. In the same year, Stephanie Harrington asked, "Does *Little Women* Belittle Women?" (*New York Times*, [10 June], Sec. 2, p. 19) and replied by describing *Little Women* as "virtually a feminist tract."

One cannot overlook Ann Douglas's introduction to the reprint of Cheney's 1889 *Louisa May Alcott* (New York: Chelsea House, 1980) and Douglas's review of Martha Saxton's *Louisa May: A Modern Biography of Louisa May Alcott* (Boston: Houghton Mifflin, 1977) which appeared in the *New York Review of Books* (28 September 1978, pp. 60-63).

This last-mentioned biography offered "modern" interpretations of themes often appearing in earlier biographies. Saxton sensed Alcott's strong antagonism to men and felt the writing of *Little Women* was "a regression for Louisa as artist and woman." Saxton saw irony in the fact that Louisa May achieved the success which her father sought.

Among the most important scholarly contributions of the last twelve years have been those in bibliography. In 1971 the second printing of Madeleine B. Stern's *Louisa May Alcott* (Norman: Univ. of Oklahoma Press, 1971), brought her bibliography up to date with the final list numbering 274, including all known poems, essays, stories, and novels chronologically arranged. Stern included reprints, later collections, and the sensational and sentimental stories published under pseudonyms. Both *Behind A Mask* (1975) and *Plots and Counterplots* (1976) included valuable bibliographies. The same is true of *Louisa's Wonder Book* (1975).

Accepting Alma J. Payne's classification of Alcott as realist, based upon "the pattern of everyday speech, the commonplace elevated to the universal, and . . . that base of personal experience . . ," *American Literary Re-*

alism included "Louisa May Alcott (1832–1888)" (6, No. 1 [Winter 1973], 27–45). Payne's in-depth bibliographical essay traced the history of Alcott criticism; evaluated bibliographical sources; reviewed editions, reprints, and published manuscript material; noted manuscript collections and current critical articles (1960–73); and closed with a discussion of areas of potential future scholarship.

From this bibliographical essay and from Payne's entry in the first volume of *American Women Writers: A Critical Reference Guide* (New York: Frederick Ungar, 1979) grew *Louisa May Alcott: A Reference Guide* (Boston: G. K. Hall & Co., 1980). In a ten-page introduction Payne indicated that the many levels upon which Alcott wrote, the many audiences to which she appealed, and the many problems and values of American society which she addressed resulted in a richly varied critical reaction. The author concluded, "With each interpretation we see a different facet of Louisa May Alcott and perhaps more importantly, a variant profile of ourselves."

Joy A. Marsella's *The Promise of Destiny: Children and Women in the Stories of Louisa May Alcott*, was published in 1983 by Greenwood Press. In a study of the sixty stories in *Aunt Jo's Scrap Bag* Marsella discovers Alcott's concern over a very modern problem—the tension between public and private, domestic roles for women. At the present time, we await the publication of a biography by Ruth MacDonald in the Twayne series. The latest entry in the field is Sarah Elbert's *A Hunger for Home: Louisa May Alcott and Little Women* (Philadelphia: Temple University Press, 1984).

It has become evident through this bibliographical review that the major themes in Alcott criticism were established early, but as in a musical composition the emphases vary according to the sociological instrument being used. The variations upon the many themes continue to appear, and the many questions posed in Alcott's works have evoked and continue to evoke many answers which change with America's changing views of itself.

INDEX

Abbott, Jacob, *Franconia* books, 166; *Rollo* books, 5, 9, 84, 122, 166, 267
Abolition, 2, 30, 33, 34, 35, 38, 101, 194, 251, 252, 280, 283
Adams, Mildred, 16–17
Adams, William Taylor ["Oliver Optic"], 122, 225
Alberghene, Janice M., 17
Alcott, Abby May (sister), 11, 51, 81, 85, 87, 90, 92, 100, 102, 133, 244, 247, 248, 282, 284
Alcott, Abigail May (mother), 40, 51, 52, 59, 90, 101, 102, 106, 108, 121, 127, 135, 137, 193, 194, 225, 232, 233, 234, 235, 240, 241, 242, 244, 247, 282
Alcott, Amos Bronson (father), 9, 10, 13, 15, 27, 28, 34, 42, 51, 53, 84, 89, 90, 101, 102, 103, 105, 106, 107, 108, 109, 121, 122, 126, 127, 137, 178, 179, 215–216, 218, 225, 227, 228, 229, 230, 231, 232, 233–234, 235, 238, 240, 241, 242, 244, 246, 249, 251, 253, 257, 258, 259, 260, 261–264, 265, 267, 269, 270, 274, 279, 280, 281, 284, 285; *Concord Days*, 261; *Conversations with Children on the Gospels*, 261 *Emerson*, 261; *Tablets*, 261
Alcott, Anna (sister), 41, 51, 53, 54, 102, 240, 244, 257, 270, 282; *see also* Pratt, Anna Alcott
Alcott, Elizabeth (sister), 51, 196, 244, 247, 270
Alcott family, 13, 15, 33, 52, 102, 200, 251, 270, 284
Alcott, Louisa May, as army nurse, 26, 27, 30, 33, 35, 74, 128; attitude toward blacks, 2, 26, 30–39, 251–252, 280–281, 283–284; autobiography in books, 10, 11, 13, 135, 196, 211, 244, 246–247, 279; bibliographies of, 15–16, 249, 279–286; biographies and reminiscences of, 15, 249, 279–286; changing reputation of, 1, 241, 249; "Children's Friend," 1, 15, 51, 168, 231, 241, 245, 249; domestic service of, 52–53, 193–194, 242; economic pressures upon, 51–52; feminism of, 4, 5, 6, 7, 8, 10, 11, 12, 13, 16, 17, 55, 61, 98, 101, 111, 112, 114–119, 127, 135, 138, 141, 142, 143–144, 172–174, 185, 191–201, 228–229, 232, 235, 249, 251, 252–254, 273, 279, 280, 282, 284, 285; literary experimentations of, 1, 2, 4, 16, 55, 241, 243–244, 249; paradoxes in, 14, 218–222; passion for theater, 13, 41, 53–54, 55, 215; pseudonyms of, 3, 15, 44, 45, 46, 48, 56, 59, 242–243, 256; realism in, 4, 17, 29, 74, 97–98, 244; reform and, 10, 11, 14, 15, 16, 17, 101, 102, 132, 191, 192, 221, 235, 245, 246–248, 250–255, 282; sentimentality of, 6, 17, 88, 93–96, 97, 100, 111, 172; and work ethic, 7, 12, 118, 127–128, 147, 187–188; works of; "The Abbot's Ghost: or, Maurice Treherne's Temptation," 47, 56–57; *Aunt Jo's Scap-Bag*, 10, 11, 177–178, 181, 248, 286; reviews of, 177–178; "Behind a Mask: or, A Woman's Power," 3, 46, 49, 58–59, 140, 141, 236–237, 256–257; *Behind a Mask*, 141, 256, 285; "The Blue and the Gray," 37; "The Brothers," 36, 251; *see also* "My Contraband"; "The Captive of Castile," 53, 242; *Comic Tragedies*, 2–3; review of, 41, 42; "The Cost of an Idea," 262; "A Country Christmas," 180; *Eight Cousins*, 8, 9, 165–169, 170, 225, 228, 232, 239, 246, 247, 253, 266–269, 273; reviews of, 165–169, 266–269; "Enigmas," 43, 60; *Flower Fables*, 1, 4, 23,

44, 242, 258–259; reviews of, 23; *A Free Bed*, 249; *Good Wives*, 77, 94, 95, 185, 276; "Happy Women," 55, 135; *Hospital Sketches*, 1, 2, 4, 25, 26–29, 30, 33, 35, 38, 44, 66, 74, 128, 243, 244, 261, 265, 283; reviews of, 25; *Hospital Sketches and Camp and Fireside Stories*, 2, 26, 30, 261; "An Hour," 2, 30–32, 37; "How I Went Out to Service," 52, 242; "In the Garret," 46; *Jack and Jill*, 8, 9, 170–171, 218, 239, 247; reviews of, 170–171; *Jo's Boys*, 8, 10, 38, 137, 138, 140, 149, 160, 171–174, 218, 225, 226, 227, 239, 240, 247–248, 250, 252, 255, 267; review of, 171–172; "Kitty's Class Day," 180; "Letters to her Laurie," 280; "Letty's Tramp," 179; *Little Men*, 8, 9, 10, 16, 136, 137, 148, 157–165, 171, 223, 225, 239, 240, 246, 247, 261, 263, 274; reviews of, 157–160; *Little Women*, 1, 4–8, 10, 11, 16, 26, 28, 41, 42, 43, 47, 51, 52, 55, 57, 58, 61, 75, 81–150, 158, 160, 172, 185, 213, 214, 215, 217, 218, 219, 221, 222–224, 225, 226, 229, 231, 232, 234, 235, 237–238, 239, 241, 244–245, 247, 248, 249, 255, 256, 259, 261, 262, 275, 276, 277, 278, 280, 282, 283, 285; collation of, 85–86; dramatizations of, 7, 88, 93–94, 95, 110, 112, 215;

reviews of, 81–83; writing and publication of, 4–5, 86–87; 89; "Love and Loyalty," 37; *Lulu's Library*, 11, 180, 248 review of, 180; "A Marble Woman; or, The Mysterious Model," 3, 45, 46, 48, 57, 258; "M.L.," 35–36, 37–38, 251; "A Modern Cinderella," 265; *A Modern Mephistopheles*, 11, 12–13, 203–207, 248–249; need for new edition of, 13, 18; reviews of, 203–207; *Moods*, 1, 3–4, 65–78, 235, 239, 244, 262, 265–266, 267, 270, 271–272, 273; need for new edition of, 18; reviews of, 66–74, 265–266; revision of, 4, 74–78; *Morning-Glories, and Other Stories*, 90; "My Contraband," 2, 32–33, 36–37; *The Mysterious Key*, 50, 57, 259; *Bachelor's Pleasure Trip*, 53; "A Night," 28; "Norna; or, The Witch's Curse," 53, 242; *An Old-Fashioned Girl*, 8, 11, 38, 77, 135, 153–157, 185, 232, 239, 245–246, 252, 253, 254, 261, 262; reviews of, 153–157; "Pauline's Passion and Punishment," 3, 43, 49, 55–56, 57, 59, 60, 141,

259; *Plots and Counterplots*, 141, 285; *Proverb Stories*, 11, 180; review of, 180; "The Rival Painters. A Tale of Rome," 124, 243; "The Rival Prima Donnas," 243; *The Rose Family*, 244; *Rose in Bloom*, 8, 9, 141, 170, 218, 226, 228, 239, 246–247, 254, 267, 268, 273–274; "The Sanitary Fair," 46; *Shawl-Straps*, 177, 181; "Silver Pitchers," 179, 254; *Silver Pitchers*, 11, 179; review of, 179; *The Skeleton in the Closet*, 50, 58; *Spinning-Wheel Stories*, 11, 248; *Success*, 11, 192, 271; *see also Work*; "Sunlight," 242–243; "Thoreau's Flute," 200; thrillers and sensationalism of, 1, 2–3, 4, 7, 8, 11, 12, 14, 41–64, 75, 140–141, 231, 232, 235–237, 243–244, 256–260, 282, 285; "To the First Robin," 241; "Transcendental Wild Oats," 10–11, 178–179; *Transcendental Wild Oats and excerpts from the Fruitlands diary*, 284; *Under the Lilacs*, 8, 9, 141, 170–171, 218, 238–239, 247, 256; review of, 170–171; "The Unloved Wife," 242; "V.V.: or, Plots and Counterplots," 3, 45–46, 47, 48, 50, 57, 75, 237; "A Whisper in the Dark," 3, 60; *Will's Wonder Book*, 244; "With a Rose, That Bloomed on the Day of John Brown's Martyrdom," 34, 243; *Work: A Story of Experience*, 11–12, 13, 16, 38, 75, 76, 126–127, 135, 136, 169, 185–202, 235, 252, 253, 271–273, 280, 284–285; reviews of, 185–191

Alger, Horatio, 7, 120–121, 125, 225; *Helen Ford*, 120; *Ragged Dick*, 7, 120, 121, 124, 125; *Timothy Crump's Ward*, 120
Allyson, June, 112
Almy, Lillie, 90
American Literary Realism, 285–286
American Revolution, 201
American Union, 44, 45, 47, 50
American Women Writers: A Critical Reference Guide, 286
Anthony, Katharine S., 282; "The Happiest Years," 281; *Louisa May Alcott*, 15, 249, 281–282
Arms, George, "The Poet As Theme Reader: William Vaughn Moody, A Student, and Louisa May Alcott," 17
Athenaeum (London), 9, 11
Atlantic Monthly, 9, 13, 36, 43, 145, 200, 280
Auerbach, Nina, 7–8, 143; "*Little Women*

[and *Pride and Prejudice*]," 129–140
Aunt Judy's Magazine, 275
Austen, Jane, 13, 96, 135, 148, 213, 228; *Pride and Prejudice*, 8, 129–136, 249
Avery, Gillian, *Childhood's Pattern: A Study of the Heroes and Heroines of Children's Fiction 1770–1950*, 278

Baker, Augusta, 99
Ballou, Maturin Murray, 43, 44, 50
Balzac, Honoré de, 230; *Le Père Goriot*, 226
"Barnard, A.M." (Alcott pseudonym), 3, 11, 15, 44, 45, 46–47, 48, 56, 59, 60, 61, 243, 244, 245, 249, 256, 258, 259, 282
Barnard, Henry, 44, 59
Barrett, C. Waller, 6; "Little Women Forever," 89–93
Barton, Bruce, *The Man Nobody Knows*, 84
Basso, Hamilton, 2; *The Light Infantry Ball*, 39
Baum, Freda, "The Scarlet Strand: Reform Motifs in the Writings of Louisa May Alcott," 15, 250–255
Baum, Vicki, *Grand Hotel*, 106
Beach, Seth Curtis, *Daughters of the Puritans*, 280
Beadle & Co., 61
Beale, Winnie, 194
Beckford, William, 54
Bedell, Jeanne F., "A Necessary Mask: The Sensation Fiction of Louisa May Alcott," 16
Bedell, Madelon, 8, 10, 284; *The Alcotts, Biography of a Family*, 15, 249, 284; "Beneath the Surface: Power and Passion in *Little Women*, 145–150
Beecher, Henry Ward, 197
Beer, Thomas, 14; "[The Influence of Louisa Alcott]," 225–226; *The Mauve Decade*, 14
Bell, Alistair, 112
Bible, 5, 44, 84, 196, 221
Bibliothèque Rose Illustrée, 217
Billings, Hammatt, 92, 93
Blanck, Jacob N., *Bibliography of American Literature*, 282
Boaden, Ann, 16
Bonstelle, Jessie, and Marian De Forest, *Little Women: Letters from the House of Alcott*, 281
"Books That Separate Parents from Their Children," 212
Boston Evening Transcript, 1, 23, 25
Boston Herald, 245

Boston, MA, 2, 3, 4, 30, 33, 38, 43, 44, 52, 53, 60, 61, 66, 84, 85, 86, 89, 90, 92, 93, 99, 100, 106, 108, 109, 110, 127, 147, 153, 215, 229, 233, 241, 242, 246, 261, 265, 270
Boston Public Library, 45
Braddon, Mary Elizabeth, 236; *Lady Audley's Secret*, 236
Brady, Mathew B., 110
Briggs, George W., & Co., 23
Brigham Young University Library, 249
Brontë, Charlotte, 126, 148; *Jane Fyre*, 268; *The Professor*, 126
Brontë, Emily, 134
Brophy, Brigid, 6, 97, 100, 102, 283; "Sentimentality and Louisa M. Alcott," 93–96, 283
Brown, John, 34, 270, 280
Brown, Mary Hosmer, *Memories of Concord*, 281
Browning, Elizabeth Barrett, 227
Browning, Robert, 68
Buffalo, N.Y., 215
Bunyan, John, 86, 92, 105, 123, 199; *Pilgrim's Progress*, 7, 84, 104, 105, 122, 126, 199, 204, 273
Burlingame, Edward R., 13; [Review of *A Modern Mephistopheles*], 204–205
Burnett, Frances Hodgson, 239

Cadogan, Mary, " 'Sweet, If Somewhat Tomboyish': The British Response to Louisa May Alcott," 15, 275–279; *You're a Brick, Angela! A New Look at Girls' Fiction from 1839 to 1975*, 278
Calvin, John, 220
Carlyle, Thomas, 54, 230, 266
Carroll, Lewis, 239, 275–276; *Alice's Adventures in Wonderland*, 85, 227, 275; *Through the Looking Glass*, 85
Carter, Henry, 59; *see also* Frank Leslie
Chambers, Jessie, 160
Chandler, Raymond, 96
Channing family, 242
Channing, William Henry, 27
Cheney, Ednah Dow Littlehale, 13, 15, 192, 215, 223, 249, 272, 279, 280, 282, 284; ["Her Works Are a Revelation of Herself"], 211; *Louisa May Alcott: The Children's Friend*, 15, 279; *Louisa May Alcott: Her Life, Letters, and Journals*, 15, 100–101, 279, 280, 281, 283, 285
Cheney, Seth, 215

Chesterton, Gilbert Keith, 13; "Louisa Alcott," 212–214
Child, Lydia Maria, 27
Childs, Mildred, 84
Choate, Joseph, 226
Christian Union, 197
Civil War, American, 2, 16, 25, 27, 28, 29, 35, 39, 55, 74, 83, 113, 122, 127, 128, 129, 135, 141, 143, 193, 195, 199, 200, 232, 238, 243, 251, 265, 270
Clark, Annie M.L., *The Alcotts in Harvard*, 15, 280
Clemens, Samuel L., 226, 237, 239; *Huckleberry Finn*, 226; *Innocents Abroad*, 225; *Tom Sawyer*, 7, 88, 128
Cobb, Sylvanus, Jr., 44
Cohn, Jan, 2, 283–284; "The Negro Character in Northern Magazine Fiction of the 1860's," 30–33, 284
Collins, Wilkie, 236; *Woman in White*, 235
Commonwealth (Boston), 26, 27, 35, 280
Concord, MA, 33, 34, 41, 42, 51, 53, 54, 107, 110, 113, 127, 131, 200, 215, 216, 218, 219, 221, 227, 230, 231, 232, 242, 244, 247, 251, 254, 259, 261, 269, 270, 281
Constanduros, Denis, 112
Conway, Moncure Daniel, 27
Coolidge, Susan, 278
Copus, E.J., *As Gold in the Furnace*, 84
Cozzens, James Gould, 2; *Guard of Honor*, 38–39
Craig, Patricia, and Mary Cadogan, *You're a Brick, Angela! A New Look at Girls' Fiction from 1839 to 1975*, 278
Crompton, Margaret, "*Little Women*: The Making of a Classic," 16
Current Literature, 84

Dante Alighieri, 54
Darton, F.J. Harvey, *Children's Books in England*, 276–277
Daudet, Alphonse, *Kings in Exile*, 226
Dedham, MA, 52, 53, 59, 242
Defoe, Daniel, *Robinson Crusoe*, 105
Delacroix, Ferdinand Victor Eugène, 227
Diamont, Sarah Elbert: *see* Sarah Elbert
Dickens, Charles, 54, 87, 127, 236, 242, 246; *David Copperfield*, 6, 88, 198; *Great Expectations*, 235; *Little Dorrit*, 235; *Nicholas Nickleby*, 247; *Pickwick Papers*, 214
Dixon, Bob, *Catching Them Young: Sex, Race and Class in Children's Fiction*, 277

Dollar Monthly, 44
Douglas, Ann, 14, 285; "Mysteries of Louisa May Alcott," 231–240
Douglass, Frederick, 251
Down, Angela, 112
Doyle, Brian, *The Who's Who of Children's Literature*, 277
Dumas, Alexandre, 230
Dumas, Alexandre, père, *The Three Musketeers*, 105
Durivage, Francis, 44

Eakins, Thomas, 110
Elbert, Sarah, 12, 16, 235, 284; *Diana and Persis*, 284; *A Hunger for Home*, 286; "Introduction to *Work: A Story of Experience*," 191–202
Eliot, George, 95, 127, 213, 227
Elliott and Thomes, 44, 50, 61
Elliott, James R., 3, 43, 44–45, 46, 47–49, 61, 140
Elliott, Thomes, and Talbot, 44, 60
Emerson, Edward, 280
Emerson, Ellen, 1, 242, 258
Emerson, Ralph Waldo, 1, 33, 34, 42, 54, 66, 101, 103, 170, 172, 178–179, 218, 219, 229, 230, 232, 233, 234, 242, 251, 259, 265, 266, 269, 273, 279; *Essays*, 170, 218; *Self-Reliance*, 247

Fairbanks, Douglas, 223
"Fairfield, Flora" (Alcott pseudonym), 15, 242, 243, 244, 245, 249, 282
Faulkner, William, *The Sound and the Fury*, 106
Fay, Janina, 112
Fenwick, Sara Innis, "American Children's Classics: Which Will Fade, Which Endure?" 16
Ferber, Edna, *So Big*, 84
Fetterley, Judith, 8; "*Little Women*: Alcott's Civil War," 140–143
Fisher, Aileen, and Olive Rabe, *We Alcotts*, 283
Fisher, Dorothy Canfield, *The Bent Twig*, 84
Fisher, Margery, 278; *Intent upon Reading*, 16; *Who's Who in Children's Books*, 278
Fitzgerald, F. Scott, "Bernice Bobs her Hair," 145
Flag of Our Union, 43, 44, 45, 46, 47–48, 56, 61, 282
Flaubert, Gustave, 230; *Madame Bovary*, 217
Foord, Sophia, 270, 274

Forrey, Caroline, "The New Woman Revisited [in *Jo's Boys*]," 10, 172–174
Frank, Anne, *The Diary of Anne Frank*, 99
Frank Leslie's Illustrated Newspaper, 43, 55, 59–60, 282
Frazer, Sir James, 161
Freud, Sigmund, 239
Fruitlands (community), 10–11, 121, 137, 178, 179, 242, 246, 262, 265, 270, 279
Fuller, Horace, 244
Fuller, Margaret, 242, 251, 272

Garland, Hamlin, *Trail Makers of the Middle Border*, 84
Garnett, Edward, 163
Garrison, William Lloyd, 33, 251
Gaskell, Elizabeth Cleghorn, 116; *Wives and Daughters*, 117
Gay, Carol, "The Philosopher and His Daughter," 284
Geismar, Maxwell, 282; "Duty's Faithful Child," 281–282
Georgetown, D.C., 2, 243, 247
Germantown, PA, 227, 240
Gerould, Katharine Fullerton, 14, 280; "Miss Alcott's New England," 217–222, 280; *Modes and Morals*, 280
Gleason, Frederick, 43, 44
Godey's Lady's Book, 10, 13
Goethe, Johann Wolfgang von, 12, 54, 206, 218, 242, 248; *Elective Affinities*, 66; *Faust*, 203; *Wilhelm Meister*, 54
Goldman, Suzy, 17
Goodrich, Samuel Griswold ("Peter Parley"), 122
Gorky, Maxim, *The Lower Depths*, 88
Gowing, Clara, *The Alcotts as I Knew Them*, 15, 280, 284
Graves & Weston, 47, 50
Greeley, Horace, 34
Gulliver, Lucile, *Louisa May Alcott: A Bibliography*, 15, 249, 281

Hale, Amanda, 44
Hamblen, Abigail Ann, 2, 284; "Louisa May Alcott and The Racial Question," 33–40, 284
Hammett, Dashiell, 148
Harding, Rebecca, 197; *Margaret Howth*, 197
Hardwick, Elizabeth, 285
Harlow, Lurabel, 90
Harper's Ferry, VA (later W VA), 34
Harper's Magazine, 12, 14

Harper's New Monthly Magazine, 9, 10, 201
Harrington, Stephanie, "Does *Little Women* Belittle Women?" 7, 110–112, 285
Harris, Joel Chandler, *Uncle Remus*, 227
Harris, William Torrey, 178, 263; *Amos Bronson Alcott: His Life and Philosophy*, 280
Harrison, William Henry, 10, 284; [Transcendental Wild Oats"], 178–179
Harvard Common Press, 10, 284
Harvard, MA, 10, 137, 234, 242
Haverstick, Iola, 17; "To See Louisa Plain," 17
Haviland, Virginia, 99
Hawthorne, Julian, 13, 203; "Woman Who Wrote *Little Women*," 281
Hawthorne, Nathaniel, 12, 54, 66, 218, 230, 248, 263, 271, 280, 283; *Scarlet Letter*, 54
Hazeltine, Mayo, 226
Heilbrun, Carolyn, 8; [Jo March: Male Model — Female Person], 143–145
Heir of Redclyffe (Yonge), 54, 114, 123
Hellman, Lillian, 148; *Julia*, 148
Hemingway, Ernest, 100, 102
Hepburn, Katharine, 94, 266
Herald (Boston), 44
Herrnstadt, Richard L., *Letters of A. Bronson Alcott*, 284
Higginson, Mary Elizabeth Channing, 262
Higginson, Thomas Wentworth, 145, 262
Hollander, Anne, 16
Holley, Sally, 194–195
Holmes, Oliver Wendell, 172
Hosmer family, 242
Howe, Julia Ward, 27
Howells, William Dean, 217, 218, 226
Hughes, Thomas, *Tom Brown's Schooldays*, 137

Ibsen, Henrik, 100
Independent, 10
Irving, Washington, 54, 55

Jackson, Helen Hunt, *Ramona*, 84, 145
James, Henry, 4, 9, 15, 226, 239, 246, 265–269;
"Benvolio," 267; *The Bostonians*, 266; "Mora Montravers," 266; Mrs. Temperley," 265; *A Passionate Pilgrim*, 266; *The Portrait of a Lady*, 271; [Review of *Eight Cousins*], 165–166, 266–269; [Review of *Moods*], 69–73, 265–266; *Roderick*

Index

Hudson, 266; "Story of A Year," 265; *Transatlantic Sketches*, 266; "The Turn of the Screw," 265, 269; *What Maisie Knew*, 265, 268
James, Henry, Sr., 28, 265
James, Mary Robertson Walsh (Mrs. Henry, Sr.), 265
Janeway, Elizabeth, 6, 139, 143; "Meg, Jo, Beth, Amy and Louisa," 6, 97–98
Jones, Bessie Z., 2; "Introduction to *Hospital Sketches*," 27–29
Journal of Negro History, 35, 280
Joyce, James, *Ulysses*, 106
Judd, Sylvester, 263

Kaledin, Eugenia, 17; "Louisa May Alcott: Success and the Sorrow of Self-denial," 17
Keats, John, *Ode To A Nightingale*, 88
Keller, Helen, *Story of My Life*, 84
Keyser, Elizabeth, "Little Women in Louisa May Alcott's *Little Men*," 17; " 'Nothing But Love': Louisa May Alcott's 'Cupid and Chow-chow,' " 17
Kierkegaard, Søren Aabye, 96
Kipling, Rudyard, 137, 212–213; *Stalky & Co.*, 137
Klemesrud, Judy, 110

Ladies' Home Journal, 280, 281
Lakeside Monthly, 12
Lamb, Charles, 69
Lancaster, MA, 196
Lane, Charles, 178
Lawrence, D.H., 9, 160, 162–165; *Sons and Lovers*, 9, 160, 162–165
Lee & Shepard, 82
Lerman, Leo, 7; "Little Women: Who's In Love With Miss Louisa May Alcott? I Am," 113–114
Leslie, Frank, 43, 46, 49, 56, 59–60, 61, 140
Levy, David W., "Racial Stereotypes in Anti-Slavery Fiction," 284
Lewis, Dio, 246
Lewis, Matthew Gregory ("Monk"), 54
Liberator, 33, 34, 243
Library of Congress, 45, 99–100, 283
Lincoln, Abraham, 227
Lincoln, M.V., 44
Linn, Edith Willis, and Henry Bazin, eds., *Alcott Memoirs*, 281
Lippincott's Magazine, 8
Little, Brown & Company, 93, 97, 99, 100, 170, 223, 281

"*Little Women* Leads Poll," 84
Locke, William John, *The Beloved Vagabond*, 106
London, Eng., 85, 86, 93, 229, 266
Loring, Aaron K., 3, 65, 66, 74, 76, 120, 125, 244; [A Letter to Louisa May Alcott by the Future Publisher of *Moods*], 65
Lothrop, Harriett Mulford Stone, 226
Lovering, Alice, 53
Lowell, Amy, 14; "Books for Children," 216

MacDonald, Ruth K., 4, 286; "*Moods*, Gothic and Domestic," 74–78
Mann, Dorothea Lawrance, "When the Alcott Books Were New," 85
Marsella, Joy A., *The Promise of Destiny*, 10, 286; "The Promise of Destiny [in *Aunt Jo's Scrap-Bags*]," 181
Martineau, Harriet, 192
Massachusetts Review, 16
May, Col. Joseph, 38, 40, 240
May family, 38, 127, 232
May, Samuel J., 251
Mazzini, Giuseppe, 57
McCarthy, Mary, *The Group*, 106
Meigs, Cornelia, 6–7, 281; "Introduction to Centennial Edition of *Little Women*," 6–7, 103–105; *The Story of the Author of Little Women: Invincible Louisa*, 15, 100, 249, 281
Melcher, Frederic G., 93
Melville, Herman, 139, 230
Merrill, Frank T., 87
Merry's Museum, 244
Milton, John, *Paradise Lost*, 216
Moers, Ellen, 7; "Money, Job, Little Women: Female Realism," 126–128
Monthly Novelette, 44
Moody, William Vaughn, 17
Morrow, Honoré Willsie, *The Father of Little Women*, 281
Moses, Belle, 280; *Louisa May Alcott, Dreamer and Worker*, 15, 280
Mott, Frank Luther, *Golden Multitudes*, 241
Moulton, W.U., 44
Mount, William Sidney, 110
Myerson, Joel, 15; " 'Our Children Are Our Best Works': Bronson and Louisa May Alcott," 261–264

Nathan, George Jean, 6; [A Dramatic Performance of *Little Women*], 88
Nation, 4, 8, 9, 145, 266, 281

Nesbit, E. (Edith Bland), 239
New England Magazine, 279
New Orleans, LA, 31
New Republic, 14
Newton, A. Edward, 88
New York Evening Mail, 92
New York Ledger, 55
New York, NY, 43, 55, 59, 61, 89, 113, 128, 130
New York Public Library, 45, 99
New York Review of Books, 285
New York Times Book Review, 97, 100, 283
New York Times Magazine, 16
New York Times Saturday Review, 13
Nice, France, 230
Nieriker, Louisa May (niece), 11, 248, 284
Niles, Thomas, 4, 28, 86, 87, 89, 90, 91, 92–93, 97, 99, 101, 109, 121, 140, 244, 246, 262
"No Name Series," 12, 140, 206, 248
Nonquitt, MA, 226
North American Review, 13, 265, 281
Northcliffe, Alfred Charles William Harmsworth, 1st viscount, 277–278

O'Brien, Sharon, "Tomboyism and Adolescent Conflict: Three Nineteenth-Century Case Studies," 17
O'Faolain, Sean, 7; "This Is Your Life . . . Louisa May Alcott," 105–110
Oldham, William, 264
Olive Branch, 243
"Oliver Optic," *see* William Taylor Adams
Overland Monthly, 9
Owen, Robert Dale, 228–229
Ozick, Cynthia, 148

Papashvily, Helen Waite, 146; *All the Happy Endings*, 15, 283; *Louisa May Alcott*, 15, 293
Papers of the Bibliographical Society of America, 3
Paris, France, 58, 92, 100, 217, 229–230
Parker, Theodore, 12, 135, 186, 192, 196, 251; "Laborious Young Women," 196; "The Public Function of Woman," 192
Pauly, Thomas H., 7; "*Ragged Dick* and *Little Women*: Idealized Homes and Unwanted Marriages," 120–125
Payne, Alma J., 15, 16, 249; "Duty's Child: Louisa May Alcott," 285; "Louisa May Alcott: A Bibliographical Essay on Secondary Sources," 279–286; "Louisa May Alcott (1832–1888)," 286; *Louisa May Alcott: A Reference Guide*, 16, 286
P., C.L., [Review of *An Old-Fashioned Girl*], 155–157
Peabody, Elizabeth Palmer, 27, 242, 251; *Record of Mr. Alcott's School*, 263; *Record of a School*, 261, 263
Perényi, Eleanor, 14; "Dear Louisa," 227–231
"Periwinkle, Nurse Tribulation," (Alcott pseudonym), 15, 26, 243, 244, 245, 249
Peterson's Magazine, 242
Phillips, Florence, 17
Pickett, La Salle Corbell, 3; [Louisa Alcott's "Natural Ambition" for the "Lurid Style" Disclosed in a Conversation], 42
Pilgrim's Progress (Bunyan), 7
Plato, 211, 218
Poe, Edgar Allan, 54, 236
Porter, Eleanor H., *Pollyanna*, 84
Porter, Maria S., 279; "Recollections of Louisa May Alcott," 279
Portland, ME, 43
Port Royal, SC, 195
Pratt, Anna Alcott, 246; see also Alcott, Anna
Pratt, John, 87, 246
Pride and Prejudice (Austen), 8, 129–136, 249
Publisher's Weekly, 93

Radcliffe, Ann, 54
Ragged Dick (Alger), 7, 120, 121, 124, 125
Randall, David A., 6; "One Hundred Good Novels," 85
Rasim, Louisa May Nieriker, *see* Louisa May Nieriker
Reader, 4
Redpath, James, 27, 28, 243, 244; *Echoes of Harper's Ferry*, 243
Reed, Mary Ann Williams, 53
Retzsch, Moritz, "The Game of Life," 204
Richards, Harriet Roosevelt, 170
Richardson, James, 52, 55, 242
Roberts Brothers, 4, 10, 12, 25, 28, 82, 85, 86, 87, 89, 90–91, 99, 121, 140, 157, 170, 177, 186, 206, 225, 244, 245, 246, 247, 248, 261, 262, 263, 280
Roe, F. Gordon, *The Victorian Child*, 276
Rollo books, 5, 9, 84, 122, 166, 267
Rome, Italy, 104, 229, 246
Rostenberg, Leona, 3, 107, 243, 256, 282; discovery of Alcott pseudonym by, 3, 61, 243, 256; "Some Anonymous and

Pseudonymous Thrillers of Louisa May Alcott," 43–50, 282
Russ, Lavinia Faxon, 6; "Not To Be Read On Sunday," 6, 99–102

Saint-Pierre, Jacques Henri Bernardin de, *Paul et Virginie*, 96
Salmon, Edward, "Should Children Have a Special Literature?" 275
Salmon, Lucy Maynard, 194
Salyer, Sandford, *Marmee: The Mother of Little Women*, 282
Sanborn, Franklin B., 13, 27, 34, 85, 280; *Amos Bronson Alcott: His Life and Philosophy*, 280; "Reminiscences of Louisa May Alcott," 215–216
Sand, George, 148, 227
Sargent, Mary Fiske, 53
Saturday Evening Gazette (Boston), 23, 43, 243
Saturday Review, 17
Saturday Review of Politics, Literature, Science, And Art, 11
Saxton, Martha, 15, 75, 231, 232, 233, 234, 235, 236, 237, 238, 249; *Louisa May: A Modern Biography of Louisa May Alcott*, 14, 15, 231, 285; "The Secret Imaginings of Louisa Alcott," 256–260
Schlesinger, Elizabeth Bancroft, 282–283; "The Alcotts through Thirty Years," 282
Schoolgirl, 277
Schreiber, Le Anne, 146
Scott, Sir Walter, *Ivanhoe*, 123
Seemüller, Anne Moncure Crane, *Emily Chester*, 266
Sewall family, 232
Shakespeare, William, 41, 50, 54; *Hamlet*, 217
Shaw, Col. Robert, 37
Shepard, Odell, *The Journals of Bronson Alcott*, 281
Shull, Martha, "The Novels of Louisa May Alcott as Commentary on the American Family," 17
Sidney, Margaret, *see* Harriett Mulford Stone Lothrop
Smith, Grover, 9; "The Doll-Burners: D.H. Lawrence and Louisa Alcott," 160–165
Smith, Jessie Willcox, 100
Southworth and Hawes, 110
Spacks, Patricia Meyer, 7, 139; [*Little Women* and the Female Imagination], 114–119
Squier, Ephraim George, 49, 60

Squier, Miriam, 60
Stephens, Alice Barber, 170
Stern, Madeleine B., 3, 14–15, 107, 140–141, 235, 256, 259, 282, 285; Alcott bibliographies of, 16, 249, 285; *Behind A Mask: The Unknown Thrillers of Louisa May Alcott*, 141, 256, 285; compiles Alcott thrillers, 14, 15, 231, 256; "Introduction to *Behind a Mask*," 50–64, 256; *Louisa May Alcott*, 15, 16, 249, 282, 285; "Louisa M. Alcott in Periodicals," 285; "Louisa M. Alcott's Contributions to Periodicals," 282; "Louisa May Alcott's Feminist Letters," 285; *Louisa's Wonder Book: An Unknown Alcott Juvenile*, 16, 285; *Plots and Counterplots: More Unknown Thrillers of Louisa May Alcott*, 141, 285; "A Writer's Progress: Louisa May Alcott at 150," 240–250
Stevenson, Robert Louis, 227, 266; *Treasure Island*, 105
Still River, MA, 270
St. Louis, MO, 263
St. Nicholas, 247
Stoehr, Taylor, *Nay-Saying Concord*, 284
Stowe, Harriet Beecher, 2, 30, 35, 172, 197, 263, 276; *We and Our Neighbors*, 197
Strickland, Charles, "Alcott, A Transcendentalist Father," 284
Stuart, Gilbert, 84
Studies in the American Renaissance, 285
Sue, Eugene, 230
Swinburne, Algernon Charles, 218

Talbot, Marion, "Glimpses of the Real Louisa May Alcott," 282
Talbot, Newton, 43, 44, 61
Tennyson, Alfred, Lord, 68
Thackeray, William Makepeace, 165, 265
Thomas, Marlo, 112
Thomes, William Henry, 43–44, 60–61
Thoreau, Henry David, 12, 15, 34, 76, 170, 199–200, 218, 227, 232, 242, 246, 251, 269–274, 279; "Friendship," 199; *Walden*, 126, 272–273; *Week on the Concord and Merrimack Rivers*, 247, 272
Thoreau, John, 270, 272
Thurber, James, 227
Ticknor, Caroline, *Classic Concord*, 281; *May Alcott: A Memoir*, 281
Tieck, Ludwig, 54
Tintner, Adeline R., 15; "A Literary Youth and A Little Woman: Henry James

Reviews Louisa Alcott," 265–269
Tolstoy, Leo, 95; *Anna Karenina*, 226; *War and Peace*, 97
Townsend, John Rowe, *Written for Children*, 276
"Trancendental Fiction," 66–69
"Transcendentalism, 84, 225
"Tribulation Periwinkle" (pseudonym of Louisa M. Alcott), 15, 26, 243, 244, 245, 249
Trollope, Anthony, 165, 265
True Flag, 44, 61
Turner, Lorenzo Dow, *Anti-Slavery Sentiment in American Literature Prior to 1865*, 35; "Louisa May Alcott's 'M.L.,'" 280–281
Turner, Stephen, 112

Ullom, Judith C., *Louisa May Alcott: A Centennial for "Little Women*," 15, 283
Urbanski, Marie Olesen, 15; "Thoreau in the Writing of Louisa May Alcott," 269–274

Van Amburgh, I.A., 247
Van Buren, Jane, "Louisa May Alcott: A Study in Persona and Idealization," 17
Vincent, Elizabeth, "Subversive Miss Alcott," 14, 222–224
Voltaire, François Marie Arouet de, 155

Wagenknecht, Edward, 6; [*Little Women* and the Domestic Sentimentalists], 88–89
Wallace, Lew, *Ben-Hur*, 84
Walpole, Horace, 54
Walpole, MA, 53
Warner, Susan, *The Wide, Wide World*, 123
Washington, D.C., 26, 28, 30, 33, 66, 128, 134, 136
Waterbury American, 2, 25
Weil, Simone, 7, 127–128; *La Condition ouvrière*, 128

Weld, Anna Minot, 257
Wells, Carolyn, 88
Wendell, Barrett, 5, 9; [*Little Women* and the *Rollo* Books], 84
Whitman, Alfred, 51, 55, 57, 280, 282
Whitman, Walt, *The Wound Dresser*, 283
Whitney, Adeline Dutton Train, 153; *Faith Gartney's Girlhood*, 65; *The Other Girls*, 185
Widener Library, 45
Willis, Frederick L.H., *Alcott Memoirs*, 281, 284
Winterich, John T., 6; "One Hundred Good Novels," 85; *Twenty-Three Books and the Stories Behind Them*, 16
Wisniewskyi, Ladislas, 280
Woman's Journal, 254
Woman Suffrage, 101, 172, 191, 221, 254, 273, 279, 280, 282
Women's Studies, 17
Wood, Mrs. Henry (Ellen), *East Lynne*, 235
Woollcott, Alexander, 87
Woolson, Constance Fenimore, "A Transplanted Boy," 226
Wordsworth, William, 242
World War I, 16
Worthington, Marjorie, *Miss Alcott of Concord: A Biography*, 15, 283
Wren, Christopher, *Beau Geste*, 106
Wright, Frances, 228
Wright, Julia McNair, 221

Yellin, Jean Fagan, 16
Yonge, Charlotte Mary, 278; *The Heir of Redclyffe*, 54, 114
Young, Agatha, *The Women and the Crisis*, 283

Zion's Herald, 91